Fear of a Black Marker

Fear of Black

Manic D Press
San Francisco

a Marker

cartoons by
Keith Knight

another  CHRONICLES compendium

Introduction by Keith's Parents

Dedicated

To my great
uncle Owen,
who makes
being a warm,
caring, loving,
and all around
snazzy human
being look so
damned easy.
I love you, sir.

Acknowledgments

Thanks again to Jennifer and Pete for this second go 'round:
to Garry Trudeau for the darn spiffy quote on the back cover:
to all the publications that run the strip; to my faithful readers; friends; and most of all, thanks to my family, Mom, Dad,
Tracy, Leslie...you guys are responsible for all of this, whether
you want to admit it or not. I love you.

Fear of a Black Marker: another K Chronicles compendium
© 2000 Keith Knight. Published by Manic D Press. All rights
reserved. No part of this publication may be reproduced, stored
in a retrieval system, or transmitted, in any form or by any
means, electronic, mechanical, photocopying, recording or
otherwise, without the prior permission of the publisher. For
more information, please contact Manic D Press, P.O. Box 410804,
San Francisco, California 94141.
ISBN 0-916397-63-7
5 4 3 2 1

Cover and book design: Pete Friedrich at Charette
Communication Design

Say hi. Keith Knight, P.O. Box 591794,
San Francisco, CA 94159-1794
keeflix@hotmail.com
www.kchronicles.com

Also by Keith Knight
Dances With Sheep: A K Chronicles Compendium (Manic D Press)

Distributed to the trade by Publishers Group West.

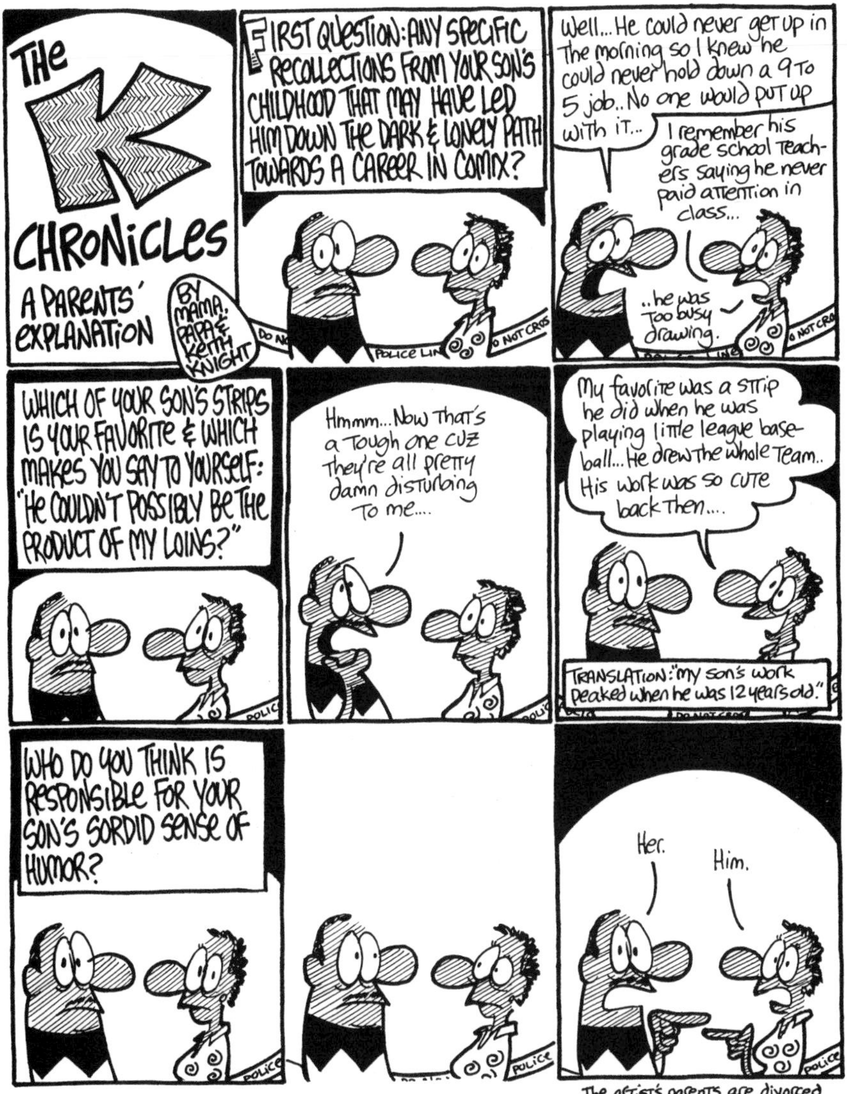
THE K CHRONICLES
A PARENTS' EXPLANATION
BY MAMA, PAPA & KEITH KNIGHT
FIRST QUESTION: ANY SPECIFIC RECOLLECTIONS FROM YOUR SON'S CHILDHOOD THAT MAY HAVE LED HIM DOWN THE DARK & LONELY PATH TOWARDS A CAREER IN COMIX?
Well... He could never get up in the morning so I knew he could never hold down a 9 to 5 job.. No one would put up with it...
I remember his grade school teachers saying he never paid attention in class...
..he was too busy drawing.
WHICH OF YOUR SON'S STRIPS IS YOUR FAVORITE & WHICH MAKES YOU SAY TO YOURSELF: "HE COULDN'T POSSIBLY BE THE PRODUCT OF MY LOINS?"
Hmmm... Now that's a tough one cuz they're all pretty damn disturbing to me....
My favorite was a strip he did when he was playing little league baseball... He drew the whole team.. His work was so cute back then....
TRANSLATION: "My son's work peaked when he was 12 years old."
WHO DO YOU THINK IS RESPONSIBLE FOR YOUR SON'S SORDID SENSE OF HUMOR?
Her.
Him.

The artist's parents are divorced.

ESTABLISHED 1850

1320 S.W. BROADWAY PORTLAND, OREGON 97201-3499

RICHARD C. JOHNSTON
ASSISTANT TO THE EDITOR

October 19, 1998

Keith Knight
PO Box 591794
San Francisco, CA 94159-1794

Dear Mr. Knight:

Thank you for sending samples of "The K Chronicles." I found them interesting.

IN A FAMILY NEWSPAPER? ARE YOU NUTS?

We've gone a long way since we first put Matt Groening's "Life in Hell" in The Oregonian, but I do not think we have gone as far as "The K Chronicles." Well, maybe we have, but I think a lot of the readers haven't, so the result is the same: Thanks, but not right now.

It is fun, though, and I would love to have a comic that makes people talk. "The K Chronicles" would certainly do that.

Again, thanks.

Sincerely,

Richard C. Johnston

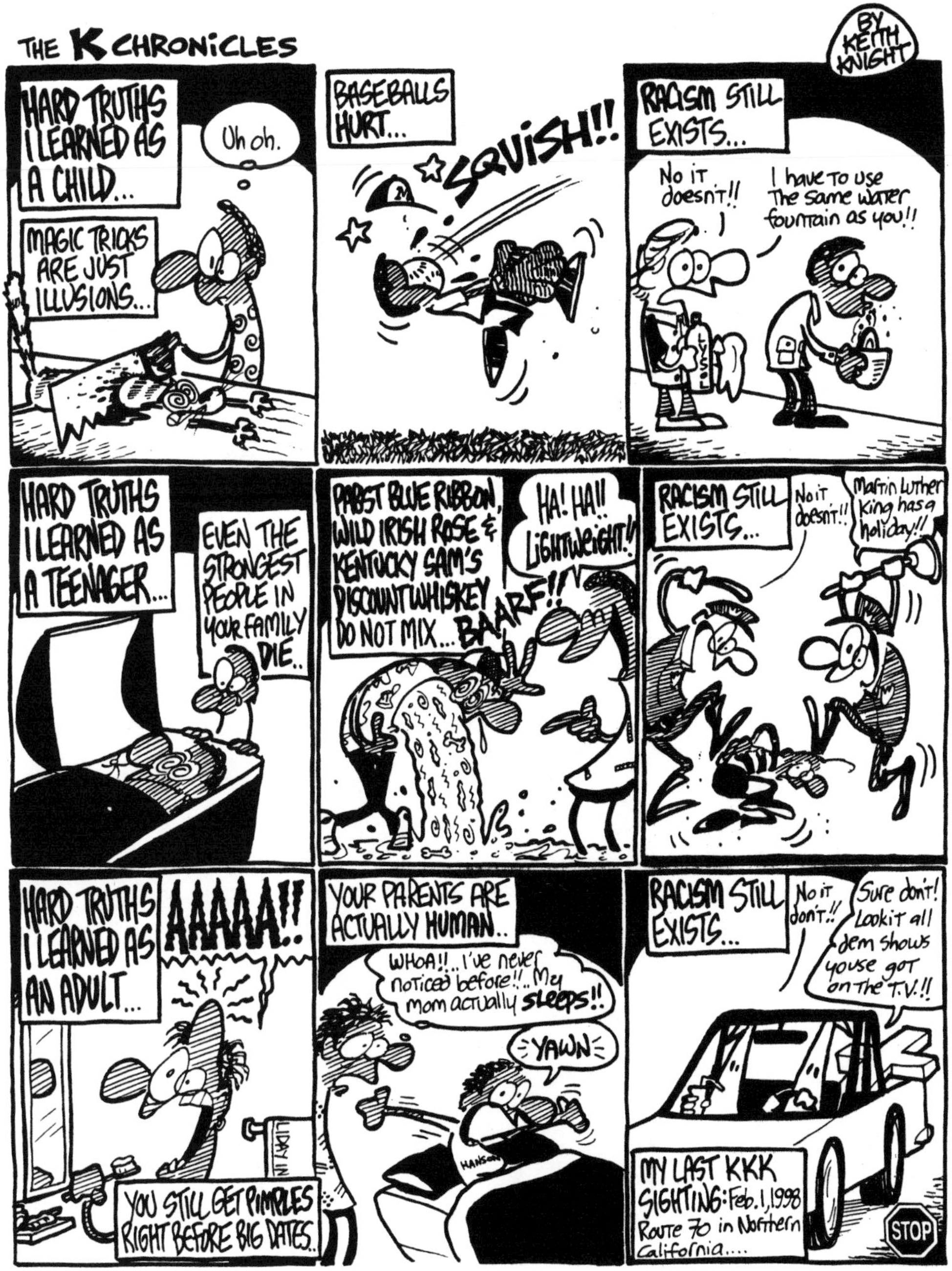
THE K CHRONICLES
BY KEITH KNIGHT
HARD TRUTHS I LEARNED AS A CHILD...
Uh oh.
MAGIC TRICKS ARE JUST ILLUSIONS...
BASEBALLS HURT...
SQUISH!!
RACISM STILL EXISTS...
No it doesn't!!
I have to use the same water fountain as you!!
LYSOL
HARD TRUTHS I LEARNED AS A TEENAGER...
EVEN THE STRONGEST PEOPLE IN YOUR FAMILY DIE..
PABST BLUE RIBBON, WILD IRISH ROSE & KENTUCKY SAM'S DISCOUNT WHISKEY DO NOT MIX...
HA! HA!! LIGHTWEIGHT!!
BAARF!!
RACISM STILL EXISTS...
No it doesn't!!
Martin Luther King has a holiday!!
HARD TRUTHS I LEARNED AS AN ADULT...
AAAAA!!
YOU STILL GET PIMPLES RIGHT BEFORE BIG DATES..
YOUR PARENTS ARE ACTUALLY HUMAN..
WHOA!!.. I've never noticed before!!.. My mom actually sleeps!!
YAWN
HANSON
RACISM STILL EXISTS...
No it don't!!
Sure don't! Lookit all dem shows youse got on the T.V.!!
MY LAST KKK SIGHTING: Feb. 1, 1998 Route 70 in Northern California....
STOP

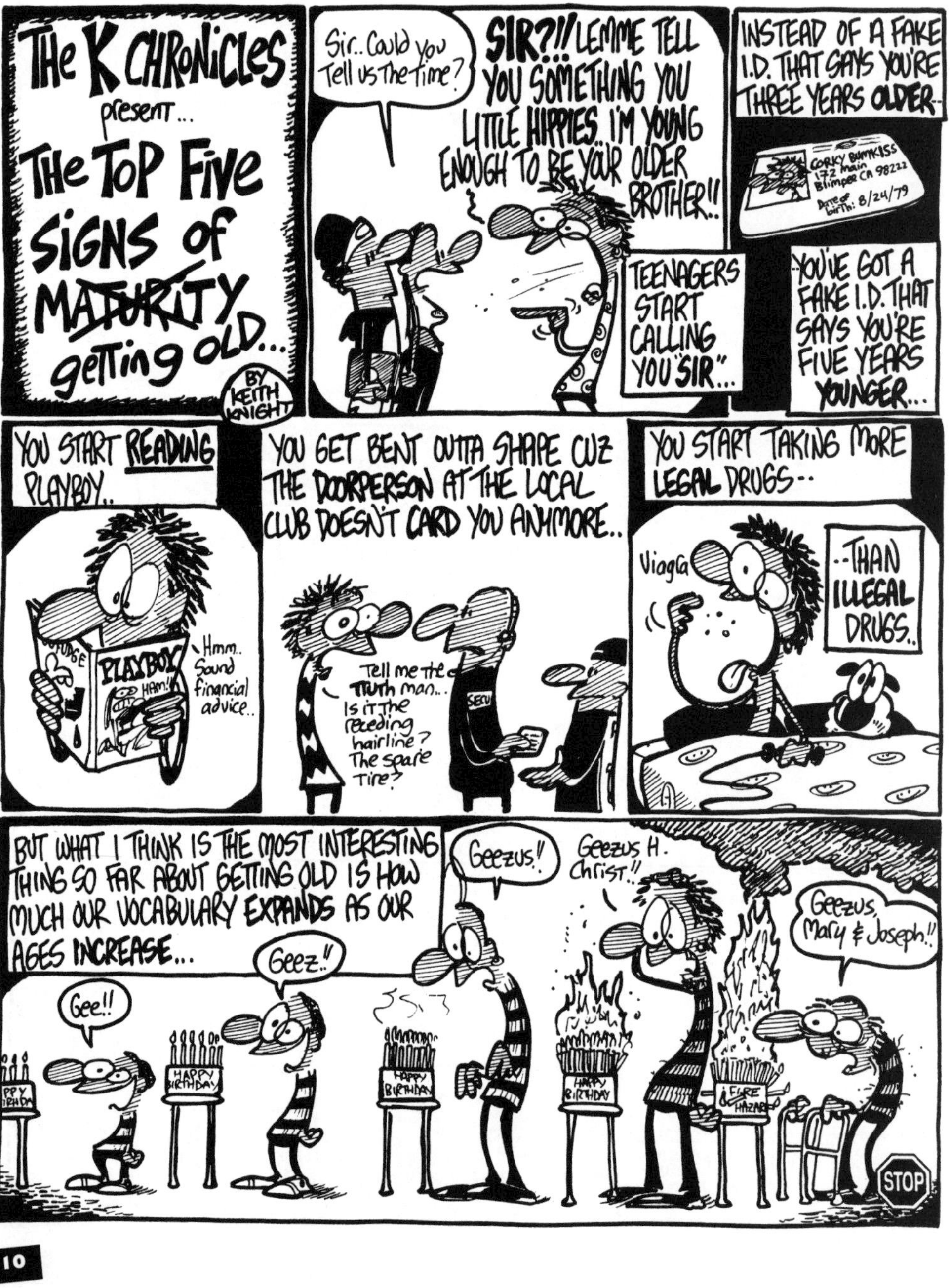
The K Chronicles
present...
The Top Five
Signs of
MATURITY
getting OLD...
BY KEITH KNIGHT
Sir.. Could you Tell us the Time?
SIR?!! LEMME TELL YOU SOMETHING YOU LITTLE HIPPIES.. I'M YOUNG ENOUGH TO BE YOUR OLDER BROTHER!!
TEENAGERS START CALLING YOU "SIR"...
INSTEAD OF A FAKE I.D. THAT SAYS YOU'RE THREE YEARS OLDER--
CORKY BUMKISS
172 Main
Blimper CA 98222
Date of birth: 8/24/79
--YOU'VE GOT A FAKE I.D. THAT SAYS YOU'RE FIVE YEARS YOUNGER...
YOU START READING PLAYBOY..
PLAYBOY
Hmm.. Sound financial advice..
YOU GET BENT OUTTA SHAPE CUZ THE DOORPERSON AT THE LOCAL CLUB DOESN'T CARD YOU ANYMORE..
Tell me the TRUTH man... Is it the receding hairline? The spare tire?
YOU START TAKING MORE LEGAL DRUGS--
Viagra
--THAN ILLEGAL DRUGS..
BUT WHAT I THINK IS THE MOST INTERESTING THING SO FAR ABOUT GETTING OLD IS HOW MUCH OUR VOCABULARY EXPANDS AS OUR AGES INCREASE...
Gee!!
HAPPY BIRTHDAY
Geez!!
HAPPY BIRTHDAY
Geezus!!
HAPPY BIRTHDAY
Geezus H. Christ!!
HAPPY BIRTHDAY
FIRE HAZARD
Geezus, Mary & Joseph!!
STOP

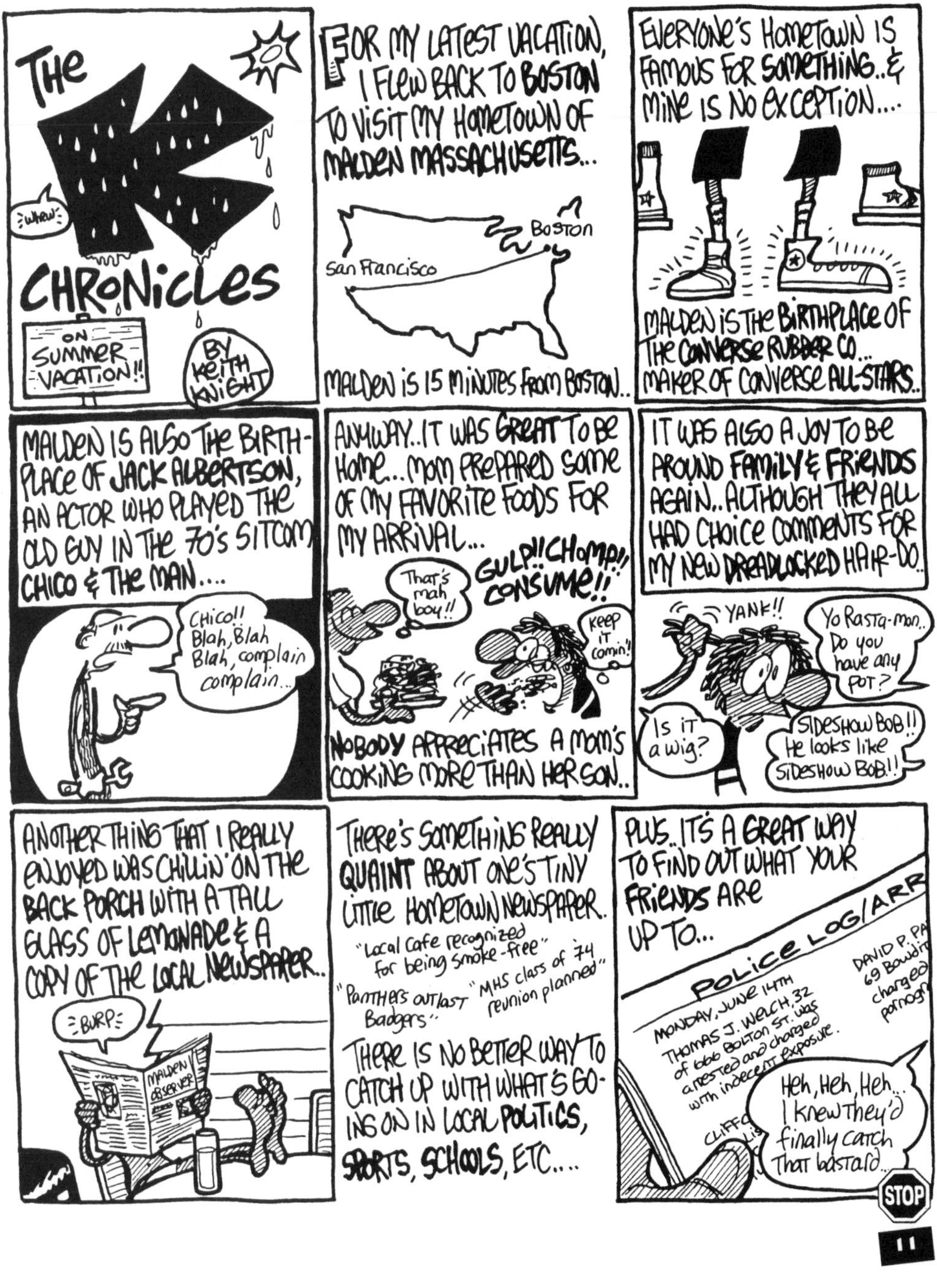

THE K CHRONICLES
WHEW
ON SUMMER VACATION!!
BY KEITH KNIGHT
FOR MY LATEST VACATION, I FLEW BACK TO BOSTON TO VISIT MY HOMETOWN OF MALDEN MASSACHUSETTS...
BOSTON
SAN FRANCISCO
MALDEN IS 15 MINUTES FROM BOSTON..
EVERYONE'S HOMETOWN IS FAMOUS FOR SOMETHING..& MINE IS NO EXCEPTION....
MALDEN IS THE BIRTHPLACE OF THE CONVERSE RUBBER CO... MAKER OF CONVERSE ALL-STARS..
MALDEN IS ALSO THE BIRTHPLACE OF JACK ALBERTSON, AN ACTOR WHO PLAYED THE OLD GUY IN THE 70'S SITCOM CHICO & THE MAN....
CHICO!! Blah, Blah Blah, complain complain...
ANYWAY..IT WAS GREAT TO BE HOME...MOM PREPARED SOME OF MY FAVORITE FOODS FOR MY ARRIVAL...
That's mah boy!!
GULP!! CHOMP!! CONSUME!!
KEEP IT COMIN'!!
NOBODY APPRECIATES A MOM'S COOKING MORE THAN HER SON..
IT WAS ALSO A JOY TO BE AROUND FAMILY & FRIENDS AGAIN..ALTHOUGH THEY ALL HAD CHOICE COMMENTS FOR MY NEW DREADLOCKED HAIR-DO..
YANK!!
Yo Rasta-man.. Do you have any POT?
Is it a wig?
SIDESHOW BOB!! He looks like SIDESHOW BOB!!
ANOTHER THING THAT I REALLY ENJOYED WAS CHILLIN' ON THE BACK PORCH WITH A TALL GLASS OF LEMONADE & A COPY OF THE LOCAL NEWSPAPER..
BURP
MALDEN OBSERVER
THERE'S SOMETHING REALLY QUAINT ABOUT ONE'S TINY LITTLE HOMETOWN NEWSPAPER..
"Local Cafe recognized for being smoke-free"
"Panthers outlast Badgers"
"MHS class of '74 reunion planned"
THERE IS NO BETTER WAY TO CATCH UP WITH WHAT'S GOING ON IN LOCAL POLITICS, SPORTS, SCHOOLS, ETC....
PLUS..IT'S A GREAT WAY TO FIND OUT WHAT YOUR FRIENDS ARE UP TO...
POLICE LOG/ARR
MONDAY, JUNE 14TH
THOMAS J. WELCH, 32 of 666 BOLTON ST. was arrested and charged with indecent exposure.
DAVID P. PA 69 Bowdo charged pornog
Heh, Heh, Heh... I knew they'd finally catch that bastard...
STOP

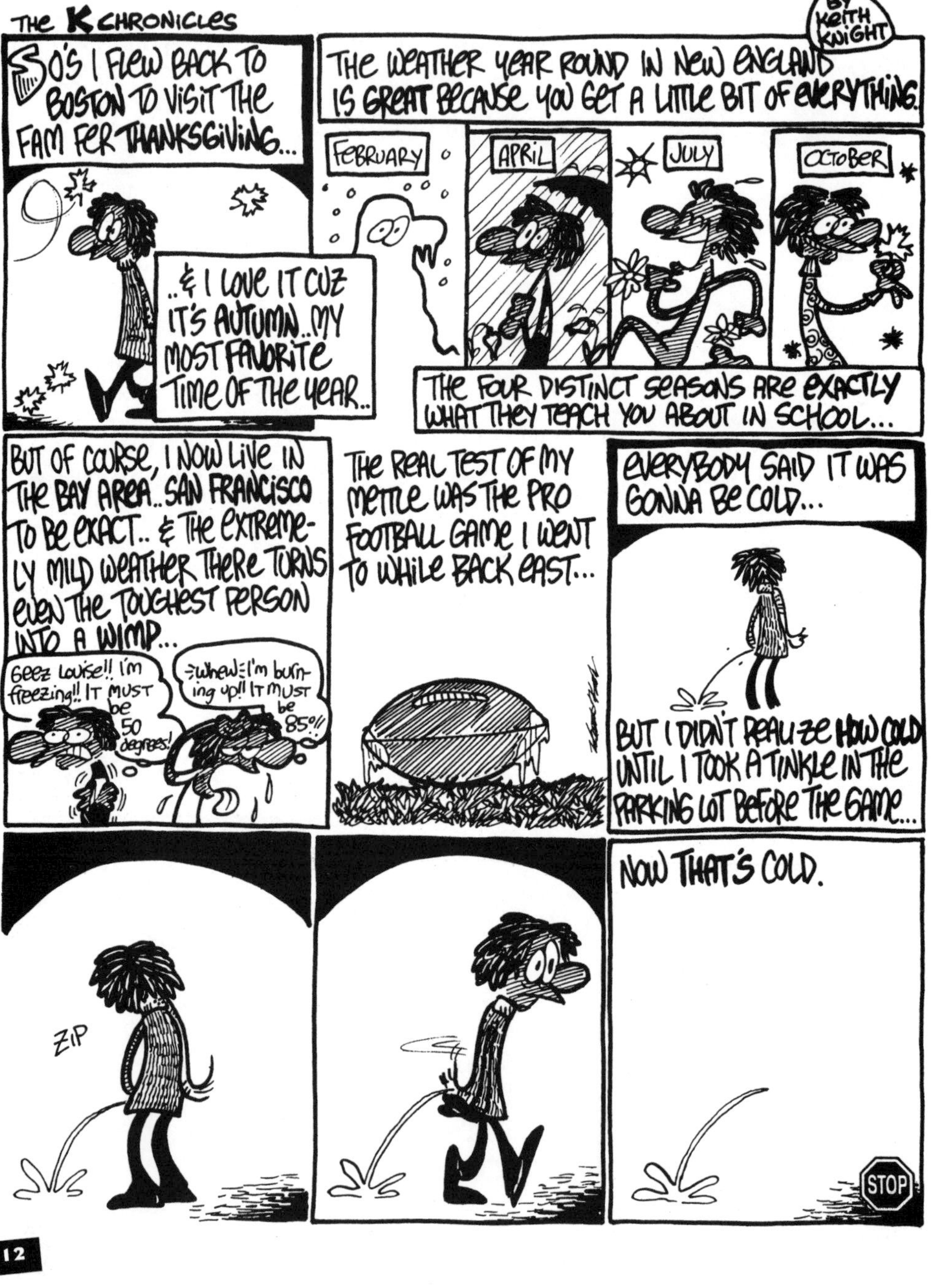
THE K CHRONICLES
BY KEITH KNIGHT
SO'S I FLEW BACK TO BOSTON TO VISIT THE FAM FER THANKSGIVING...
..& I LOVE IT CUZ IT'S AUTUMN..MY MOST FAVORITE TIME OF THE YEAR..
THE WEATHER YEAR ROUND IN NEW ENGLAND IS GREAT BECAUSE YOU GET A LITTLE BIT OF EVERYTHING.
FEBRUARY
APRIL
JULY
OCTOBER
THE FOUR DISTINCT SEASONS ARE EXACTLY WHAT THEY TEACH YOU ABOUT IN SCHOOL...
BUT OF COURSE, I NOW LIVE IN THE BAY AREA..SAN FRANCISCO TO BE EXACT.. & THE EXTREMELY MILD WEATHER THERE TURNS EVEN THE TOUGHEST PERSON INTO A WIMP...
GEEZ LOUISE!! I'M FREEZING!! IT MUST BE 50 DEGREES!
=WHEW= I'M BURNING UP!! IT MUST BE 85°!!
THE REAL TEST OF MY METTLE WAS THE PRO FOOTBALL GAME I WENT TO WHILE BACK EAST...
EVERYBODY SAID IT WAS GONNA BE COLD...
BUT I DIDN'T REALIZE HOW COLD UNTIL I TOOK A TINKLE IN THE PARKING LOT BEFORE THE GAME...
ZIP
NOW THAT'S COLD.
STOP

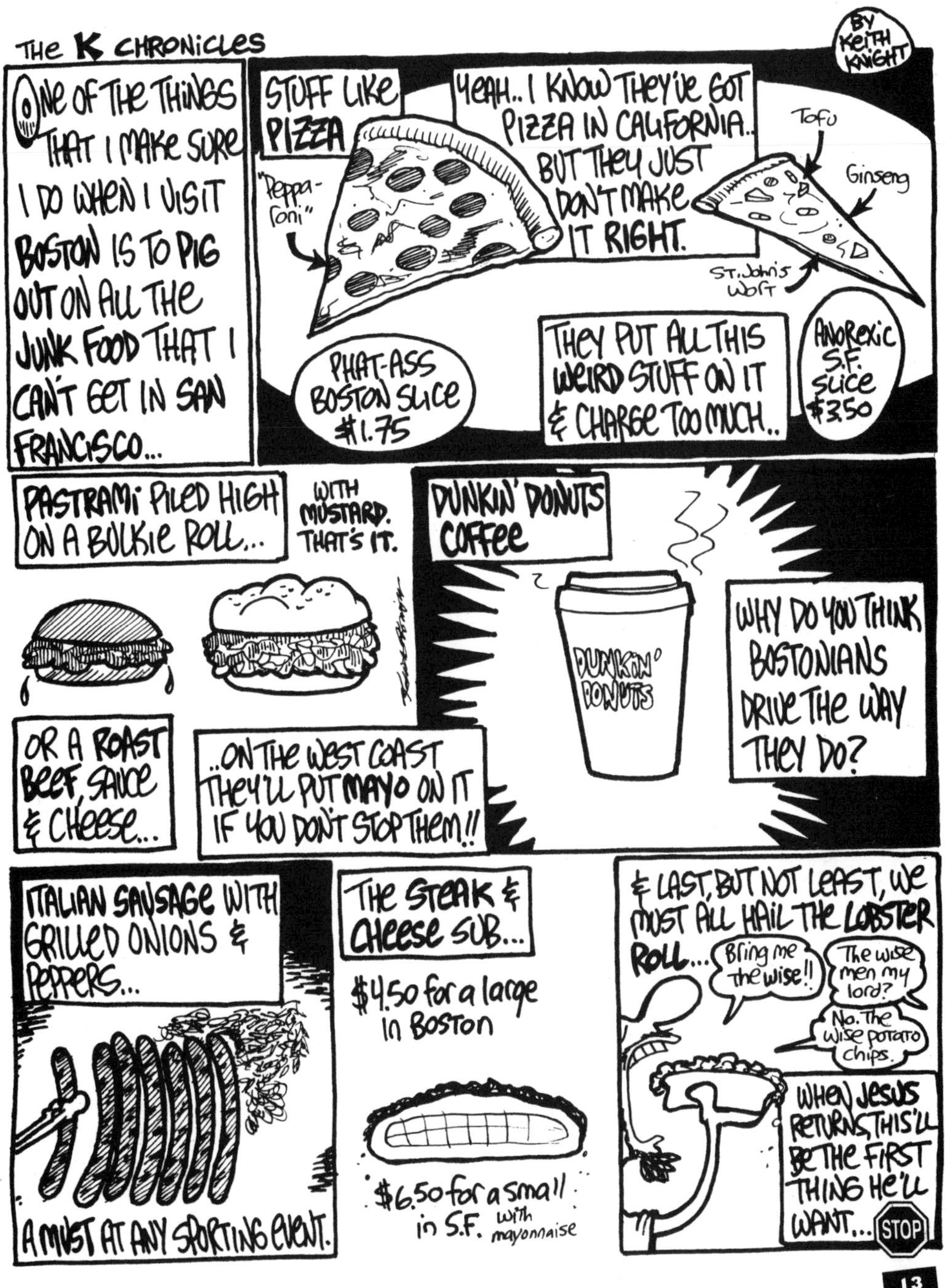

THE K CHRONICLES
BY KEITH KNIGHT
ONE OF THE THINGS THAT I MAKE SURE I DO WHEN I VISIT BOSTON IS TO PIG OUT ON ALL THE JUNK FOOD THAT I CAN'T GET IN SAN FRANCISCO...
STUFF LIKE PIZZA
YEAH.. I KNOW THEY'VE GOT PIZZA IN CALIFORNIA.. BUT THEY JUST DON'T MAKE IT RIGHT.
"Peppa-roni"
Tofu
Ginseng
St. John's Wort
PHAT-ASS BOSTON SLICE $1.75
THEY PUT ALL THIS WEIRD STUFF ON IT & CHARGE TOO MUCH..
ANOREXIC S.F. SLICE $3.50
PASTRAMI PILED HIGH ON A BULKIE ROLL...
WITH MUSTARD. THAT'S IT.
OR A ROAST BEEF, SAUCE & CHEESE...
..ON THE WEST COAST THEY'LL PUT MAYO ON IT IF YOU DON'T STOP THEM!!
DUNKIN' DONUTS COFFEE
DUNKIN' DONUTS
WHY DO YOU THINK BOSTONIANS DRIVE THE WAY THEY DO?
ITALIAN SAUSAGE WITH GRILLED ONIONS & PEPPERS...
A MUST AT ANY SPORTING EVENT.
THE STEAK & CHEESE SUB...
$4.50 for a large in Boston
$6.50 for a small in S.F. with mayonnaise
& LAST, BUT NOT LEAST, WE MUST ALL HAIL THE LOBSTER ROLL...
Bring me the wise!!
The wise men my lord?
No. The wise potato chips.
WHEN JESUS RETURNS, THIS'LL BE THE FIRST THING HE'LL WANT...
STOP

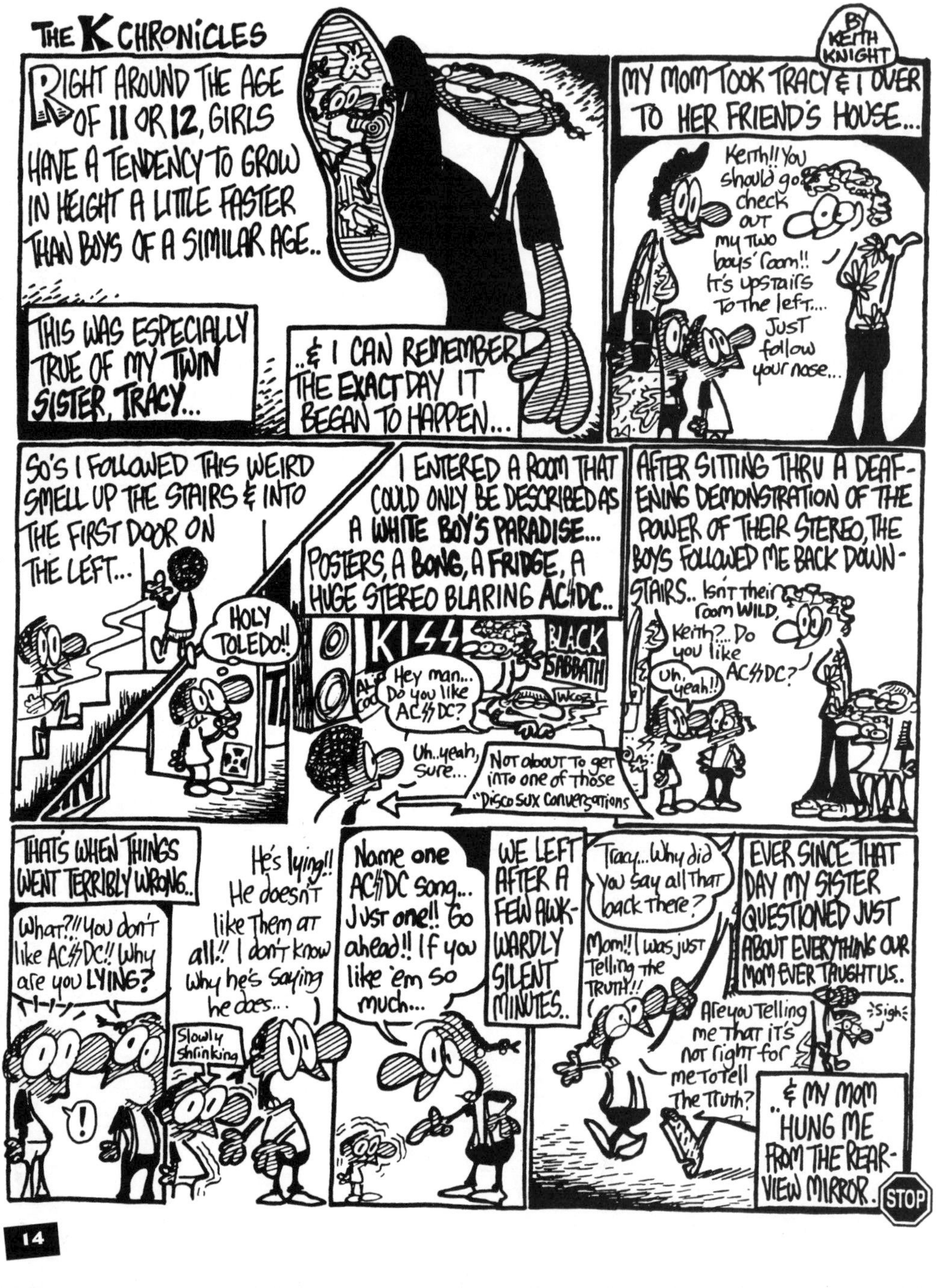
THE K CHRONICLES
BY KEITH KNIGHT
RIGHT AROUND THE AGE OF 11 OR 12, GIRLS HAVE A TENDENCY TO GROW IN HEIGHT A LITTLE FASTER THAN BOYS OF A SIMILAR AGE..
THIS WAS ESPECIALLY TRUE OF MY TWIN SISTER, TRACY...
..& I CAN REMEMBER THE EXACT DAY IT BEGAN TO HAPPEN...
MY MOM TOOK TRACY & I OVER TO HER FRIEND'S HOUSE...
Keith!! You should go check out my two boys' room!! It's upstairs to the left.... Just follow your nose...
SO'S I FOLLOWED THIS WEIRD SMELL UP THE STAIRS & INTO THE FIRST DOOR ON THE LEFT...
HOLY TOLEDO!!
I ENTERED A ROOM THAT COULD ONLY BE DESCRIBED AS A WHITE BOY'S PARADISE... POSTERS, A BONG, A FRIDGE, A HUGE STEREO BLARING AC/DC..
KISS
BLACK SABBATH
Hey man... Do you like AC/DC?
Uh..yeah, sure...
Not about to get into one of those "Disco Sux Conversations
AFTER SITTING THRU A DEAFENING DEMONSTRATION OF THE POWER OF THEIR STEREO, THE BOYS FOLLOWED ME BACK DOWNSTAIRS..
Isn't their room WILD, Keith?... Do you like AC/DC?
Uh, yeah!!
THAT'S WHEN THINGS WENT TERRIBLY WRONG..
What?!! You don't like AC/DC!! Why are you LYING?
!
He's lying!! He doesn't like them at all!! I don't know why he's saying he does...
Slowly shrinking
Name one AC/DC song... Just one!! Go ahead!! If you like 'em so much...
WE LEFT AFTER A FEW AWKWARDLY SILENT MINUTES..
Tracy...Why did you say all that back there?
Mom!! I was just telling the TRUTH!!
Are you telling me that it's not right for me to tell the truth?
EVER SINCE THAT DAY MY SISTER QUESTIONED JUST ABOUT EVERYTHING OUR MOM EVER TAUGHT US..
Sigh
..& MY MOM HUNG ME FROM THE REARVIEW MIRROR.
STOP

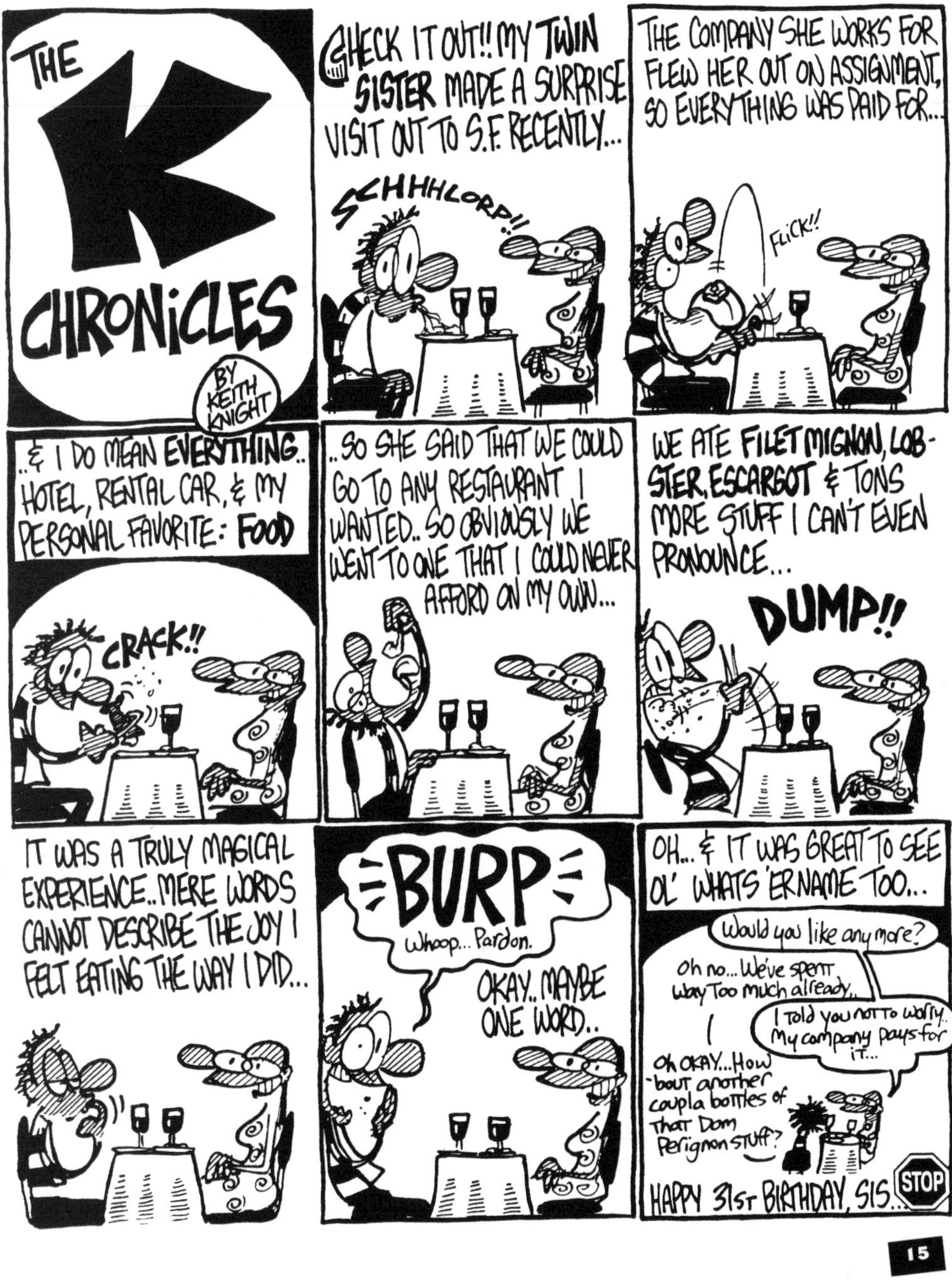
THE K CHRONICLES
BY KEITH KNIGHT
CHECK IT OUT!! MY TWIN SISTER MADE A SURPRISE VISIT OUT TO S.F. RECENTLY...
SCHHHLORP!!
THE COMPANY SHE WORKS FOR FLEW HER OUT ON ASSIGNMENT, SO EVERYTHING WAS PAID FOR...
FLICK!!
..& I DO MEAN EVERYTHING.. HOTEL, RENTAL CAR, & MY PERSONAL FAVORITE: FOOD
CRACK!!
..SO SHE SAID THAT WE COULD GO TO ANY RESTAURANT I WANTED.. SO OBVIOUSLY WE WENT TO ONE THAT I COULD NEVER AFFORD ON MY OWN...
WE ATE FILET MIGNON, LOBSTER, ESCARGOT & TONS MORE STUFF I CAN'T EVEN PRONOUNCE...
DUMP!!
IT WAS A TRULY MAGICAL EXPERIENCE.. MERE WORDS CANNOT DESCRIBE THE JOY I FELT EATING THE WAY I DID...
BURP
Whoop... Pardon.
OKAY.. MAYBE ONE WORD..
OH... & IT WAS GREAT TO SEE OL' WHATS 'ER NAME TOO...
Would you like any more?
Oh no... We've spent way too much already..
I told you not to worry.. My company pays for it...
Oh OKAY... How 'bout another coupla bottles of that Dom Perignon stuff?
HAPPY 31ST BIRTHDAY, SIS...
STOP

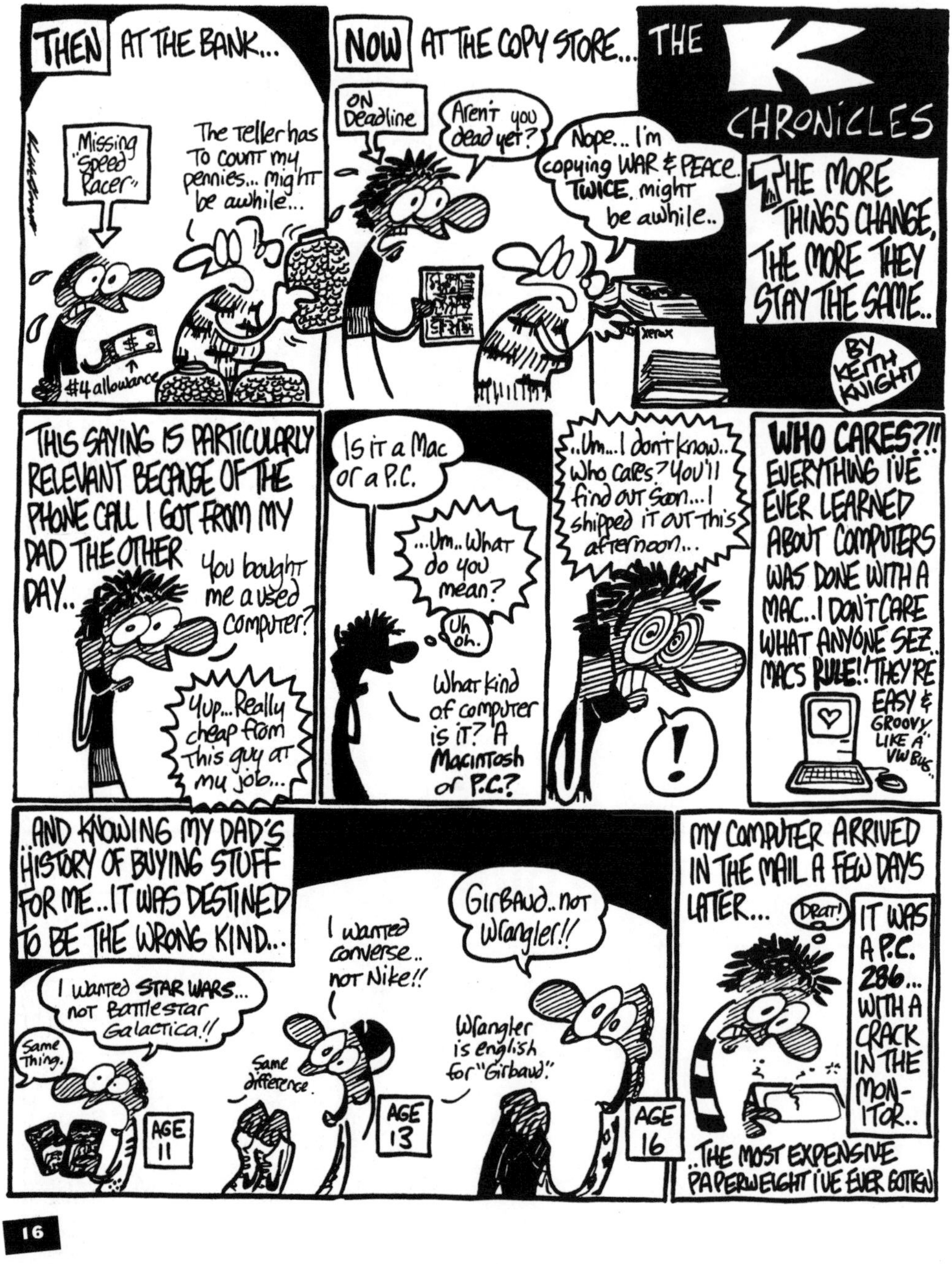
THEN AT THE BANK...
"Missing "Speed Racer."
$4 allowance
The teller has to count my pennies... might be awhile...
NOW AT THE COPY STORE...
ON Deadline
Aren't you dead yet?
Nope... I'm copying WAR & PEACE. TWICE. might be awhile..
XEROX
THE K CHRONICLES
THE MORE THINGS CHANGE, THE MORE THEY STAY THE SAME..
BY KEITH KNIGHT
THIS SAYING IS PARTICULARLY RELEVANT BECAUSE OF THE PHONE CALL I GOT FROM MY DAD THE OTHER DAY..
You bought me a used computer?
Yup... Really cheap from this guy at my job...
Is it a Mac or a P.C.
...Um.. What do you mean?
Uh oh.
What kind of computer is it? A Macintosh or P.C.?
..Um... I don't know.. Who cares? You'll find out soon... I shipped it out this afternoon...
!
WHO CARES?!! EVERYTHING I'VE EVER LEARNED ABOUT COMPUTERS WAS DONE WITH A MAC.. I DON'T CARE WHAT ANYONE SEZ.. MACS RULE!! THEY'RE EASY & GROOVY.. LIKE A VW BUS..
..AND KNOWING MY DAD'S HISTORY OF BUYING STUFF FOR ME.. IT WAS DESTINED TO BE THE WRONG KIND...
I wanted STAR WARS... not Battlestar Galactica!!
Same Thing.
AGE 11
I wanted converse.. not Nike!!
Same difference.
AGE 13
Girbaud.. not Wrangler!!
Wrangler is english for "Girbaud."
AGE 16
MY COMPUTER ARRIVED IN THE MAIL A FEW DAYS LATER...
DRAT!
IT WAS A P.C. 286... WITH A CRACK IN THE MONITOR..
..THE MOST EXPENSIVE PAPERWEIGHT I'VE EVER GOTTEN

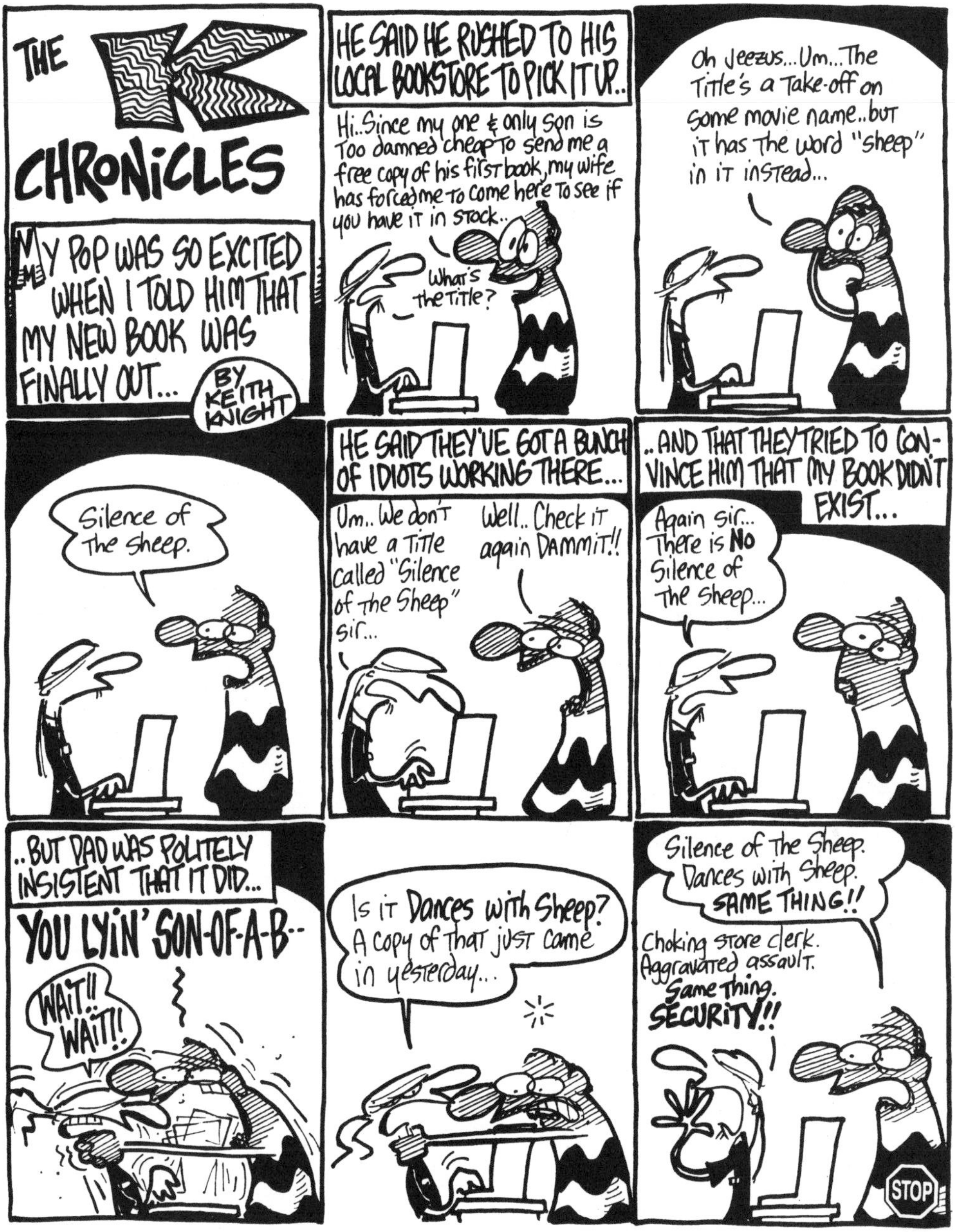
THE K CHRONICLES
MY POP WAS SO EXCITED WHEN I TOLD HIM THAT MY NEW BOOK WAS FINALLY OUT...
BY KEITH KNIGHT
HE SAID HE RUSHED TO HIS LOCAL BOOKSTORE TO PICK IT UP..
Hi..Since my one & only son is Too damned cheap To send me a free copy of his first book, my wife has forced me To come here To see if you have it in stock..
What's the Title?
Oh Jeezus...Um...The Title's a Take-off on some movie name..but it has The word "sheep" in it instead...
Silence of The sheep.
HE SAID THEY'VE GOT A BUNCH OF IDIOTS WORKING THERE...
Um..We don't have a Title called "Silence of The Sheep" sir...
Well.. Check it again DAMMIT!!
..AND THAT THEY TRIED TO CONVINCE HIM THAT MY BOOK DIDN'T EXIST...
Again sir... There is NO Silence of The Sheep...
..BUT DAD WAS POLITELY INSISTENT THAT IT DID...
YOU LYIN' SON-OF-A-B--
WAIT!! WAIT!!
Is it Dances with Sheep? A copy of That just came in yesterday...
Silence of The Sheep. Dances with Sheep. SAME THING!!
Choking store clerk. Aggravated assault. Same thing. SECURITY!!
STOP

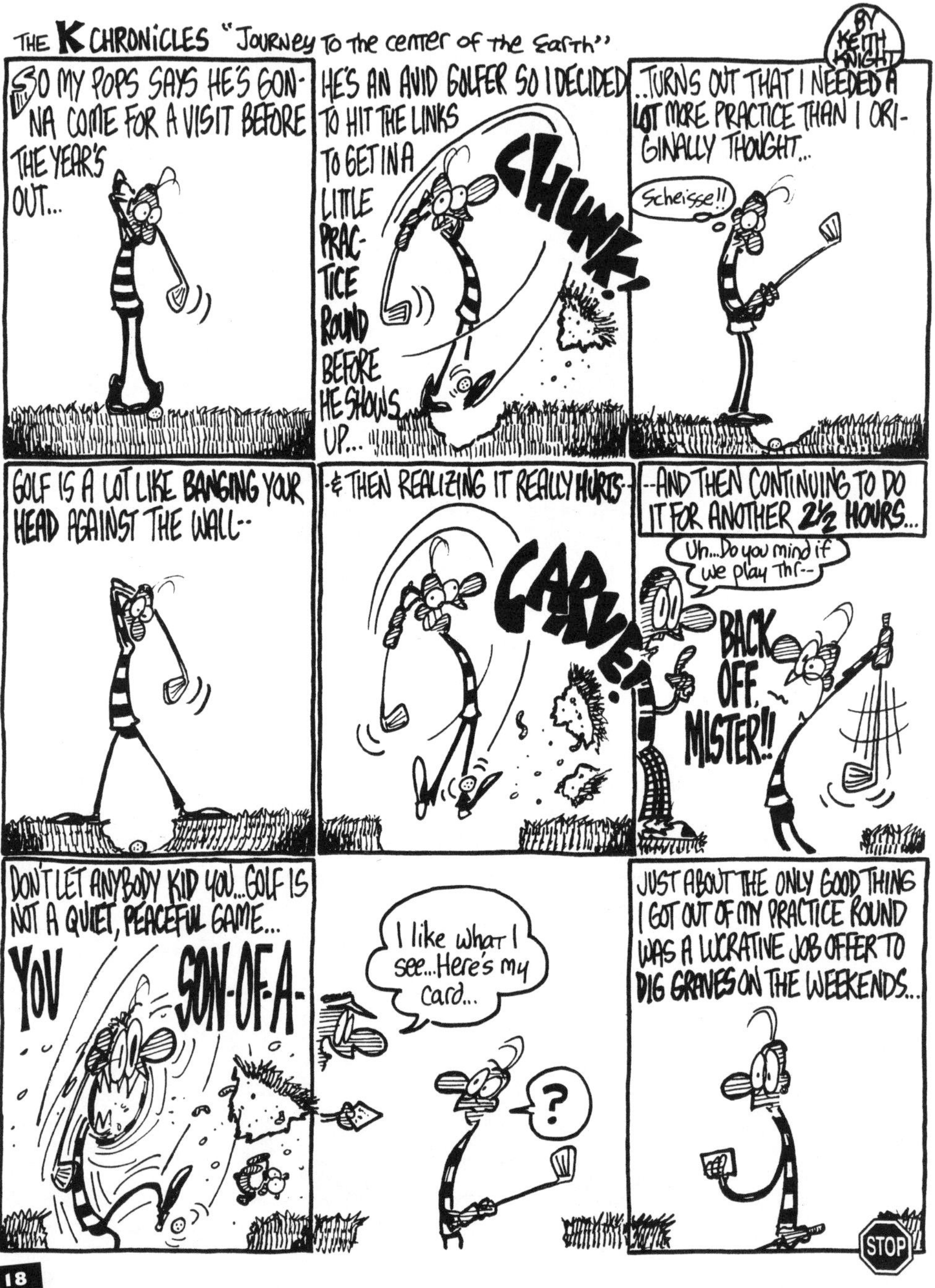
THE K CHRONICLES "Journey to the center of the earth"
BY KEITH KNIGHT
SO MY POPS SAYS HE'S GONNA COME FOR A VISIT BEFORE THE YEAR'S OUT...
HE'S AN AVID GOLFER SO I DECIDED TO HIT THE LINKS TO GET IN A LITTLE PRACTICE ROUND BEFORE HE SHOWS UP...
CHUNK!
...TURNS OUT THAT I NEEDED A LOT MORE PRACTICE THAN I ORIGINALLY THOUGHT...
Scheisse!!
GOLF IS A LOT LIKE BANGING YOUR HEAD AGAINST THE WALL--
-& THEN REALIZING IT REALLY HURTS-
CARVE!
--AND THEN CONTINUING TO DO IT FOR ANOTHER 2½ HOURS...
Uh...Do you mind if we play thr--
BACK OFF, MISTER!!
DON'T LET ANYBODY KID YOU...GOLF IS NOT A QUIET, PEACEFUL GAME...
YOU SON-OF-A-
I like what I see...Here's my card...
?
JUST ABOUT THE ONLY GOOD THING I GOT OUT OF MY PRACTICE ROUND WAS A LUCRATIVE JOB OFFER TO DIG GRAVES ON THE WEEKENDS...
STOP

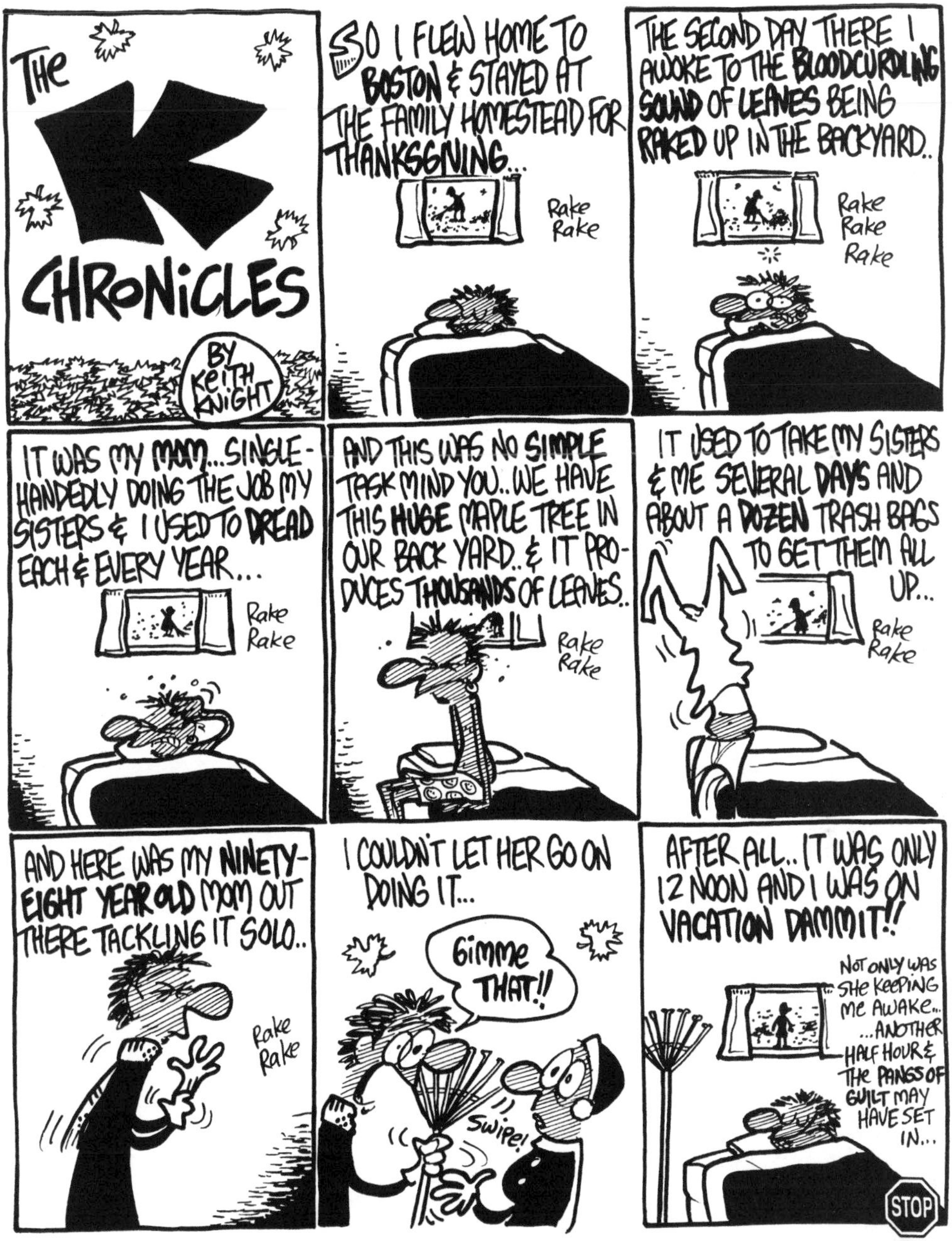
THE K CHRONICLES
BY KEITH KNIGHT
SO I FLEW HOME TO BOSTON & STAYED AT THE FAMILY HOMESTEAD FOR THANKSGIVING...
Rake Rake
THE SECOND DAY THERE I AWOKE TO THE BLOODCURDLING SOUND OF LEAVES BEING RAKED UP IN THE BACKYARD..
Rake Rake Rake
IT WAS MY MOM...SINGLE-HANDEDLY DOING THE JOB MY SISTERS & I USED TO DREAD EACH & EVERY YEAR...
Rake Rake
AND THIS WAS NO SIMPLE TASK MIND YOU.. WE HAVE THIS HUGE MAPLE TREE IN OUR BACK YARD.. & IT PRODUCES THOUSANDS OF LEAVES..
Rake Rake
IT USED TO TAKE MY SISTERS & ME SEVERAL DAYS AND ABOUT A DOZEN TRASH BAGS TO GET THEM ALL UP...
Rake Rake
AND HERE WAS MY NINETY-EIGHT YEAR OLD MOM OUT THERE TACKLING IT SOLO..
Rake Rake
I COULDN'T LET HER GO ON DOING IT...
Gimme THAT!!
Swipe!
AFTER ALL.. IT WAS ONLY 12 NOON AND I WAS ON VACATION DAMMIT!!
NOT ONLY WAS SHE KEEPING ME AWAKE... ...ANOTHER HALF HOUR & THE PANGS OF GUILT MAY HAVE SET IN...
STOP

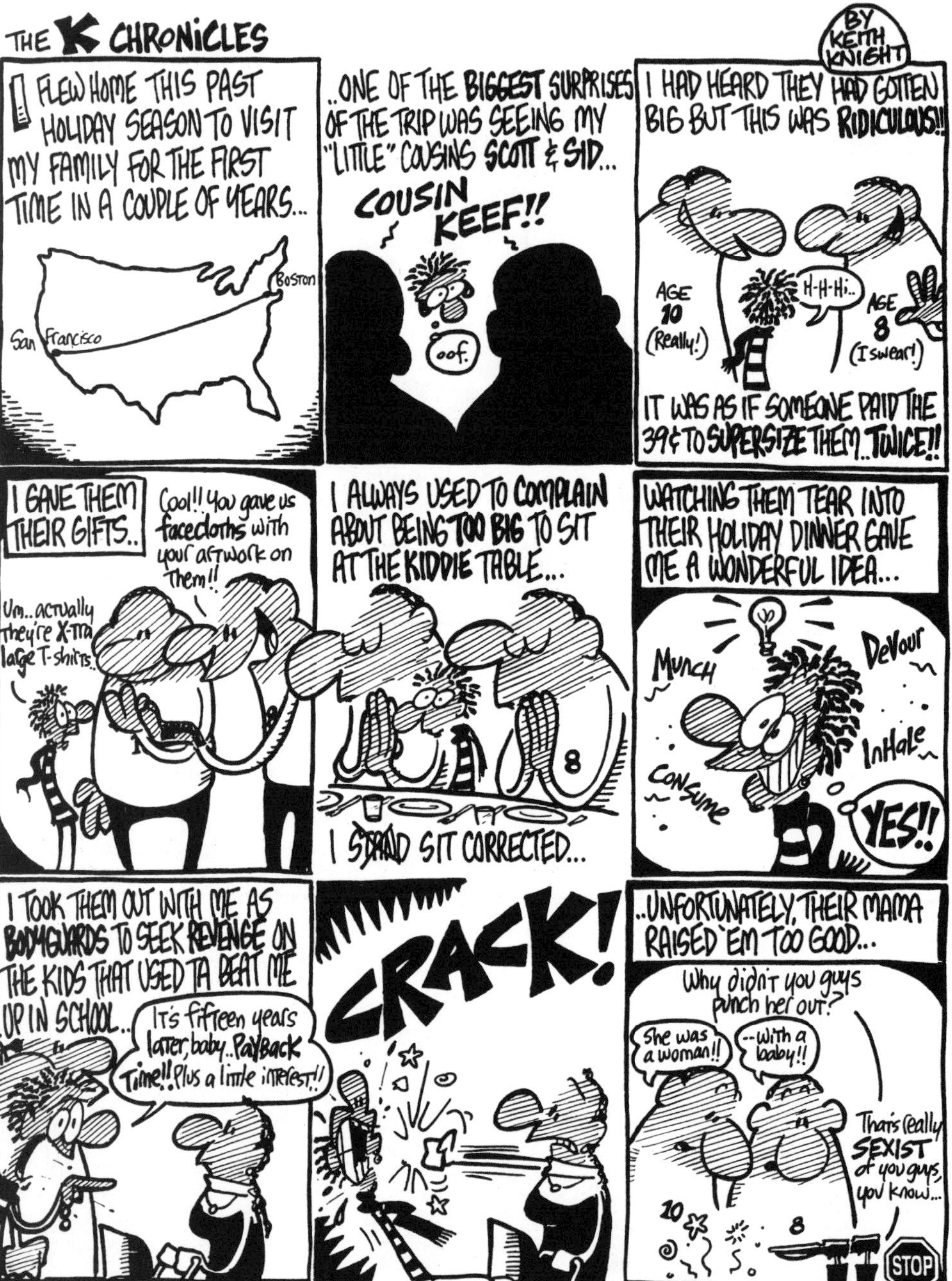
THE K CHRONICLES
BY KEITH KNIGHT
I FLEW HOME THIS PAST HOLIDAY SEASON TO VISIT MY FAMILY FOR THE FIRST TIME IN A COUPLE OF YEARS...
Boston
San Francisco
..ONE OF THE BIGGEST SURPRISES OF THE TRIP WAS SEEING MY "LITTLE" COUSINS SCOTT & SID...
COUSIN KEEF!!
oof.
I HAD HEARD THEY HAD GOTTEN BIG BUT THIS WAS RIDICULOUS!!
AGE 10 (Really!)
H-H-Hi..
AGE 8 (I swear!)
IT WAS AS IF SOMEONE PAID THE 39¢ TO SUPERSIZE THEM..TWICE!!
I GAVE THEM THEIR GIFTS..
Cool!! You gave us facecloths with your artwork on Them!!
Um...actually they're X-tra large T-shirts..
I ALWAYS USED TO COMPLAIN ABOUT BEING TOO BIG TO SIT AT THE KIDDIE TABLE...
8
I STAND SIT CORRECTED...
WATCHING THEM TEAR INTO THEIR HOLIDAY DINNER GAVE ME A WONDERFUL IDEA...
Munch
DeVour
InHale
ConSume
YES!!
I TOOK THEM OUT WITH ME AS BODYGUARDS TO SEEK REVENGE ON THE KIDS THAT USED TA BEAT ME UP IN SCHOOL...
It's fifteen years later, baby..Payback Time!! Plus a little interest!!
CRACK!
..UNFORTUNATELY, THEIR MAMA RAISED 'EM TOO GOOD...
Why didn't you guys punch her out?
She was a woman!!
--With a baby!!
That's really SEXIST of you guys, you know...
10
8
STOP

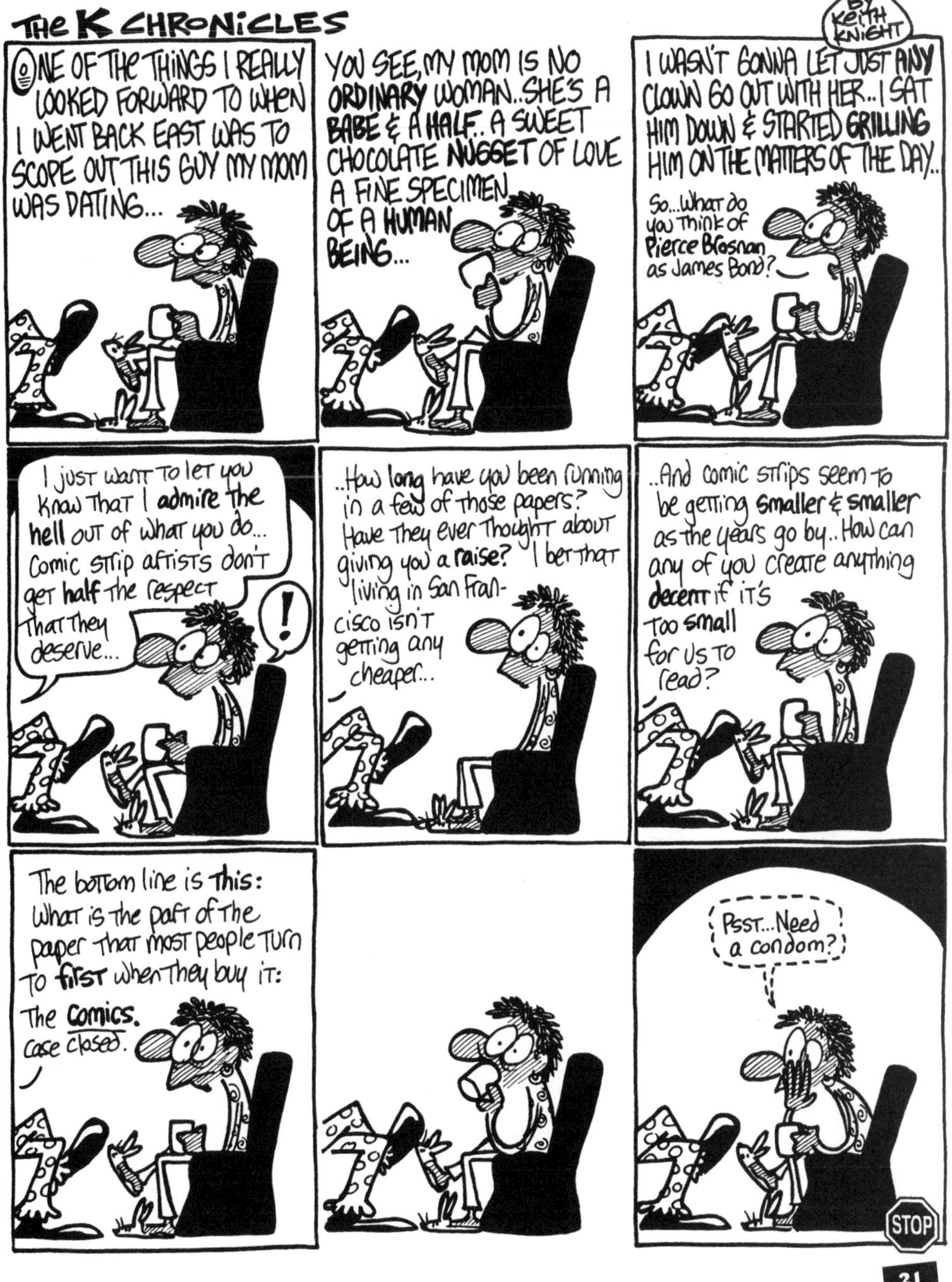

THE K CHRONICLES
BY KEITH KNIGHT
ONE OF THE THINGS I REALLY LOOKED FORWARD TO WHEN I WENT BACK EAST WAS TO SCOPE OUT THIS GUY MY MOM WAS DATING...
YOU SEE, MY MOM IS NO ORDINARY WOMAN..SHE'S A BABE & A HALF.. A SWEET CHOCOLATE NUGGET OF LOVE A FINE SPECIMEN OF A HUMAN BEING...
I WASN'T GONNA LET JUST ANY CLOWN GO OUT WITH HER.. I SAT HIM DOWN & STARTED GRILLING HIM ON THE MATTERS OF THE DAY..
So...What do you Think of Pierce Brosnan as James Bond?
I just want to let you know that I admire the hell out of what you do... Comic strip artists don't get half the respect that they deserve...
!
..How long have you been running in a few of those papers? Have they ever thought about giving you a raise? I bet that living in San Francisco isn't getting any cheaper...
..And comic strips seem to be getting smaller & smaller as the years go by.. How can any of you create anything decent if it's too small for us to read?
The bottom line is this: What is the part of the paper that most people turn to first when they buy it: The comics. Case closed.
Psst...Need a condom?
STOP

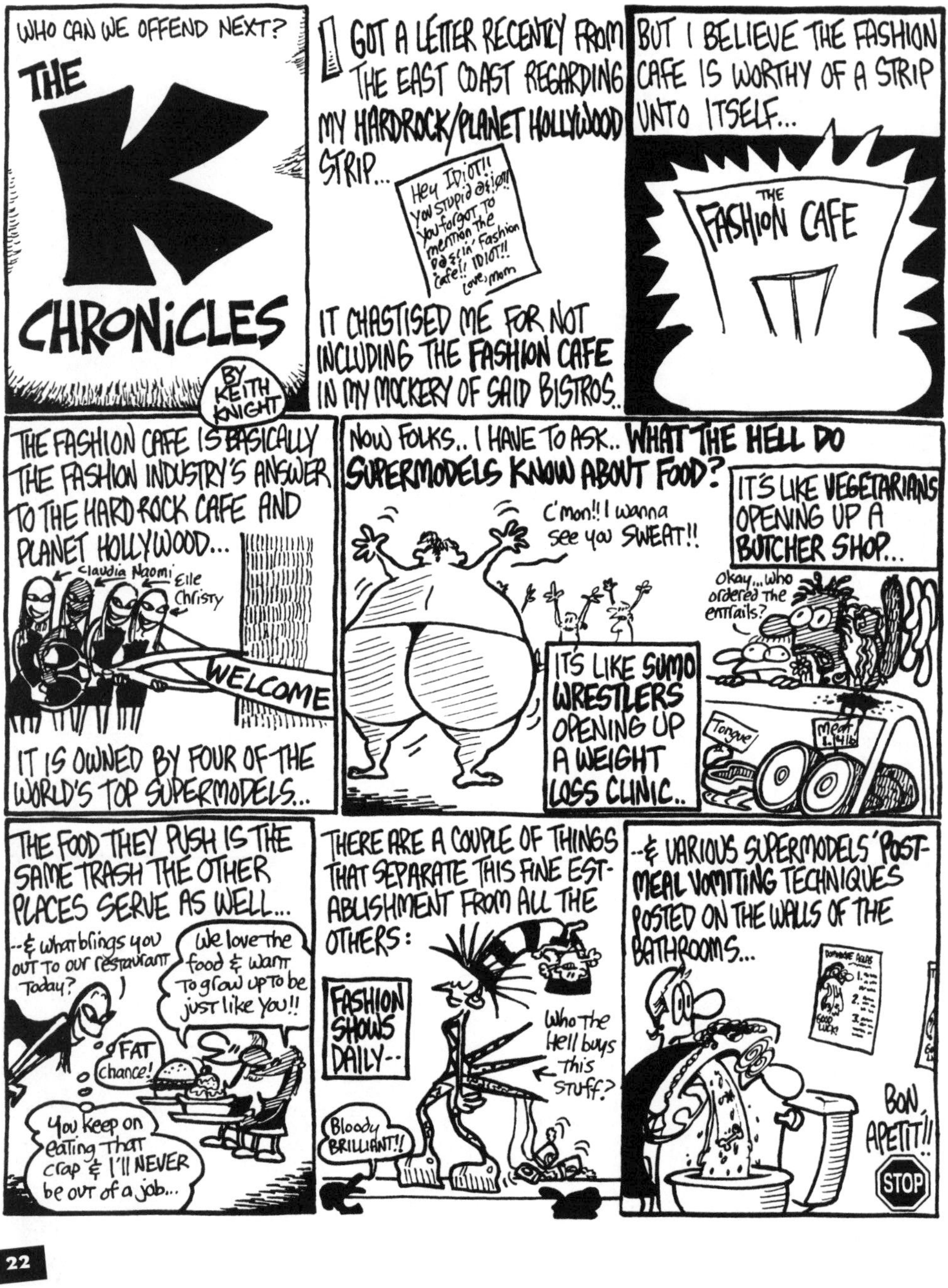
WHO CAN WE OFFEND NEXT?
THE K CHRONICLES
BY KEITH KNIGHT
I GOT A LETTER RECENTLY FROM THE EAST COAST REGARDING MY HARDROCK/PLANET HOLLYWOOD STRIP...
Hey IDIOT!! You stupid @$!@!! You forgot to mention the @$$%in' Fashion Cafe!! IDIOT!! Love, mom
IT CHASTISED ME FOR NOT INCLUDING THE FASHION CAFE IN MY MOCKERY OF SAID BISTROS..
BUT I BELIEVE THE FASHION CAFE IS WORTHY OF A STRIP UNTO ITSELF...
THE FASHION CAFE
THE FASHION CAFE IS BASICALLY THE FASHION INDUSTRY'S ANSWER TO THE HARD ROCK CAFE AND PLANET HOLLYWOOD...
Claudia
Naomi
Elle
Christy
WELCOME
IT IS OWNED BY FOUR OF THE WORLD'S TOP SUPERMODELS...
NOW FOLKS.. I HAVE TO ASK.. WHAT THE HELL DO SUPERMODELS KNOW ABOUT FOOD?
C'mon!! I wanna see you SWEAT!!
IT'S LIKE SUMO WRESTLERS OPENING UP A WEIGHT LOSS CLINIC..
IT'S LIKE VEGETARIANS OPENING UP A BUTCHER SHOP...
Okay... who ordered the entrails?
Tongue
Meat
THE FOOD THEY PUSH IS THE SAME TRASH THE OTHER PLACES SERVE AS WELL...
--& what brings you out to our restaurant today?
We love the food & want to grow up to be just like you!!
FAT chance!
You keep on eating that crap & I'll NEVER be out of a job...
THERE ARE A COUPLE OF THINGS THAT SEPARATE THIS FINE ESTABLISHMENT FROM ALL THE OTHERS:
FASHION SHOWS DAILY--
Who the Hell buys this stuff?
Bloody BRILLIANT!!
--& VARIOUS SUPERMODELS' POST-MEAL VOMITING TECHNIQUES POSTED ON THE WALLS OF THE BATHROOMS...
GOOD LUCK!
BON APETIT!!
STOP

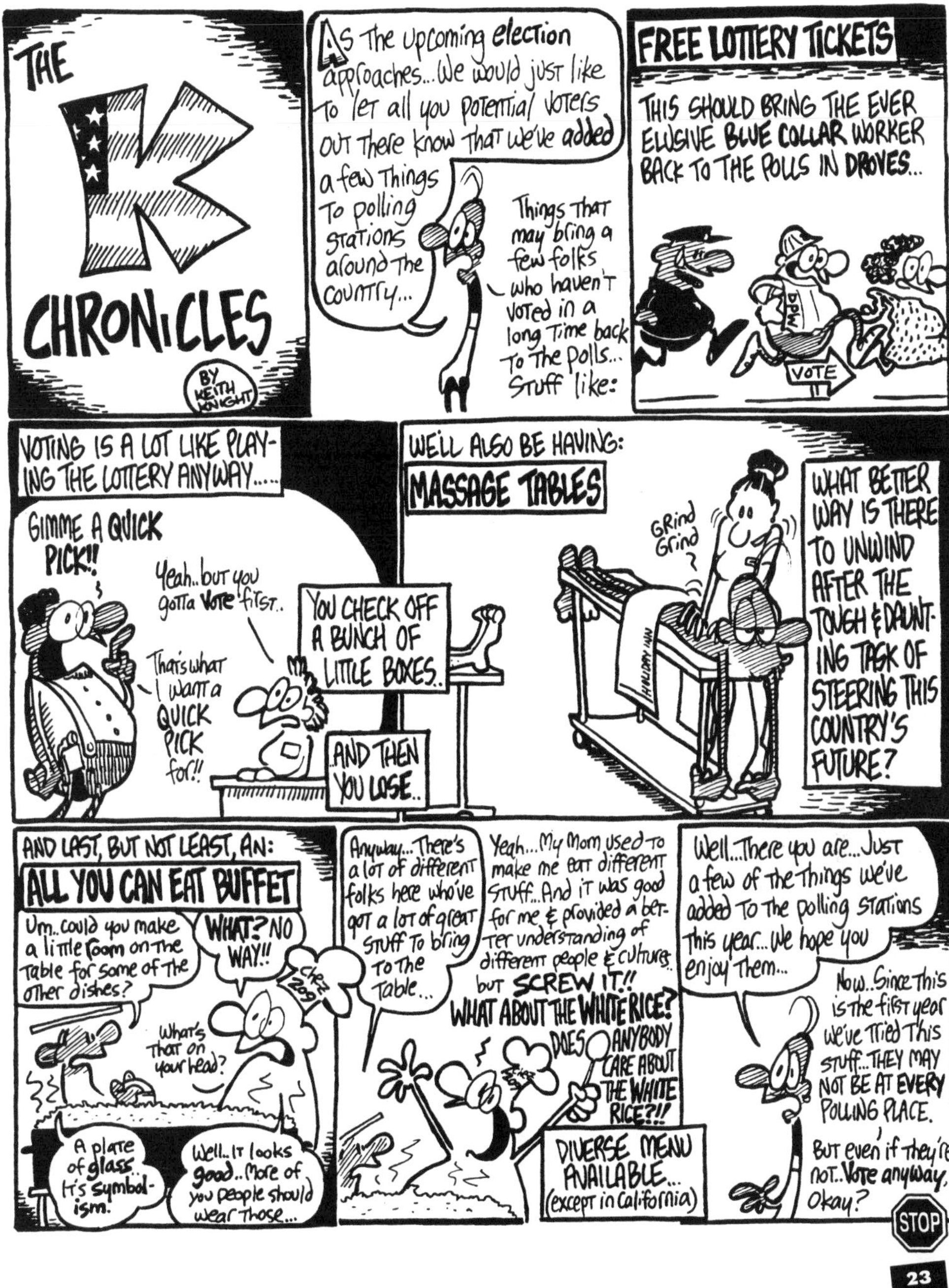
THE K CHRONICLES
BY KEITH KNIGHT
AS THE UPCOMING ELECTION APPROACHES... WE WOULD JUST LIKE TO LET ALL YOU POTENTIAL VOTERS OUT THERE KNOW THAT WE'VE ADDED A FEW THINGS TO POLLING STATIONS AROUND THE COUNTRY...
THINGS THAT MAY BRING A FEW FOLKS WHO HAVEN'T VOTED IN A LONG TIME BACK TO THE POLLS... STUFF LIKE:
FREE LOTTERY TICKETS
THIS SHOULD BRING THE EVER ELUSIVE BLUE COLLAR WORKER BACK TO THE POLLS IN DROVES...
DPW
VOTE
VOTING IS A LOT LIKE PLAYING THE LOTTERY ANYWAY.....
GIMME A QUICK PICK!!
YEAH.. BUT YOU GOTTA VOTE FIRST..
THAT'S WHAT I WANT A QUICK PICK FOR!!
YOU CHECK OFF A BUNCH OF LITTLE BOXES..
..AND THEN YOU LOSE..
WE'LL ALSO BE HAVING:
MASSAGE TABLES
GRIND GRIND
HOLIDAY INN
WHAT BETTER WAY IS THERE TO UNWIND AFTER THE TOUGH & DAUNTING TASK OF STEERING THIS COUNTRY'S FUTURE?
AND LAST, BUT NOT LEAST, AN:
ALL YOU CAN EAT BUFFET
UM.. COULD YOU MAKE A LITTLE ROOM ON THE TABLE FOR SOME OF THE OTHER DISHES?
WHAT? NO WAY!!
CHEZ ZOG
WHAT'S THAT ON YOUR HEAD?
A PLATE OF GLASS.. IT'S SYMBOLISM.
WELL.. IT LOOKS GOOD.. MORE OF YOU PEOPLE SHOULD WEAR THOSE...
ANYWAY... THERE'S A LOT OF DIFFERENT FOLKS HERE WHO'VE GOT A LOT OF GREAT STUFF TO BRING TO THE TABLE...
YEAH... MY MOM USED TO MAKE ME EAT DIFFERENT STUFF... AND IT WAS GOOD FOR ME & PROVIDED A BETTER UNDERSTANDING OF DIFFERENT PEOPLE & CULTURES.. BUT SCREW IT!!
WHAT ABOUT THE WHITE RICE?
DOES ANYBODY CARE ABOUT THE WHITE RICE?!!
DIVERSE MENU AVAILABLE... (EXCEPT IN CALIFORNIA)
WELL... THERE YOU ARE... JUST A FEW OF THE THINGS WE'VE ADDED TO THE POLLING STATIONS THIS YEAR... WE HOPE YOU ENJOY THEM...
NOW.. SINCE THIS IS THE FIRST YEAR WE'VE TRIED THIS STUFF... THEY MAY NOT BE AT EVERY POLLING PLACE.
BUT EVEN IF THEY'RE NOT.. VOTE ANYWAY, OKAY?
STOP

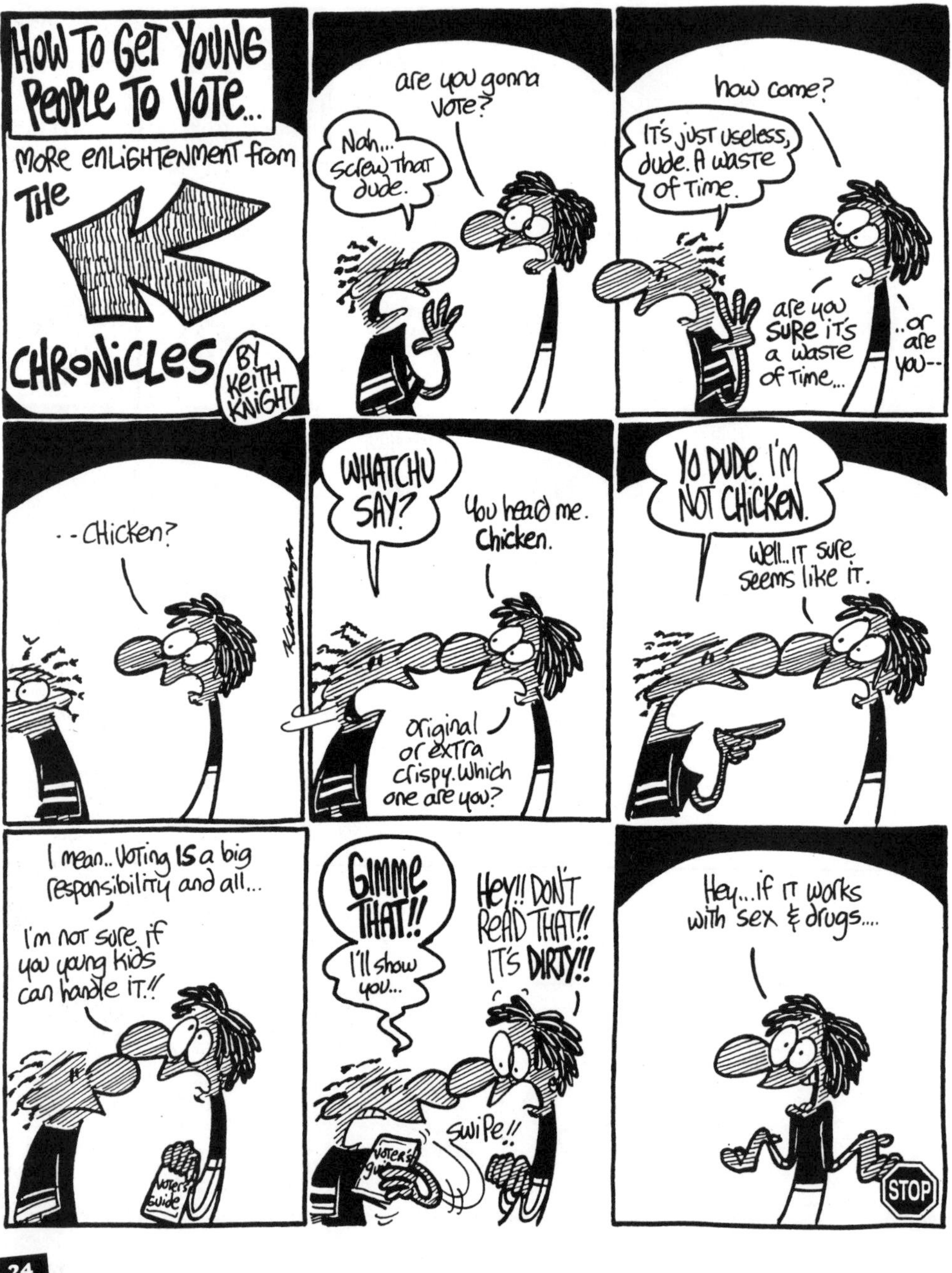

HOW TO GET YOUNG PEOPLE TO VOTE...
MORE ENLIGHTENMENT FROM THE (K) CHRONICLES
BY KEITH KNIGHT
are you gonna vote?
Nah... screw that dude.
how come?
IT'S JUST USELESS, DUDE. A WASTE OF TIME.
are you SURE IT'S a waste of time...
..or are you--
- - CHICKEN?
WHATCHU SAY?
You heard me. Chicken.
original or extra crispy. Which one are you?
YO DUDE. I'M NOT CHICKEN.
Well.. IT sure seems like IT.
I mean.. Voting IS a big responsibility and all...
I'm not sure if you young kids can handle IT!!
Voter's Guide
GIMME THAT!!
I'll show you...
HEY!! DON'T READ THAT!! IT'S DIRTY!!
SWIPE!!
Hey...if IT works with sex & drugs....
STOP

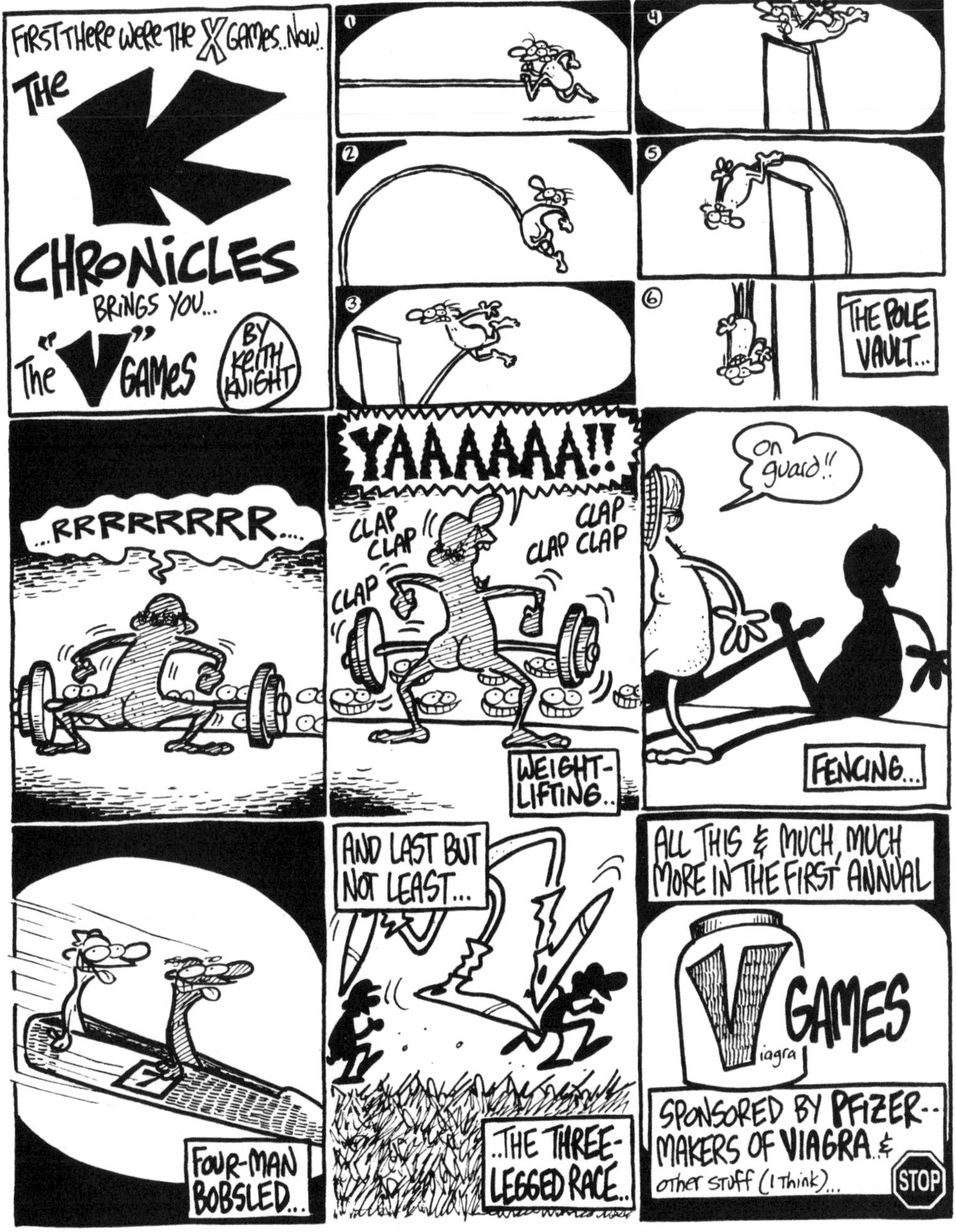
FIRST THERE WERE THE X GAMES.. NOW..
THE K CHRONICLES
BRINGS YOU...
The "V" GAMES
BY KEITH KNIGHT
THE POLE VAULT...
...RRRRRRRR....
YAAAAAA!!
CLAP CLAP
CLAP CLAP
CLAP
WEIGHT-LIFTING..
On guard!!
FENCING...
FOUR-MAN BOBSLED...
AND LAST BUT NOT LEAST...
..THE THREE-LEGGED RACE..
ALL THIS & MUCH, MUCH MORE IN THE FIRST ANNUAL
V GAMES
Viagra
SPONSORED BY PFIZER.. MAKERS OF VIAGRA..&
other stuff (I think)...
STOP

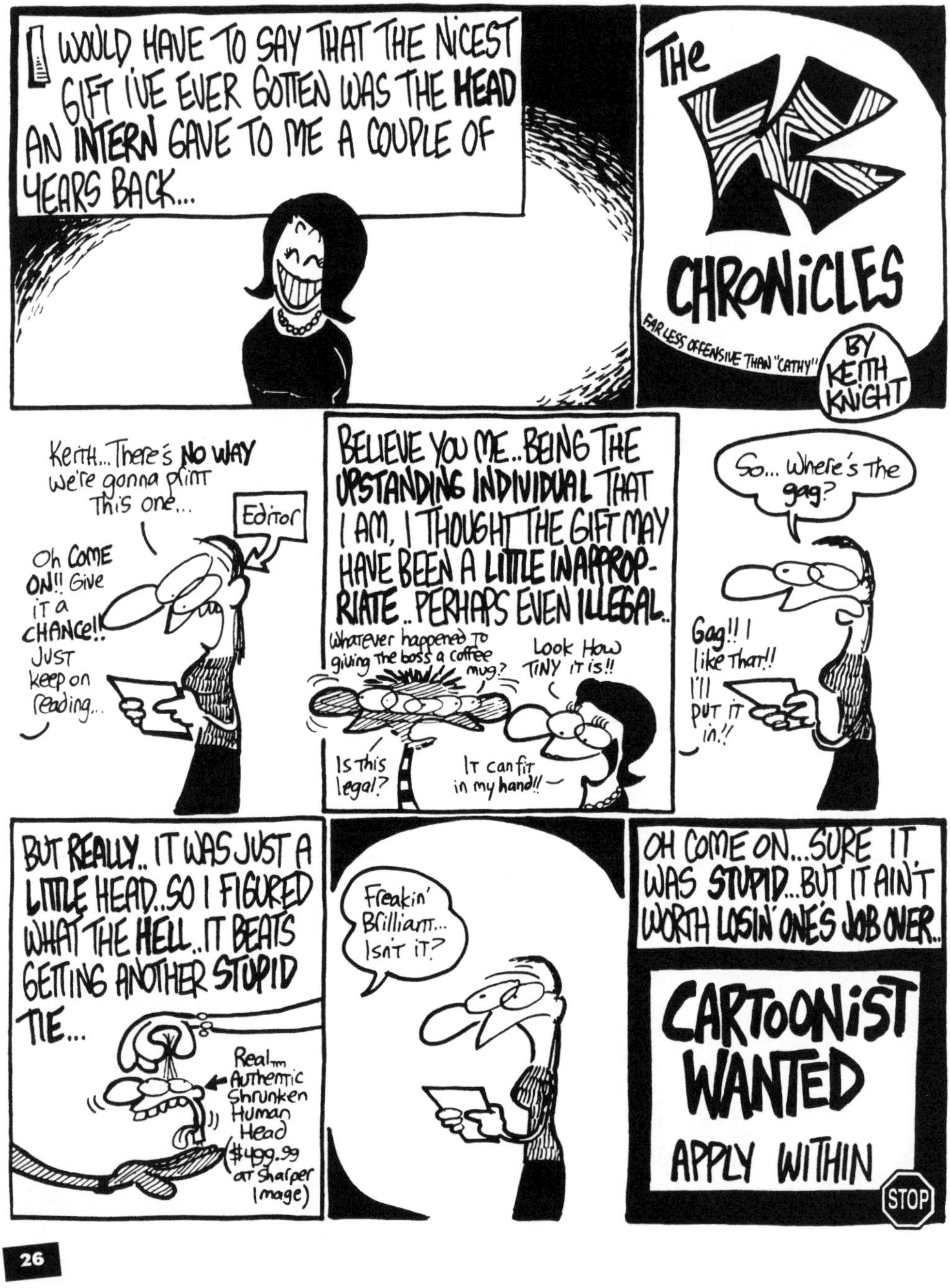

I WOULD HAVE TO SAY THAT THE NICEST GIFT I'VE EVER GOTTEN WAS THE HEAD AN INTERN GAVE TO ME A COUPLE OF YEARS BACK...
THE K CHRONICLES
FAR LESS OFFENSIVE THAN "CATHY"
BY KEITH KNIGHT
Keith... There's NO WAY we're gonna print This one...
Editor
Oh COME ON!! Give it a CHANCE!! JUST keep on reading...
BELIEVE YOU ME... BEING THE UPSTANDING INDIVIDUAL THAT I AM, I THOUGHT THE GIFT MAY HAVE BEEN A LITTLE INAPPROPRIATE.. PERHAPS EVEN ILLEGAL..
Whatever happened to giving the boss a coffee mug?
Look How TINY it is!!
Is this legal?
It can fit in my hand!!
So... where's the gag?
Gag!! I like That!! I'll put it in!!
BUT REALLY.. IT WAS JUST A LITTLE HEAD.. SO I FIGURED WHAT THE HELL.. IT BEATS GETTING ANOTHER STUPID TIE...
Real™ Authentic Shrunken Human Head ($499.99 at Sharper Image)
Freakin' Brilliant... Isn't it?
OH COME ON... SURE IT WAS STUPID... BUT IT AIN'T WORTH LOSIN' ONE'S JOB OVER..
CARTOONIST WANTED
APPLY WITHIN
STOP

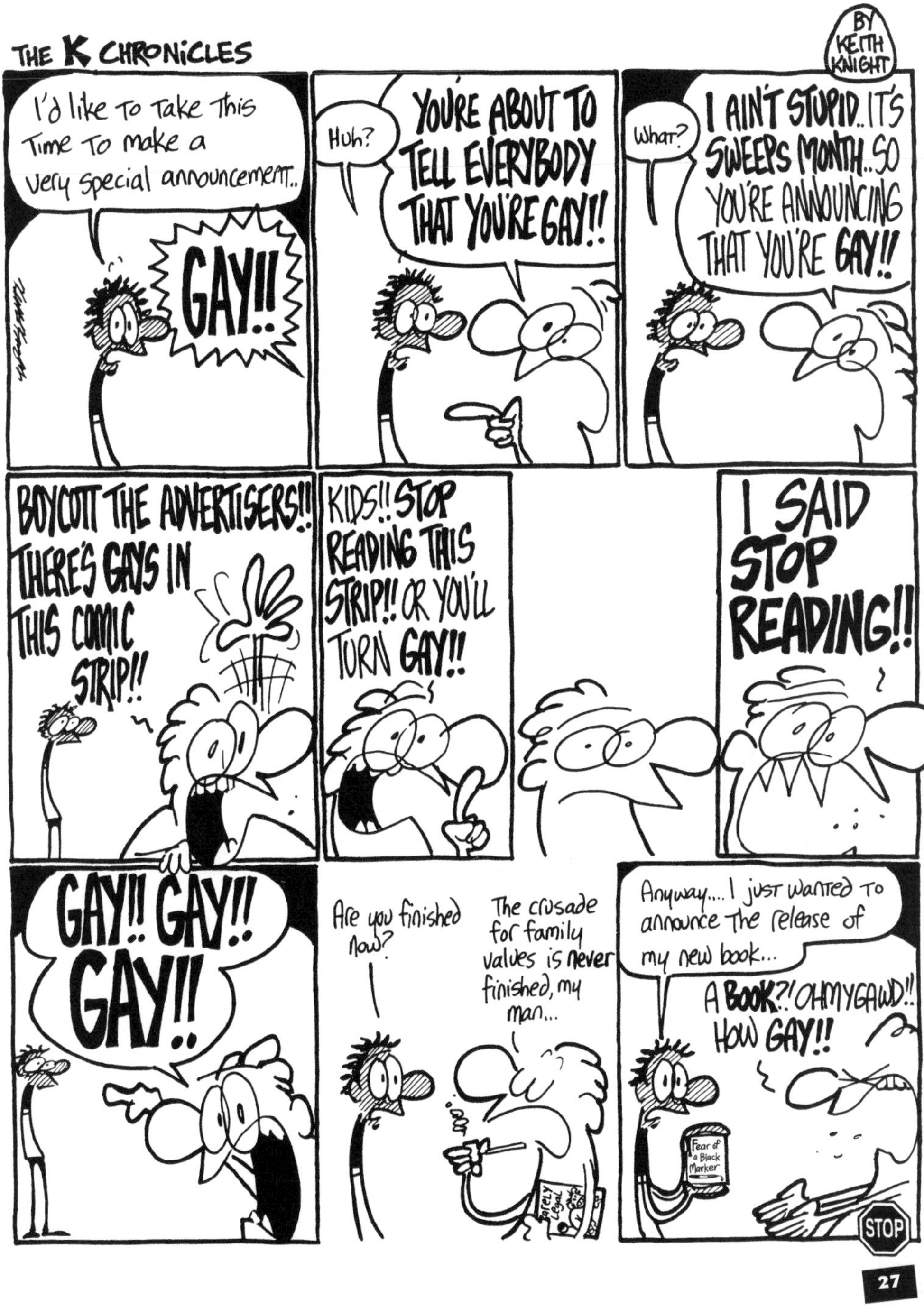
THE K CHRONICLES
BY KEITH KNIGHT
I'd like to take this time to make a very special announcement..
GAY!!
Huh?
YOU'RE ABOUT TO TELL EVERYBODY THAT YOU'RE GAY!!
What?
I AIN'T STUPID.. IT'S SWEEPS MONTH.. SO YOU'RE ANNOUNCING THAT YOU'RE GAY!!
BOYCOTT THE ADVERTISERS!! THERE'S GAYS IN THIS COMIC STRIP!!
KIDS!! STOP READING THIS STRIP!! OR YOU'LL TURN GAY!!
I SAID STOP READING!!
GAY!! GAY!! GAY!!
Are you finished now?
The crusade for family values is never finished, my man...
Barely Legal
Anyway.... I just wanted to announce the release of my new book...
A BOOK?! OHMYGAWD!! HOW GAY!!
Fear of a Black Marker
STOP

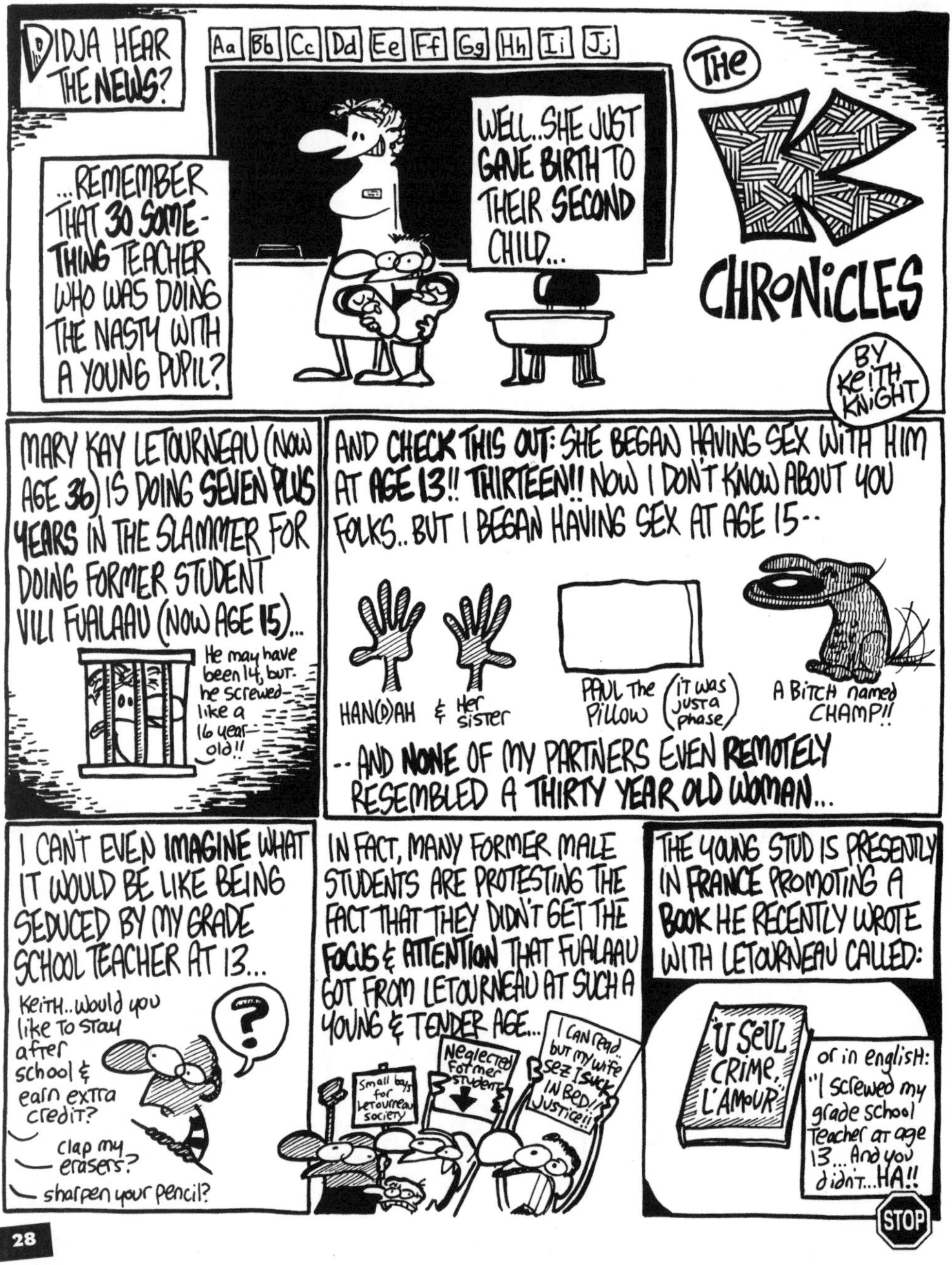
DIDJA HEAR THE NEWS?
Aa Bb Cc Dd Ee Ff Gg Hh Ii Jj
...REMEMBER THAT 30 SOME-THING TEACHER WHO WAS DOING THE NASTY WITH A YOUNG PUPIL?
WELL..SHE JUST GAVE BIRTH TO THEIR SECOND CHILD...
THE K CHRONICLES
BY KEITH KNIGHT
MARY KAY LETOURNEAU (NOW AGE 36) IS DOING SEVEN PLUS YEARS IN THE SLAMMER FOR DOING FORMER STUDENT VILI FUALAAU (NOW AGE 15)...
He may have been 14, but... he screwed like a 16 year old!!
AND CHECK THIS OUT: SHE BEGAN HAVING SEX WITH HIM AT AGE 13!! THIRTEEN!! NOW I DON'T KNOW ABOUT YOU FOLKS.. BUT I BEGAN HAVING SEX AT AGE 15--
HAN(D)AH & Her sister
PAUL The Pillow
(it was just a phase)
A BITCH named CHAMP!!
--AND NONE OF MY PARTNERS EVEN REMOTELY RESEMBLED A THIRTY YEAR OLD WOMAN...
I CAN'T EVEN IMAGINE WHAT IT WOULD BE LIKE BEING SEDUCED BY MY GRADE SCHOOL TEACHER AT 13...
KEITH...Would you like to stay after school & earn extra credit?
?
clap my erasers?
sharpen your pencil?
IN FACT, MANY FORMER MALE STUDENTS ARE PROTESTING THE FACT THAT THEY DIDN'T GET THE FOCUS & ATTENTION THAT FUALAAU GOT FROM LETOURNEAU AT SUCH A YOUNG & TENDER AGE...
Small boys for Letourneau society
Neglected Former Students
I can read.. but my wife sez I SUCK IN BED!! JUSTICE!!
THE YOUNG STUD IS PRESENTLY IN FRANCE PROMOTING A BOOK HE RECENTLY WROTE WITH LETOURNEAU CALLED:
"U SEUL CRIME, L'AMOUR"
or in english: "I screwed my grade school Teacher at age 13... And you didn't...HA!!
STOP

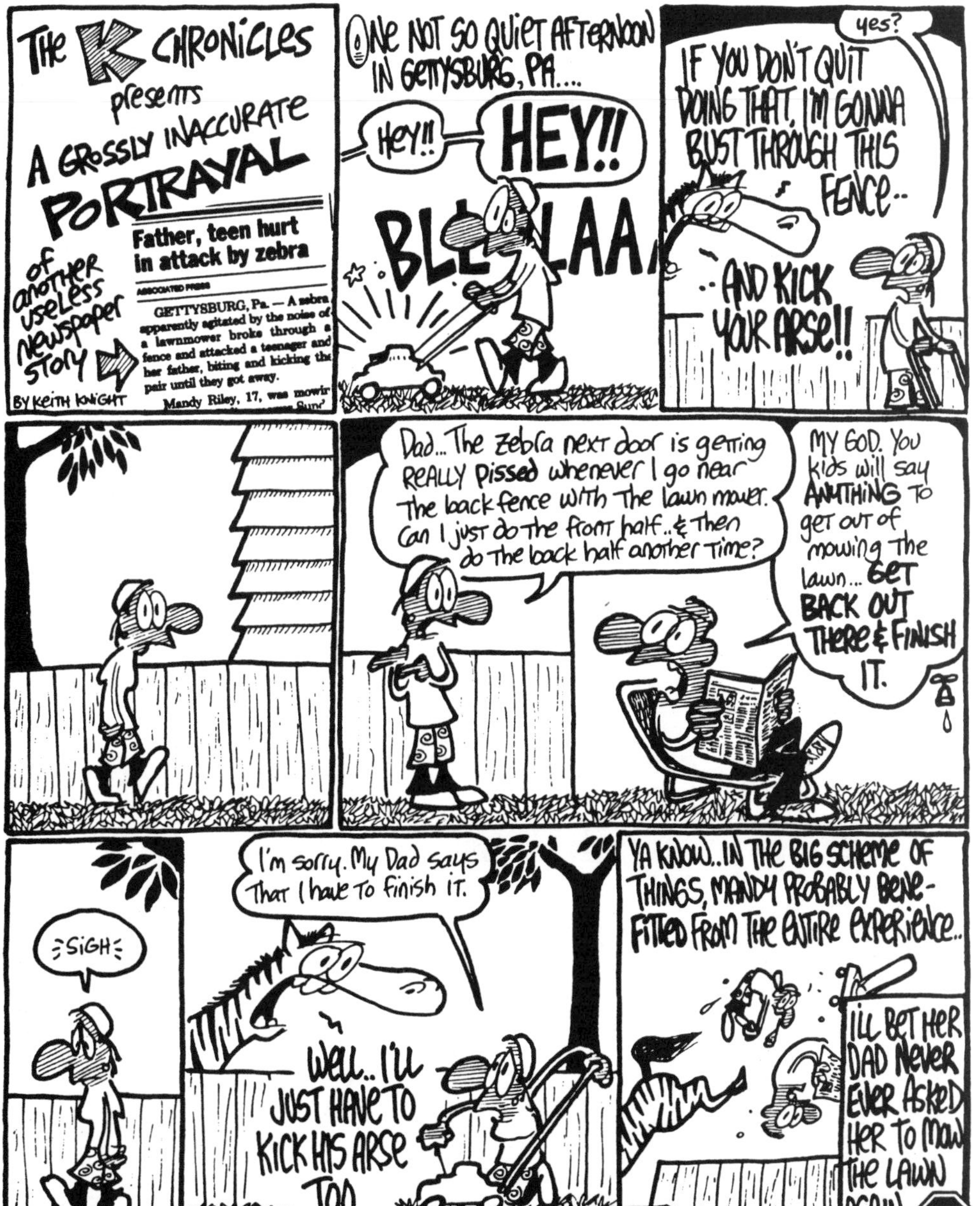
THE K CHRONICLES presents
A GROSSLY INACCURATE PORTRAYAL
of another useless newspaper story
BY KEITH KNIGHT
Father, teen hurt in attack by zebra
ASSOCIATED PRESS
GETTYSBURG, Pa. — A zebra apparently agitated by the noise of a lawnmower broke through a fence and attacked a teenager and her father, biting and kicking the pair until they got away.
Mandy Riley, 17, was mowir
ONE NOT SO QUIET AFTERNOON IN GETTYSBURG, PA....
HEY!!
HEY!!
BLLLAAA
yes?
IF YOU DON'T QUIT DOING THAT, I'M GONNA BUST THROUGH THIS FENCE..
AND KICK YOUR ARSE!!
Dad... The zebra next door is getting REALLY pissed whenever I go near The back fence with The lawn mower. Can I just do the front half.. & Then do The back half another Time?
MY GOD. You kids will say ANYTHING To get out of mowing The lawn... GET BACK OUT THERE & FINISH IT.
SIGH
I'm sorry. My Dad says That I have To finish IT.
WELL.. I'LL JUST HAVE TO KICK HIS ARSE TOO...
YA KNOW.. IN THE BIG SCHEME OF THINGS, MANDY PROBABLY BENEFITTED FROM THE ENTIRE EXPERIENCE..
I'LL BET HER DAD NEVER EVER ASKED HER TO MOW THE LAWN AGAIN..
STOP

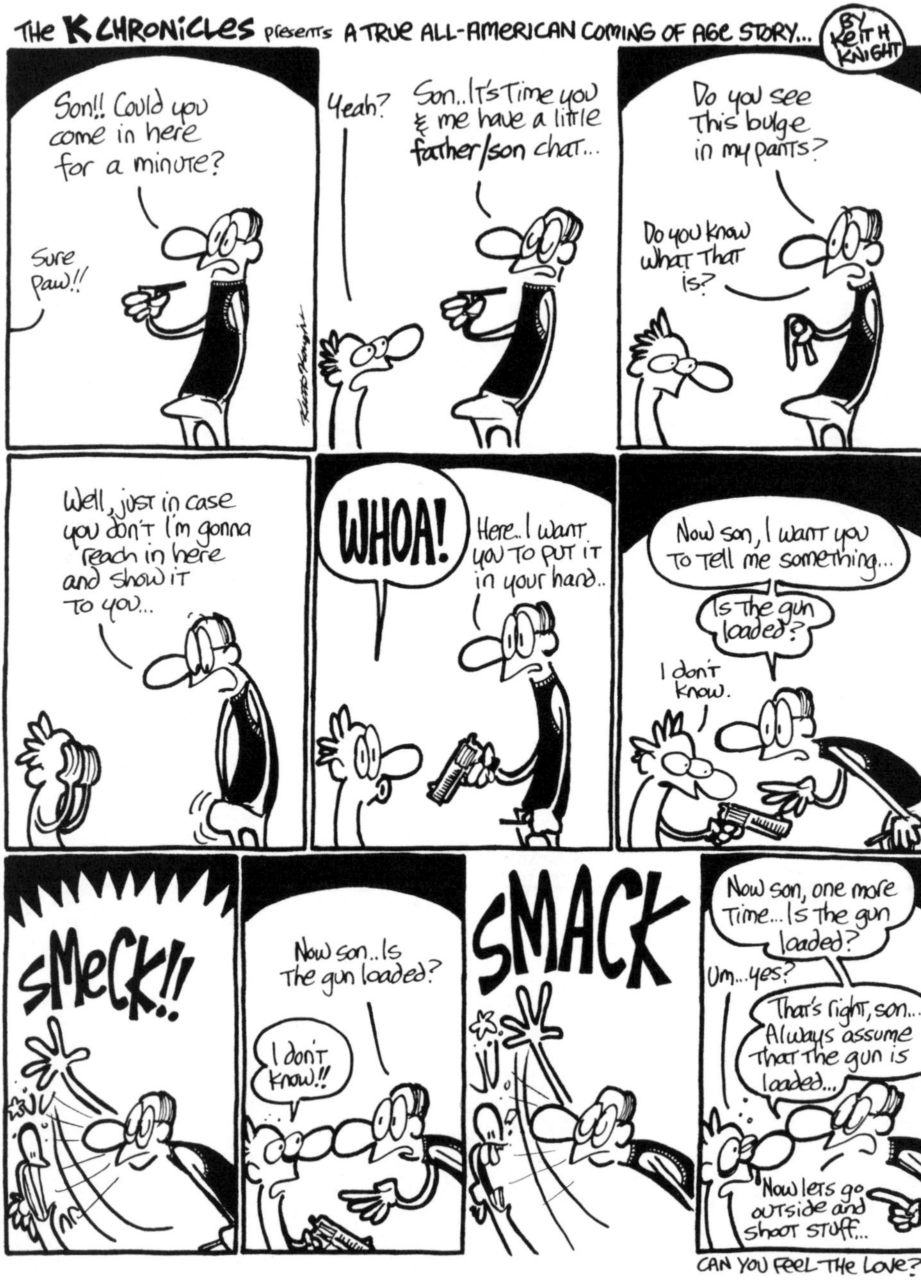
THE K CHRONICLES presents A TRUE ALL-AMERICAN COMING OF AGE STORY...
BY KEITH KNIGHT
Son!! Could you come in here for a minute?
Sure Paw!!
Yeah?
Son.. It's Time you & me have a little father/son chat...
Do you see This bulge in my pants?
Do you know what That is?
Well, just in case you don't I'm gonna reach in here and show it to you...
WHOA!
Here.. I want you to put it in your hand..
Now son, I want you to tell me something...
Is The gun loaded?
I don't know.
SMECK!!
Now son.. Is The gun loaded?
I don't know!!
SMACK
Now son, one more Time... Is The gun loaded?
Um...yes?
That's right, son... Always assume That The gun is loaded...
Now lets go outside and shoot stuff...
CAN YOU FEEL THE LOVE?

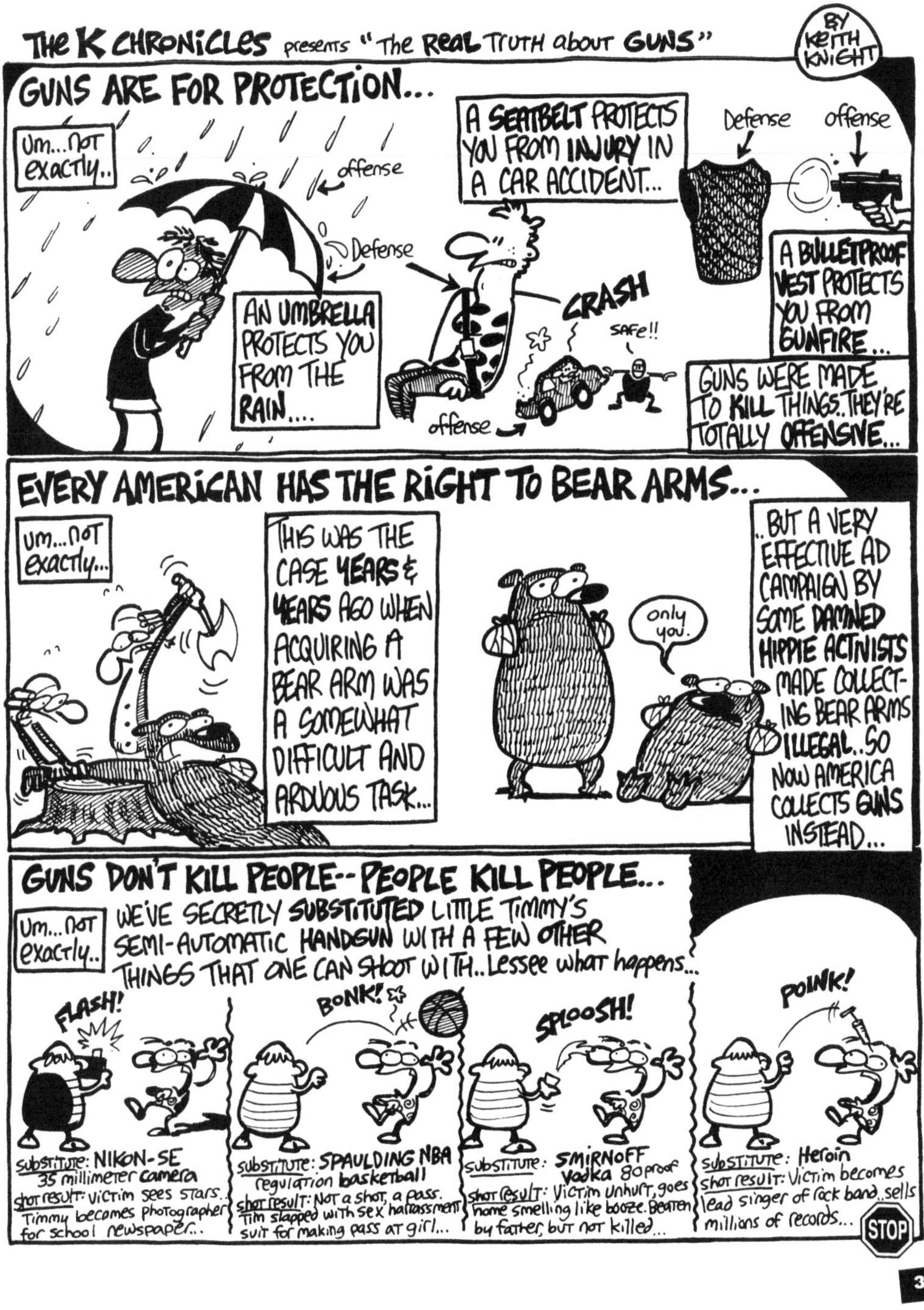
THE K CHRONICLES presents "The REAL TRUTH about GUNS"
BY KEITH KNIGHT
GUNS ARE FOR PROTECTION...
Um...not exactly..
offense
Defense
AN UMBRELLA PROTECTS YOU FROM THE RAIN....
A SEATBELT PROTECTS YOU FROM INJURY IN A CAR ACCIDENT...
CRASH
SAFE!!
offense
Defense
offense
A BULLETPROOF VEST PROTECTS YOU FROM GUNFIRE...
GUNS WERE MADE TO KILL THINGS..THEY'RE TOTALLY OFFENSIVE...
EVERY AMERICAN HAS THE RIGHT TO BEAR ARMS...
Um...not exactly...
THIS WAS THE CASE YEARS & YEARS AGO WHEN ACQUIRING A BEAR ARM WAS A SOMEWHAT DIFFICULT AND ARDUOUS TASK...
only you.
..BUT A VERY EFFECTIVE AD CAMPAIGN BY SOME DAMNED HIPPIE ACTIVISTS MADE COLLECTING BEAR ARMS ILLEGAL..SO NOW AMERICA COLLECTS GUNS INSTEAD...
GUNS DON'T KILL PEOPLE--PEOPLE KILL PEOPLE...
Um...not exactly..
WE'VE SECRETLY SUBSTITUTED LITTLE TIMMY'S SEMI-AUTOMATIC HANDGUN WITH A FEW OTHER THINGS THAT ONE CAN SHOOT WITH.. Lessee what happens...
FLASH!
SUBSTITUTE: NIKON-SE 35 millimeter camera
shot result: Victim sees stars.. Timmy becomes photographer for school newspaper..
BONK!
SUBSTITUTE: SPAULDING NBA regulation basketball
shot result: Not a shot, a pass. Tim slapped with sex harassment suit for making pass at girl...
SPLOOSH!
SUBSTITUTE: SMIRNOFF Vodka 80 proof
shot result: Victim unhurt, goes home smelling like booze. Beaten by father, but not killed...
POINK!
SUBSTITUTE: Heroin
shot result: Victim becomes lead singer of rock band..sells millions of records...
STOP

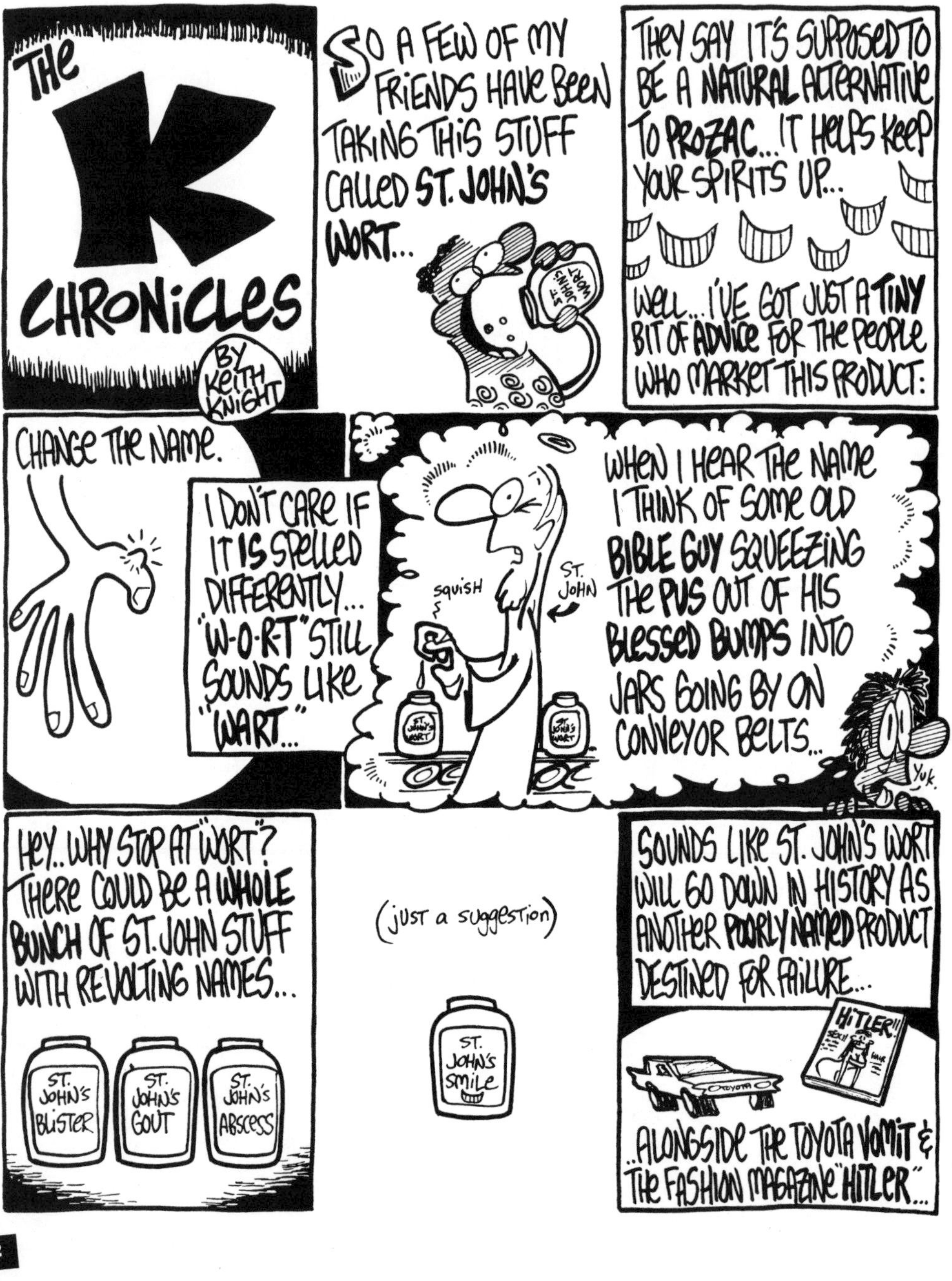

THE K CHRONICLES
BY KEITH KNIGHT
SO A FEW OF MY FRIENDS HAVE BEEN TAKING THIS STUFF CALLED ST. JOHN'S WORT...
ST. JOHN'S WORT
THEY SAY IT'S SUPPOSED TO BE A NATURAL ALTERNATIVE TO PROZAC... IT HELPS KEEP YOUR SPIRITS UP...
WELL... I'VE GOT JUST A TINY BIT OF ADVICE FOR THE PEOPLE WHO MARKET THIS PRODUCT:
CHANGE THE NAME.
I DON'T CARE IF IT IS SPELLED DIFFERENTLY... "W-O-R-T" STILL SOUNDS LIKE "WART"...
SQUISH
ST. JOHN
ST. JOHN'S WORT
ST. JOHN'S WORT
WHEN I HEAR THE NAME I THINK OF SOME OLD BIBLE GUY SQUEEZING THE PUS OUT OF HIS BLESSED BUMPS INTO JARS GOING BY ON CONVEYOR BELTS...
YUK.
HEY.. WHY STOP AT "WORT"? THERE COULD BE A WHOLE BUNCH OF ST. JOHN STUFF WITH REVOLTING NAMES...
ST. JOHN'S BLISTER
ST. JOHN'S GOUT
ST. JOHN'S ABSCESS
(JUST A SUGGESTION)
ST. JOHN'S SMILE
SOUNDS LIKE ST. JOHN'S WORT WILL GO DOWN IN HISTORY AS ANOTHER POORLY NAMED PRODUCT DESTINED FOR FAILURE...
HITLER!!
TOYOTA
...ALONGSIDE THE TOYOTA VOMIT & THE FASHION MAGAZINE "HITLER"...

THE **K** CHRONICLES

BY KEITH KNIGHT

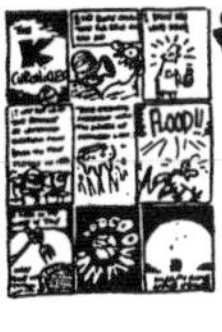

HELLO FOLKS!! YOU MAY HAVE NOTICED SOMETHING A LITTLE **DIFFERENT** ABOUT THIS WEEK'S STRIP... IT'S A BIT **SMALLER** THAN USUAL...ABOUT **90%** SMALLER. WHY?... WELL, THE **U.S. HOUSE INTERIOR APPROPRIATION SUBCOMMITTEE** APPROVED A PROPOSED **90% BUDGET CUT** TO THE **NATIONAL ENDOWMENT FOR THE ARTS**...**THIS AFTER ALREADY CUTTING THE NEA BUDGET BY 40% IN 1995**. THE NEA IS A MAJOR FUNDING RESOURCE FOR **HUNDREDS**, PERHAPS **THOUSANDS** OF ARTISTS AND ARTS ORGANIZATIONS THAT CREATE BEAUTY, PROVOKE THOUGHT & ADD CULTURAL RICHNESS TO COMMUNITIES BOTH RICH AND POOR, SMALL AND LARGE, **NATIONWIDE**. I JUST WANTED TO SHOW EVERYBODY HOW BIG A REDUCTION THIS WOULD BE BY SHRINKING MY COMIC BY THE **SAME** PERCENTAGE.... SORRY ABOUT THIS BUT I THOUGHT THAT IT WOULD BE THE BEST WAY TO GET THE POINT ACROSS.

BY THE WAY, THIS WEEK'S STRIP WAS PROBABLY MY **BEST** SO FAR... A HYSTERICAL **TOUR DE FORCE** FEATURING **MIKE TYSON, 27 LACTATING HOLSTEIN COWS**, AND A **HALF EATEN PIECE OF DAY OLD FUDGE**..ANYWAY, TO PREVENT THIS CUT FROM OCCURING, **CALL (202) 225-3121**, & ASK TO BE CONNECTED TO **YOUR** MEMBER OF CONGRESS & **TELL 'EM NOT TO DO IT!!** Thanks!! STOP

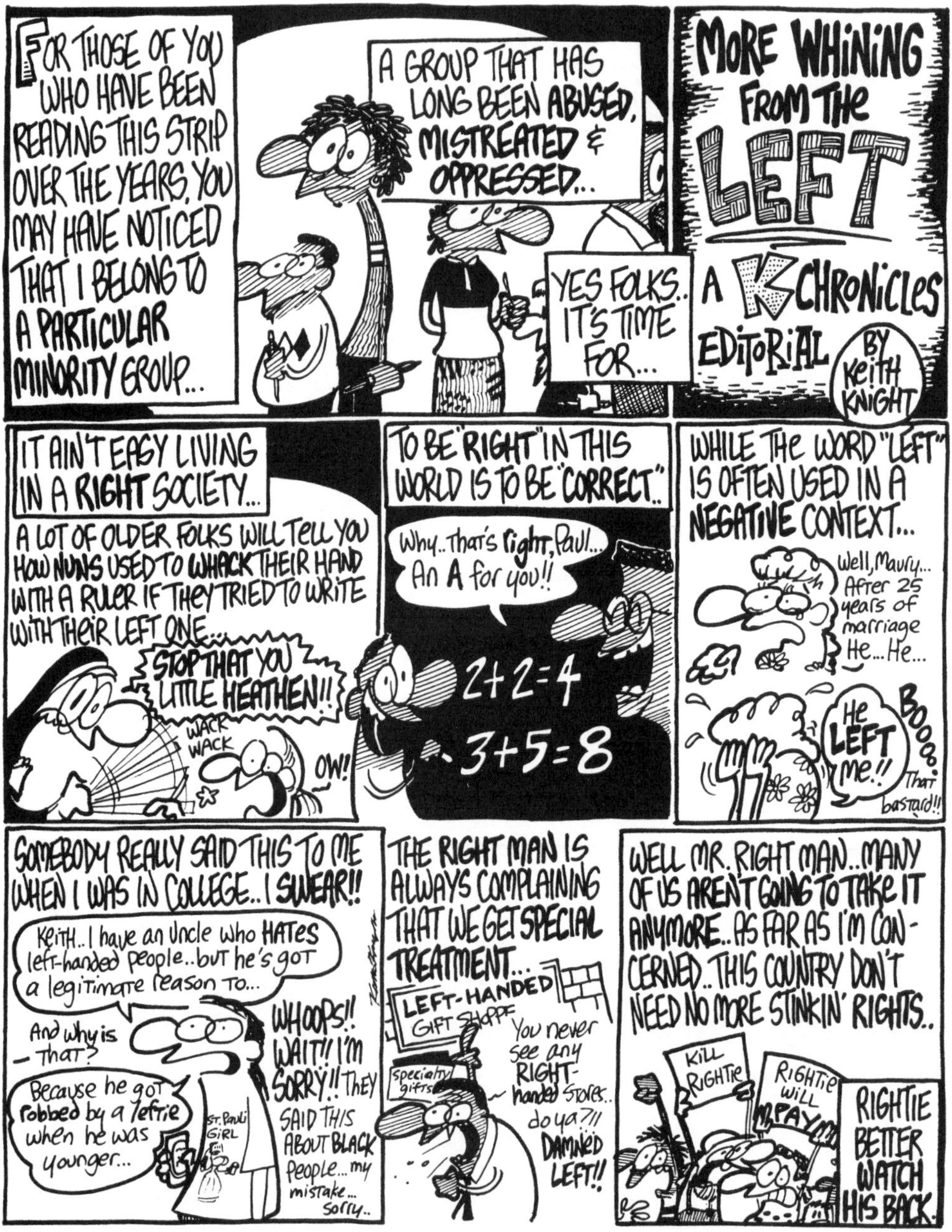
FOR THOSE OF YOU WHO HAVE BEEN READING THIS STRIP OVER THE YEARS, YOU MAY HAVE NOTICED THAT I BELONG TO A PARTICULAR MINORITY GROUP...
A GROUP THAT HAS LONG BEEN ABUSED, MISTREATED & OPPRESSED...
YES FOLKS.. IT'S TIME FOR...
MORE WHINING FROM THE LEFT
A K CHRONICLES EDITORIAL
BY KEITH KNIGHT
IT AIN'T EASY LIVING IN A RIGHT SOCIETY...
A LOT OF OLDER FOLKS WILL TELL YOU HOW NUNS USED TO WHACK THEIR HAND WITH A RULER IF THEY TRIED TO WRITE WITH THEIR LEFT ONE...
STOP THAT YOU LITTLE HEATHEN!!
WACK WACK
OW!
TO BE "RIGHT" IN THIS WORLD IS TO BE "CORRECT."
Why.. That's right, Paul... An A for you!!
2+2=4
3+5=8
WHILE THE WORD "LEFT" IS OFTEN USED IN A NEGATIVE CONTEXT...
Well, Maury... After 25 years of marriage He... He...
He LEFT me!!
Boooo.
That bastard!!
SOMEBODY REALLY SAID THIS TO ME WHEN I WAS IN COLLEGE.. I SWEAR!!
Keith.. I have an Uncle who HATES left-handed people.. but he's got a legitimate reason to...
And why is that?
Because he got robbed by a leftie when he was younger...
ST. PAULI GIRL
WHOOPS!! WAIT!! I'M SORRY!! THEY SAID THIS ABOUT BLACK people... my mistake... sorry..
THE RIGHT MAN IS ALWAYS COMPLAINING THAT WE GET SPECIAL TREATMENT...
LEFT-HANDED GIFT SHOPPE
specialty gifts
You never see any RIGHT-handed Stores.. do ya?!!
DAMNED LEFT!!
WELL MR. RIGHT MAN.. MANY OF US AREN'T GOING TO TAKE IT ANYMORE.. AS FAR AS I'M CONCERNED.. THIS COUNTRY DON'T NEED NO MORE STINKIN' RIGHTS..
KILL RIGHTIE
RIGHTIE WILL PAY
RIGHTIE BETTER WATCH HIS BACK.

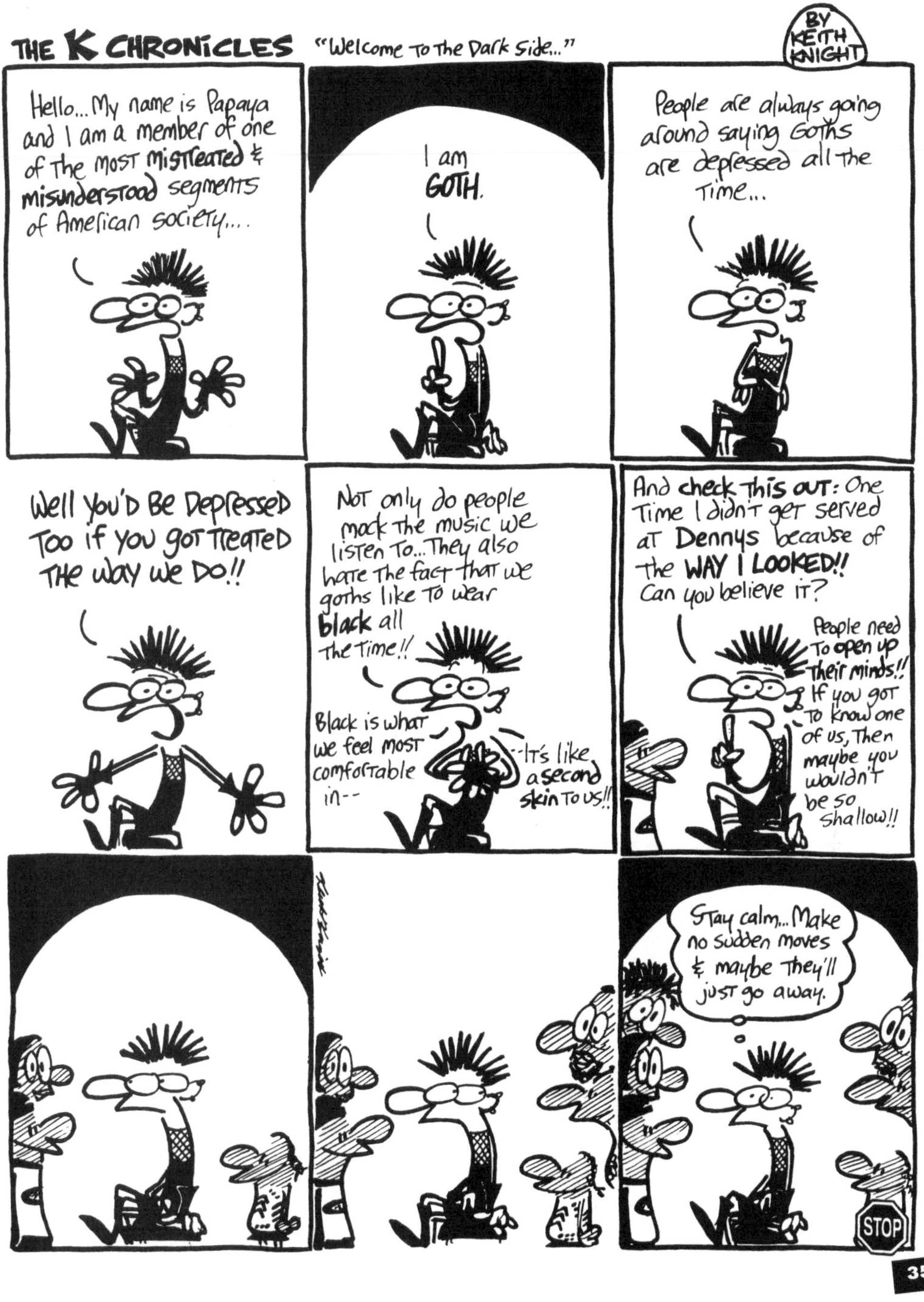
THE K CHRONICLES "Welcome To The Dark Side..."
BY KEITH KNIGHT
Hello... My name is Papaya and I am a member of one of the most mistreated & misunderstood segments of American society....
I am GOTH.
People are always going around saying Goths are depressed all the time...
Well you'd be depressed too if you got treated the way we do!!
Not only do people mock the music we listen to... They also hate the fact that we goths like to wear black all the time!!
Black is what we feel most comfortable in--
--It's like a second skin to us!!
And check this out: One time I didn't get served at Dennys because of the WAY I LOOKED!! Can you believe it?
People need to open up their minds!! If you got to know one of us, then maybe you wouldn't be so shallow!!
Stay calm... Make no sudden moves & maybe they'll just go away.
STOP

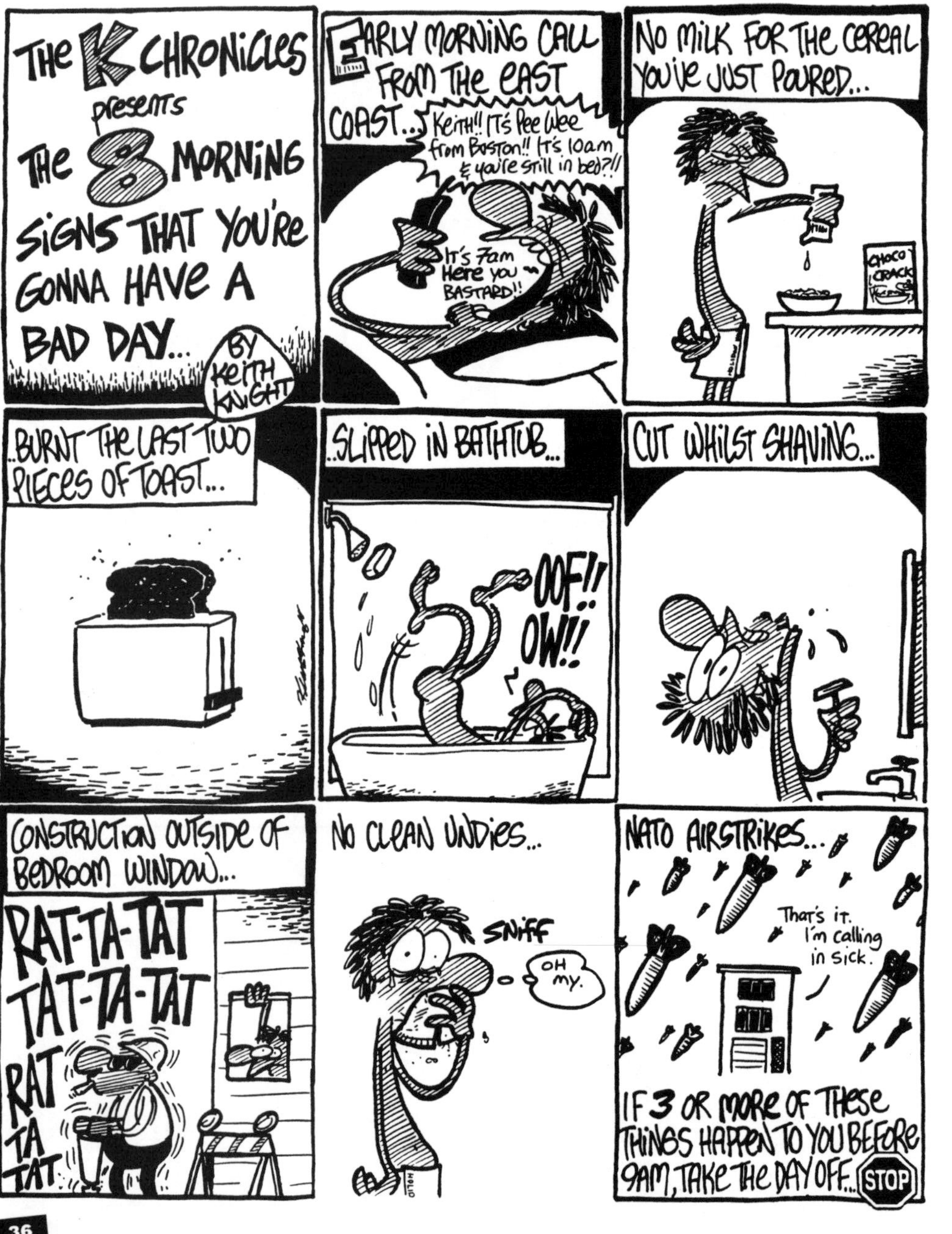
THE K CHRONICLES
presents
THE 8 MORNING SIGNS THAT YOU'RE GONNA HAVE A BAD DAY...
BY KEITH KNIGHT
EARLY MORNING CALL FROM THE EAST COAST...
KEITH!! IT'S Pee Wee from Boston!! It's 10am & you're still in bed?!!
It's 7am Here you BASTARD!!
NO MILK FOR THE CEREAL YOU'VE JUST POURED...
CHOCO CRACK
..BURNT THE LAST TWO PIECES OF TOAST...
..SLIPPED IN BATHTUB...
OOF!! OW!!
CUT WHILST SHAVING...
CONSTRUCTION OUTSIDE OF BEDROOM WINDOW...
RAT-TA-TAT TAT-TA-TAT RAT TA TAT
NO CLEAN UNDIES...
SNIFF
OH MY.
NATO AIRSTRIKES...
That's it. I'm calling in sick.
IF 3 OR MORE OF THESE THINGS HAPPEN TO YOU BEFORE 9AM, TAKE THE DAY OFF...
STOP

BY KEITH KNIGHT

1 JUST VISITED YOSEMITE NATIONAL PARK RECENTLY...

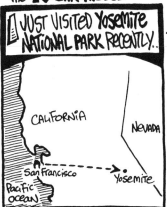

CALIFORNIA

NEVADA

San Francisco

Pacific Ocean

Yosemite

I WAS OUT THERE ATTENDING THE WEDDING OF STARK RAVING BRAD GONZO PERCUSSIONIST OF THE WORLD'S MOST INCREDIBLE BAND, THE MARGINAL PROPHETS*...

BRAD

ANDIE

* MY BAND!

YOSEMITE IS A GREAT PLACE TO GET MARRIED... HELL...IT'S A GREAT PLACE TO DO ANYTHING...

Grand Canyon of the Tuolumne

Hetch Hetchy Res.

Tuolumne Meadows

1189 SQUARE MILES OF STUNNING WATERFALLS, RUSHING RIVERS, ALPINE MEADOWS, HUNGRY BEARS & GRANITE CLIFFS...

A BUNCH OF FOLKS FROM THE WEDDING PARTY WENT ON A HIKE ALONG THE HETCH HETCHY RESERVOIR THE DAY BEFORE THE CEREMONY...

I WAS PSYCHED BECAUSE I COULD FINALLY PUT MY HIKING BOOTS TO GOOD USE...

HIKING BOOTS ARE LIKE THE SPORT UTILITY VEHICLES OF FOOTWEAR...

PEOPLE DON'T BUY THEM TO GO OUT INTO THE WOODS... THEY BUY THEM BECAUSE THEY LOOK COOL...

SITTING IN CITY TRAFFIC

7 MILES TO THE GALLON

BEEP!

ANYWAYS...AFTER ABOUT **20** MINUTES OF HIKING, OUR EXPEDITION CAME TO AN ABRUPT HALT...

WHOA!!

Rattle Rattle

I WAS A **HALF-STEP** AWAY FROM AN INTIMATE ENCOUNTER WITH A 2-FOOT LONG RATTLESNAKE!!

RATTLE

..IT WAS GIVING ME A "DON'T TREAD ON ME" WARNING RATTLE

YEESH...I GOTTA TELL YA.. I DIG THE GREAT OUTDOORS & ALL...

VH1 Behind the Music

..BUT IT'S INCIDENTS LIKE THAT THAT MAKE ME THINK CABLE T.V. AIN'T REALLY THAT BAD...

STOP

37

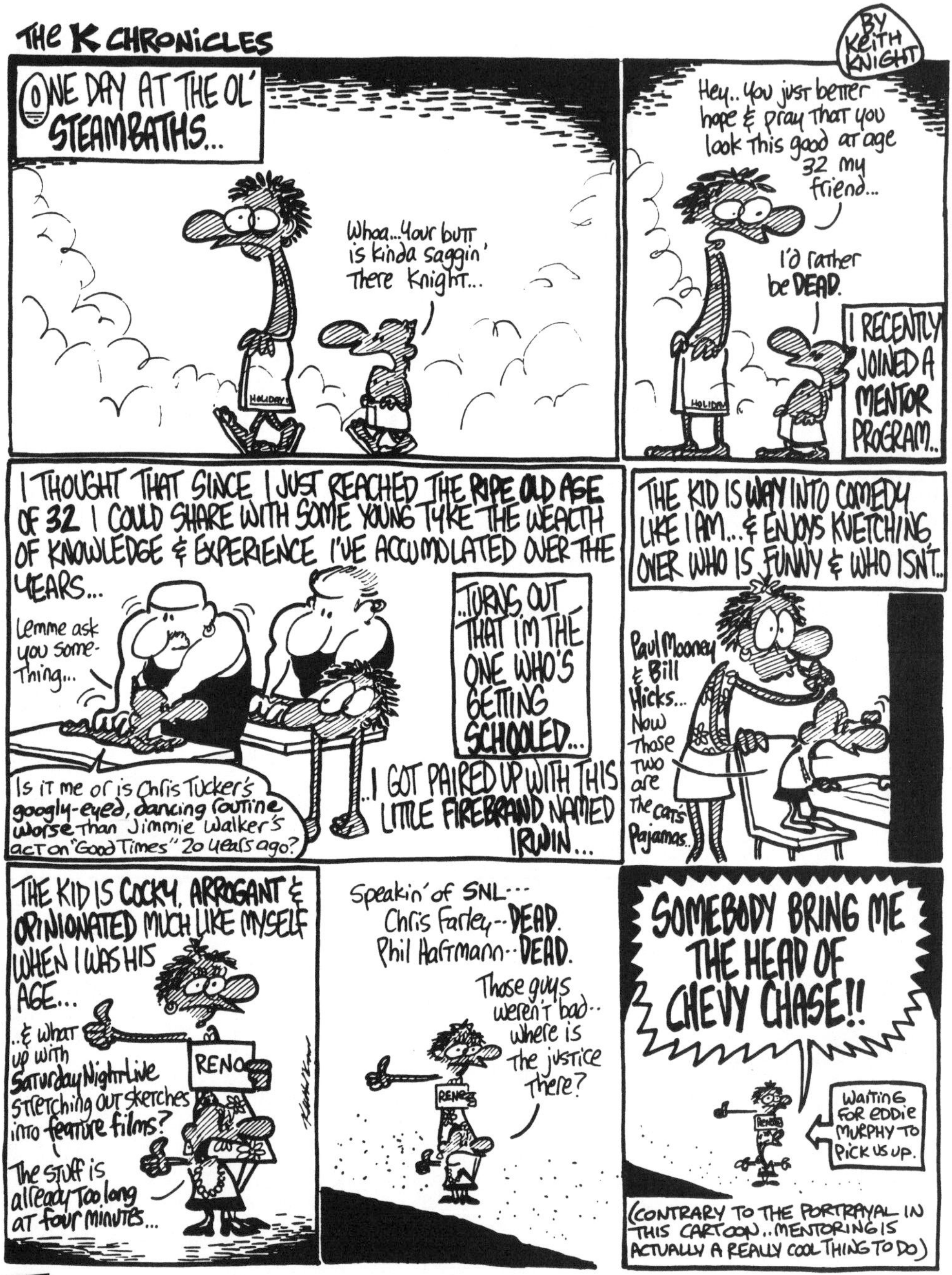
THE K CHRONICLES
BY KEITH KNIGHT
ONE DAY AT THE OL' STEAMBATHS...
Whoa...Your butt is kinda saggin' there Knight...
HOLIDAY
Hey.. you just better hope & pray that you look this good at age 32 my friend...
I'd rather be DEAD.
I RECENTLY JOINED A MENTOR PROGRAM..
I THOUGHT THAT SINCE I JUST REACHED THE RIPE OLD AGE OF 32 I COULD SHARE WITH SOME YOUNG TYKE THE WEALTH OF KNOWLEDGE & EXPERIENCE I'VE ACCUMULATED OVER THE YEARS...
Lemme ask you some-thing...
..TURNS OUT THAT I'M THE ONE WHO'S GETTING SCHOOLED...
Is it me or is Chris Tucker's googly-eyed, dancing routine worse than Jimmie Walker's act on "Good Times" 20 years ago?
..I GOT PAIRED UP WITH THIS LITTLE FIREBRAND NAMED IRWIN...
THE KID IS WAY INTO COMEDY LIKE I AM... & ENJOYS KVETCHING OVER WHO IS FUNNY & WHO ISN'T..
Paul Mooney & Bill Hicks... Now those two are the cat's Pajamas..
THE KID IS COCKY, ARROGANT & OPINIONATED MUCH LIKE MYSELF WHEN I WAS HIS AGE...
..& what up with Saturday Night Live stretching out sketches into feature films?
RENO
The stuff is already too long at four minutes...
Speakin' of SNL...
Chris Farley--DEAD.
Phil Hartmann--DEAD.
Those guys weren't bad.. where is the justice there?
RENO
SOMEBODY BRING ME THE HEAD OF CHEVY CHASE!!
WAITING FOR EDDIE MURPHY TO PICK US UP.
(CONTRARY TO THE PORTRAYAL IN THIS CARTOON..MENTORING IS ACTUALLY A REALLY COOL THING TO DO)

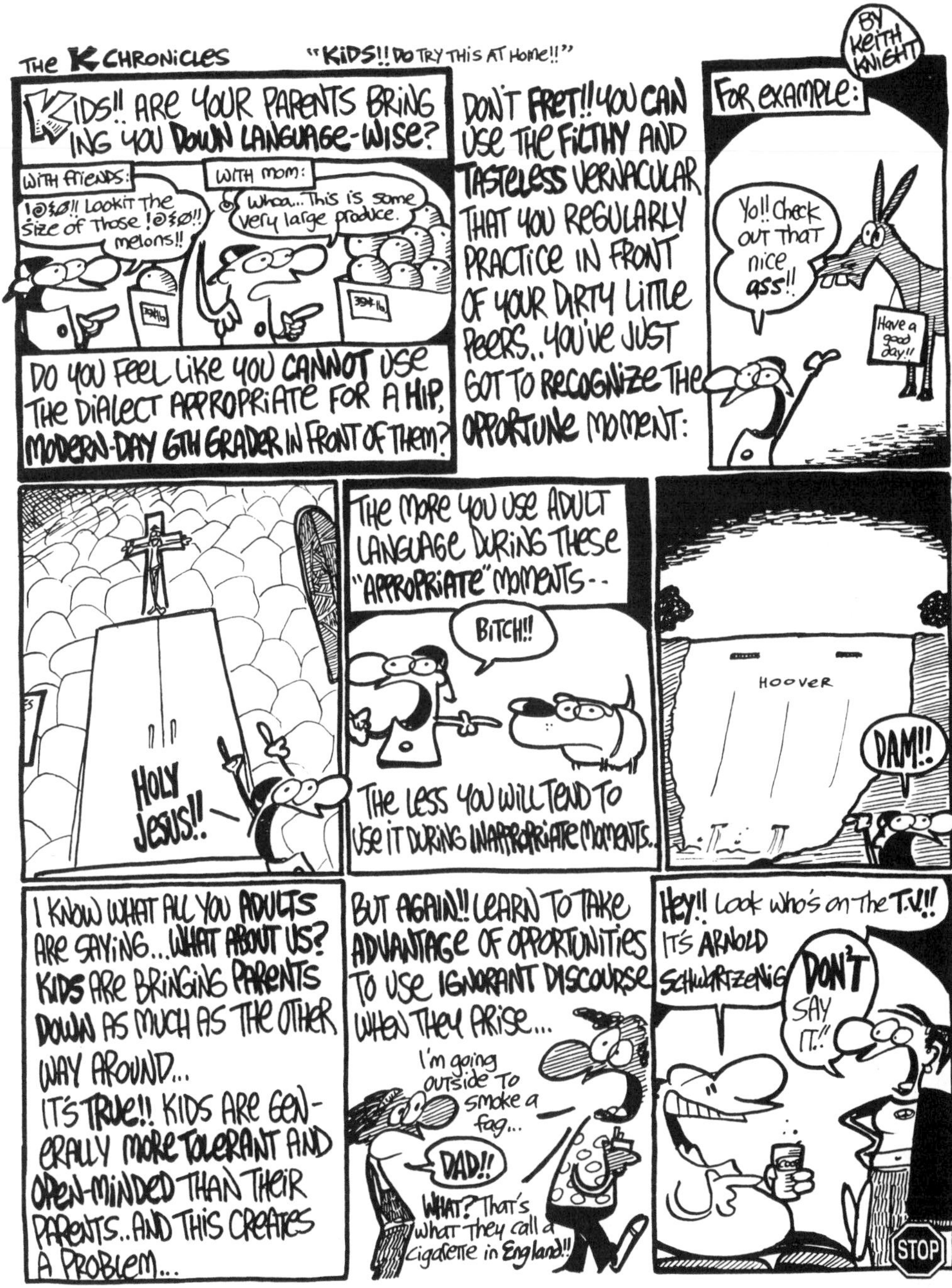
THE K CHRONICLES
"KIDS!! DO TRY THIS AT HOME!!"
BY KEITH KNIGHT
KIDS!! ARE YOUR PARENTS BRINGING YOU DOWN LANGUAGE-WISE?
WITH FRIENDS:
!@$%!! LOOKIT THE SIZE OF THOSE !@$%!! MELONS!!
WITH MOM:
WHOA... THIS IS SOME VERY LARGE PRODUCE.
DO YOU FEEL LIKE YOU CANNOT USE THE DIALECT APPROPRIATE FOR A HIP, MODERN-DAY 6TH GRADER IN FRONT OF THEM?
DON'T FRET!! YOU CAN USE THE FILTHY AND TASTELESS VERNACULAR THAT YOU REGULARLY PRACTICE IN FRONT OF YOUR DIRTY LITTLE PEERS.. YOU'VE JUST GOT TO RECOGNIZE THE OPPORTUNE MOMENT:
FOR EXAMPLE:
YO!! CHECK OUT THAT NICE ASS!!
HAVE A GOOD DAY!!
HOLY JESUS!!
THE MORE YOU USE ADULT LANGUAGE DURING THESE "APPROPRIATE" MOMENTS--
BITCH!!
THE LESS YOU WILL TEND TO USE IT DURING INAPPROPRIATE MOMENTS..
HOOVER
DAM!!
I KNOW WHAT ALL YOU ADULTS ARE SAYING... WHAT ABOUT US? KIDS ARE BRINGING PARENTS DOWN AS MUCH AS THE OTHER WAY AROUND...
IT'S TRUE!! KIDS ARE GENERALLY MORE TOLERANT AND OPEN-MINDED THAN THEIR PARENTS.. AND THIS CREATES A PROBLEM...
BUT AGAIN!! LEARN TO TAKE ADVANTAGE OF OPPORTUNITIES TO USE IGNORANT DISCOURSE WHEN THEY ARISE...
I'M GOING OUTSIDE TO SMOKE A FAG...
DAD!!
WHAT? THAT'S WHAT THEY CALL A CIGARETTE IN ENGLAND!!
HEY!! LOOK WHO'S ON THE T.V.!! IT'S ARNOLD SCHWARTZENIG
DON'T SAY IT!!
STOP

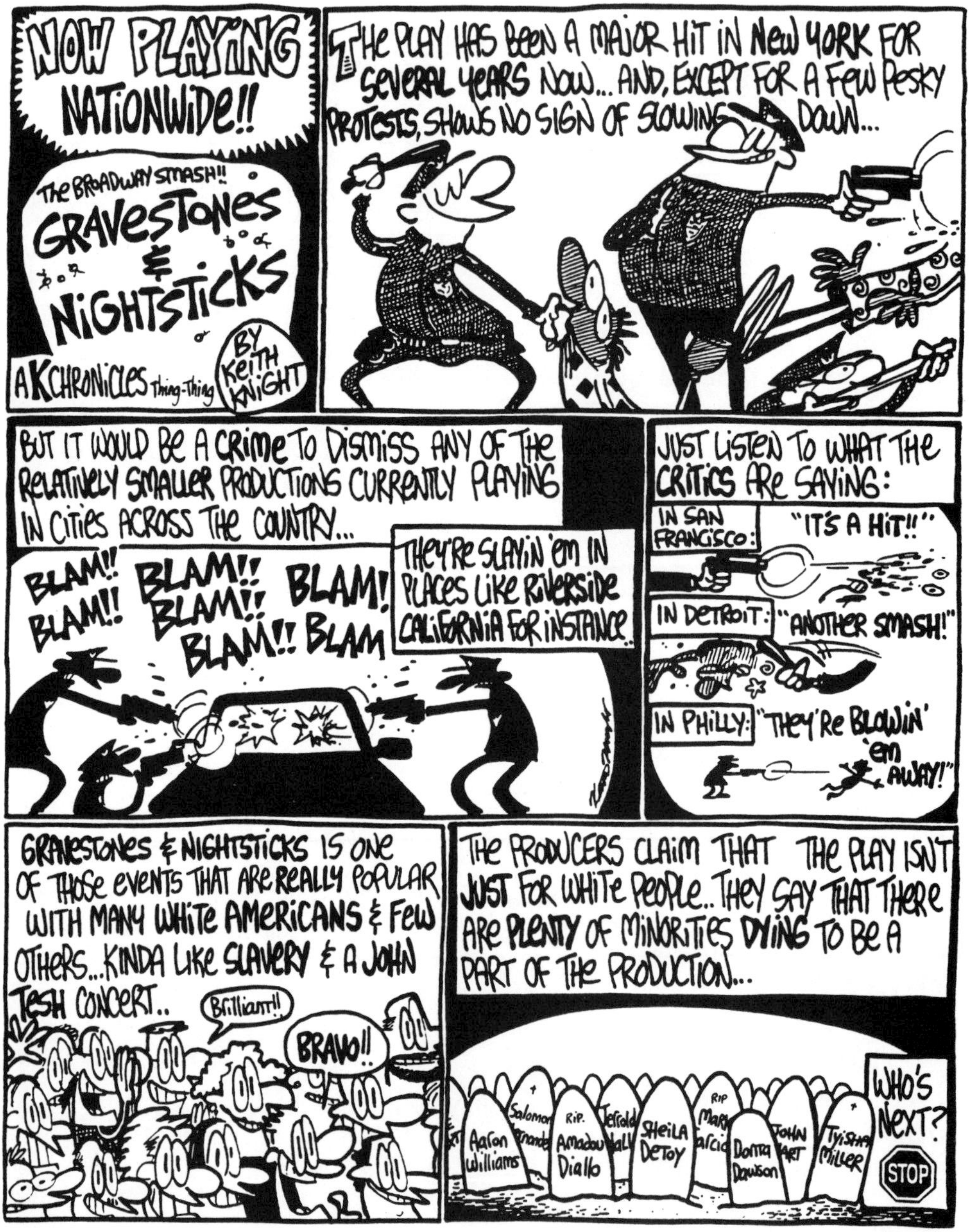
NOW PLAYING NATIONWIDE!!
The BROADWAY SMASH!!
GRAVESTONES & NIGHTSTICKS
or
A K CHRONICLES thing-thing
BY KEITH KNIGHT
THE PLAY HAS BEEN A MAJOR HIT IN NEW YORK FOR SEVERAL YEARS NOW... AND, EXCEPT FOR A FEW PESKY PROTESTS, SHOWS NO SIGN OF SLOWING DOWN...
BUT IT WOULD BE A CRIME TO DISMISS ANY OF THE RELATIVELY SMALLER PRODUCTIONS CURRENTLY PLAYING IN CITIES ACROSS THE COUNTRY...
BLAM!! BLAM!!
BLAM!! BLAM!!
BLAM!! BLAM
BLAM!
THEY'RE SLAYIN' 'EM IN PLACES LIKE RIVERSIDE CALIFORNIA FOR INSTANCE..
JUST LISTEN TO WHAT THE CRITICS ARE SAYING:
IN SAN FRANCISCO: "IT'S A HIT!!"
IN DETROIT: "ANOTHER SMASH!"
IN PHILLY: "THEY'RE BLOWIN' 'EM AWAY!"
GRAVESTONES & NIGHTSTICKS IS ONE OF THOSE EVENTS THAT ARE REALLY POPULAR WITH MANY WHITE AMERICANS & FEW OTHERS...KINDA LIKE SLAVERY & A JOHN TESH CONCERT..
Brilliant!!
BRAVO!!
THE PRODUCERS CLAIM THAT THE PLAY ISN'T JUST FOR WHITE PEOPLE.. THEY SAY THAT THERE ARE PLENTY OF MINORITIES DYING TO BE A PART OF THE PRODUCTION...
Aaron Williams
Salomon
R.I.P. Amadou Diallo
Jerrold
SHEILA DETOY
RIP
Donta Dawson
JOHN
Tyisha Miller
WHO'S NEXT?
STOP

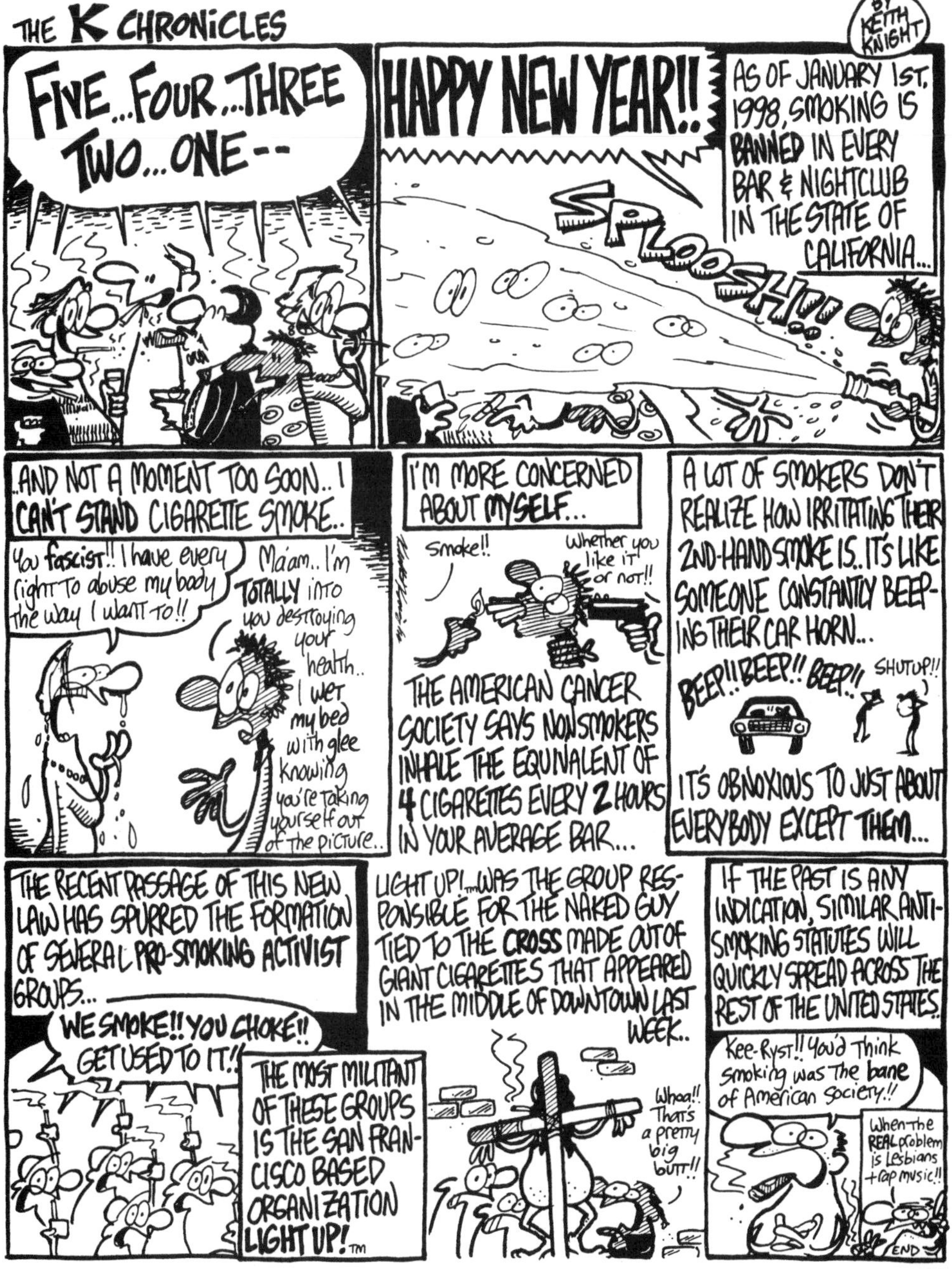

THE K CHRONICLES
BY KEITH KNIGHT
FIVE...FOUR...THREE TWO...ONE--
HAPPY NEW YEAR!!
AS OF JANUARY 1ST, 1998, SMOKING IS BANNED IN EVERY BAR & NIGHTCLUB IN THE STATE OF CALIFORNIA...
SPLOOSH!!!
..AND NOT A MOMENT TOO SOON.. I CAN'T STAND CIGARETTE SMOKE..
You fascist!! I have every right to abuse my body the way I want to!!
Ma'am.. I'm TOTALLY into you destroying your health.. I wet my bed with glee knowing you're taking yourself out of the picture..
I'M MORE CONCERNED ABOUT MYSELF...
Smoke!!
Whether you like it or not!!
THE AMERICAN CANCER SOCIETY SAYS NONSMOKERS INHALE THE EQUIVALENT OF 4 CIGARETTES EVERY 2 HOURS IN YOUR AVERAGE BAR...
A LOT OF SMOKERS DON'T REALIZE HOW IRRITATING THEIR 2ND-HAND SMOKE IS.. IT'S LIKE SOMEONE CONSTANTLY BEEPING THEIR CAR HORN...
BEEP!! BEEP!! BEEP!!
SHUTUP!!
IT'S OBNOXIOUS TO JUST ABOUT EVERYBODY EXCEPT THEM...
THE RECENT PASSAGE OF THIS NEW LAW HAS SPURRED THE FORMATION OF SEVERAL PRO-SMOKING ACTIVIST GROUPS...
WE SMOKE!! YOU CHOKE!! GET USED TO IT!!
THE MOST MILITANT OF THESE GROUPS IS THE SAN FRANCISCO BASED ORGANIZATION LIGHT UP!™
LIGHT UP!™ WAS THE GROUP RESPONSIBLE FOR THE NAKED GUY TIED TO THE CROSS MADE OUT OF GIANT CIGARETTES THAT APPEARED IN THE MIDDLE OF DOWNTOWN LAST WEEK..
Whoa!! That's a pretty big butt!!
IF THE PAST IS ANY INDICATION, SIMILAR ANTI-SMOKING STATUTES WILL QUICKLY SPREAD ACROSS THE REST OF THE UNITED STATES..
Kee-Ryst!! You'd Think smoking was The bane of American society!!
When the REAL problem is Lesbians + rap music!!
END

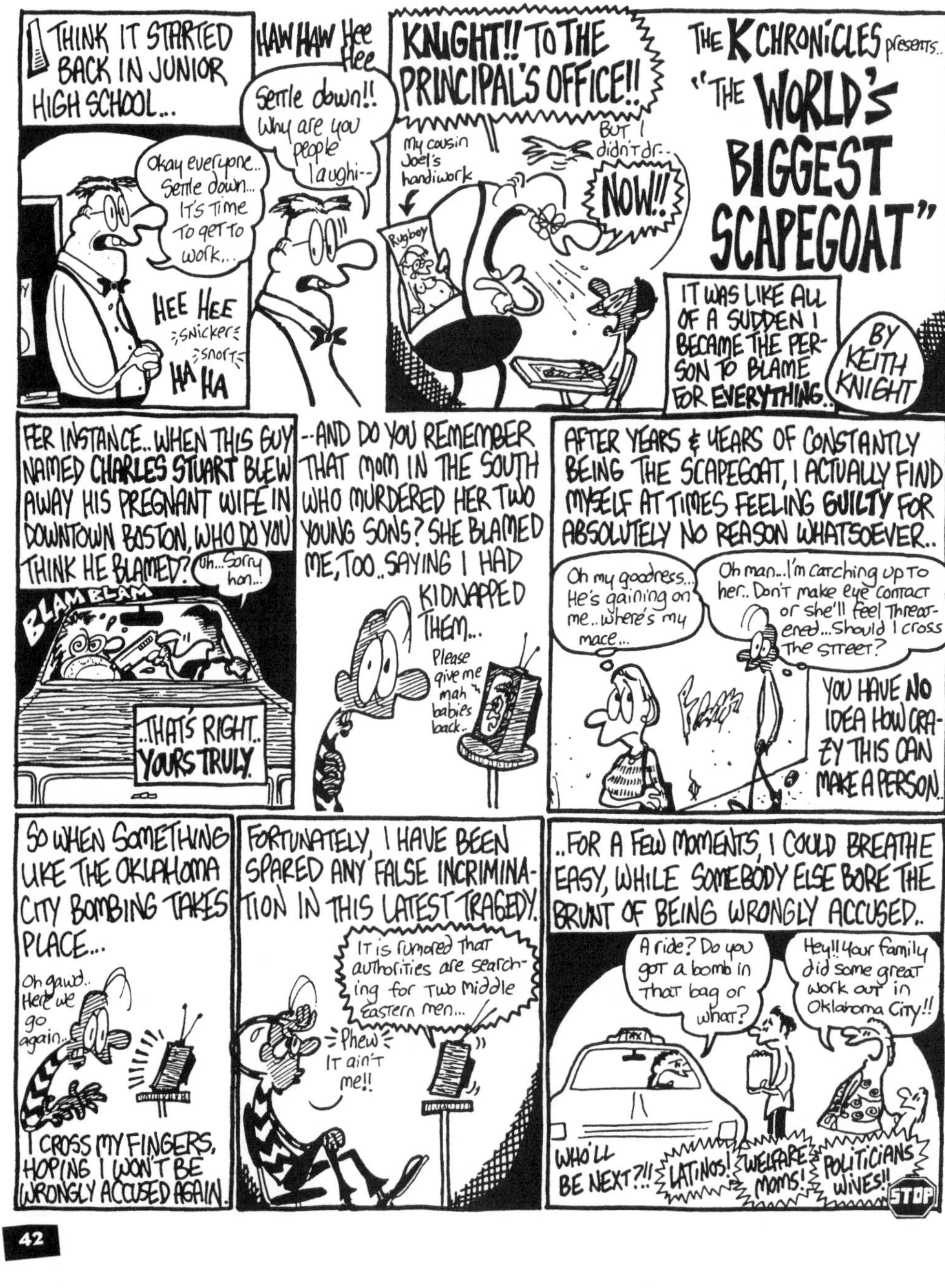
I THINK IT STARTED BACK IN JUNIOR HIGH SCHOOL...
Okay everyone.. Settle down... It's time to get to work...
HEE HEE
snicker
snort
HA HA
HAW HAW Hee Hee
Settle down!! Why are you people laughi--
KNIGHT!! TO THE PRINCIPAL'S OFFICE!!
My cousin Joel's handiwork
Rugboy
But I didn't dr--
NOW!!
THE K CHRONICLES presents..
"THE WORLD'S BIGGEST SCAPEGOAT"
IT WAS LIKE ALL OF A SUDDEN I BECAME THE PERSON TO BLAME FOR EVERYTHING..
BY KEITH KNIGHT
FER INSTANCE.. WHEN THIS GUY NAMED CHARLES STUART BLEW AWAY HIS PREGNANT WIFE IN DOWNTOWN BOSTON, WHO DO YOU THINK HE BLAMED?
Uh... Sorry hon...
BLAM BLAM
..THAT'S RIGHT.. YOURS TRULY.
--AND DO YOU REMEMBER THAT MOM IN THE SOUTH WHO MURDERED HER TWO YOUNG SONS? SHE BLAMED ME, TOO.. SAYING I HAD KIDNAPPED THEM...
Please give me mah babies back..
AFTER YEARS & YEARS OF CONSTANTLY BEING THE SCAPEGOAT, I ACTUALLY FIND MYSELF AT TIMES FEELING GUILTY FOR ABSOLUTELY NO REASON WHATSOEVER..
Oh my goodness... He's gaining on me.. where's my mace...
Oh man... I'm catching up to her.. Don't make eye contact or she'll feel threatened... Should I cross the street?
YOU HAVE NO IDEA HOW CRAZY THIS CAN MAKE A PERSON..
SO WHEN SOMETHING LIKE THE OKLAHOMA CITY BOMBING TAKES PLACE...
Oh gawd.. Here we go again..
I CROSS MY FINGERS, HOPING I WON'T BE WRONGLY ACCUSED AGAIN.
FORTUNATELY, I HAVE BEEN SPARED ANY FALSE INCRIMINATION IN THIS LATEST TRAGEDY.
It is rumored that authorities are searching for two Middle Eastern men...
Phew It ain't me!!
..FOR A FEW MOMENTS, I COULD BREATHE EASY, WHILE SOMEBODY ELSE BORE THE BRUNT OF BEING WRONGLY ACCUSED..
A ride? Do you got a bomb in that bag or what?
Hey!! Your family did some great work out in Oklahoma City!!
TAXI
WHO'LL BE NEXT?!!
LATINOS!
WELFARE MOMS!
POLITICIANS WIVES!!
STOP

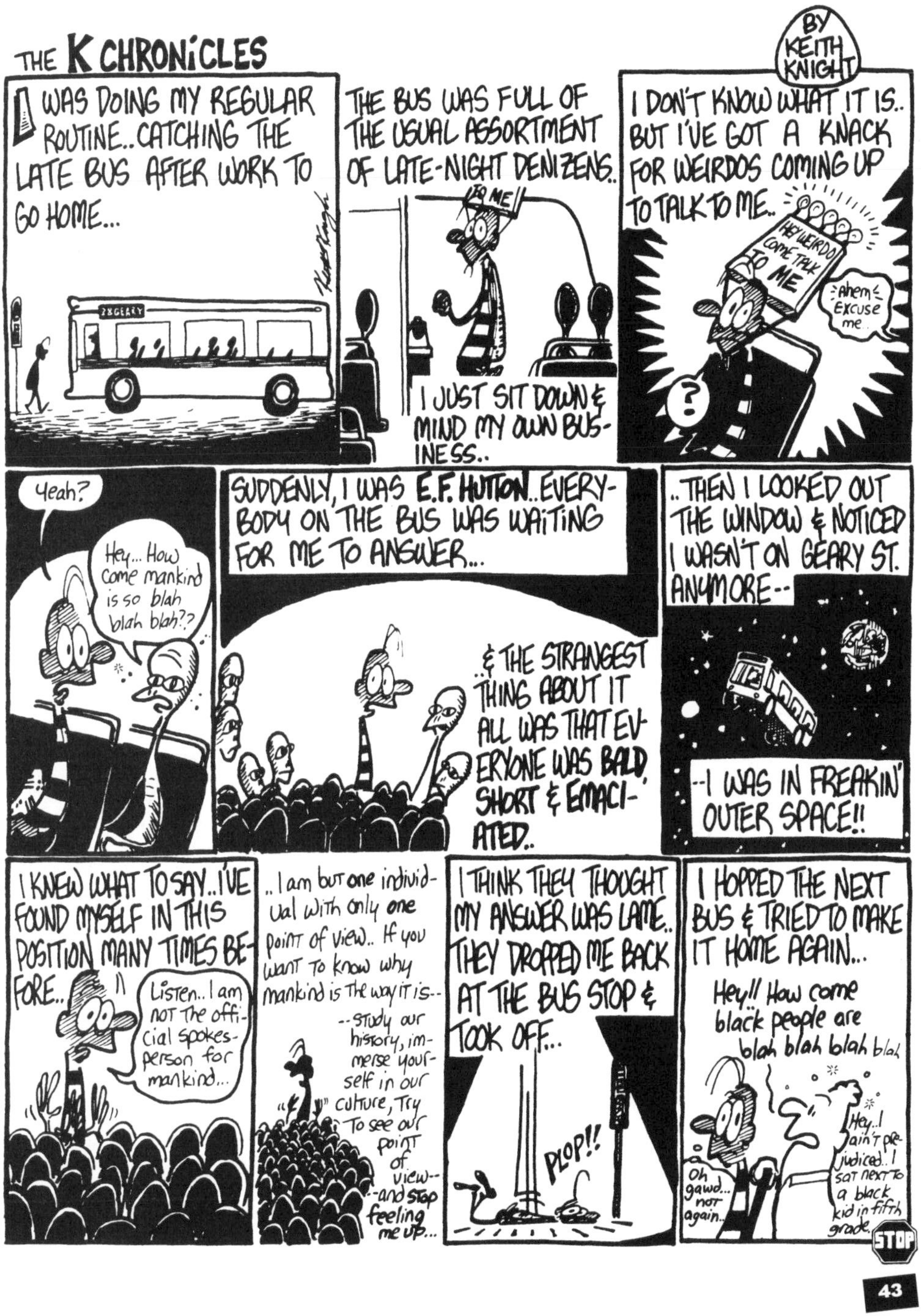
THE K CHRONICLES
BY KEITH KNIGHT
I WAS DOING MY REGULAR ROUTINE.. CATCHING THE LATE BUS AFTER WORK TO GO HOME...
38 GEARY
THE BUS WAS FULL OF THE USUAL ASSORTMENT OF LATE-NIGHT DENIZENS..
TO ME
I JUST SIT DOWN & MIND MY OWN BUSINESS..
I DON'T KNOW WHAT IT IS.. BUT I'VE GOT A KNACK FOR WEIRDOS COMING UP TO TALK TO ME..
HEY WEIRDO COME TALK TO ME
ahem Excuse me..
?
Yeah?
Hey... How come mankind is so blah blah blah?
SUDDENLY, I WAS E.F. HUTTON.. EVERYBODY ON THE BUS WAS WAITING FOR ME TO ANSWER...
...& THE STRANGEST THING ABOUT IT ALL WAS THAT EVERYONE WAS BALD, SHORT & EMACIATED..
..THEN I LOOKED OUT THE WINDOW & NOTICED I WASN'T ON GEARY ST. ANYMORE--
--I WAS IN FREAKIN' OUTER SPACE!!
I KNEW WHAT TO SAY.. I'VE FOUND MYSELF IN THIS POSITION MANY TIMES BEFORE..
Listen.. I am not the official spokesperson for mankind...
.. I am but one individual with only one point of view.. If you want to know why mankind is the way it is--
--study our history, immerse yourself in our culture, try to see our point of view--
--and stop feeling me up...
I THINK THEY THOUGHT MY ANSWER WAS LAME.. THEY DROPPED ME BACK AT THE BUS STOP & TOOK OFF...
PLOP!!
I HOPPED THE NEXT BUS & TRIED TO MAKE IT HOME AGAIN...
Hey!! How come black people are blah blah blah blah
Oh gawd... not again..
Hey..I ain't prejudiced.. I sat next to a black kid in fifth grade.
STOP

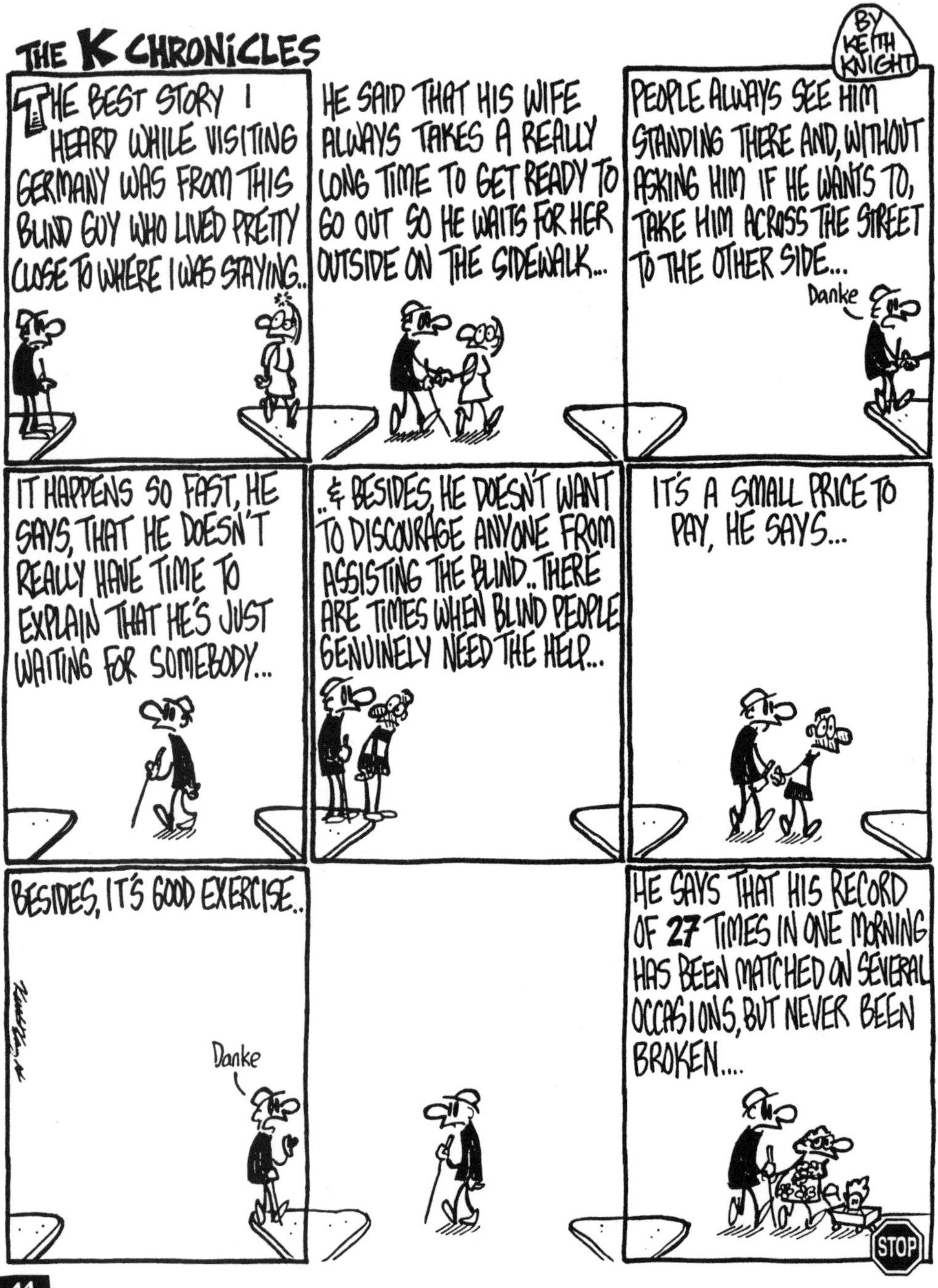
THE K CHRONICLES
BY KEITH KNIGHT
THE BEST STORY I HEARD WHILE VISITING GERMANY WAS FROM THIS BLIND GUY WHO LIVED PRETTY CLOSE TO WHERE I WAS STAYING..
HE SAID THAT HIS WIFE ALWAYS TAKES A REALLY LONG TIME TO GET READY TO GO OUT SO HE WAITS FOR HER OUTSIDE ON THE SIDEWALK...
PEOPLE ALWAYS SEE HIM STANDING THERE AND, WITHOUT ASKING HIM IF HE WANTS TO, TAKE HIM ACROSS THE STREET TO THE OTHER SIDE...
Danke
IT HAPPENS SO FAST, HE SAYS, THAT HE DOESN'T REALLY HAVE TIME TO EXPLAIN THAT HE'S JUST WAITING FOR SOMEBODY...
..& BESIDES, HE DOESN'T WANT TO DISCOURAGE ANYONE FROM ASSISTING THE BLIND.. THERE ARE TIMES WHEN BLIND PEOPLE GENUINELY NEED THE HELP...
IT'S A SMALL PRICE TO PAY, HE SAYS...
BESIDES, IT'S GOOD EXERCISE..
Danke
HE SAYS THAT HIS RECORD OF 27 TIMES IN ONE MORNING HAS BEEN MATCHED ON SEVERAL OCCASIONS, BUT NEVER BEEN BROKEN....
STOP

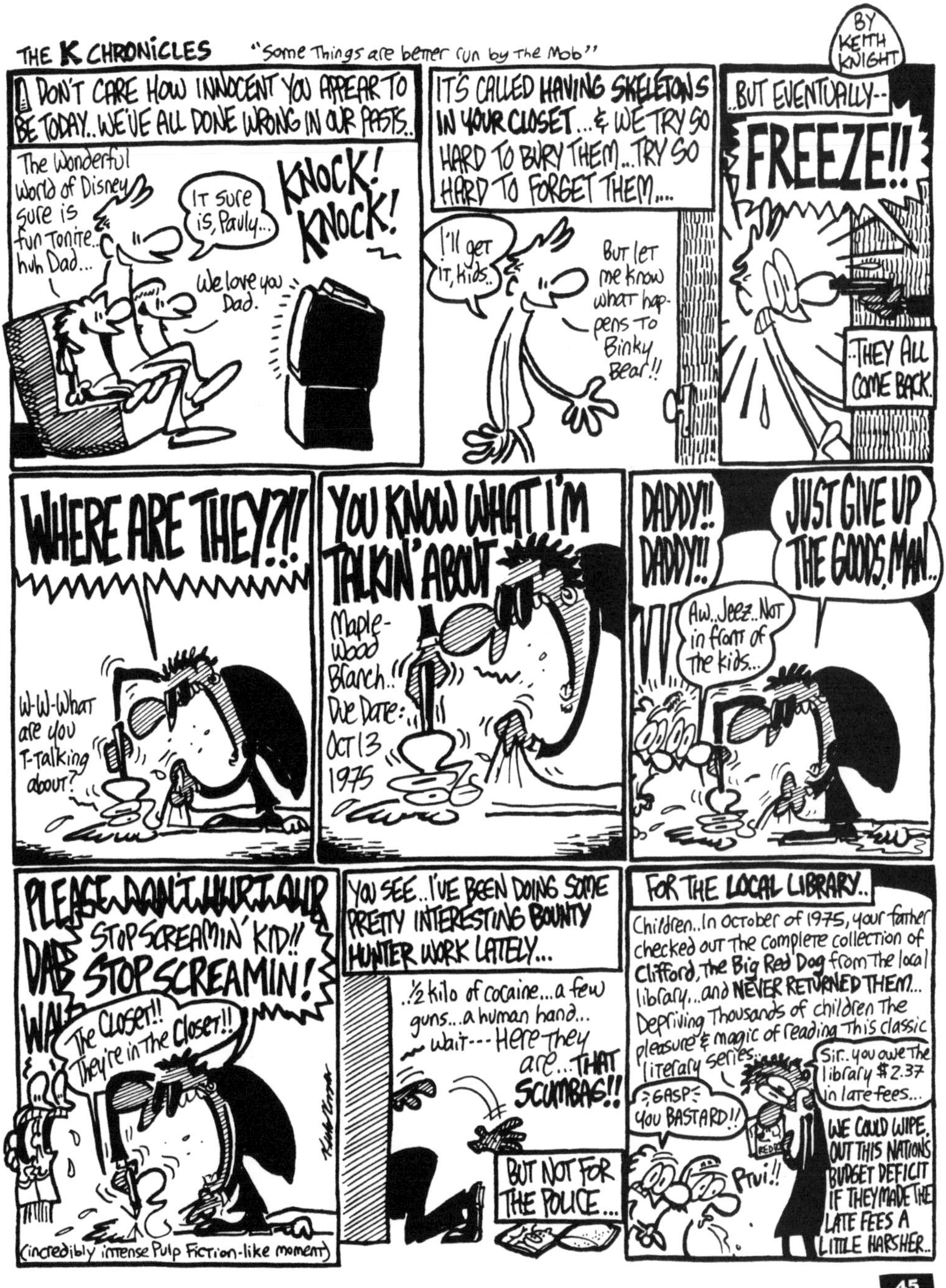
THE K CHRONICLES
"Some Things are better run by the Mob"
BY KEITH KNIGHT
I DON'T CARE HOW INNOCENT YOU APPEAR TO BE TODAY.. WE'VE ALL DONE WRONG IN OUR PASTS..
The Wonderful World of Disney sure is fun Tonite.. huh Dad...
It sure is, Pauly...
We love you Dad.
KNOCK! KNOCK!
IT'S CALLED HAVING SKELETONS IN YOUR CLOSET... & WE TRY SO HARD TO BURY THEM... TRY SO HARD TO FORGET THEM....
I'll get it, kids..
But let me know what happens to Binky Bear!!
..BUT EVENTUALLY--
FREEZE!!
..THEY ALL COME BACK.
WHERE ARE THEY?!!
W-W-What are you T-Talking about?
YOU KNOW WHAT I'M TALKIN' ABOUT
Maple-Wood Branch..! Due Date: Oct 13 1975
DADDY!! DADDY!!
JUST GIVE UP THE GOODS, MAN..
Aw..Jeez..Not in front of the kids...
PLEASE DON'T HURT OUR DAD
STOP SCREAMIN' KID!! STOP SCREAMIN'!
The Closet!! They're in The Closet!!
(incredibly intense Pulp Fiction-like moment)
YOU SEE.. I'VE BEEN DOING SOME PRETTY INTERESTING BOUNTY HUNTER WORK LATELY...
..½ kilo of cocaine...a few guns...a human hand... wait--- Here They are... THAT SCUMBAG!!
BUT NOT FOR THE POLICE...
FOR THE LOCAL LIBRARY..
Children..In October of 1975, your father checked out the complete collection of Clifford, the Big Red Dog from the local library...and NEVER RETURNED THEM... Depriving Thousands of children The pleasure & magic of reading This classic literary series...
Sir.. you owe The library $2.37 in late fees...
GASP You BASTARD!!
Ptui!!
WE COULD WIPE OUT THIS NATION'S BUDGET DEFICIT IF THEY MADE THE LATE FEES A LITTLE HARSHER...

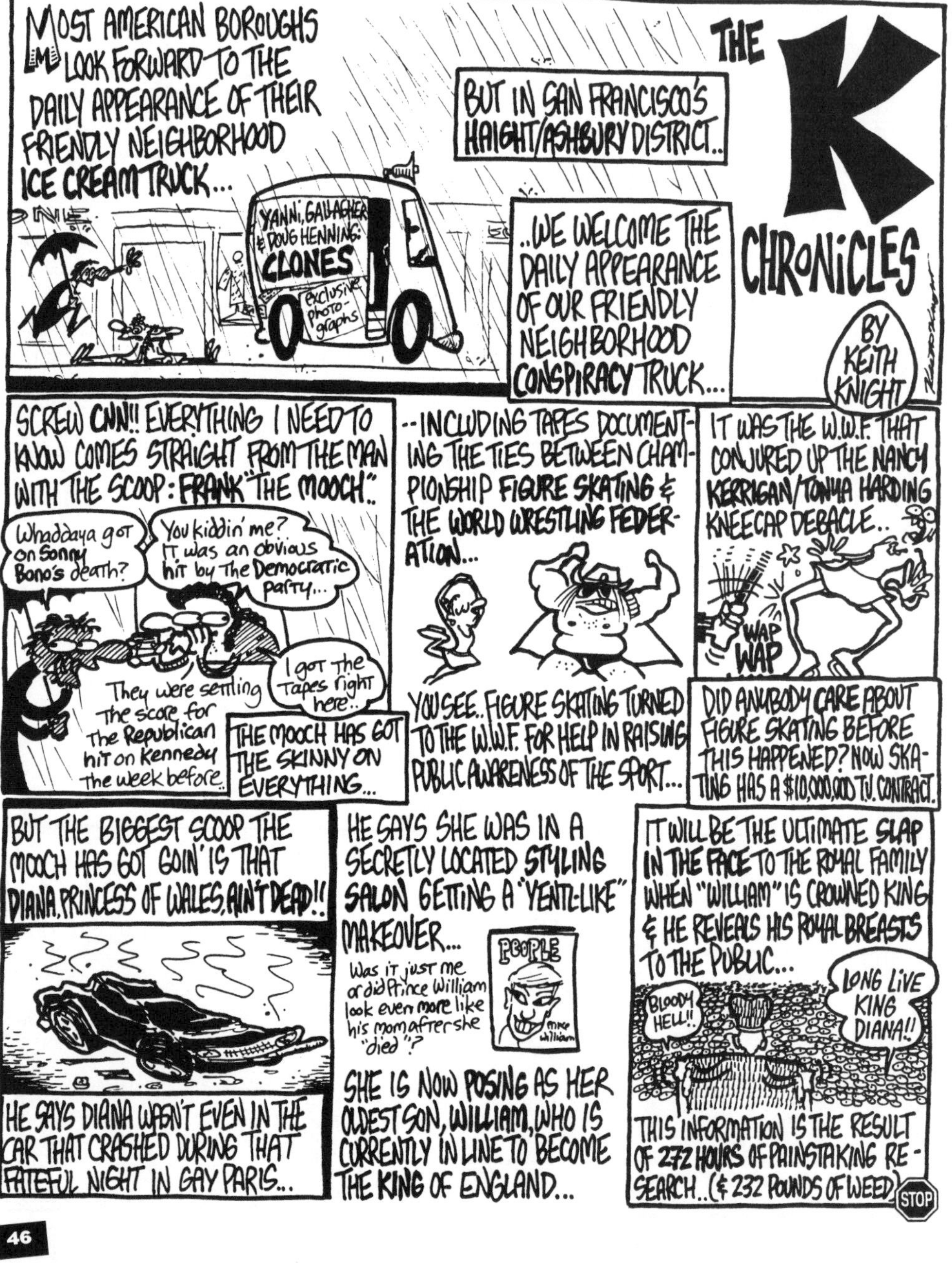

MOST AMERICAN BOROUGHS LOOK FORWARD TO THE DAILY APPEARANCE OF THEIR FRIENDLY NEIGHBORHOOD ICE CREAM TRUCK...
BUT IN SAN FRANCISCO'S HAIGHT/ASHBURY DISTRICT..
THE K CHRONICLES
BY KEITH KNIGHT
YANNI, GALLAGHER & DOUG HENNING: CLONES
exclusive photographs
..WE WELCOME THE DAILY APPEARANCE OF OUR FRIENDLY NEIGHBORHOOD CONSPIRACY TRUCK...
SCREW CNN!! EVERYTHING I NEED TO KNOW COMES STRAIGHT FROM THE MAN WITH THE SCOOP: FRANK "THE MOOCH"..
Whaddaya got on Sonny Bono's death?
You kiddin' me? It was an obvious hit by the Democratic party...
They were settling the score for the Republican hit on Kennedy the week before..
I got the Tapes right here..
THE MOOCH HAS GOT THE SKINNY ON EVERYTHING...
--INCLUDING TAPES DOCUMENTING THE TIES BETWEEN CHAMPIONSHIP FIGURE SKATING & THE WORLD WRESTLING FEDERATION...
YOU SEE.. FIGURE SKATING TURNED TO THE W.W.F. FOR HELP IN RAISING PUBLIC AWARENESS OF THE SPORT...
IT WAS THE W.W.F. THAT CONJURED UP THE NANCY KERRIGAN/TONYA HARDING KNEECAP DEBACLE...
WAP WAP
DID ANYBODY CARE ABOUT FIGURE SKATING BEFORE THIS HAPPENED? NOW SKATING HAS A $10,000,000 T.V. CONTRACT.
BUT THE BIGGEST SCOOP THE MOOCH HAS GOT GOIN' IS THAT DIANA, PRINCESS OF WALES, AIN'T DEAD!!
HE SAYS DIANA WASN'T EVEN IN THE CAR THAT CRASHED DURING THAT FATEFUL NIGHT IN GAY PARIS...
HE SAYS SHE WAS IN A SECRETLY LOCATED STYLING SALON GETTING A "YENTL-LIKE" MAKEOVER...
Was it just me or did Prince William look even more like his mom after she "died"?
PEOPLE
SHE IS NOW POSING AS HER OLDEST SON, WILLIAM, WHO IS CURRENTLY IN LINE TO BECOME THE KING OF ENGLAND...
IT WILL BE THE ULTIMATE SLAP IN THE FACE TO THE ROYAL FAMILY WHEN "WILLIAM" IS CROWNED KING & HE REVEALS HIS ROYAL BREASTS TO THE PUBLIC...
BLOODY HELL!!
LONG LIVE KING DIANA!!
THIS INFORMATION IS THE RESULT OF 272 HOURS OF PAINSTAKING RESEARCH..(& 232 POUNDS OF WEED)
STOP

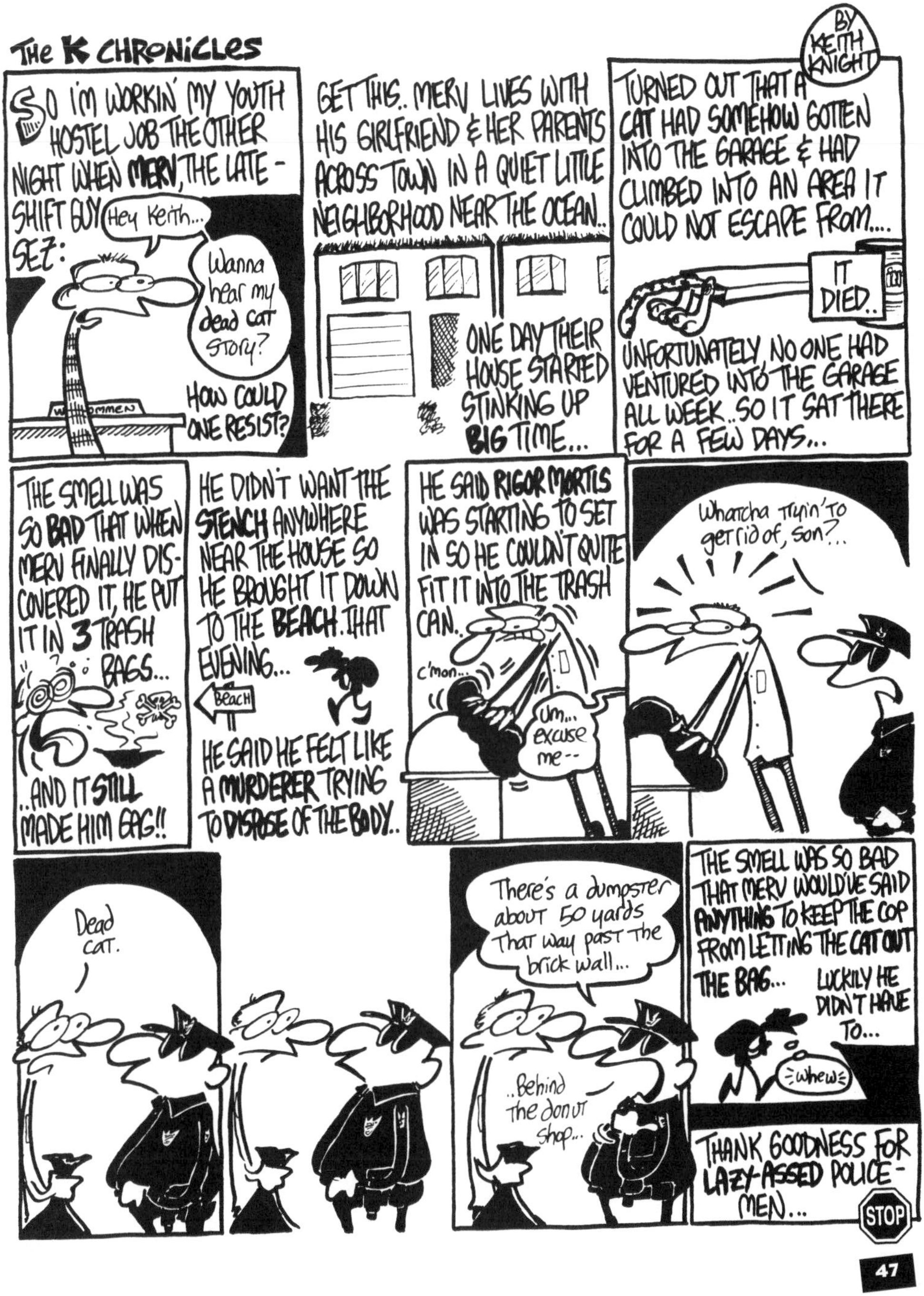
The K CHRONICLES
BY KEITH KNIGHT
SO I'M WORKIN' MY YOUTH HOSTEL JOB THE OTHER NIGHT WHEN MERV, THE LATE-SHIFT GUY SEZ:
Hey Keith...
Wanna hear my dead cat story?
HOW COULD ONE RESIST?
GET THIS.. MERV LIVES WITH HIS GIRLFRIEND & HER PARENTS ACROSS TOWN IN A QUIET LITTLE NEIGHBORHOOD NEAR THE OCEAN..
ONE DAY THEIR HOUSE STARTED STINKING UP BIG TIME...
TURNED OUT THAT A CAT HAD SOMEHOW GOTTEN INTO THE GARAGE & HAD CLIMBED INTO AN AREA IT COULD NOT ESCAPE FROM....
IT DIED..
UNFORTUNATELY, NO ONE HAD VENTURED INTO THE GARAGE ALL WEEK..SO IT SAT THERE FOR A FEW DAYS...
THE SMELL WAS SO BAD THAT WHEN MERV FINALLY DISCOVERED IT, HE PUT IT IN 3 TRASH BAGS...
..AND IT STILL MADE HIM GAG!!
HE DIDN'T WANT THE STENCH ANYWHERE NEAR THE HOUSE SO HE BROUGHT IT DOWN TO THE BEACH. THAT EVENING...
BEACH
HE SAID HE FELT LIKE A MURDERER TRYING TO DISPOSE OF THE BODY..
HE SAID RIGOR MORTIS WAS STARTING TO SET IN SO HE COULDN'T QUITE FIT IT INTO THE TRASH CAN..
c'mon...
Um... excuse me--
Whatcha tryin' to get rid of, son?...
Dead cat.
There's a dumpster about 50 yards that way past the brick wall...
..Behind the donut shop...
THE SMELL WAS SO BAD THAT MERV WOULD'VE SAID ANYTHING TO KEEP THE COP FROM LETTING THE CAT OUT THE BAG...
LUCKILY HE DIDN'T HAVE TO...
whew
THANK GOODNESS FOR LAZY-ASSED POLICEMEN...
STOP

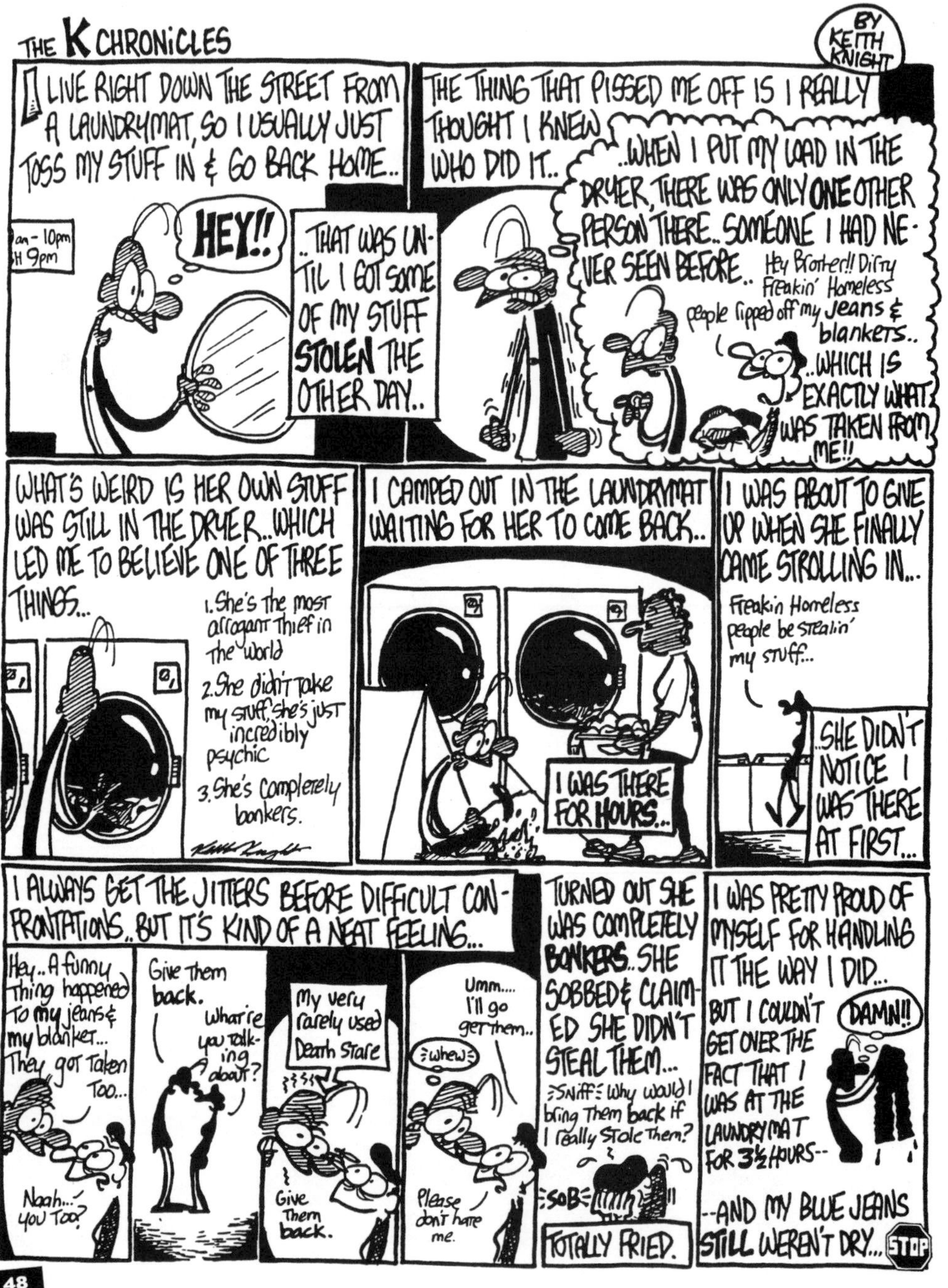
THE K CHRONICLES
BY KEITH KNIGHT
I LIVE RIGHT DOWN THE STREET FROM A LAUNDRYMAT, SO I USUALLY JUST TOSS MY STUFF IN & GO BACK HOME..
HEY!!
..THAT WAS UNTIL I GOT SOME OF MY STUFF STOLEN THE OTHER DAY..
THE THING THAT PISSED ME OFF IS I REALLY THOUGHT I KNEW WHO DID IT..
..WHEN I PUT MY LOAD IN THE DRYER, THERE WAS ONLY ONE OTHER PERSON THERE.. SOMEONE I HAD NEVER SEEN BEFORE..
Hey Brother!! Dirty Freakin' Homeless people ripped off my jeans & blankets..
..WHICH IS EXACTLY WHAT WAS TAKEN FROM ME!!
WHAT'S WEIRD IS HER OWN STUFF WAS STILL IN THE DRYER...WHICH LED ME TO BELIEVE ONE OF THREE THINGS...
1. She's the most arrogant thief in the world
2. She didn't take my stuff, she's just incredibly psychic
3. She's completely bonkers.
I CAMPED OUT IN THE LAUNDRYMAT WAITING FOR HER TO COME BACK..
I WAS THERE FOR HOURS...
I WAS ABOUT TO GIVE UP WHEN SHE FINALLY CAME STROLLING IN...
Freakin Homeless people be stealin' my stuff...
..SHE DIDN'T NOTICE I WAS THERE AT FIRST...
I ALWAYS GET THE JITTERS BEFORE DIFFICULT CONFRONTATIONS.. BUT IT'S KIND OF A NEAT FEELING...
Hey.. A funny thing happened to my jeans & my blanket... They got taken too...
Naah...! you too?
Give them back.
What're you talking about?
My very rarely used Death Stare
Give them back.
whew
Umm.... I'll go get them..
Please don't hate me.
TURNED OUT SHE WAS COMPLETELY BONKERS.. SHE SOBBED & CLAIMED SHE DIDN'T STEAL THEM...
SNIFF Why would I bring them back if I really stole them?
SOB
TOTALLY FRIED.
I WAS PRETTY PROUD OF MYSELF FOR HANDLING IT THE WAY I DID...
BUT I COULDN'T GET OVER THE FACT THAT I WAS AT THE LAUNDRYMAT FOR 3½ HOURS--
DAMN!!
--AND MY BLUE JEANS STILL WEREN'T DRY...
STOP

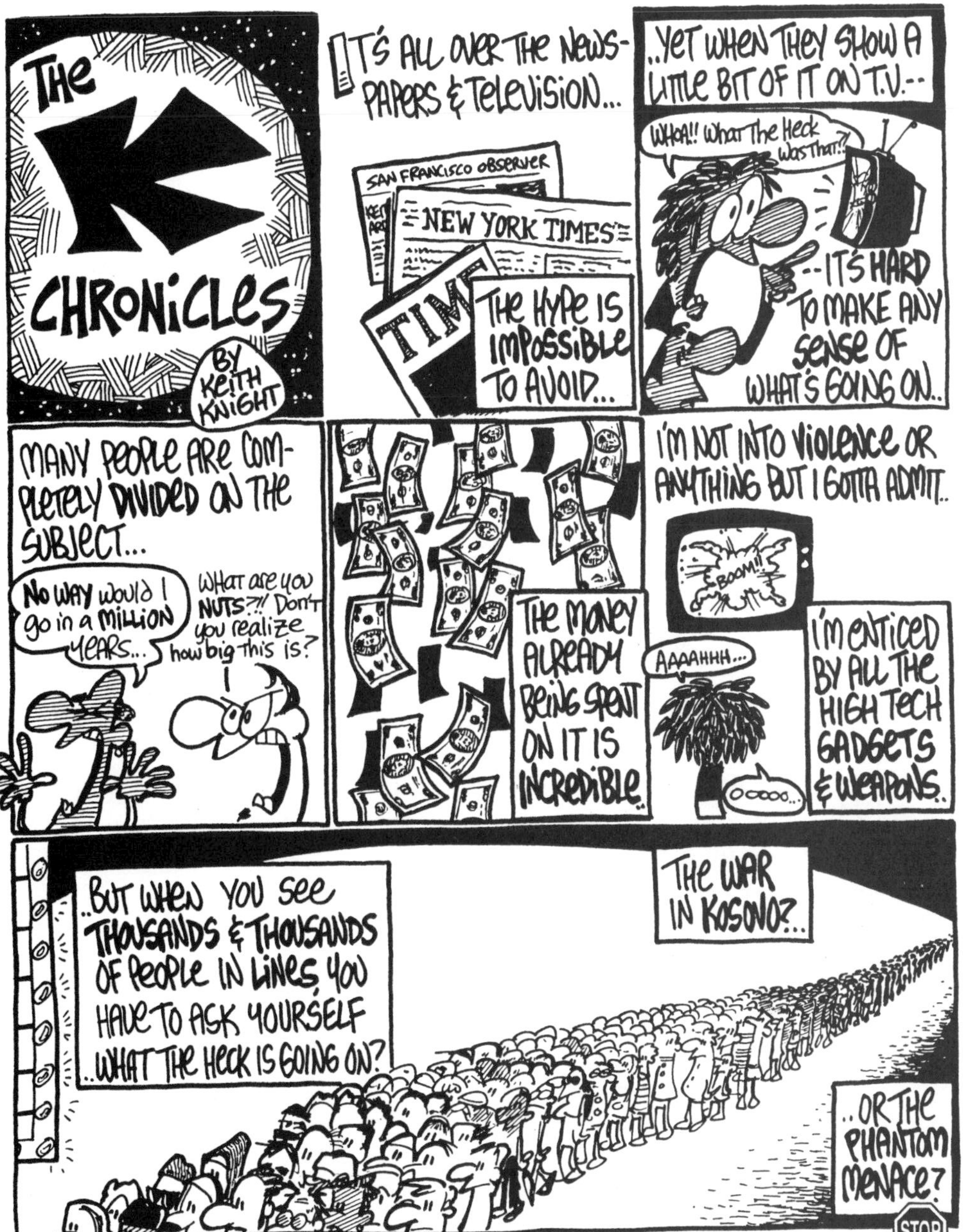

THE K CHRONICLES
BY KEITH KNIGHT
IT'S ALL OVER THE NEWSPAPERS & TELEVISION...
SAN FRANCISCO OBSERVER
NEW YORK TIMES
TIME
THE HYPE IS IMPOSSIBLE TO AVOID...
..YET WHEN THEY SHOW A LITTLE BIT OF IT ON T.V.--
WHOA!! What The Heck Was That?!
--IT'S HARD TO MAKE ANY SENSE OF WHAT'S GOING ON..
MANY PEOPLE ARE COMPLETELY DIVIDED ON THE SUBJECT...
No WAY would I go in a MILLION YEARS...
WHAT are you NUTS?!! Don't you realize how big this is?
THE MONEY ALREADY BEING SPENT ON IT IS INCREDIBLE..
I'M NOT INTO VIOLENCE OR ANYTHING BUT I GOTTA ADMIT..
BOOM!!
AAAAHHH...
Ooooo...
I'M ENTICED BY ALL THE HIGH TECH GADGETS & WEAPONS..
..BUT WHEN YOU SEE THOUSANDS & THOUSANDS OF PEOPLE IN LINES, YOU HAVE TO ASK YOURSELF ..WHAT THE HECK IS GOING ON?
THE WAR IN KOSOVO?...
..OR THE PHANTOM MENACE?
STOP

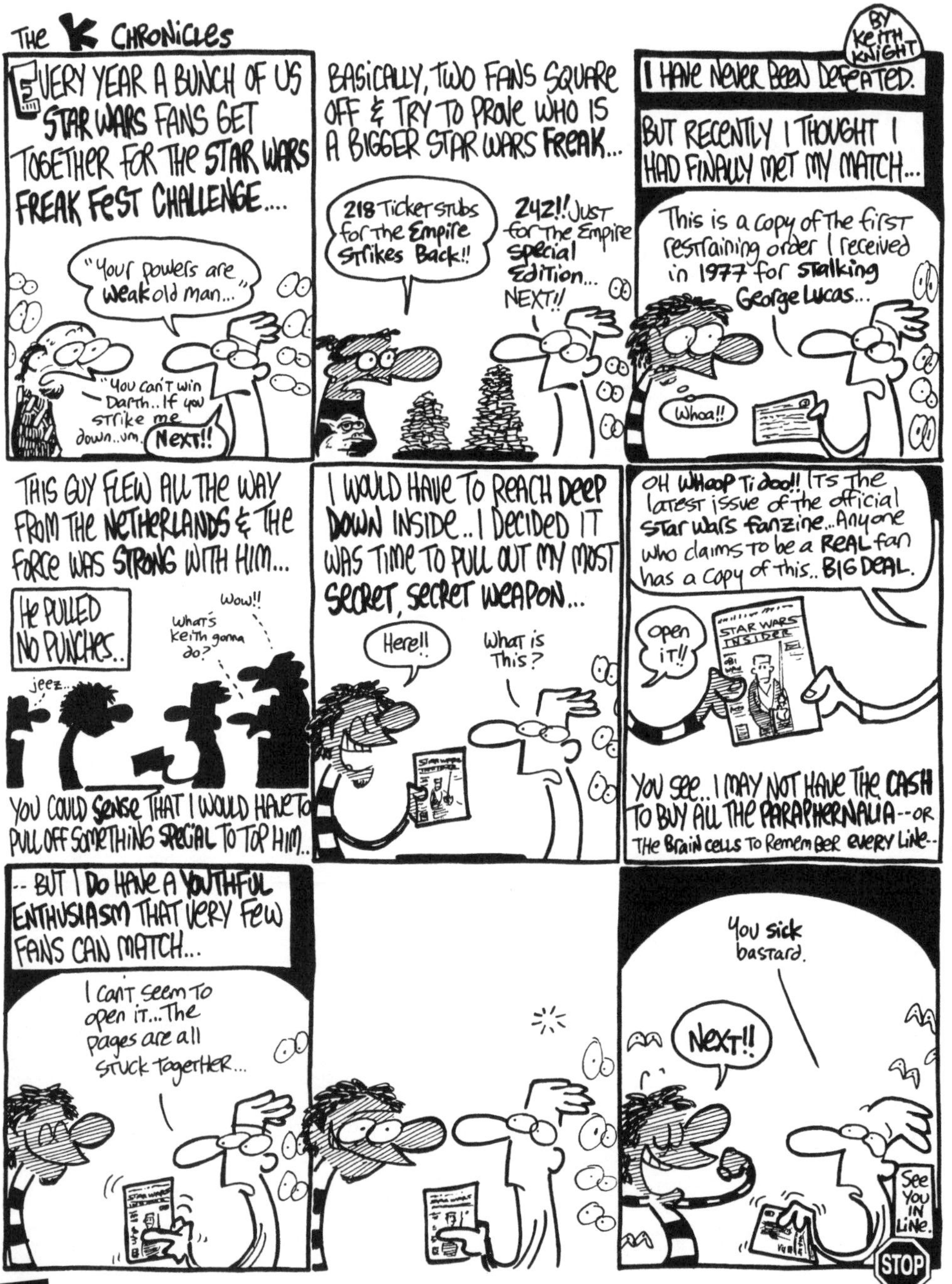
THE K CHRONICLES
BY KEITH KNIGHT
EVERY YEAR A BUNCH OF US STAR WARS FANS GET TOGETHER FOR THE STAR WARS FREAK FEST CHALLENGE....
"Your powers are weak old man..."
"You can't win Darth.. If you strike me down..um..
NEXT!!
BASICALLY, TWO FANS SQUARE OFF & TRY TO PROVE WHO IS A BIGGER STAR WARS FREAK...
218 Ticket stubs for the Empire Strikes Back!!
242!! Just for the Empire special Edition... NEXT!!
I HAVE NEVER BEEN DEFEATED.
BUT RECENTLY I THOUGHT I HAD FINALLY MET MY MATCH...
This is a copy of the first restraining order I received in 1977 for stalking George Lucas...
Whoa!!
THIS GUY FLEW ALL THE WAY FROM THE NETHERLANDS & THE FORCE WAS STRONG WITH HIM...
He PULLED NO PUNCHES..
jeez..
What's keith gonna do?
Wow!!
YOU COULD SENSE THAT I WOULD HAVE TO PULL OFF SOMETHING SPECIAL TO TOP HIM...
I WOULD HAVE TO REACH DEEP DOWN INSIDE.. I DECIDED IT WAS TIME TO PULL OUT MY MOST SECRET, SECRET WEAPON...
Here!!
What is This?
OH WHOOP TI DOO!! ITS THE latest issue of the official Star Wars fanzine...Anyone who claims to be a REAL fan has a copy of this.. BIG DEAL.
open it!!
STAR WARS INSIDER
YOU SEE.. I MAY NOT HAVE THE CASH TO BUY ALL THE PARAPHERNALIA--OR THE BRAIN CELLS TO REMEMBER EVERY LINE--
-- BUT I DO HAVE A YOUTHFUL ENTHUSIASM THAT VERY FEW FANS CAN MATCH...
I can't seem to open it... The pages are all stuck together...
You sick bastard.
NEXT!!
See You IN LINE.
STOP

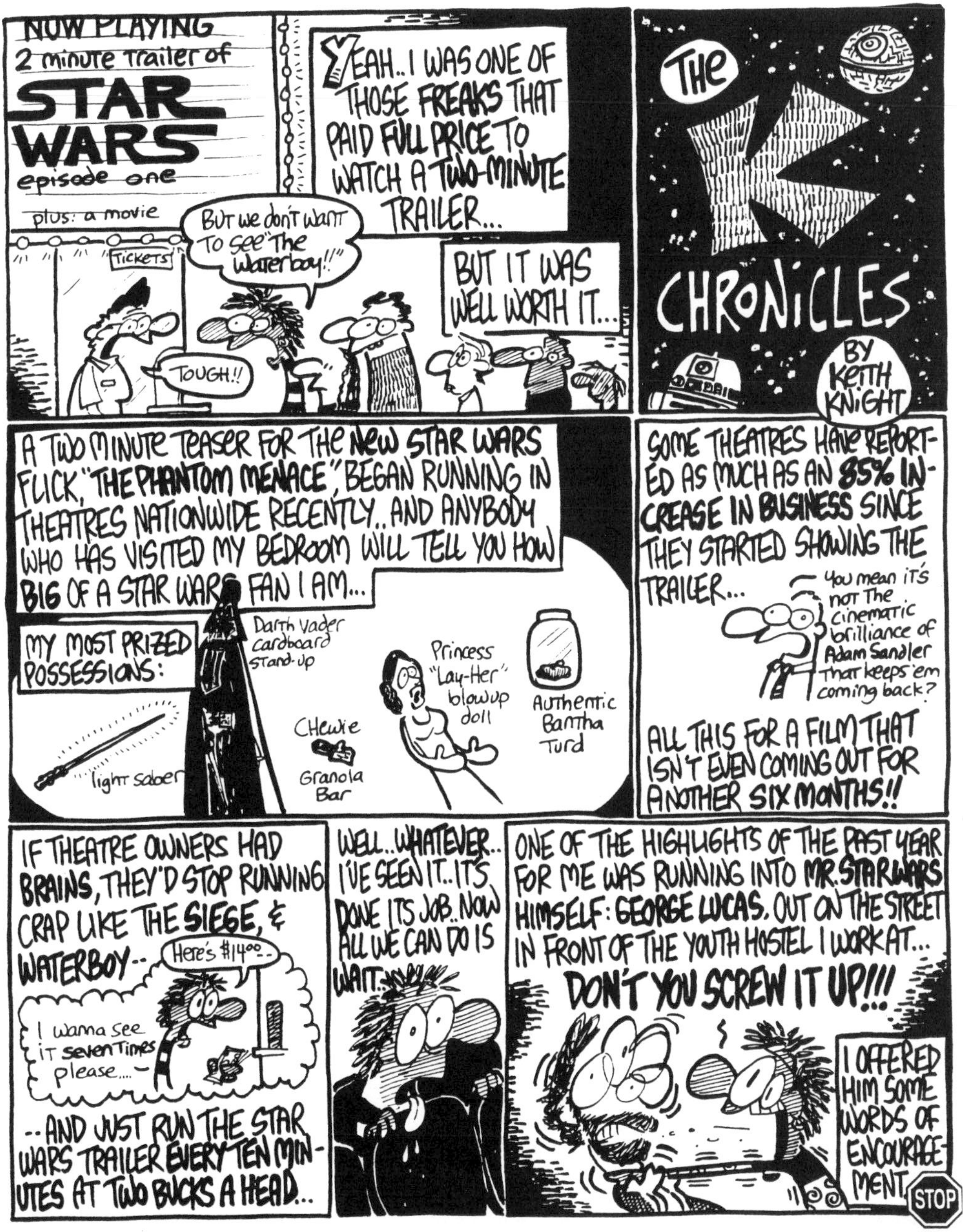
NOW PLAYING
2 minute trailer of
STAR WARS
episode one
plus: a movie
YEAH.. I WAS ONE OF THOSE FREAKS THAT PAID FULL PRICE TO WATCH A TWO-MINUTE TRAILER...
BUT we don't want to see "The Waterboy!!"
TICKETS
TOUGH!!
BUT IT WAS WELL WORTH IT...
THE K CHRONICLES
BY KEITH KNIGHT
A TWO MINUTE TEASER FOR THE NEW STAR WARS FLICK, "THE PHANTOM MENACE", BEGAN RUNNING IN THEATRES NATIONWIDE RECENTLY.. AND ANYBODY WHO HAS VISITED MY BEDROOM WILL TELL YOU HOW BIG OF A STAR WARS FAN I AM...
MY MOST PRIZED POSSESSIONS:
Darth Vader cardboard stand-up
light saber
Chewie Granola Bar
Princess "Lay-Her" blowup doll
Authentic Bantha Turd
SOME THEATRES HAVE REPORTED AS MUCH AS AN 85% INCREASE IN BUSINESS SINCE THEY STARTED SHOWING THE TRAILER...
You mean it's not the cinematic brilliance of Adam Sandler that keeps 'em coming back?
ALL THIS FOR A FILM THAT ISN'T EVEN COMING OUT FOR ANOTHER SIX MONTHS!!
IF THEATRE OWNERS HAD BRAINS, THEY'D STOP RUNNING CRAP LIKE THE SIEGE, & WATERBOY--
Here's $14.00..
I wanna see it seven times please....
--AND JUST RUN THE STAR WARS TRAILER EVERY TEN MINUTES AT TWO BUCKS A HEAD...
WELL.. WHATEVER.. I'VE SEEN IT.. IT'S DONE ITS JOB.. NOW ALL WE CAN DO IS WAIT...
ONE OF THE HIGHLIGHTS OF THE PAST YEAR FOR ME WAS RUNNING INTO MR. STAR WARS HIMSELF: GEORGE LUCAS. OUT ON THE STREET IN FRONT OF THE YOUTH HOSTEL I WORK AT...
DON'T YOU SCREW IT UP!!!
I OFFERED HIM SOME WORDS OF ENCOURAGEMENT.
STOP

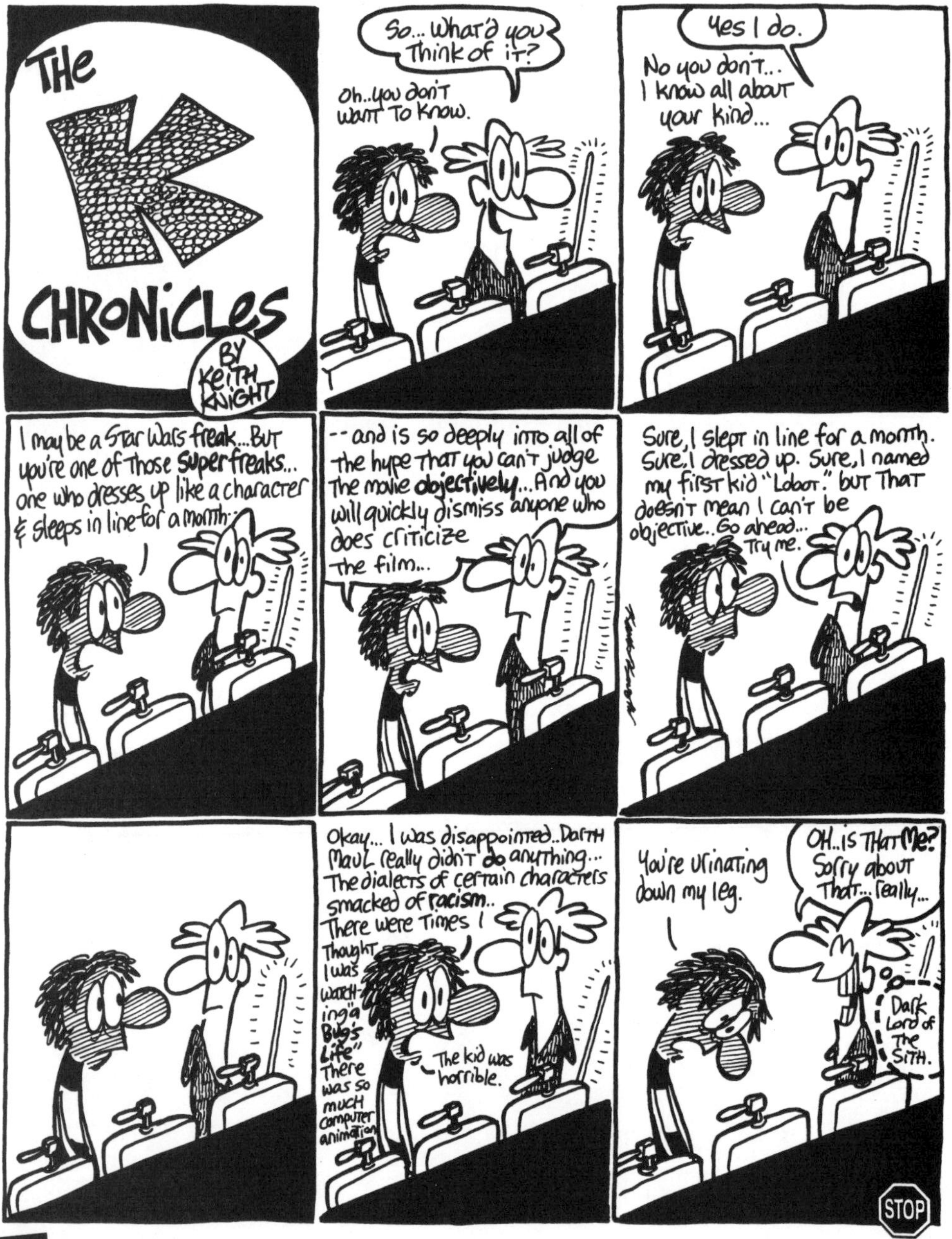
THE K CHRONICLES
BY KEITH KNIGHT
So... What'd you Think of it?
Oh..you don't want To Know.
Yes I do.
No you don't... I know all about your kind...
I may be a Star Wars freak...But you're one of those superfreaks... one who dresses up like a character & sleeps in line for a month--
-- and is so deeply into all of the hype that you can't judge the movie objectively...And you will quickly dismiss anyone who does criticize the film...
Sure, I slept in line for a month. Sure, I dressed up. Sure, I named my first kid "Lobot." but That doesn't mean I can't be objective.. Go ahead... Try me.
Okay... I was disappointed..Darth Maul really didn't do anything... The dialects of certain characters smacked of racism.. There were Times I Thought I was watching a "Bug's Life" There was so much computer animation
The kid was horrible.
You're urinating down my leg.
OH..is That Me? Sorry about That... really...
Dark Lord of The Sith.
STOP

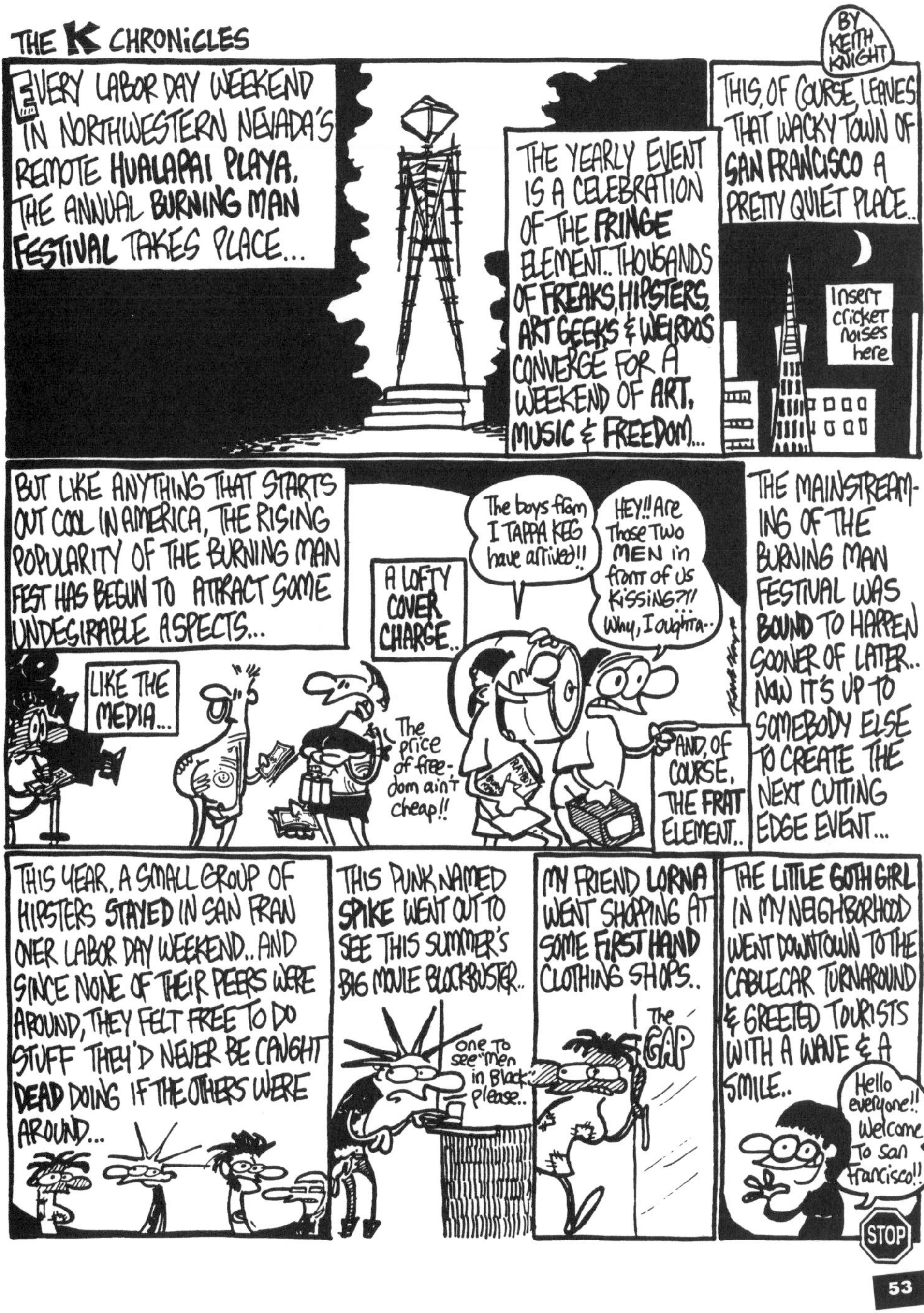
THE K CHRONICLES
BY KEITH KNIGHT
EVERY LABOR DAY WEEKEND IN NORTHWESTERN NEVADA'S REMOTE HUALAPAI PLAYA, THE ANNUAL BURNING MAN FESTIVAL TAKES PLACE...
THE YEARLY EVENT IS A CELEBRATION OF THE FRINGE ELEMENT.. THOUSANDS OF FREAKS, HIPSTERS, ART GEEKS & WEIRDOS CONVERGE FOR A WEEKEND OF ART, MUSIC & FREEDOM...
THIS, OF COURSE, LEAVES THAT WACKY TOWN OF SAN FRANCISCO A PRETTY QUIET PLACE..
Insert cricket noises here
BUT LIKE ANYTHING THAT STARTS OUT COOL IN AMERICA, THE RISING POPULARITY OF THE BURNING MAN FEST HAS BEGUN TO ATTRACT SOME UNDESIRABLE ASPECTS...
LIKE THE MEDIA...
A LOFTY COVER CHARGE..
The price of free-dom ain't cheap!!
The boys from I TAPPA KEG have arrived!!
HEY!! Are Those Two MEN in front of us Kissing?!! Why, I oughta..
AND, OF COURSE, THE FRAT ELEMENT..
THE MAINSTREAMING OF THE BURNING MAN FESTIVAL WAS BOUND TO HAPPEN SOONER OF LATER.. NOW IT'S UP TO SOMEBODY ELSE TO CREATE THE NEXT CUTTING EDGE EVENT...
THIS YEAR, A SMALL GROUP OF HIPSTERS STAYED IN SAN FRAN OVER LABOR DAY WEEKEND.. AND SINCE NONE OF THEIR PEERS WERE AROUND, THEY FELT FREE TO DO STUFF THEY'D NEVER BE CAUGHT DEAD DOING IF THE OTHERS WERE AROUND...
THIS PUNK NAMED SPIKE WENT OUT TO SEE THIS SUMMER'S BIG MOVIE BLOCKBUSTER..
One to see "Men in Black" please..
MY FRIEND LORNA WENT SHOPPING AT SOME FIRST HAND CLOTHING SHOPS..
The GAP
THE LITTLE GOTH GIRL IN MY NEIGHBORHOOD WENT DOWNTOWN TO THE CABLECAR TURNAROUND & GREETED TOURISTS WITH A WAVE & A SMILE..
Hello everyone!! Welcome To San Francisco!!
STOP

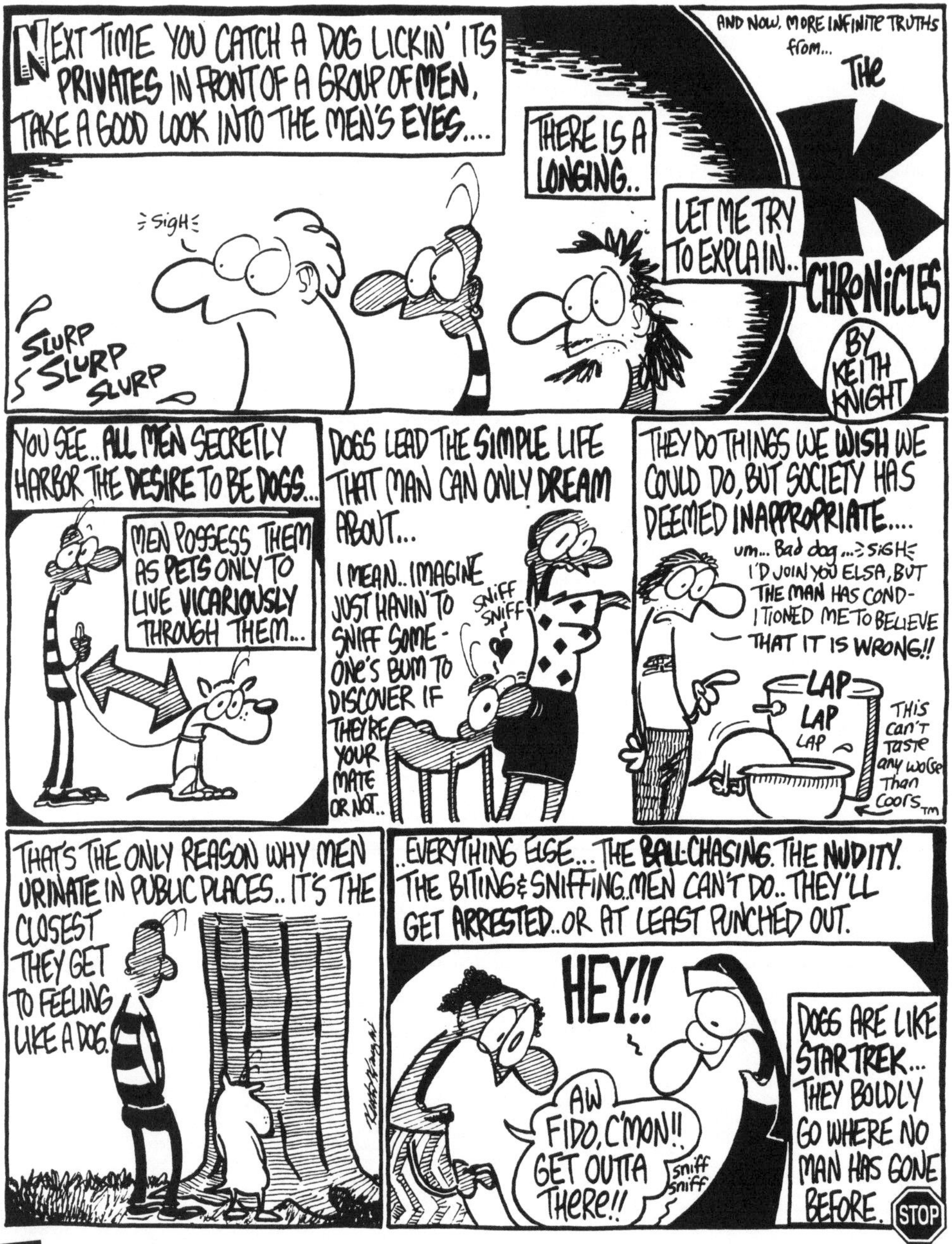
NEXT TIME YOU CATCH A DOG LICKIN' ITS PRIVATES IN FRONT OF A GROUP OF MEN, TAKE A GOOD LOOK INTO THE MEN'S EYES....
AND NOW, MORE INFINITE TRUTHS FROM... THE K CHRONICLES BY KEITH KNIGHT
THERE IS A LONGING..
LET ME TRY TO EXPLAIN..
SIGH
SLURP SLURP SLURP
YOU SEE.. ALL MEN SECRETLY HARBOR THE DESIRE TO BE DOGS...
MEN POSSESS THEM AS PETS ONLY TO LIVE VICARIOUSLY THROUGH THEM...
DOGS LEAD THE SIMPLE LIFE THAT MAN CAN ONLY DREAM ABOUT...
I MEAN.. IMAGINE JUST HAVIN' TO SNIFF SOME-ONE'S BUM TO DISCOVER IF THEY'RE YOUR MATE OR NOT..
SNIFF SNIFF
THEY DO THINGS WE WISH WE COULD DO, BUT SOCIETY HAS DEEMED INAPPROPRIATE.....
um... Bad dog... SIGH I'D JOIN YOU ELSA, BUT THE MAN HAS CONDITIONED ME TO BELIEVE THAT IT IS WRONG!!
LAP LAP LAP
THIS can't Taste any worse Than Coors TM
THAT'S THE ONLY REASON WHY MEN URINATE IN PUBLIC PLACES.. IT'S THE CLOSEST THEY GET TO FEELING LIKE A DOG.
..EVERYTHING ELSE... THE BALL-CHASING. THE NUDITY. THE BITING & SNIFFING. MEN CAN'T DO.. THEY'LL GET ARRESTED.. OR AT LEAST PUNCHED OUT.
HEY!!
AW FIDO, C'MON!! GET OUTTA THERE!!
sniff sniff
DOGS ARE LIKE STAR TREK... THEY BOLDLY GO WHERE NO MAN HAS GONE BEFORE.
STOP

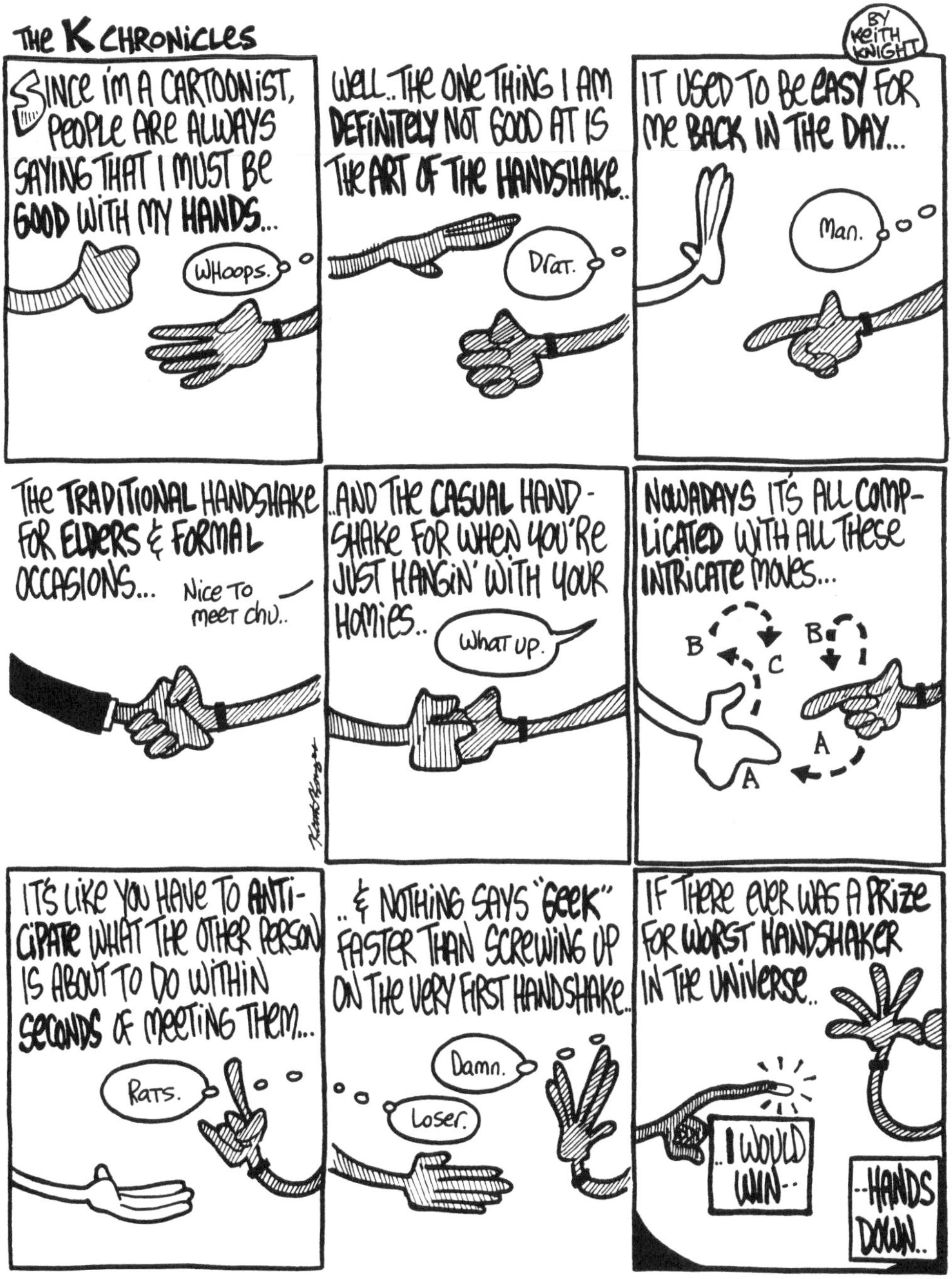
THE K CHRONICLES
BY KEITH KNIGHT
SINCE I'M A CARTOONIST, PEOPLE ARE ALWAYS SAYING THAT I MUST BE GOOD WITH MY HANDS...
WHOOPS.
WELL.. THE ONE THING I AM DEFINITELY NOT GOOD AT IS THE ART OF THE HANDSHAKE..
DRAT.
IT USED TO BE EASY FOR ME BACK IN THE DAY...
MAN.
THE TRADITIONAL HANDSHAKE FOR ELDERS & FORMAL OCCASIONS...
NICE TO MEET CHU..
..AND THE CASUAL HANDSHAKE FOR WHEN YOU'RE JUST HANGIN' WITH YOUR HOMIES..
WHAT UP.
NOWADAYS IT'S ALL COMPLICATED WITH ALL THESE INTRICATE MOVES...
B
C
B
A
A
IT'S LIKE YOU HAVE TO ANTICIPATE WHAT THE OTHER PERSON IS ABOUT TO DO WITHIN SECONDS OF MEETING THEM...
RATS.
..& NOTHING SAYS "GEEK" FASTER THAN SCREWING UP ON THE VERY FIRST HANDSHAKE..
DAMN.
LOSER.
IF THERE EVER WAS A PRIZE FOR WORST HANDSHAKER IN THE UNIVERSE..
..I WOULD WIN--
--HANDS DOWN..

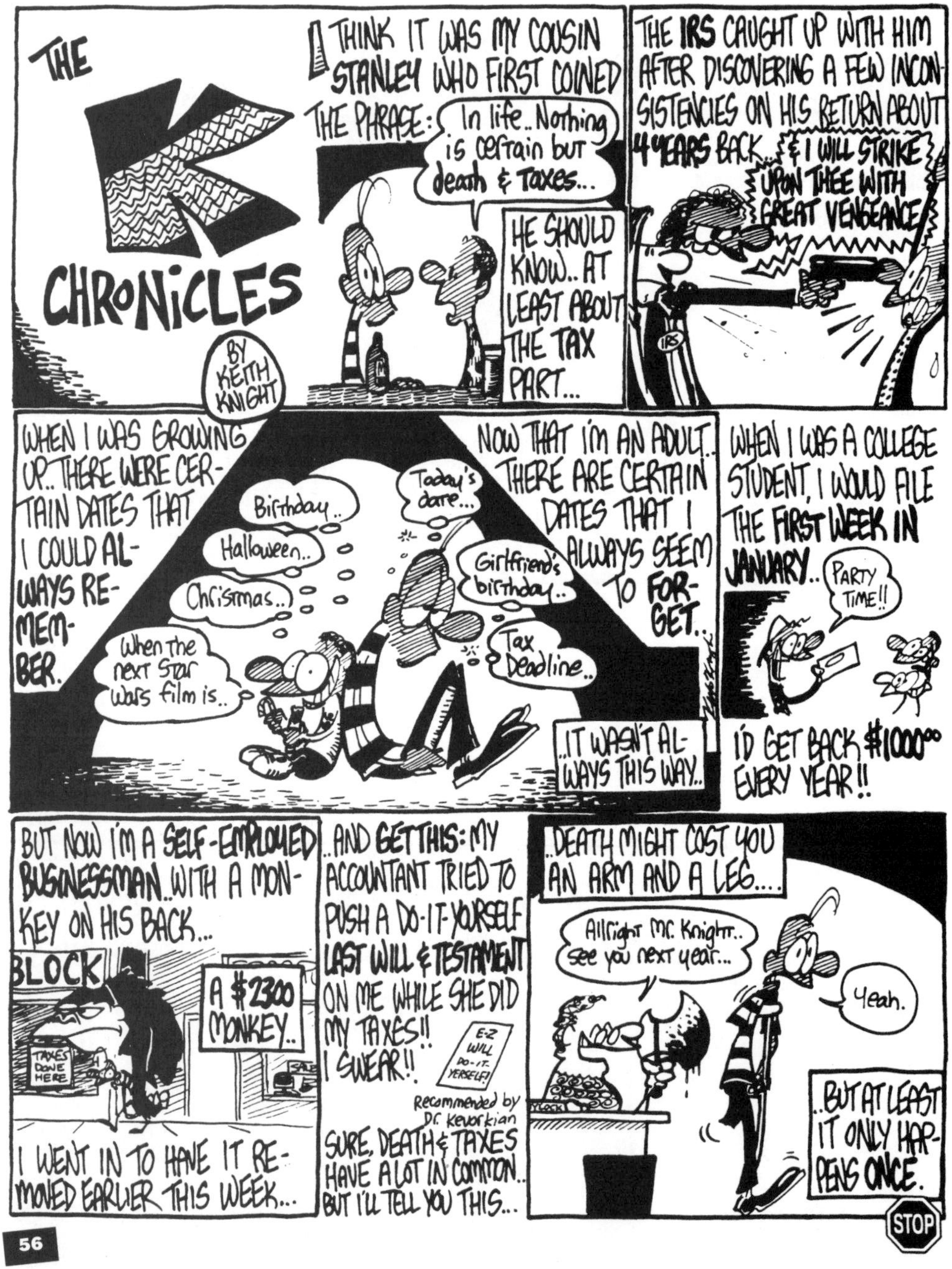
THE K CHRONICLES
BY KEITH KNIGHT
I THINK IT WAS MY COUSIN STANLEY WHO FIRST COINED THE PHRASE:
In life.. Nothing is certain but death & Taxes...
HE SHOULD KNOW.. AT LEAST ABOUT THE TAX PART...
THE IRS CAUGHT UP WITH HIM AFTER DISCOVERING A FEW INCONSISTENCIES ON HIS RETURN ABOUT 4 YEARS BACK...
& I WILL STRIKE UPON THEE WITH GREAT VENGEANCE
IRS
WHEN I WAS GROWING UP.. THERE WERE CERTAIN DATES THAT I COULD ALWAYS REMEMBER.
Birthday..
Halloween..
Chrismas..
When the next Star Wars film is..
Today's date...
Girlfriend's birthday..
Tax Deadline..
NOW THAT I'M AN ADULT.. THERE ARE CERTAIN DATES THAT I ALWAYS SEEM TO FORGET..
..IT WASN'T ALWAYS THIS WAY..
WHEN I WAS A COLLEGE STUDENT, I WOULD FILE THE FIRST WEEK IN JANUARY..
PARTY TIME!!
I'D GET BACK $1000.00 EVERY YEAR!!
BUT NOW I'M A SELF-EMPLOYED BUSINESSMAN.. WITH A MONKEY ON HIS BACK...
BLOCK
TAXES DONE HERE
A $2300 MONKEY..
I WENT IN TO HAVE IT REMOVED EARLIER THIS WEEK...
..AND GET THIS: MY ACCOUNTANT TRIED TO PUSH A DO-IT-YOURSELF LAST WILL & TESTAMENT ON ME WHILE SHE DID MY TAXES!! I SWEAR!!
E-Z WILL DO-IT-YERSELF!
Recommended by Dr. Kevorkian
SURE, DEATH & TAXES HAVE A LOT IN COMMON.. BUT I'LL TELL YOU THIS...
..DEATH MIGHT COST YOU AN ARM AND A LEG....
Allright Mr. Knight.. see you next year...
Yeah.
..BUT AT LEAST IT ONLY HAPPENS ONCE.
STOP

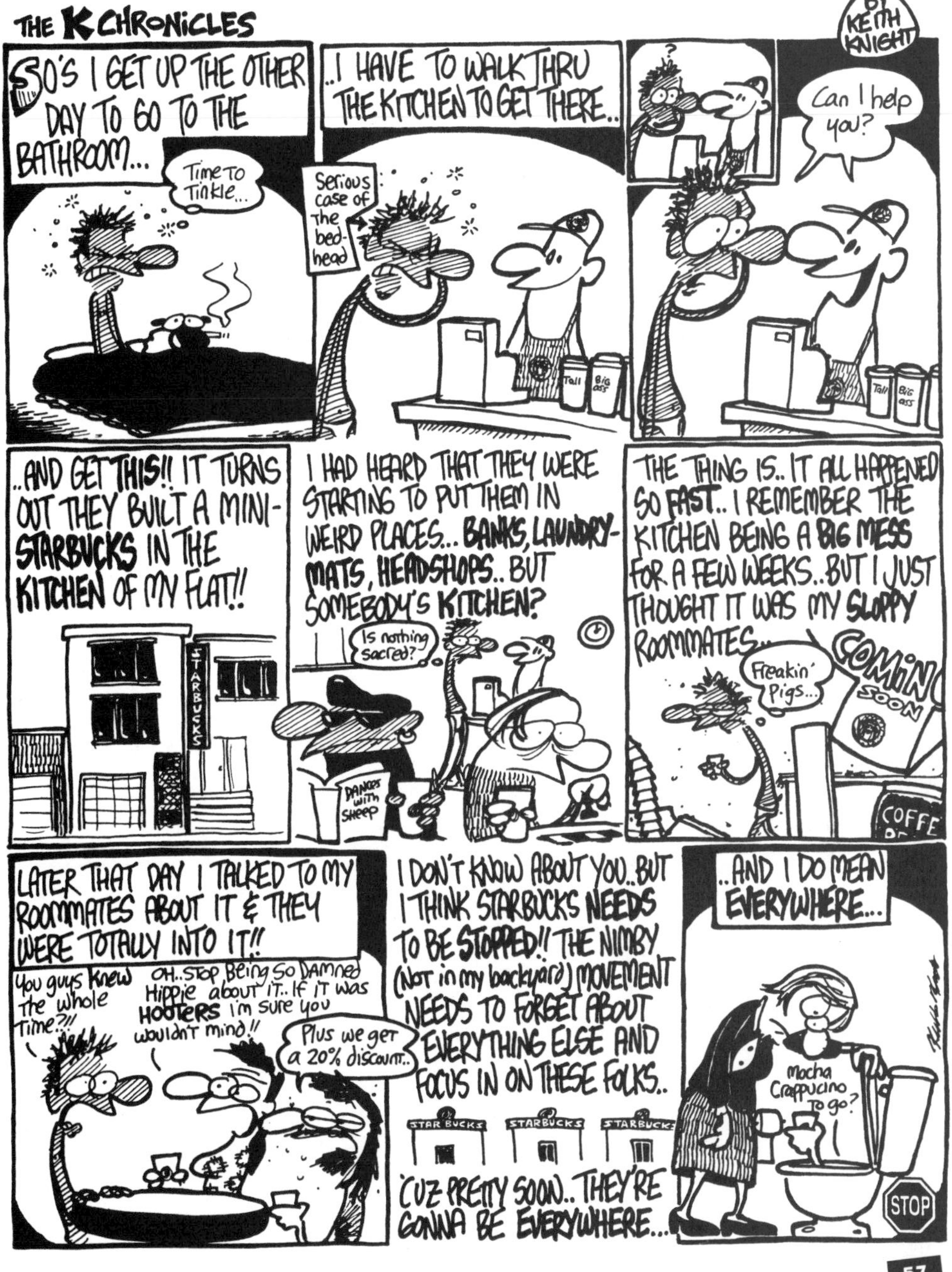
THE K CHRONICLES
BY KEITH KNIGHT
SO'S I GET UP THE OTHER DAY TO GO TO THE BATHROOM...
Time to Tinkle...
..I HAVE TO WALK THRU THE KITCHEN TO GET THERE..
Serious case of the bed-head
Tall
Big ass
?
Can I help you?
..AND GET THIS!! IT TURNS OUT THEY BUILT A MINI-STARBUCKS IN THE KITCHEN OF MY FLAT!!
STARBUCKS
I HAD HEARD THAT THEY WERE STARTING TO PUT THEM IN WEIRD PLACES... BANKS, LAUNDRY-MATS, HEADSHOPS.. BUT SOMEBODY'S KITCHEN?
Is nothing sacred?
DANCES WITH SHEEP
THE THING IS.. IT ALL HAPPENED SO FAST.. I REMEMBER THE KITCHEN BEING A BIG MESS FOR A FEW WEEKS..BUT I JUST THOUGHT IT WAS MY SLOPPY ROOMMATES..
Freakin' Pigs...
COMING SOON
COFFE
LATER THAT DAY I TALKED TO MY ROOMMATES ABOUT IT & THEY WERE TOTALLY INTO IT!!
You guys knew the whole time?!!
OH..STOP Being So Damned Hippie about it.. If it was HOOTERS i'm sure you wouldn't mind!!
Plus we get a 20% discount..
I DON'T KNOW ABOUT YOU..BUT I THINK STARBUCKS NEEDS TO BE STOPPED!! THE NIMBY (Not in my backyard) MOVEMENT NEEDS TO FORGET ABOUT EVERYTHING ELSE AND FOCUS IN ON THESE FOLKS..
STARBUCKS
STARBUCKS
STARBUCKS
'CUZ PRETTY SOON.. THEY'RE GONNA BE EVERYWHERE...
..AND I DO MEAN EVERYWHERE...
Mocha Crappucino to go?
STOP

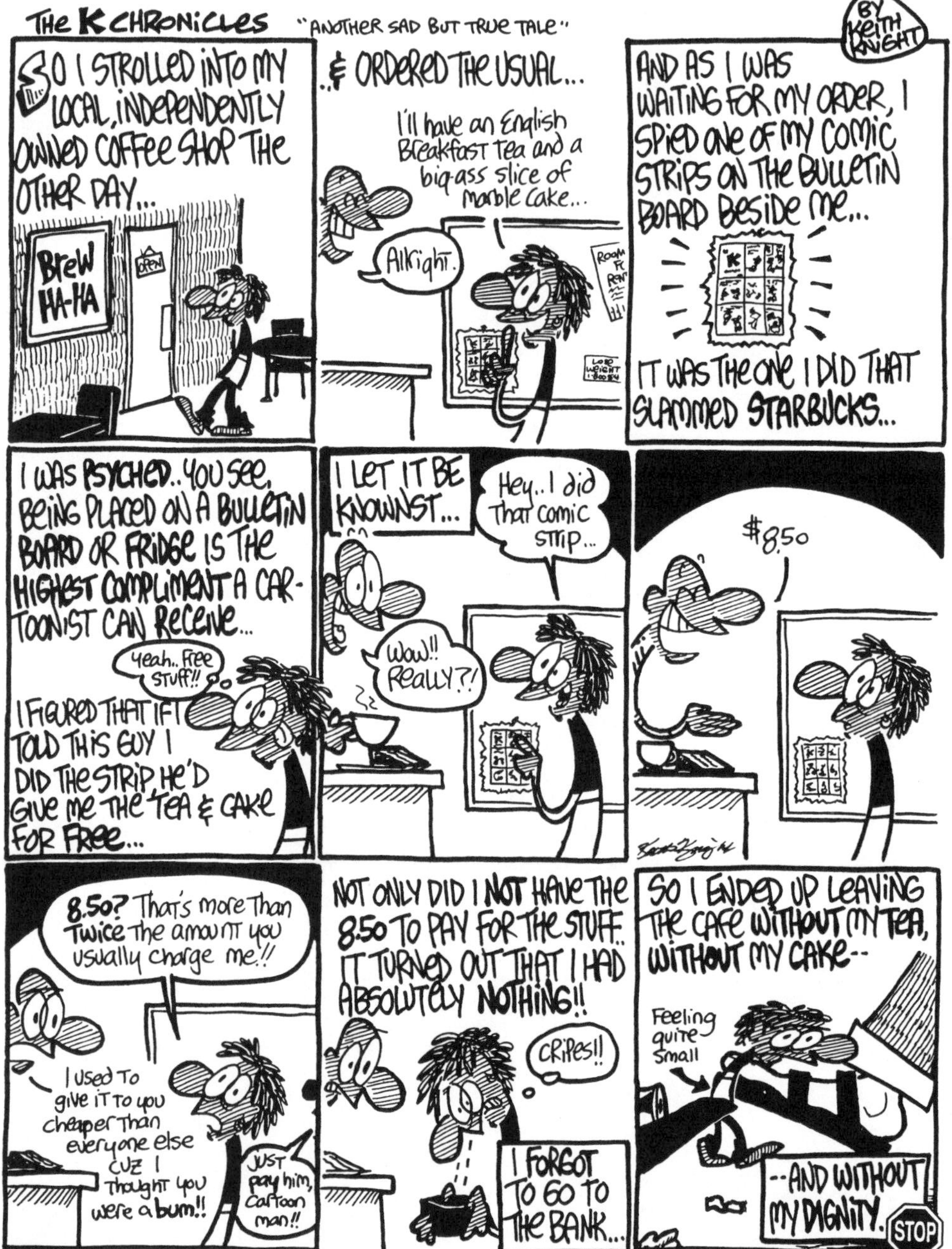
THE K CHRONICLES
"ANOTHER SAD BUT TRUE TALE"
BY KEITH KNIGHT
SO I STROLLED INTO MY LOCAL, INDEPENDENTLY OWNED COFFEE SHOP THE OTHER DAY...
BREW HA-HA
OPEN
...& ORDERED THE USUAL...
I'll have an English Breakfast Tea and a big-ass slice of Marble Cake...
Allright.
AND AS I WAS WAITING FOR MY ORDER, I SPIED ONE OF MY COMIC STRIPS ON THE BULLETIN BOARD BESIDE ME...
IT WAS THE ONE I DID THAT SLAMMED STARBUCKS...
I WAS PSYCHED.. YOU SEE, BEING PLACED ON A BULLETIN BOARD OR FRIDGE IS THE HIGHEST COMPLIMENT A CARTOONIST CAN RECEIVE...
Yeah.. Free STUFF!!
I FIGURED THAT IF I TOLD THIS GUY I DID THE STRIP HE'D GIVE ME THE TEA & CAKE FOR FREE...
I LET IT BE KNOWNST...
Hey.. I did That comic strip...
Wow!! Really?!
$8.50
8.50? That's more Than Twice the amount you usually charge me!!
I used To give iT To you cheaper Than everyone else cuz I Thought you were a bum!!
JUST pay him, Cartoon man!!
NOT ONLY DID I NOT HAVE THE 8.50 TO PAY FOR THE STUFF.. IT TURNED OUT THAT I HAD ABSOLUTELY NOTHING!!
Cripes!!
I FORGOT TO GO TO THE BANK...
SO I ENDED UP LEAVING THE CAFE WITHOUT MY TEA, WITHOUT MY CAKE--
Feeling quite small
--AND WITHOUT MY DIGNITY.
STOP

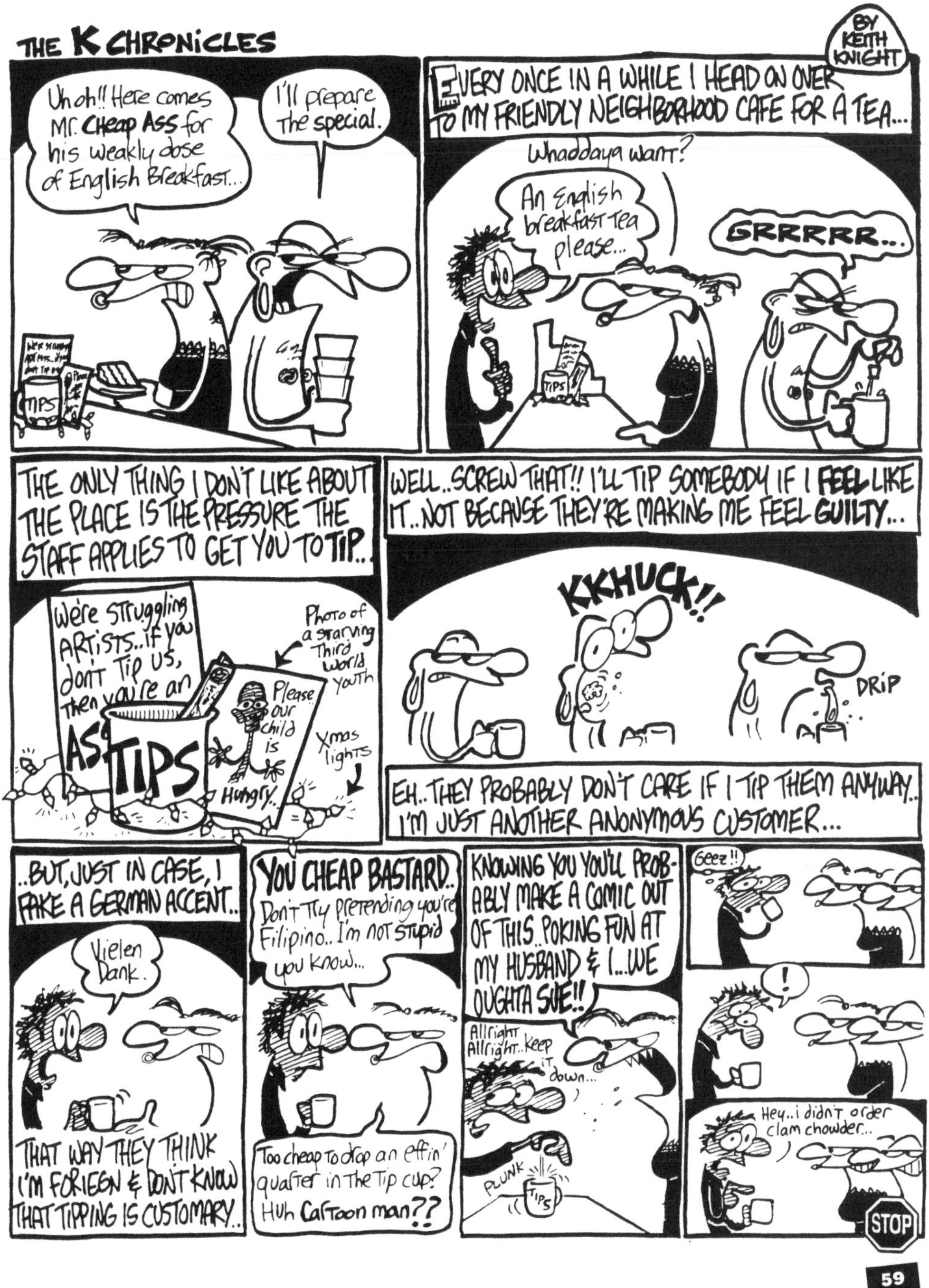
THE K CHRONICLES
BY KEITH KNIGHT
Uh oh!! Here comes Mr. CHEAP ASS for his weakly dose of English Breakfast...
I'll prepare the special.
EVERY ONCE IN A WHILE I HEAD ON OVER TO MY FRIENDLY NEIGHBORHOOD CAFE FOR A TEA...
Whaddaya want?
An English breakfast tea please...
GRRRRR...
TIPS
THE ONLY THING I DON'T LIKE ABOUT THE PLACE IS THE PRESSURE THE STAFF APPLIES TO GET YOU TO TIP...
We're struggling ARTISTS.. if you don't Tip us, then you're an ASS
TIPS
Photo of a starving Third World Youth
Please our child is Hungry..
Xmas lights
WELL.. SCREW THAT!! I'LL TIP SOMEBODY IF I FEEL LIKE IT.. NOT BECAUSE THEY'RE MAKING ME FEEL GUILTY...
KKHUCK!!
DRIP
EH.. THEY PROBABLY DON'T CARE IF I TIP THEM ANYWAY.. I'M JUST ANOTHER ANONYMOUS CUSTOMER...
..BUT, JUST IN CASE, I FAKE A GERMAN ACCENT..
Vielen Dank.
THAT WAY THEY THINK I'M FORIEGN & DON'T KNOW THAT TIPPING IS CUSTOMARY..
YOU CHEAP BASTARD.. Don't Try pretending you're Filipino.. I'm not stupid you know...
Too cheap to drop an effin' quarter in the Tip cup? Huh Cartoon man??
KNOWING YOU YOU'LL PROB-ABLY MAKE A COMIC OUT OF THIS.. POKING FUN AT MY HUSBAND & I...WE OUGHTA SUE!!
Allright Allright.. Keep it down...
PLUNK
TIPS
Geez!!
!
Hey.. i didn't order clam chowder...
STOP

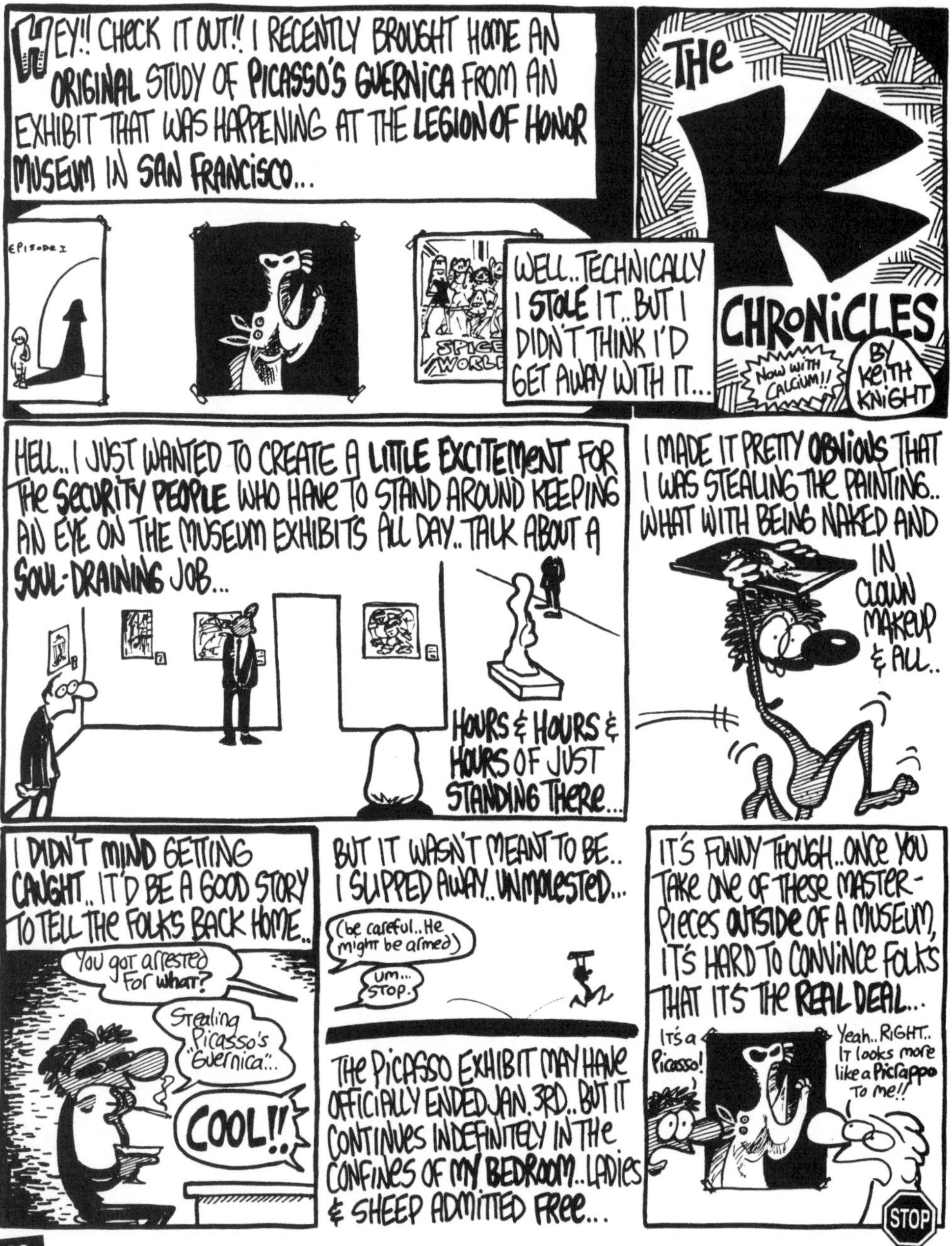
HEY!! CHECK IT OUT!! I RECENTLY BROUGHT HOME AN ORIGINAL STUDY OF PICASSO'S GUERNICA FROM AN EXHIBIT THAT WAS HAPPENING AT THE LEGION OF HONOR MUSEUM IN SAN FRANCISCO...
THE K CHRONICLES
NOW WITH CALCIUM!!
BY KEITH KNIGHT
WELL.. TECHNICALLY I STOLE IT.. BUT I DIDN'T THINK I'D GET AWAY WITH IT...
HELL.. I JUST WANTED TO CREATE A LITTLE EXCITEMENT FOR THE SECURITY PEOPLE WHO HAVE TO STAND AROUND KEEPING AN EYE ON THE MUSEUM EXHIBITS ALL DAY.. TALK ABOUT A SOUL-DRAINING JOB...
HOURS & HOURS & HOURS OF JUST STANDING THERE...
I MADE IT PRETTY OBVIOUS THAT I WAS STEALING THE PAINTING.. WHAT WITH BEING NAKED AND IN CLOWN MAKEUP & ALL..
I DIDN'T MIND GETTING CAUGHT.. IT'D BE A GOOD STORY TO TELL THE FOLKS BACK HOME..
You got arrested for what?
Stealing Picasso's "Guernica"...
COOL!!
BUT IT WASN'T MEANT TO BE.. I SLIPPED AWAY.. UNMOLESTED...
(be careful.. He might be armed)
Um... stop.
THE PICASSO EXHIBIT MAY HAVE OFFICIALLY ENDED JAN. 3RD.. BUT IT CONTINUES INDEFINITELY IN THE CONFINES OF MY BEDROOM.. LADIES & SHEEP ADMITTED FREE...
IT'S FUNNY THOUGH.. ONCE YOU TAKE ONE OF THESE MASTER-PIECES OUTSIDE OF A MUSEUM, IT'S HARD TO CONVINCE FOLKS THAT IT'S THE REAL DEAL...
It's a Picasso!
Yeah.. RIGHT.. It looks more like a Picrappo to me!!
STOP

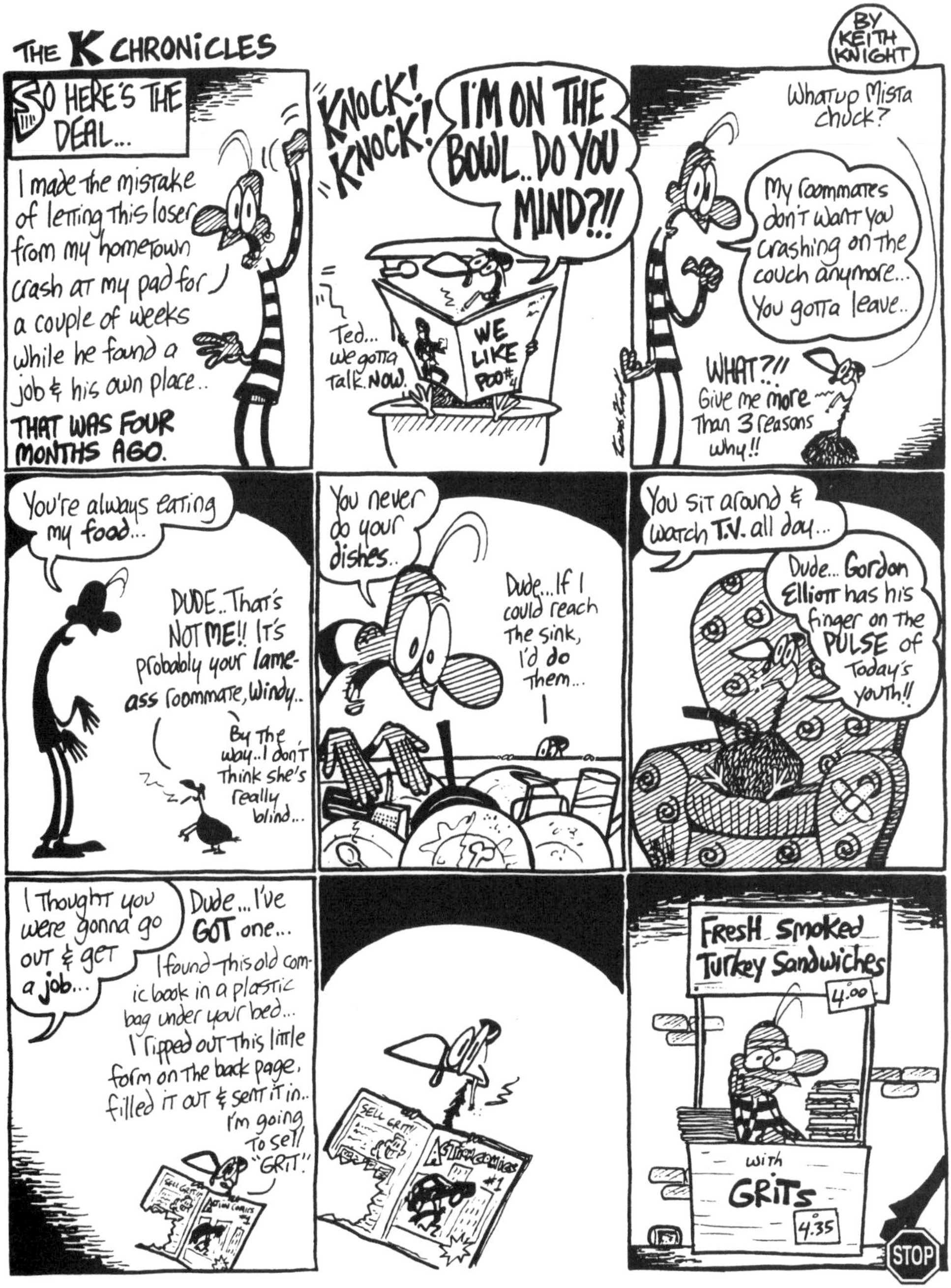
THE K CHRONICLES
BY KEITH KNIGHT
SO HERE'S THE DEAL...
I made the mistake of letting this loser from my hometown crash at my pad for a couple of weeks while he found a job & his own place..
THAT WAS FOUR MONTHS AGO.
KNOCK! KNOCK!
I'M ON THE BOWL.. DO YOU MIND?!!
Ted... we gotta talk. NOW.
WE LIKE POO #4
Whatup Mista Chuck?
My roommates don't want you crashing on the couch anymore... You gotta leave..
WHAT?!! Give me more than 3 reasons why!!
You're always eating my food...
DUDE.. That's NOT ME!! It's probably your lame-ass roommate, Windy..
By the way.. I don't think she's really blind...
You never do your dishes..
Dude... If I could reach the sink, I'd do them...
You sit around & watch T.V. all day...
Dude... Gordon Elliott has his finger on the PULSE of today's youth!!
I thought you were gonna go out & get a job...
Dude... I've GOT one... I found this old comic book in a plastic bag under your bed... I ripped out this little form on the back page, filled it out & sent it in.. I'm going to sell "GRIT."
SELL GRIT
ACTION COMICS #1
FRESH SMOKED TURKEY SANDWICHES 4.00
WITH GRITS 4.35
STOP

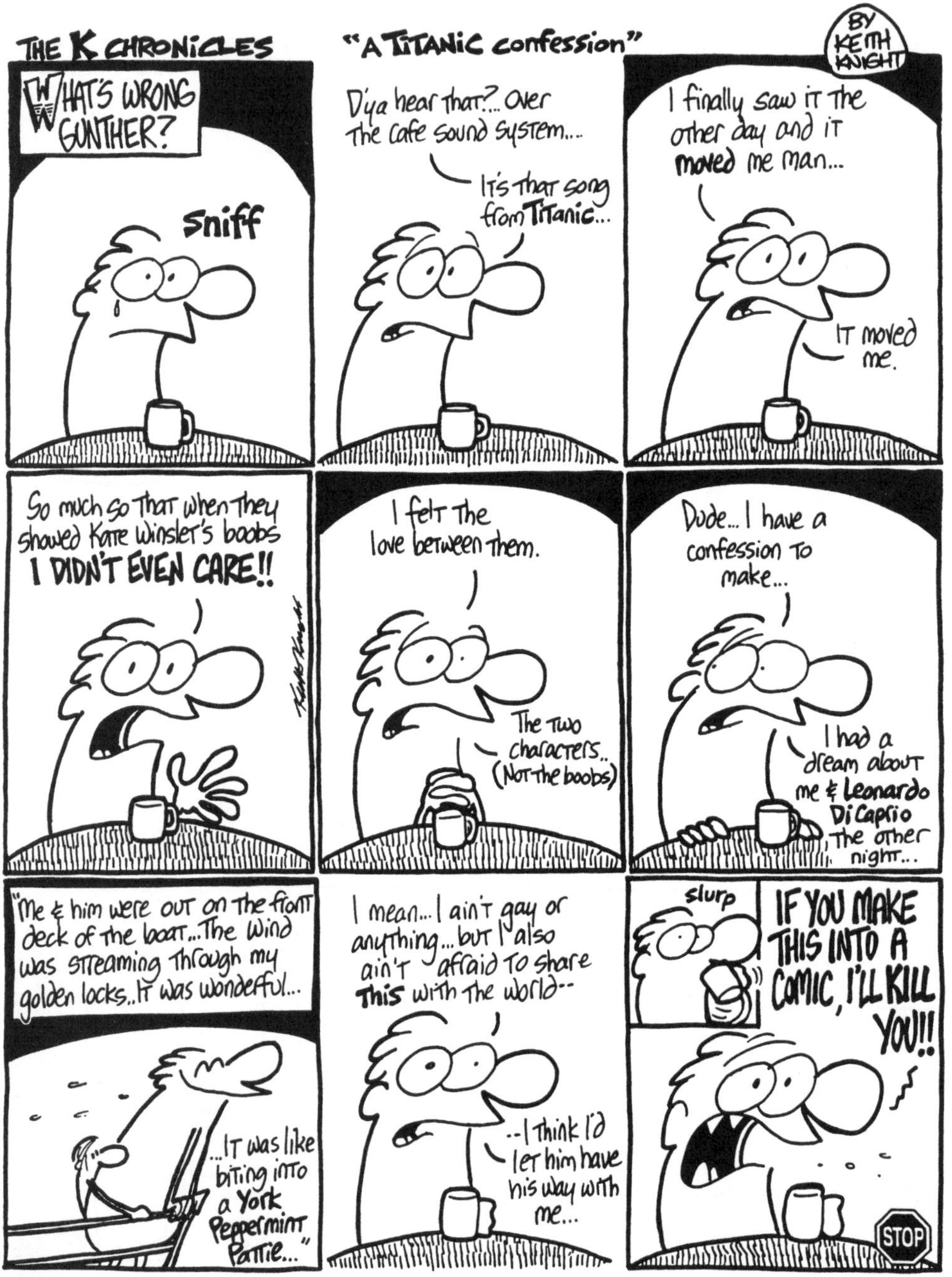
THE K CHRONICLES
"A TITANIC confession"
BY KEITH KNIGHT
WHAT'S WRONG GUNTHER?
Sniff
D'ya hear that?... Over the cafe sound system...
It's that song from Titanic...
I finally saw it the other day and it moved me man...
It moved me.
So much so that when they showed Kate Winslet's boobs I DIDN'T EVEN CARE!!
I felt the love between them.
The two characters.. (Not the boobs)
Dude... I have a confession to make...
I had a dream about me & Leonardo DiCaprio the other night...
"Me & him were out on the front deck of the boat... The wind was streaming through my golden locks.. It was wonderful...
...It was like biting into a York Peppermint Pattie..."
I mean... I ain't gay or anything... but I also ain't afraid to share this with the world--
--I think I'd let him have his way with me...
slurp
IF YOU MAKE THIS INTO A COMIC, I'LL KILL YOU!!
STOP

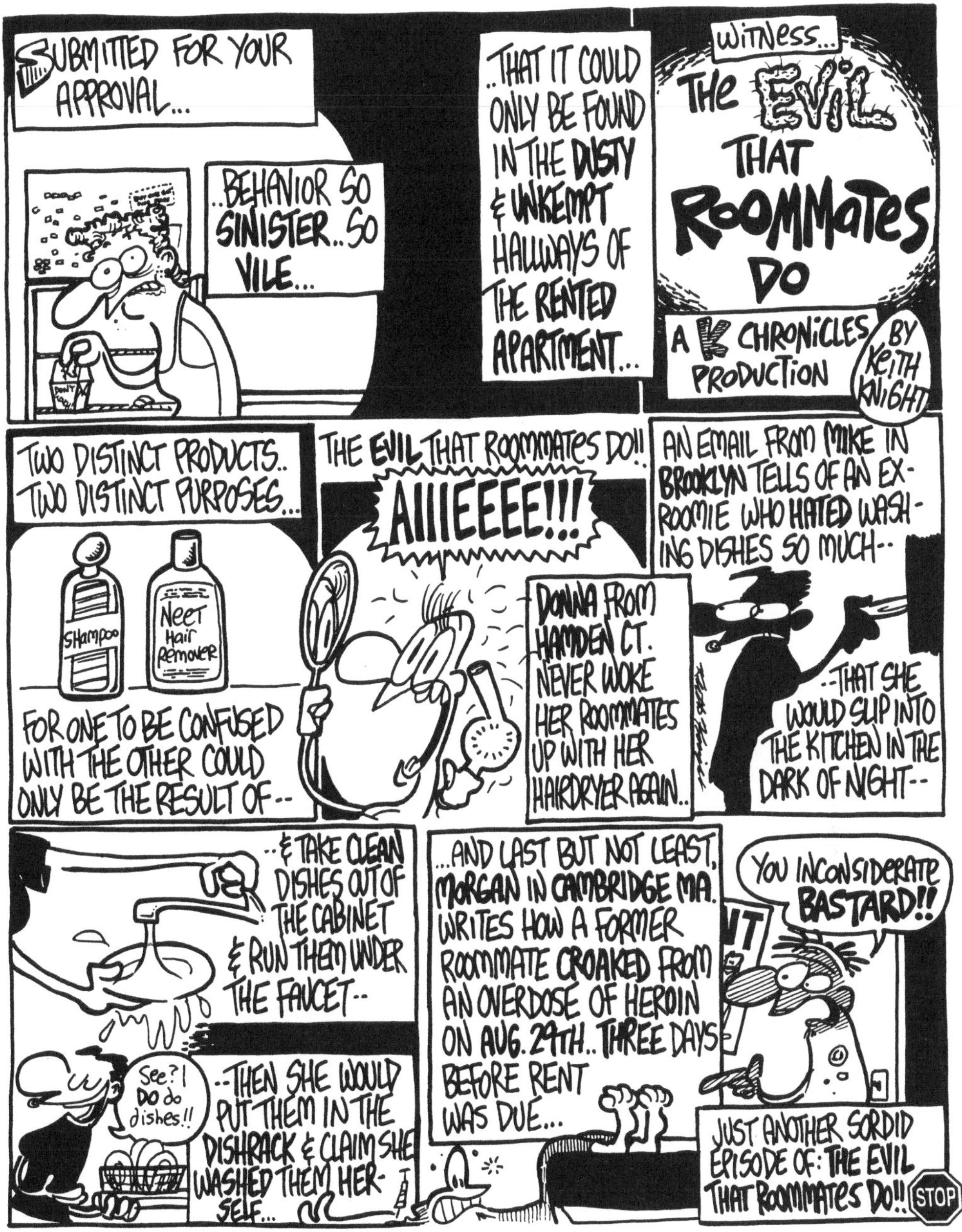
SUBMITTED FOR YOUR APPROVAL...
..BEHAVIOR SO SINISTER...SO VILE...
DON'T TOUCH
..THAT IT COULD ONLY BE FOUND IN THE DUSTY & UNKEMPT HALLWAYS OF THE RENTED APARTMENT...
WITNESS...
THE EVIL THAT ROOMMATES DO
A K CHRONICLES PRODUCTION
BY KEITH KNIGHT
TWO DISTINCT PRODUCTS.. TWO DISTINCT PURPOSES...
SHampoo
Neet Hair Remover
FOR ONE TO BE CONFUSED WITH THE OTHER COULD ONLY BE THE RESULT OF--
THE EVIL THAT ROOMMATES DO!!
AIIIEEEE!!!
DONNA FROM HAMDEN CT. NEVER WOKE HER ROOMMATES UP WITH HER HAIRDRYER AGAIN..
AN EMAIL FROM MIKE IN BROOKLYN TELLS OF AN EX-ROOMIE WHO HATED WASHING DISHES SO MUCH--
--THAT SHE WOULD SLIP INTO THE KITCHEN IN THE DARK OF NIGHT--
--& TAKE CLEAN DISHES OUT OF THE CABINET & RUN THEM UNDER THE FAUCET--
See?! DO do dishes!!
--THEN SHE WOULD PUT THEM IN THE DISHRACK & CLAIM SHE WASHED THEM HER-SELF...
...AND LAST BUT NOT LEAST, MORGAN IN CAMBRIDGE MA. WRITES HOW A FORMER ROOMMATE CROAKED FROM AN OVERDOSE OF HEROIN ON AUG. 29TH.. THREE DAYS BEFORE RENT WAS DUE...
YOU INCONSIDERATE BASTARD!!
NT
JUST ANOTHER SORDID EPISODE OF: THE EVIL THAT ROOMMATES DO!!
STOP

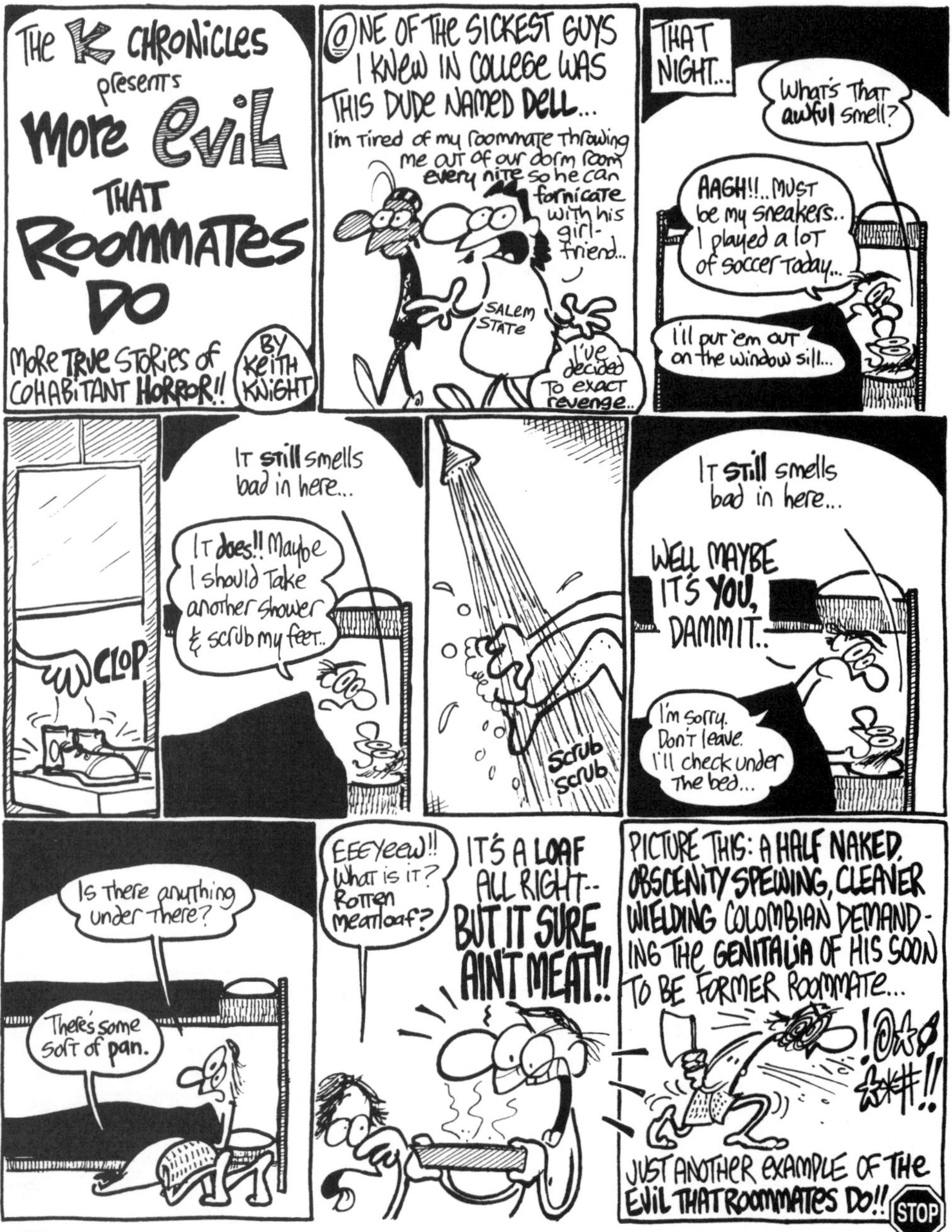
The K Chronicles presents
More Evil That Roommates Do
More TRUE stories of cohabitant HORROR!!
By Keith Knight
One of the sickest guys I knew in college was this dude named DELL...
I'm tired of my roommate throwing me out of our dorm room every nite so he can fornicate with his girl-friend...
SALEM STATE
I've decided to exact revenge...
THAT NIGHT...
What's that awful smell?
AAGH!!.. MUST be my sneakers.. I played a lot of soccer today...
I'll put 'em out on the window sill...
CLOP
It still smells bad in here...
It does!! Maybe I should take another shower & scrub my feet..
Scrub scrub
It still smells bad in here...
WELL MAYBE IT'S YOU, DAMMIT..
I'm sorry. Don't leave. I'll check under the bed...
Is there anything under there?
There's some sort of pan.
EEEYeew!! What is it? Rotten meatloaf?
IT'S A LOAF ALL RIGHT-- BUT IT SURE AIN'T MEAT!!
PICTURE THIS: A HALF NAKED, OBSCENITY SPEWING, CLEAVER WIELDING COLOMBIAN DEMANDING THE GENITALIA OF HIS SOON TO BE FORMER ROOMMATE...
JUST ANOTHER EXAMPLE OF THE EVIL THAT ROOMMATES DO!!
STOP

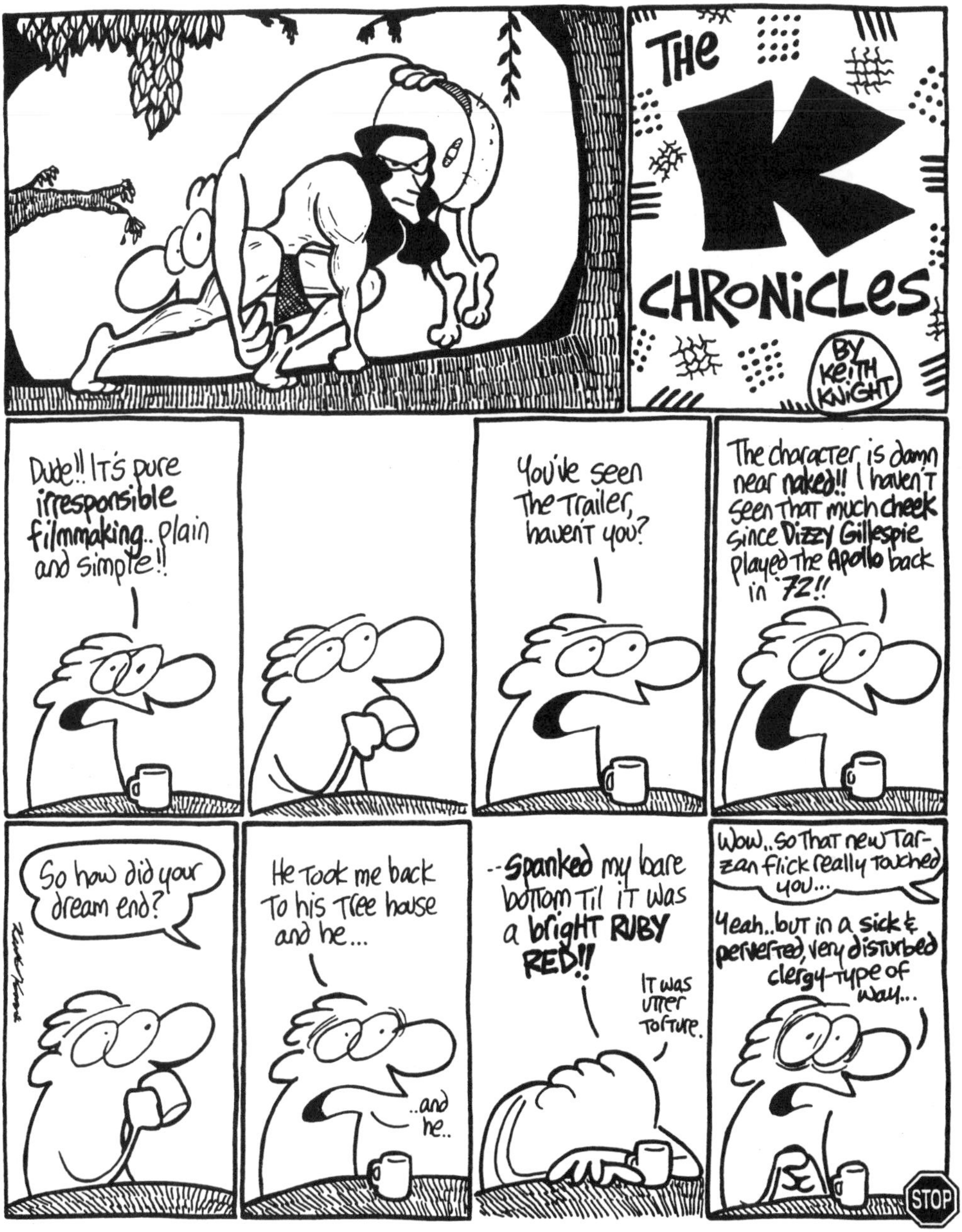

THE K CHRONICLES
BY KEITH KNIGHT
Dude!! It's pure irresponsible filmmaking.. plain and simple!!
You've seen the trailer, haven't you?
The character is damn near naked!! I haven't seen that much cheek since Dizzy Gillespie played the Apollo back in '72!!
So how did your dream end?
He took me back to his tree house and he...
..and he..
--Spanked my bare bottom til it was a bright RUBY RED!!
It was utter torture.
Wow.. so that new Tarzan flick really touched you...
Yeah.. but in a sick & perverted, very disturbed clergy-type of way...
STOP

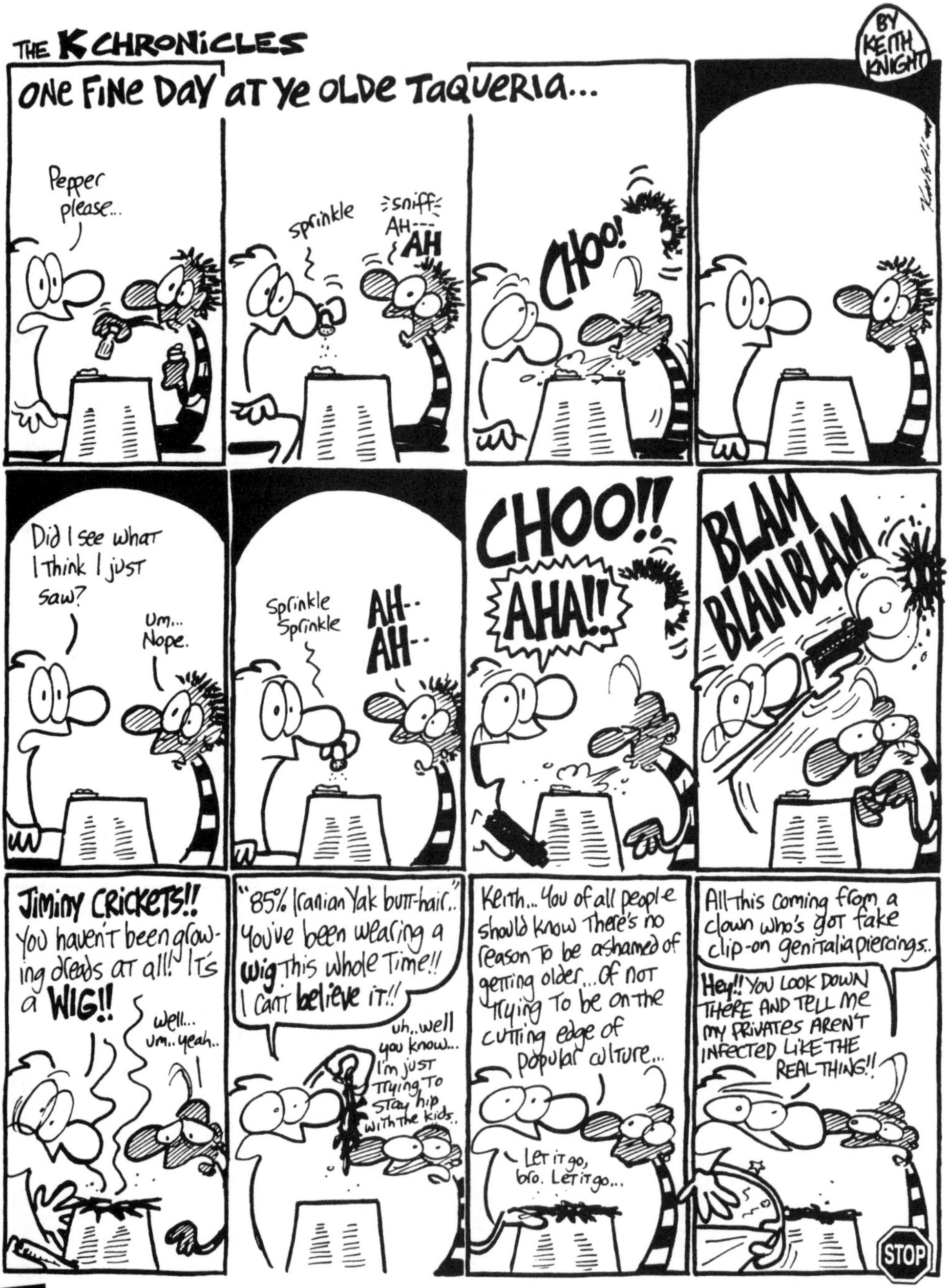
THE K CHRONICLES
BY KEITH KNIGHT
ONE FINE DAY AT YE OLDE TAQUERIA...
Pepper please...
sprinkle
sniff AH--- AH
CHOO!
Did I see what I think I just saw?
Um... Nope.
Sprinkle Sprinkle
AH-- AH--
CHOO!!
AHA!!
BLAM BLAM BLAM BLAM
JIMINY CRICKETS!! You haven't been growing dreads at all! It's a WIG!!
well... um.. yeah..
"85% Iranian Yak butt-hair.." You've been wearing a wig this whole time!! I can't believe it!!
uh.. well you know... I'm just trying to stay hip with the kids..
Keith... You of all people should know there's no reason to be ashamed of getting older... of not trying to be on the cutting edge of popular culture...
Let it go, bro. Let it go...
All this coming from a clown who's got fake clip-on genitalia piercings..
Hey!! You look down there and tell me my privates aren't infected like the real thing!!
STOP

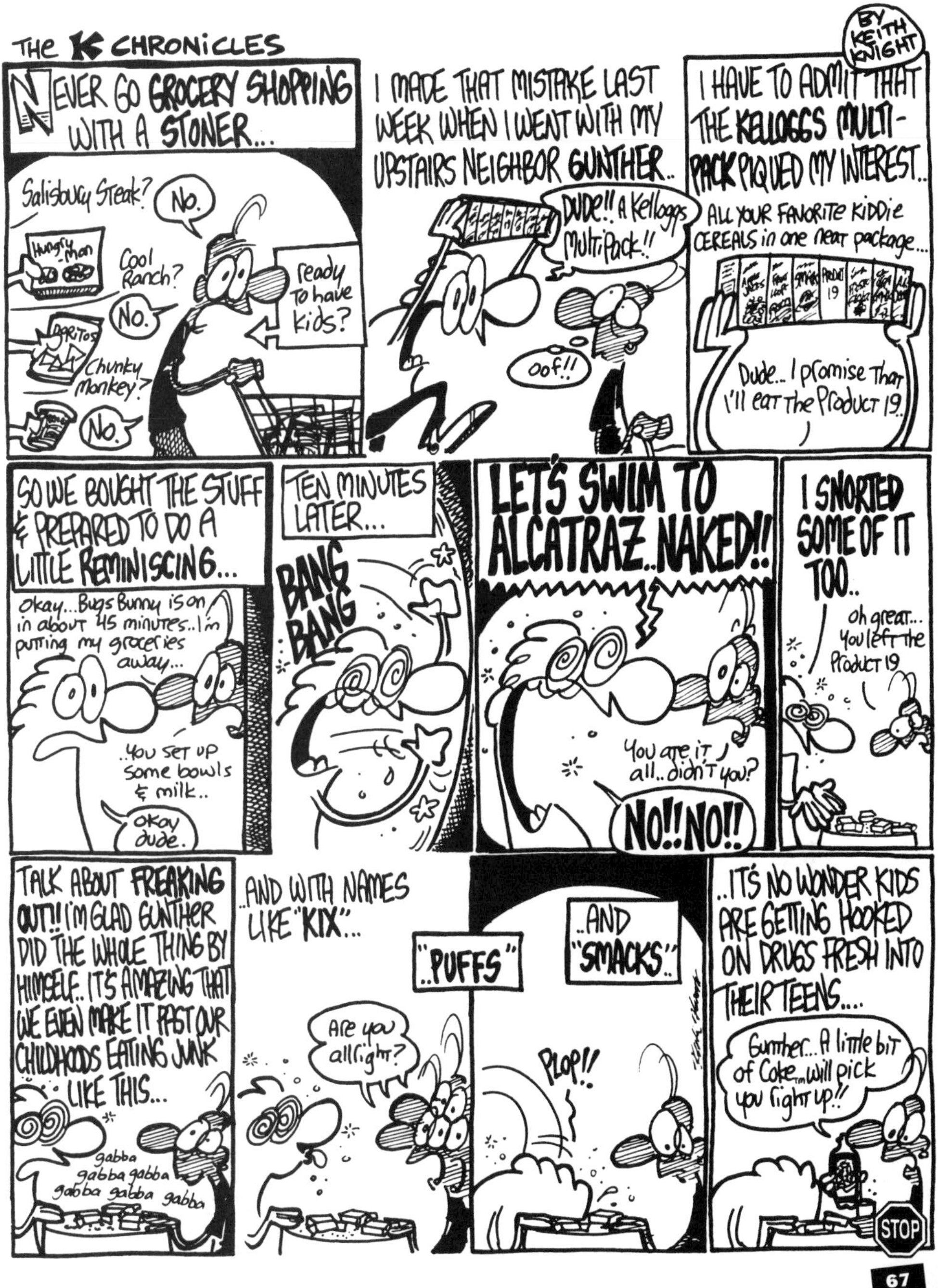
THE K CHRONICLES
BY KEITH KNIGHT
NEVER GO GROCERY SHOPPING WITH A STONER...
Salisbury Steak?
No.
Hungry-Man
Cool Ranch?
No.
DORITOS
Chunky Monkey?
No.
ready to have kids?
I MADE THAT MISTAKE LAST WEEK WHEN I WENT WITH MY UPSTAIRS NEIGHBOR GUNTHER..
DUDE!! A Kelloggs MultiPack!!
oof!!
I HAVE TO ADMIT THAT THE KELLOGGS MULTI-PACK PIQUED MY INTEREST...
ALL YOUR FAVORITE KIDDIE CEREALS in one neat package...
Dude.. I promise That I'll eat The Product 19..
SO WE BOUGHT THE STUFF & PREPARED TO DO A LITTLE REMINISCING...
Okay... Bugs Bunny is on in about 45 minutes.. I'm putting my groceries away...
..You set up some bowls & milk..
okay dude.
TEN MINUTES LATER...
BANG BANG
LET'S SWIM TO ALCATRAZ..NAKED!!
You ate it all.. didn't you?
NO!! NO!!
I SNORTED SOME OF IT TOO..
oh great... You left the Product 19
TALK ABOUT FREAKING OUT!! I'M GLAD GUNTHER DID THE WHOLE THING BY HIMSELF.. IT'S AMAZING THAT WE EVEN MAKE IT PAST OUR CHILDHOODS EATING JUNK LIKE THIS...
gabba gabba gabba gabba gabba gabba
..AND WITH NAMES LIKE "KIX"...
"PUFFS"
Are you allright?
..AND "SMACKS"..
PLOP!!
..IT'S NO WONDER KIDS ARE GETTING HOOKED ON DRUGS FRESH INTO THEIR TEENS....
Gunther... A little bit of Coke™ will pick you right up!!
STOP

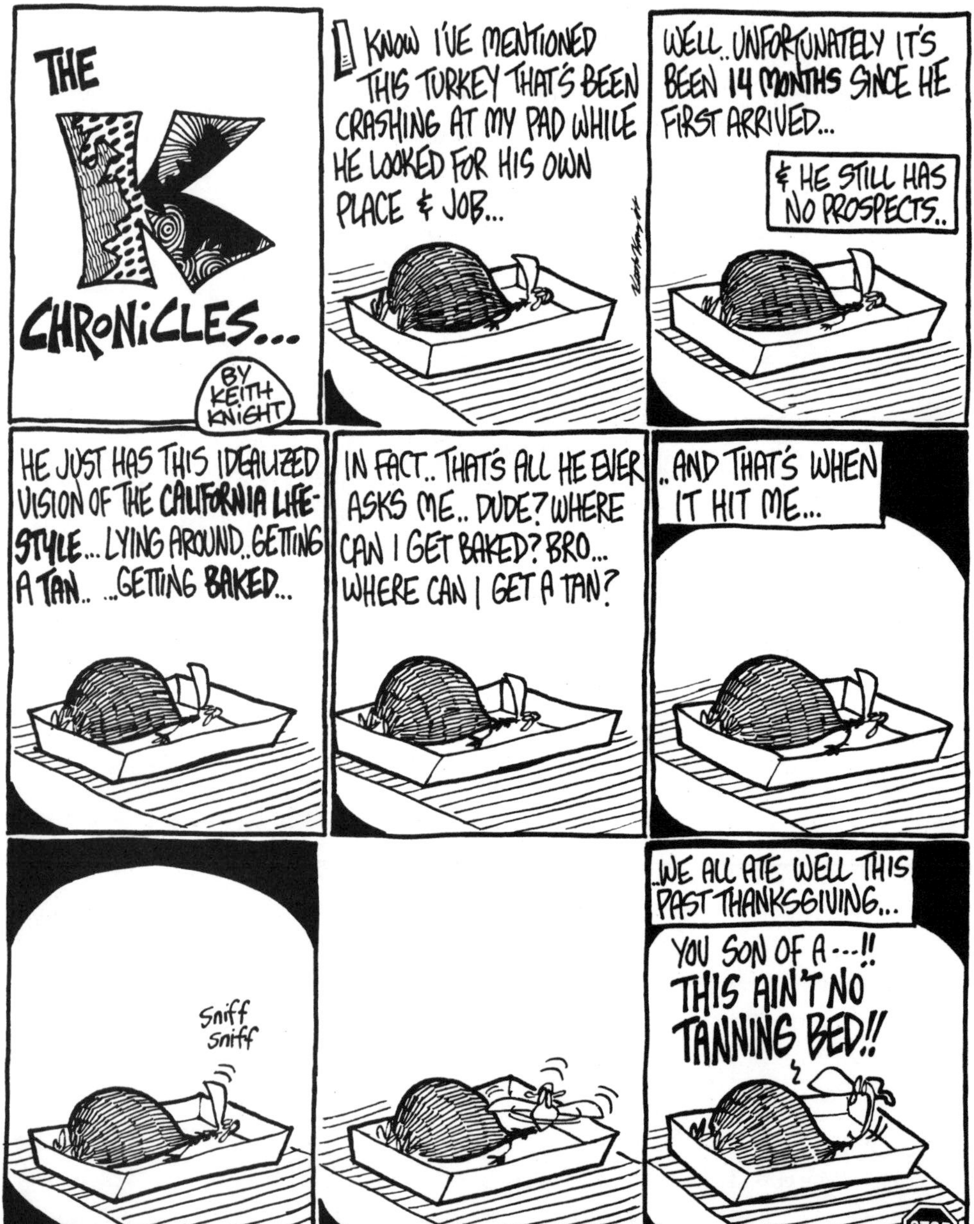
THE K CHRONICLES...
BY KEITH KNIGHT
I KNOW I'VE MENTIONED THIS TURKEY THAT'S BEEN CRASHING AT MY PAD WHILE HE LOOKED FOR HIS OWN PLACE & JOB...
WELL.. UNFORTUNATELY IT'S BEEN 14 MONTHS SINCE HE FIRST ARRIVED...
& HE STILL HAS NO PROSPECTS..
HE JUST HAS THIS IDEALIZED VISION OF THE CALIFORNIA LIFE-STYLE... LYING AROUND.. GETTING A TAN.. ...GETTING BAKED...
IN FACT.. THAT'S ALL HE EVER ASKS ME.. DUDE? WHERE CAN I GET BAKED? BRO... WHERE CAN I GET A TAN?
..AND THAT'S WHEN IT HIT ME...
Sniff sniff
..WE ALL ATE WELL THIS PAST THANKSGIVING...
YOU SON OF A ---!! THIS AIN'T NO TANNING BED!!
STOP

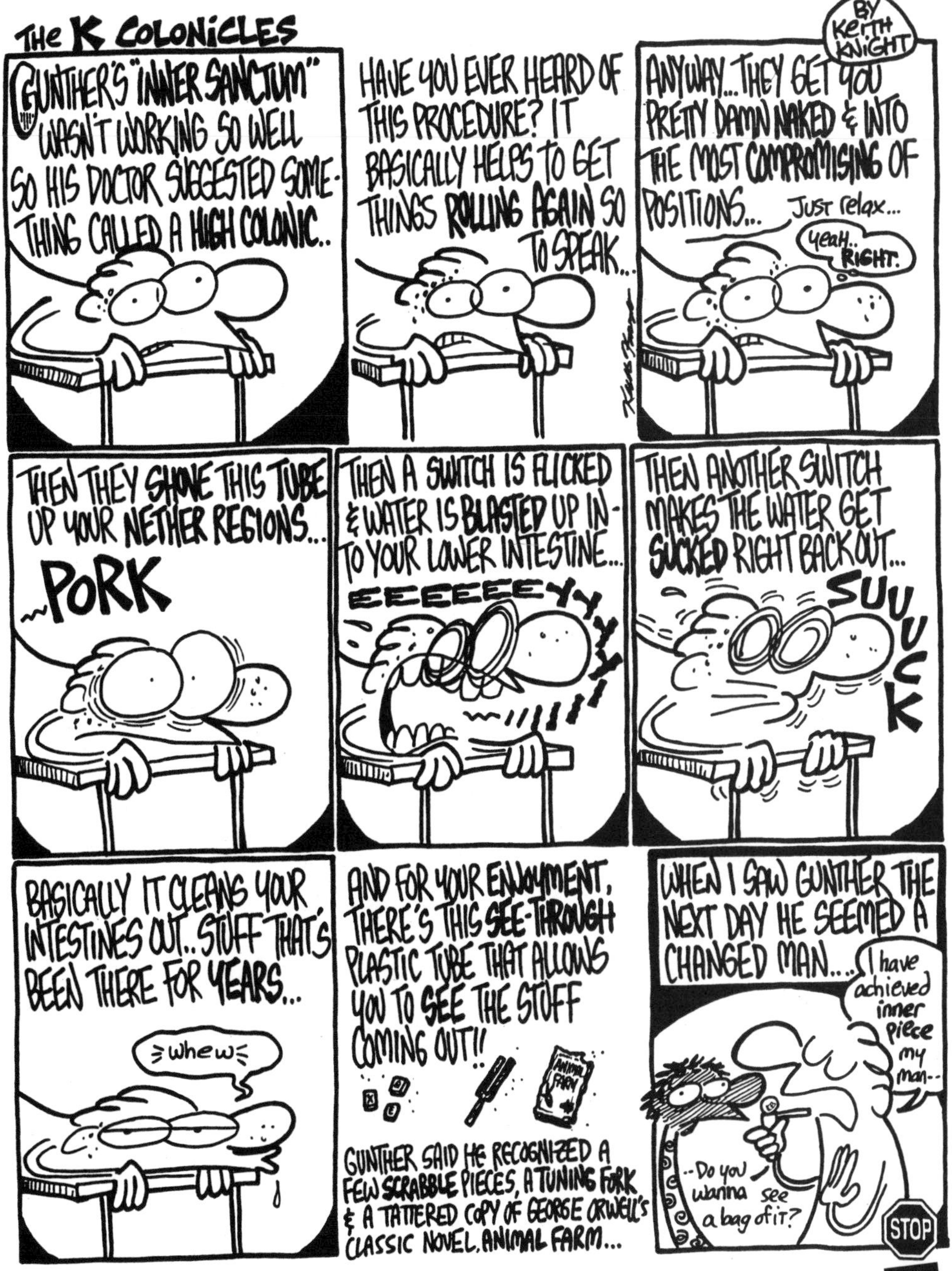
THE K COLONICLES
BY KEITH KNIGHT
GUNTHER'S "INNER SANCTUM" WASN'T WORKING SO WELL SO HIS DOCTOR SUGGESTED SOME-THING CALLED A HIGH COLONIC..
HAVE YOU EVER HEARD OF THIS PROCEDURE? IT BASICALLY HELPS TO GET THINGS ROLLING AGAIN SO TO SPEAK...
ANYWAY... THEY GET YOU PRETTY DAMN NAKED & INTO THE MOST COMPROMISING OF POSITIONS...
Just relax...
yeah.. RIGHT.
THEN THEY SHOVE THIS TUBE UP YOUR NETHER REGIONS...
~PORK
THEN A SWITCH IS FLICKED & WATER IS BLASTED UP IN-TO YOUR LOWER INTESTINE...
EEEEEEYYYY
THEN ANOTHER SWITCH MAKES THE WATER GET SUCKED RIGHT BACK OUT...
SUUUUCK
BASICALLY IT CLEANS YOUR INTESTINES OUT.. STUFF THAT'S BEEN THERE FOR YEARS...
whew
AND FOR YOUR ENJOYMENT, THERE'S THIS SEE-THROUGH PLASTIC TUBE THAT ALLOWS YOU TO SEE THE STUFF COMING OUT!!
ANIMAL FARM
GUNTHER SAID HE RECOGNIZED A FEW SCRABBLE PIECES, A TUNING FORK & A TATTERED COPY OF GEORGE ORWELL'S CLASSIC NOVEL, ANIMAL FARM...
WHEN I SAW GUNTHER THE NEXT DAY HE SEEMED A CHANGED MAN....
I have achieved inner piece my man--
--Do you wanna see a bag of IT?
STOP

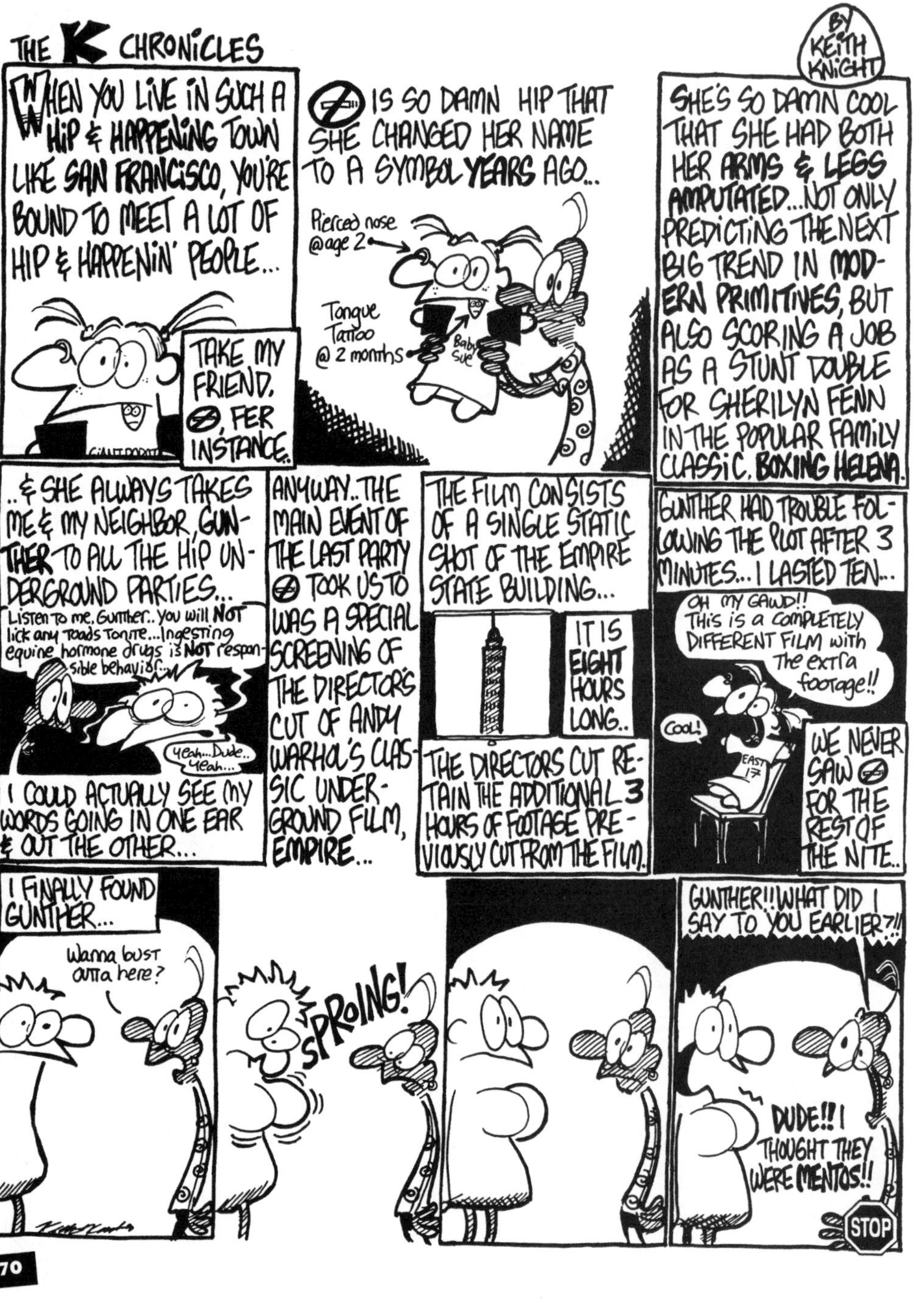

THE K CHRONICLES
BY KEITH KNIGHT
WHEN YOU LIVE IN SUCH A HIP & HAPPENING TOWN LIKE SAN FRANCISCO, YOU'RE BOUND TO MEET A LOT OF HIP & HAPPENIN' PEOPLE...
TAKE MY FRIEND, , FER INSTANCE..
IS SO DAMN HIP THAT SHE CHANGED HER NAME TO A SYMBOL YEARS AGO...
Pierced nose @age 2
Tongue Tattoo @ 2 months
Baby Sue
SHE'S SO DAMN COOL THAT SHE HAD BOTH HER ARMS & LEGS AMPUTATED...NOT ONLY PREDICTING THE NEXT BIG TREND IN MODERN PRIMITIVES, BUT ALSO SCORING A JOB AS A STUNT DOUBLE FOR SHERILYN FENN IN THE POPULAR FAMILY CLASSIC, BOXING HELENA.
..& SHE ALWAYS TAKES ME & MY NEIGHBOR, GUNTHER TO ALL THE HIP UNDERGROUND PARTIES...
Listen to me, Gunther.. you will NOT lick any Toads Tonite...Ingesting equine hormone drugs is NOT responsible behavior...
Yeah...Dude.. Yeah...
I COULD ACTUALLY SEE MY WORDS GOING IN ONE EAR & OUT THE OTHER...
ANYWAY..THE MAIN EVENT OF THE LAST PARTY TOOK US TO WAS A SPECIAL SCREENING OF THE DIRECTOR'S CUT OF ANDY WARHOL'S CLASSIC UNDERGROUND FILM, EMPIRE...
THE FILM CONSISTS OF A SINGLE STATIC SHOT OF THE EMPIRE STATE BUILDING...
IT IS EIGHT HOURS LONG..
THE DIRECTORS CUT RETAIN THE ADDITIONAL 3 HOURS OF FOOTAGE PREVIOUSLY CUT FROM THE FILM.
GUNTHER HAD TROUBLE FOLLOWING THE PLOT AFTER 3 MINUTES... I LASTED TEN...
OH MY GAWD!! This is a COMPLETELY DIFFERENT FILM with the extra footage!!
Cool!
EAST 17
WE NEVER SAW FOR THE REST OF THE NITE..
I FINALLY FOUND GUNTHER...
Wanna bust outta here?
SPROING!
GUNTHER!! WHAT DID I SAY TO YOU EARLIER?!!
DUDE!! I THOUGHT THEY WERE MENTOS!!
STOP

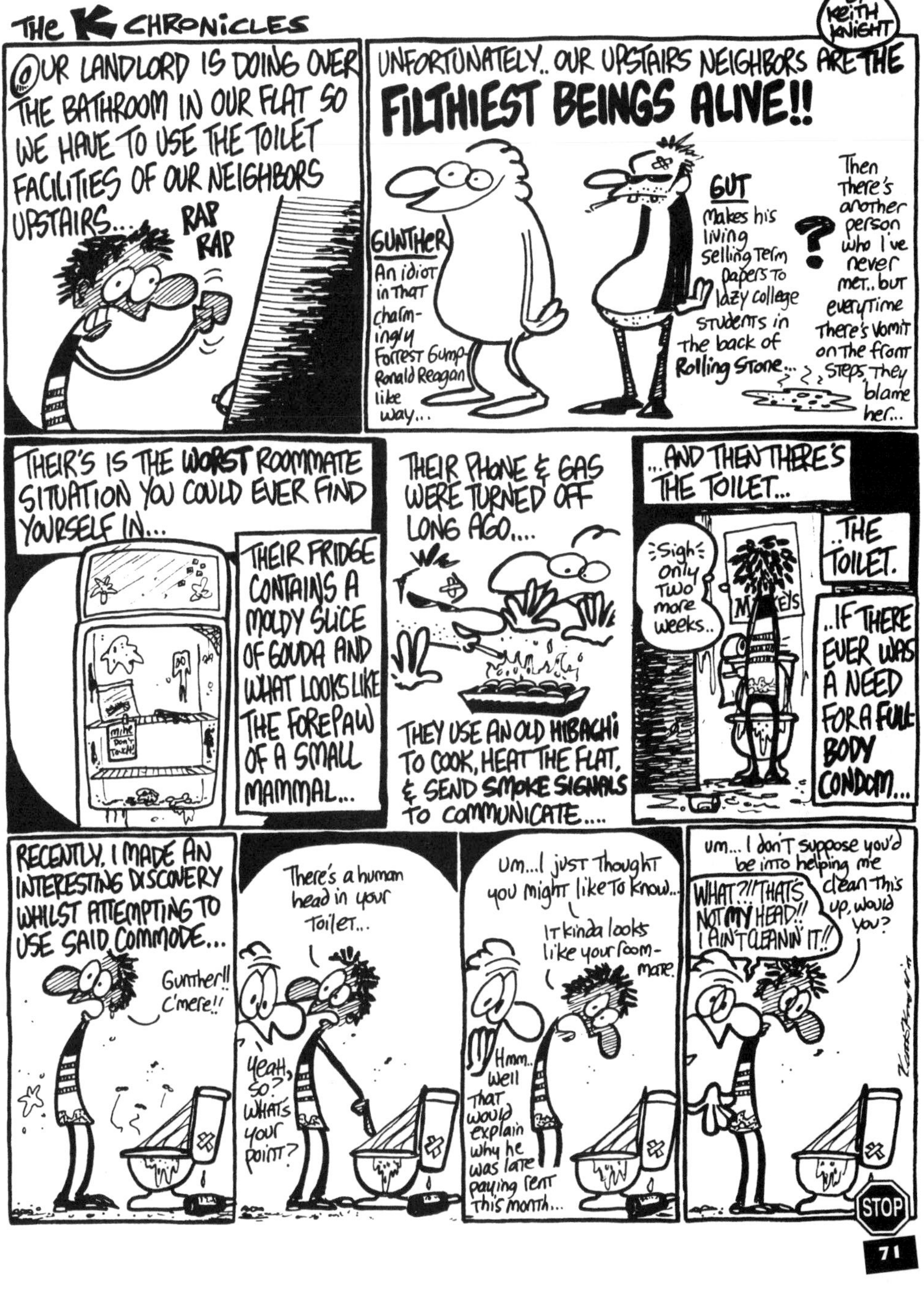
THE K CHRONICLES
BY KEITH KNIGHT
OUR LANDLORD IS DOING OVER THE BATHROOM IN OUR FLAT SO WE HAVE TO USE THE TOILET FACILITIES OF OUR NEIGHBORS UPSTAIRS...
RAP RAP
UNFORTUNATELY.. OUR UPSTAIRS NEIGHBORS ARE THE
FILTHIEST BEINGS ALIVE!!
GUNTHER
An idiot in that charm-ingly Forrest Gump-Ronald Reagan like way...
GUT
Makes his living selling term papers to lazy college students in the back of Rolling Stone...
?
Then there's another person who I've never met.. but everytime there's vomit on the front steps, they blame her...
THEIR'S IS THE WORST ROOMMATE SITUATION YOU COULD EVER FIND YOURSELF IN...
THEIR FRIDGE CONTAINS A MOLDY SLICE OF GOUDA AND WHAT LOOKS LIKE THE FOREPAW OF A SMALL MAMMAL...
mine Don't Touch!
THEIR PHONE & GAS WERE TURNED OFF LONG AGO....
THEY USE AN OLD HIBACHI TO COOK, HEAT THE FLAT, & SEND SMOKE SIGNALS TO COMMUNICATE....
...AND THEN THERE'S THE TOILET...
Sigh only two more weeks..
..THE TOILET.
..IF THERE EVER WAS A NEED FOR A FULL BODY CONDOM...
RECENTLY, I MADE AN INTERESTING DISCOVERY WHILST ATTEMPTING TO USE SAID COMMODE...
Gunther!! C'mere!!
There's a human head in your toilet...
Yeah, so? What's your point?
Um...I just thought you might like to know...
It kinda looks like your room-mate.
Hmm.. Well that would explain why he was late paying rent this month...
Um... I don't suppose you'd be into helping me clean this up, would you?
WHAT?!! THAT'S NOT MY HEAD!! I AIN'T CLEANIN' IT!!
STOP

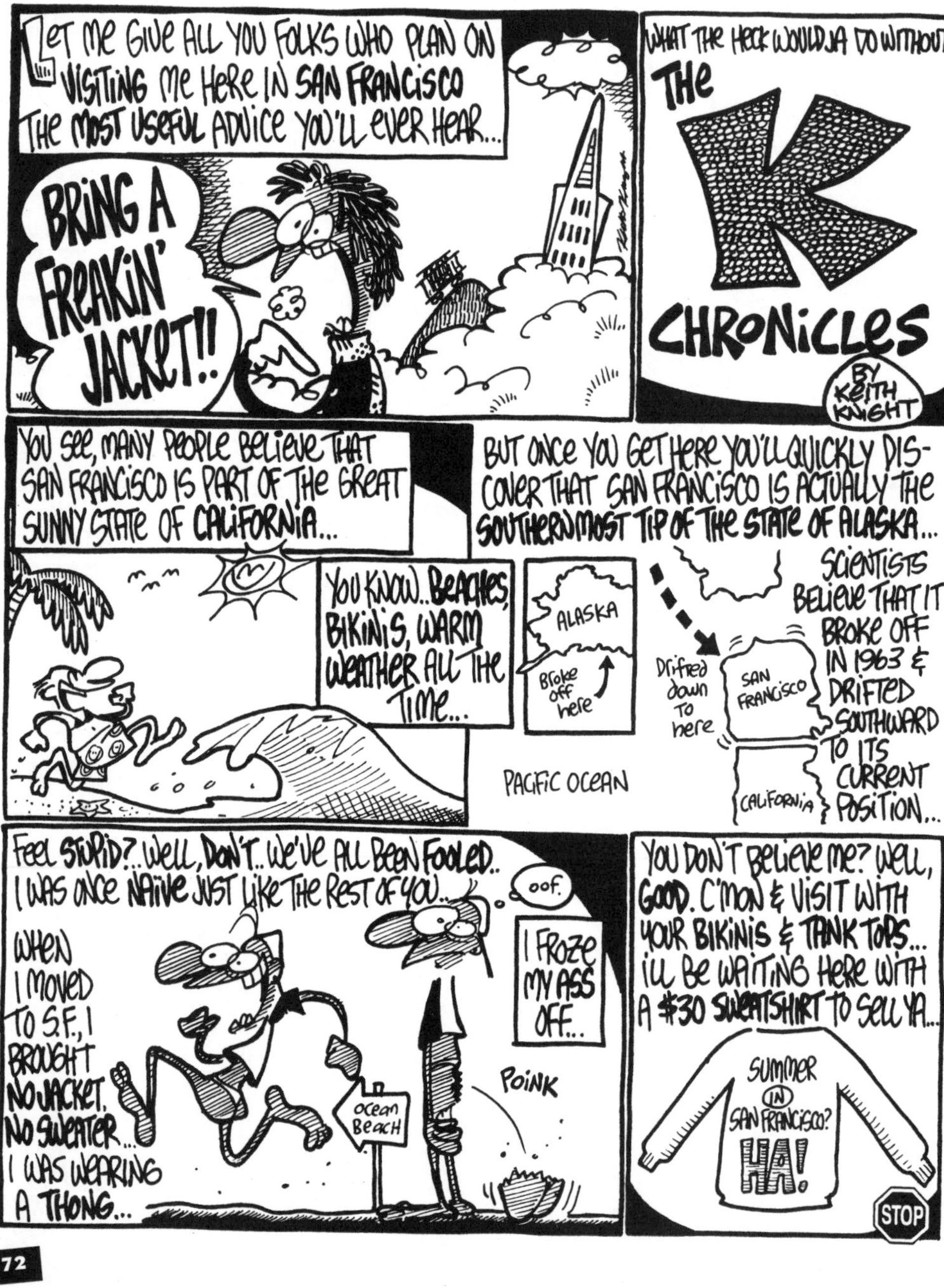
Let me give all you folks who plan on visiting me here in San Francisco the most useful advice you'll ever hear...
Bring a freakin' jacket!!..
What the heck would ja do without
The K Chronicles
By Keith Knight
You see, many people believe that San Francisco is part of the great sunny state of California...
You know.. beaches, bikinis, warm weather all the time...
But once you get here you'll quickly discover that San Francisco is actually the southernmost tip of the state of Alaska...
Alaska
Broke off here
Drifted down to here
San Francisco
California
Pacific Ocean
Scientists believe that it broke off in 1963 & drifted southward to its current position...
Feel stupid?.. Well, don't.. We've all been fooled.. I was once naïve just like the rest of you...
When I moved to S.F., I brought no jacket, no sweater... I was wearing a thong...
oof.
I froze my ass off...
Ocean Beach
Poink
You don't believe me? Well, good. C'mon & visit with your bikinis & tank tops... I'll be waiting here with a $30 sweatshirt to sell ya...
Summer in San Francisco? HA!
STOP

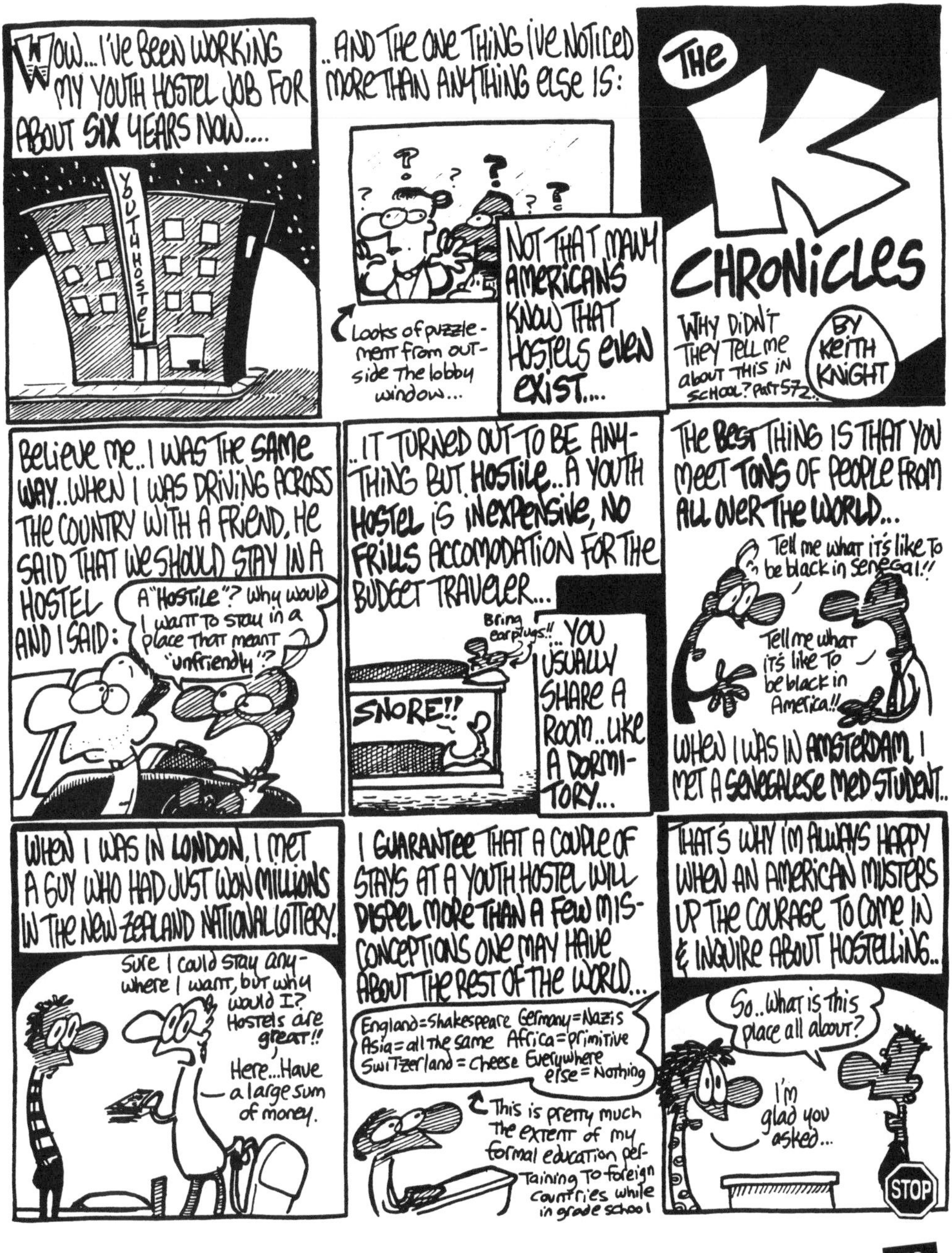
WOW... I'VE BEEN WORKING MY YOUTH HOSTEL JOB FOR ABOUT SIX YEARS NOW....
YOUTH HOSTEL
..AND THE ONE THING I'VE NOTICED MORE THAN ANYTHING ELSE IS:
Looks of puzzlement from outside the lobby window...
NOT THAT MANY AMERICANS KNOW THAT HOSTELS EVEN EXIST....
THE K CHRONICLES
WHY DIDN'T THEY TELL ME ABOUT THIS IN SCHOOL? PART 572..
BY KEITH KNIGHT
BELIEVE ME.. I WAS THE SAME WAY.. WHEN I WAS DRIVING ACROSS THE COUNTRY WITH A FRIEND, HE SAID THAT WE SHOULD STAY IN A HOSTEL AND I SAID:
A "HOSTILE"? Why would I want to stay in a place that meant "unfriendly"?
..IT TURNED OUT TO BE ANYTHING BUT HOSTILE.. A YOUTH HOSTEL IS INEXPENSIVE, NO FRILLS ACCOMODATION FOR THE BUDGET TRAVELER...
Bring earplugs!!
...YOU USUALLY SHARE A ROOM.. LIKE A DORMITORY...
SNORE!!
THE BEST THING IS THAT YOU MEET TONS OF PEOPLE FROM ALL OVER THE WORLD...
Tell me what it's like to be black in Senegal!!
Tell me what it's like to be black in America!!
WHEN I WAS IN AMSTERDAM, I MET A SENEGALESE MED STUDENT..
WHEN I WAS IN LONDON, I MET A GUY WHO HAD JUST WON MILLIONS IN THE NEW ZEALAND NATIONAL LOTTERY.
Sure I could stay anywhere I want, but why would I? Hostels are great!!
Here...Have a large sum of money.
I GUARANTEE THAT A COUPLE OF STAYS AT A YOUTH HOSTEL WILL DISPEL MORE THAN A FEW MISCONCEPTIONS ONE MAY HAVE ABOUT THE REST OF THE WORLD...
England=Shakespeare Germany=Nazis Asia=all the same Africa=primitive Switzerland=Cheese Everywhere else=Nothing
This is pretty much the extent of my formal education pertaining to foreign countries while in grade school
THAT'S WHY I'M ALWAYS HAPPY WHEN AN AMERICAN MUSTERS UP THE COURAGE TO COME IN & INQUIRE ABOUT HOSTELLING..
So.. What is this place all about?
I'm glad you asked...
STOP

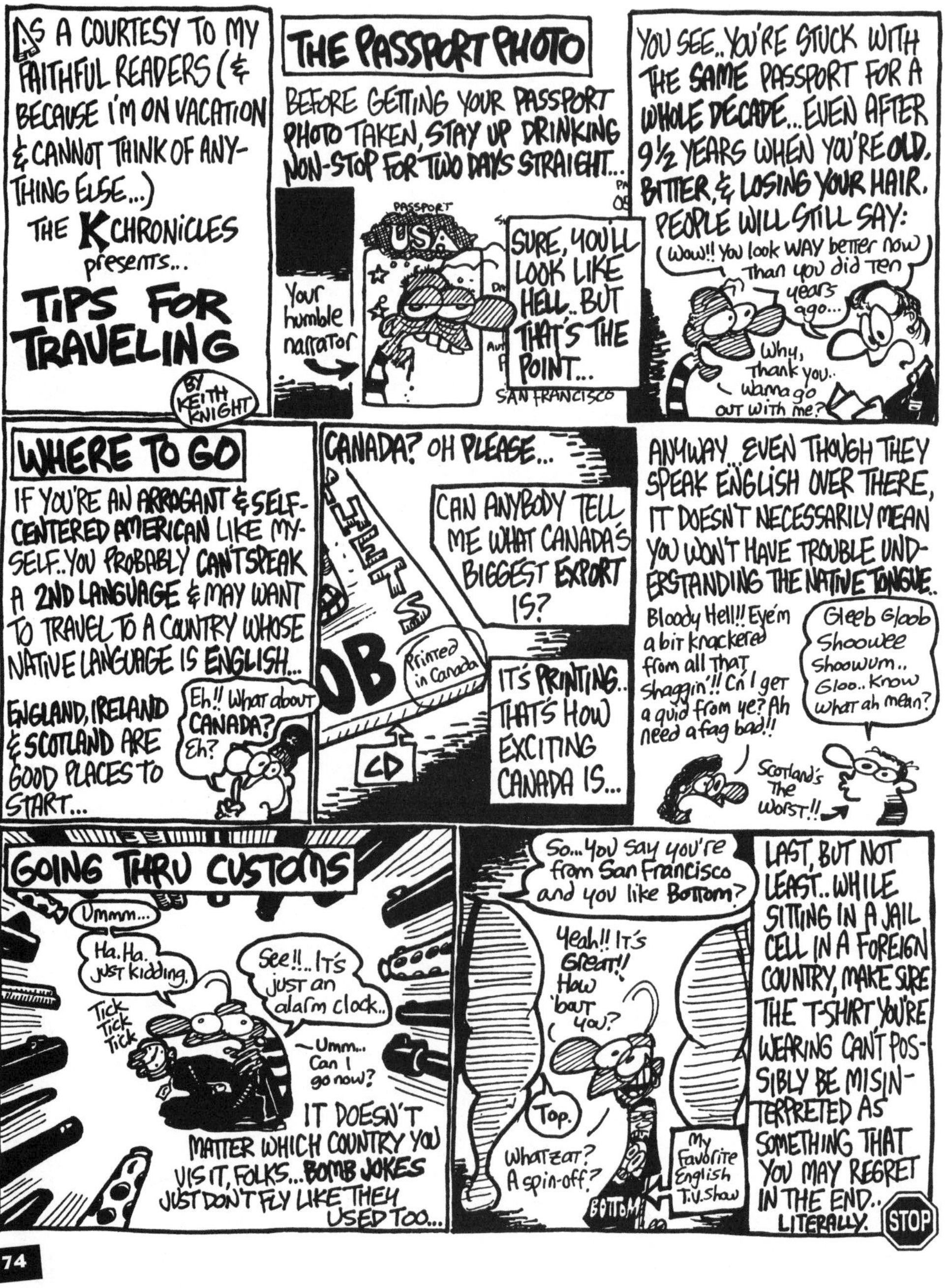

AS A COURTESY TO MY FAITHFUL READERS (& BECAUSE I'M ON VACATION & CANNOT THINK OF ANYTHING ELSE...)
THE K CHRONICLES presents...
TIPS FOR TRAVELING
BY KEITH KNIGHT
THE PASSPORT PHOTO
BEFORE GETTING YOUR PASSPORT PHOTO TAKEN, STAY UP DRINKING NON-STOP FOR TWO DAYS STRAIGHT...
PASSPORT
USA
Your humble narrator
SURE, YOU'LL LOOK LIKE HELL.. BUT THAT'S THE POINT...
SAN FRANCISCO
YOU SEE.. YOU'RE STUCK WITH THE SAME PASSPORT FOR A WHOLE DECADE... EVEN AFTER 9½ YEARS WHEN YOU'RE OLD, BITTER, & LOSING YOUR HAIR, PEOPLE WILL STILL SAY:
Wow!! You look WAY better now than you did ten years ago...
Why, thank you.. Wanna go out with me?
WHERE TO GO
IF YOU'RE AN ARROGANT & SELF-CENTERED AMERICAN LIKE MYSELF.. YOU PROBABLY CAN'T SPEAK A 2ND LANGUAGE & MAY WANT TO TRAVEL TO A COUNTRY WHOSE NATIVE LANGUAGE IS ENGLISH...
ENGLAND, IRELAND & SCOTLAND ARE GOOD PLACES TO START...
Eh!! What about CANADA? Eh?
CANADA? OH PLEASE...
CAN ANYBODY TELL ME WHAT CANADA'S BIGGEST EXPORT IS?
Printed in Canada
CD
IT'S PRINTING.. THAT'S HOW EXCITING CANADA IS...
ANYWAY... EVEN THOUGH THEY SPEAK ENGLISH OVER THERE, IT DOESN'T NECESSARILY MEAN YOU WON'T HAVE TROUBLE UNDERSTANDING THE NATIVE TONGUE..
Bloody Hell!! Eye'm a bit knackered from all that shaggin'!! Cn'I get a quid from ye? Ah need a fag bad!!
Gleeb Gloob Shoowee Showum.. Gloo.. Know what ah mean?
Scotland's The Worst!!
GOING THRU CUSTOMS
Ummm...
Ha. Ha. Just kidding.
See!!.. It's just an alarm clock..
Tick Tick Tick
Umm... Can I go now?
IT DOESN'T MATTER WHICH COUNTRY YOU VISIT, FOLKS... BOMB JOKES JUST DON'T FLY LIKE THEY USED TOO...
So... You say you're from San Francisco and you like Bottom?
Yeah!! It's Great!! How 'bout you?
Top.
Whatzat? A spin-off?
My Favorite English T.V. Show
BOTTOM
LAST, BUT NOT LEAST.. WHILE SITTING IN A JAIL CELL IN A FOREIGN COUNTRY, MAKE SURE THE T-SHIRT YOU'RE WEARING CAN'T POSSIBLY BE MISINTERPRETED AS SOMETHING THAT YOU MAY REGRET IN THE END.. LITERALLY.
STOP

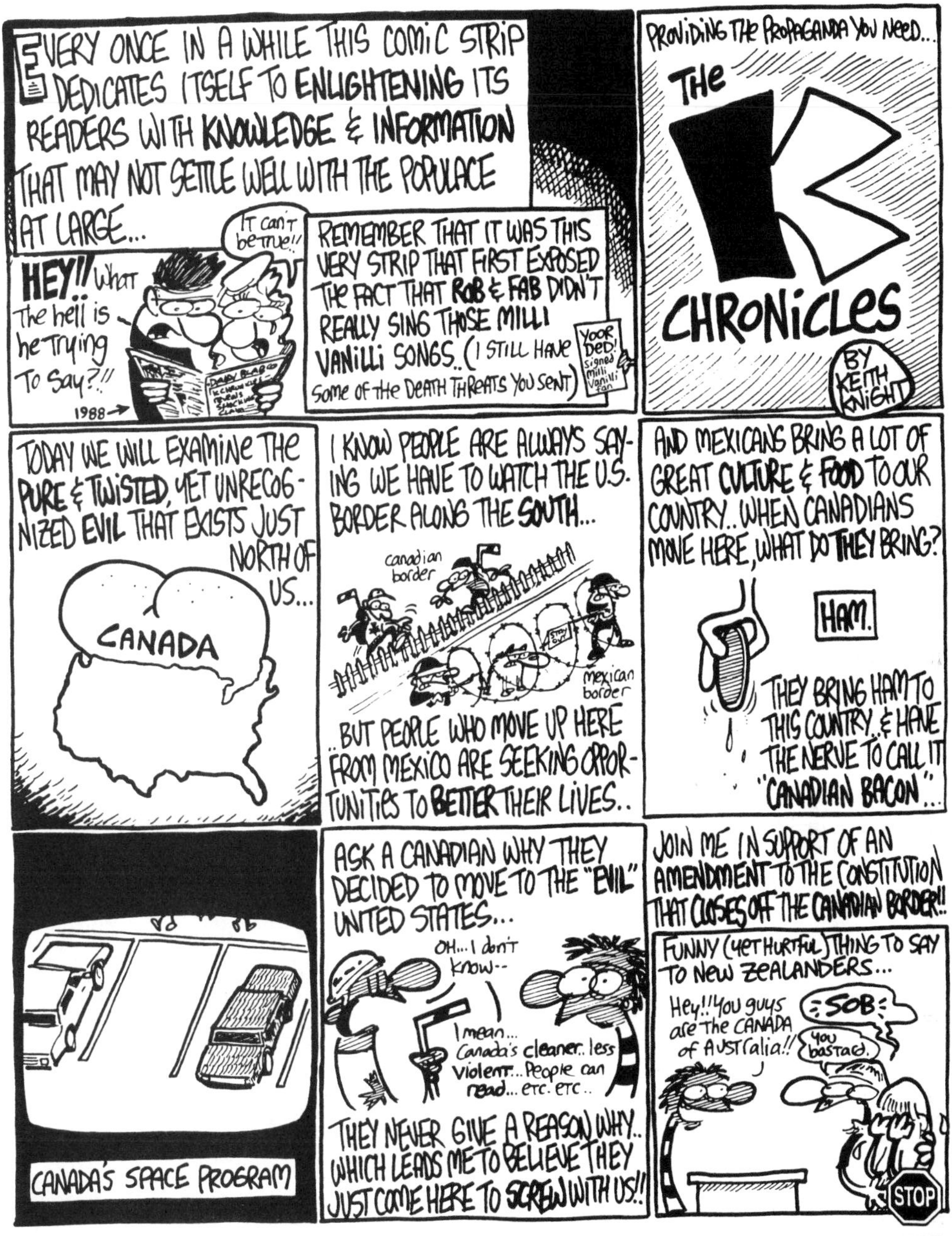
EVERY ONCE IN A WHILE THIS COMIC STRIP DEDICATES ITSELF TO ENLIGHTENING ITS READERS WITH KNOWLEDGE & INFORMATION THAT MAY NOT SETTLE WELL WITH THE POPULACE AT LARGE...
HEY!! What the hell is he trying to say?!!
It can't be true!!
1988
REMEMBER THAT IT WAS THIS VERY STRIP THAT FIRST EXPOSED THE FACT THAT ROB & FAB DIDN'T REALLY SING THOSE MILLI VANILLI SONGS.. (I STILL HAVE SOME OF THE DEATH THREATS YOU SENT)
YOOR DED! signed Milli Vanilli fan
PROVIDING THE PROPAGANDA YOU NEED...
THE K CHRONICLES
BY KEITH KNIGHT
TODAY WE WILL EXAMINE THE PURE & TWISTED, YET UNRECOGNIZED EVIL THAT EXISTS JUST NORTH OF US...
CANADA
I KNOW PEOPLE ARE ALWAYS SAYING WE HAVE TO WATCH THE U.S. BORDER ALONG THE SOUTH...
canadian border
mexican border
..BUT PEOPLE WHO MOVE UP HERE FROM MEXICO ARE SEEKING OPPORTUNITIES TO BETTER THEIR LIVES..
AND MEXICANS BRING A LOT OF GREAT CULTURE & FOOD TO OUR COUNTRY.. WHEN CANADIANS MOVE HERE, WHAT DO THEY BRING?
HAM.
THEY BRING HAM TO THIS COUNTRY & HAVE THE NERVE TO CALL IT "CANADIAN BACON"...
CANADA'S SPACE PROGRAM
ASK A CANADIAN WHY THEY DECIDED TO MOVE TO THE "EVIL" UNITED STATES...
OH... I don't know--
I mean... Canada's cleaner.. less violent... People can read... etc. etc..
THEY NEVER GIVE A REASON WHY.. WHICH LEADS ME TO BELIEVE THEY JUST COME HERE TO SCREW WITH US!!
JOIN ME IN SUPPORT OF AN AMENDMENT TO THE CONSTITUTION THAT CLOSES OFF THE CANADIAN BORDER!!
FUNNY (YET HURTFUL) THING TO SAY TO NEW ZEALANDERS...
Hey!! You guys are the CANADA of AUSTRALIA!!
SOB
You bastard.
STOP

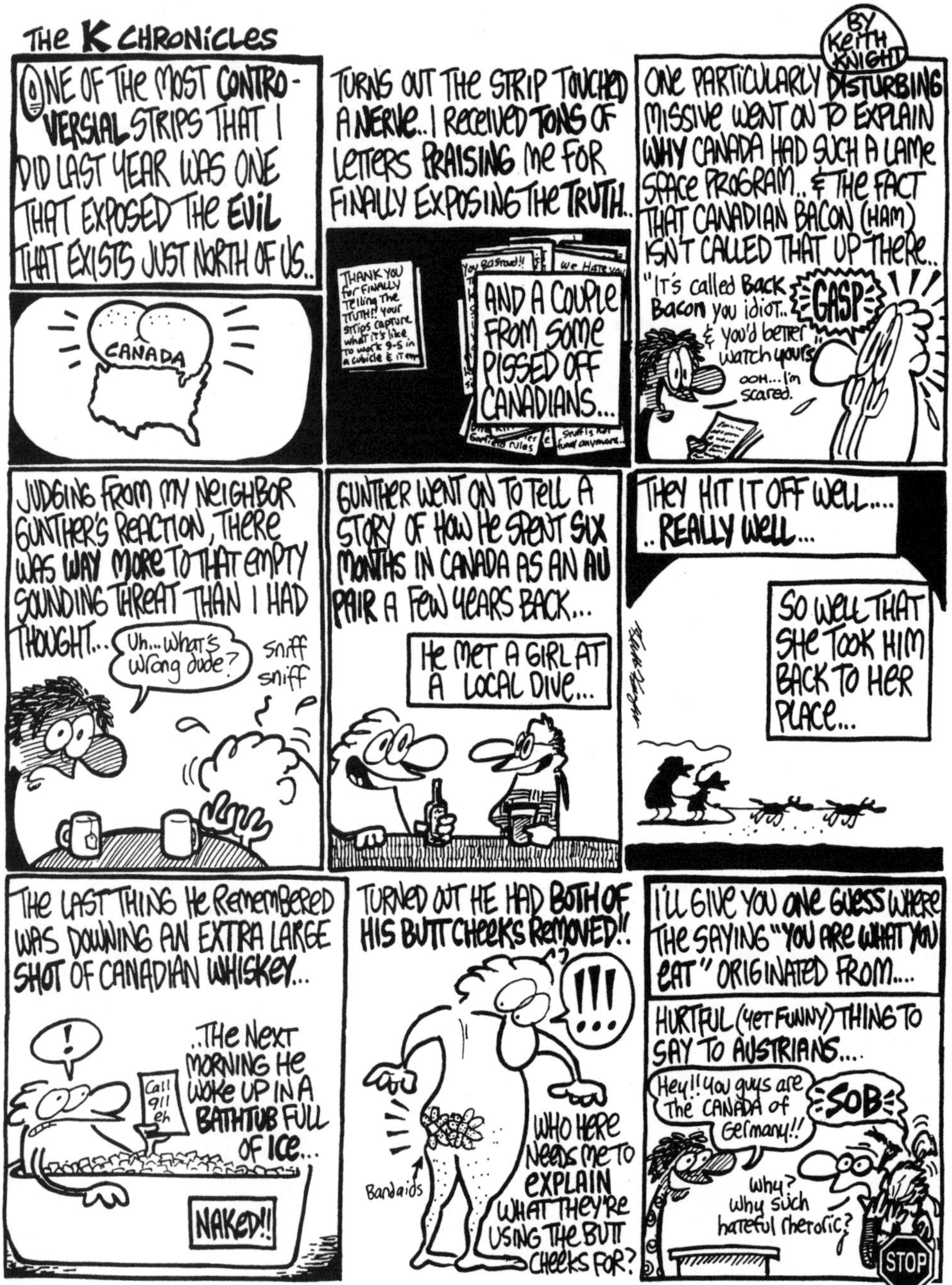

THE K CHRONICLES
BY KEITH KNIGHT
ONE OF THE MOST CONTROVERSIAL STRIPS THAT I DID LAST YEAR WAS ONE THAT EXPOSED THE EVIL THAT EXISTS JUST NORTH OF US..
CANADA
TURNS OUT THE STRIP TOUCHED A NERVE.. I RECEIVED TONS OF LETTERS PRAISING ME FOR FINALLY EXPOSING THE TRUTH..
THANK YOU for FINALLY Telling The TRUTH!! your strips capture what it's like to work 9-5 in a cubicle & it
You Bastard!!
We Hate you
Stuff is not funny anymore...
AND A COUPLE FROM SOME PISSED OFF CANADIANS...
ONE PARTICULARLY DISTURBING MISSIVE WENT ON TO EXPLAIN WHY CANADA HAD SUCH A LAME SPACE PROGRAM.. & THE FACT THAT CANADIAN BACON (HAM) ISN'T CALLED THAT UP THERE..
"It's called Back Bacon you idiot.. & you'd better watch yours"
GASP
OOH... I'm scared.
JUDGING FROM MY NEIGHBOR GUNTHER'S REACTION, THERE WAS WAY MORE TO THAT EMPTY SOUNDING THREAT THAN I HAD THOUGHT...
Uh... What's wrong dude?
sniff sniff
GUNTHER WENT ON TO TELL A STORY OF HOW HE SPENT SIX MONTHS IN CANADA AS AN AU PAIR A FEW YEARS BACK...
HE MET A GIRL AT A LOCAL DIVE...
THEY HIT IT OFF WELL.... ..REALLY WELL...
SO WELL THAT SHE TOOK HIM BACK TO HER PLACE...
THE LAST THING HE REMEMBERED WAS DOWNING AN EXTRA LARGE SHOT OF CANADIAN WHISKEY...
!
..THE NEXT MORNING HE WOKE UP IN A BATHTUB FULL OF ICE...
Call 911 eh
NAKED!!
TURNED OUT HE HAD BOTH OF HIS BUTT CHEEKS REMOVED!!
!!!...
Bandaids
WHO HERE NEEDS ME TO EXPLAIN WHAT THEY'RE USING THE BUTT CHEEKS FOR?
I'LL GIVE YOU ONE GUESS WHERE THE SAYING "YOU ARE WHAT YOU EAT" ORIGINATED FROM....
HURTFUL (YET FUNNY) THING TO SAY TO AUSTRIANS....
Hey!! You guys are The CANADA of Germany!!
SOB
Why? Why such hateful rhetoric?
STOP

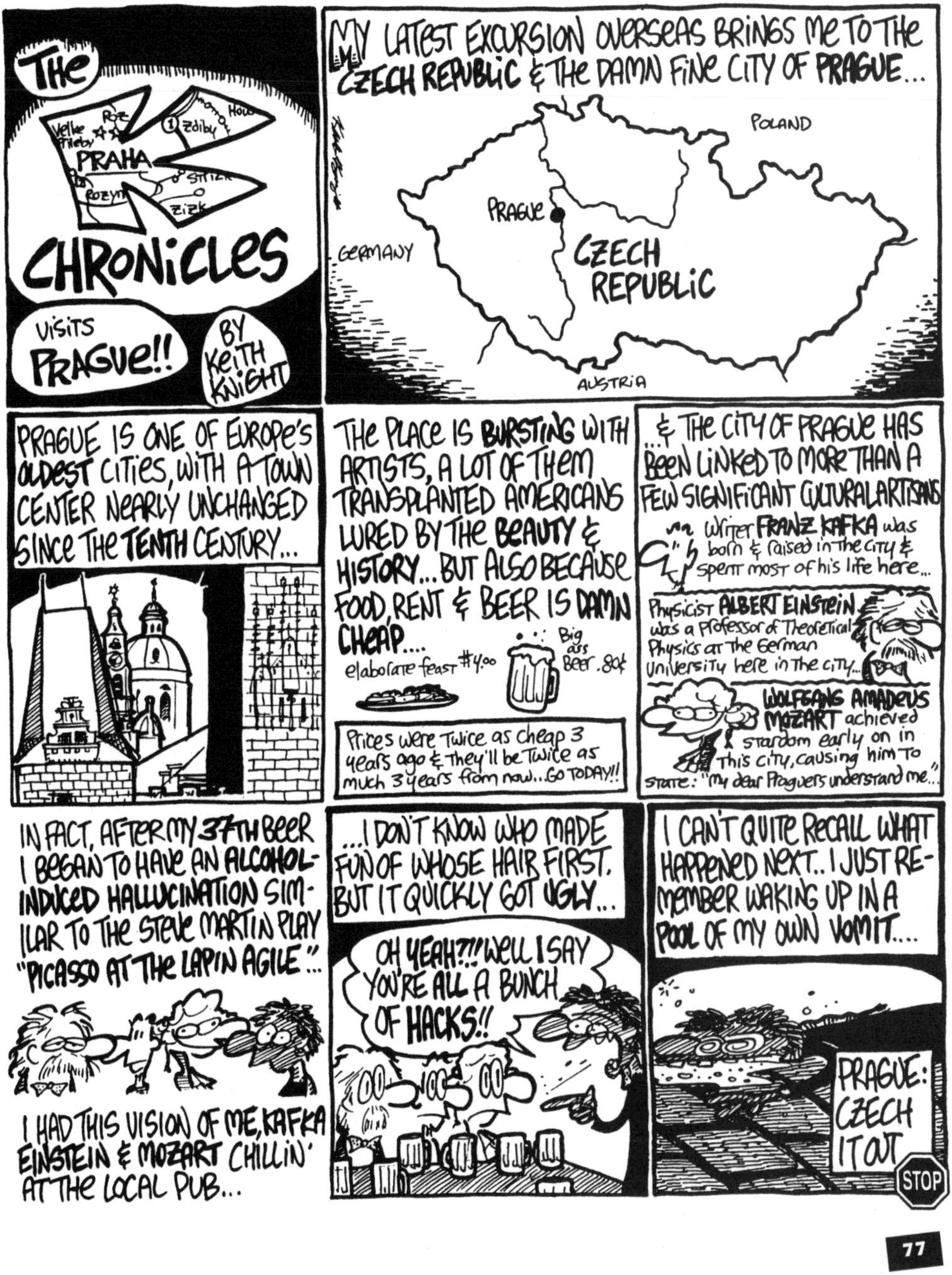
THE
PRAHA
CHRONICLES
VISITS PRAGUE!!
BY KEITH KNIGHT
MY LATEST EXCURSION OVERSEAS BRINGS ME TO THE CZECH REPUBLIC & THE DAMN FINE CITY OF PRAGUE...
POLAND
PRAGUE
GERMANY
CZECH REPUBLIC
AUSTRIA
PRAGUE IS ONE OF EUROPE'S OLDEST CITIES, WITH A TOWN CENTER NEARLY UNCHANGED SINCE THE TENTH CENTURY...
THE PLACE IS BURSTING WITH ARTISTS, A LOT OF THEM TRANSPLANTED AMERICANS LURED BY THE BEAUTY & HISTORY... BUT ALSO BECAUSE FOOD, RENT & BEER IS DAMN CHEAP....
elaborate feast $4.00
Big ass Beer .80¢
Prices were twice as cheap 3 years ago & they'll be twice as much 3 years from now... GO TODAY!!
...& THE CITY OF PRAGUE HAS BEEN LINKED TO MORE THAN A FEW SIGNIFICANT CULTURAL ARTISANS
Writer FRANZ KAFKA was born & raised in the city & spent most of his life here...
Physicist ALBERT EINSTEIN was a professor of Theoretical Physics at the German University here in the city...
WOLFGANG AMADEUS MOZART achieved stardom early on in this city, causing him to state: "My dear Praguers understand me."
IN FACT, AFTER MY 37TH BEER I BEGAN TO HAVE AN ALCOHOL-INDUCED HALLUCINATION SIMILAR TO THE STEVE MARTIN PLAY "PICASSO AT THE LAPIN AGILE"...
I HAD THIS VISION OF ME, KAFKA EINSTEIN & MOZART CHILLIN' AT THE LOCAL PUB...
...I DON'T KNOW WHO MADE FUN OF WHOSE HAIR FIRST, BUT IT QUICKLY GOT UGLY...
OH YEAH?!! WELL I SAY YOU'RE ALL A BUNCH OF HACKS!!
I CAN'T QUITE RECALL WHAT HAPPENED NEXT.. I JUST REMEMBER WAKING UP IN A POOL OF MY OWN VOMIT....
PRAGUE: CZECH IT OUT
STOP

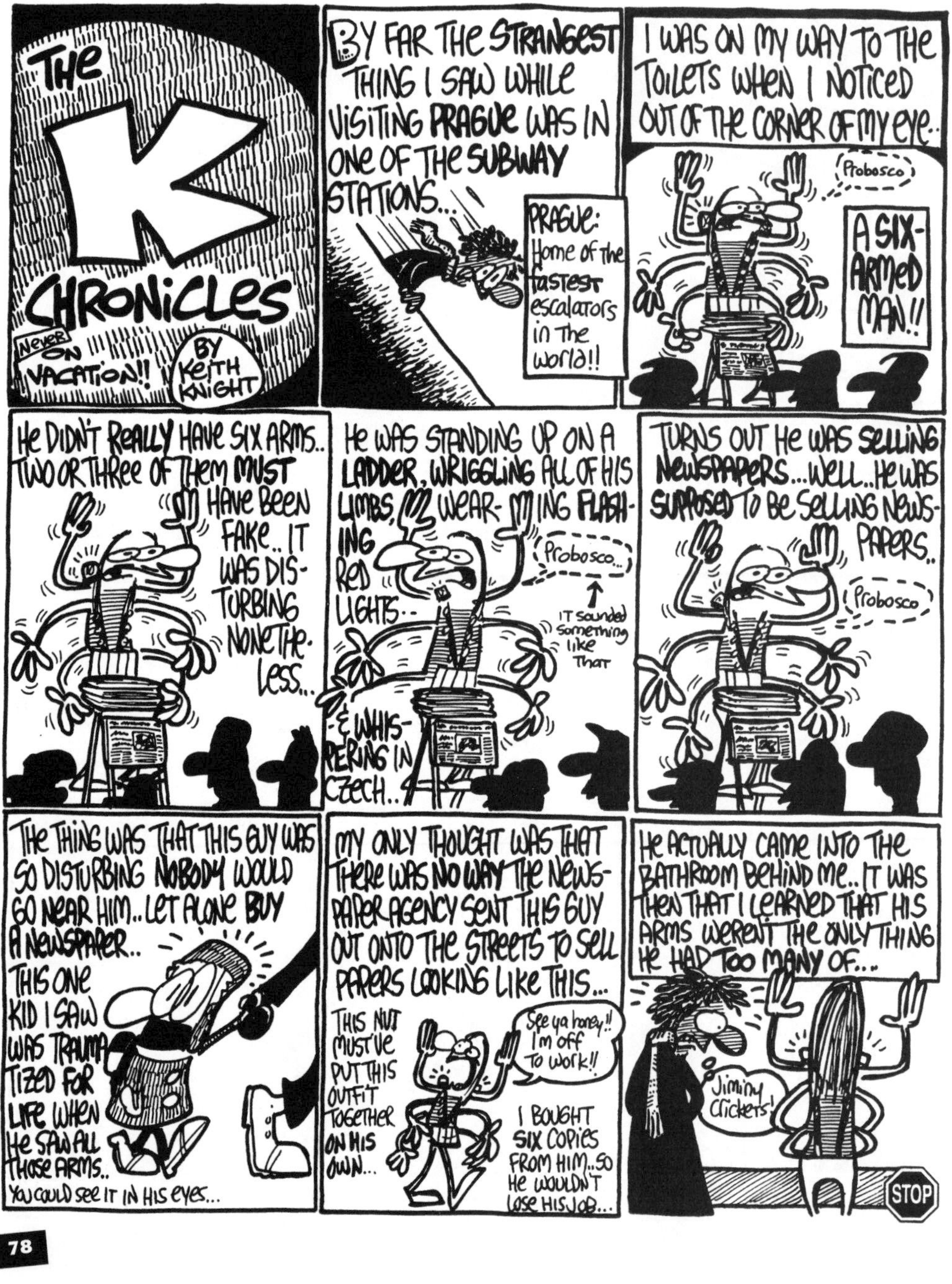
THE K CHRONICLES
NEVER ON VACATION!!
BY KEITH KNIGHT
BY FAR THE STRANGEST THING I SAW WHILE VISITING PRAGUE WAS IN ONE OF THE SUBWAY STATIONS...
PRAGUE: Home of the fastest escalators in the world!!
I WAS ON MY WAY TO THE TOILETS WHEN I NOTICED OUT OF THE CORNER OF MY EYE..
Probosco
A SIX-ARMED MAN!!
HE DIDN'T REALLY HAVE SIX ARMS.. TWO OR THREE OF THEM MUST HAVE BEEN FAKE.. IT WAS DISTURBING NONETHELESS...
HE WAS STANDING UP ON A LADDER, WRIGGLING ALL OF HIS LIMBS, WEARING FLASHING RED LIGHTS..
Probosco..
IT sounded something like That
& WHISPERING IN CZECH..
TURNS OUT HE WAS SELLING NEWSPAPERS...WELL..HE WAS SUPPOSED TO BE SELLING NEWSPAPERS..
Probosco
THE THING WAS THAT THIS GUY WAS SO DISTURBING NOBODY WOULD GO NEAR HIM..LET ALONE BUY A NEWSPAPER..
THIS ONE KID I SAW WAS TRAUMATIZED FOR LIFE WHEN HE SAW ALL THOSE ARMS..
YOU COULD SEE IT IN HIS EYES...
MY ONLY THOUGHT WAS THAT THERE WAS NO WAY THE NEWSPAPER AGENCY SENT THIS GUY OUT ONTO THE STREETS TO SELL PAPERS LOOKING LIKE THIS...
THIS NUT MUST'VE PUT THIS OUTFIT TOGETHER ON HIS OWN...
See ya honey!! I'm off to work!!
I BOUGHT SIX COPIES FROM HIM..SO HE WOULDN'T LOSE HIS JOB...
HE ACTUALLY CAME INTO THE BATHROOM BEHIND ME.. IT WAS THEN THAT I LEARNED THAT HIS ARMS WEREN'T THE ONLY THING HE HAD TOO MANY OF...
Jiminy Crickets!
STOP

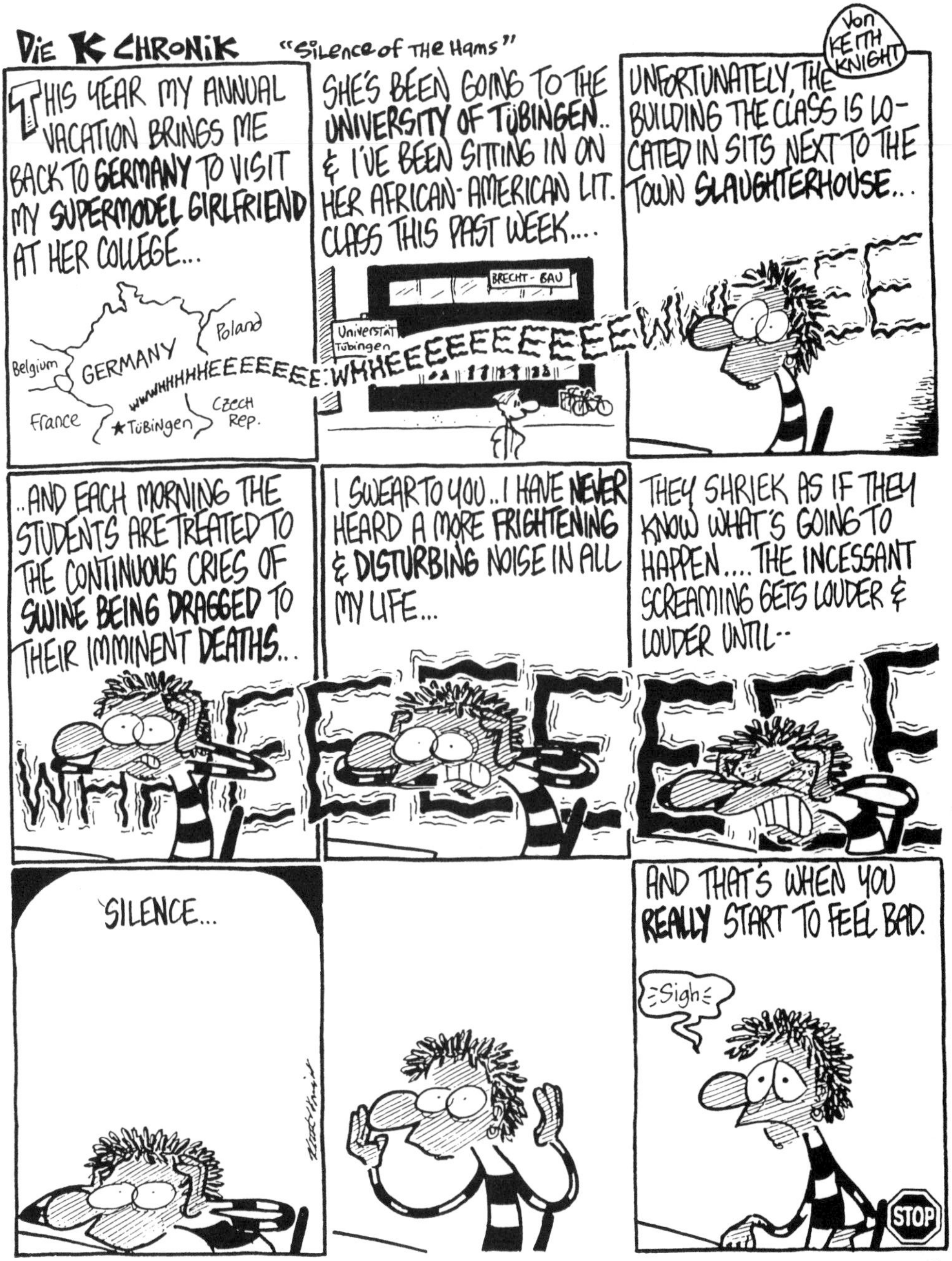
DIE K CHRONIK
"SILENCE OF THE HAMS"
VON KEITH KNIGHT
THIS YEAR MY ANNUAL VACATION BRINGS ME BACK TO GERMANY TO VISIT MY SUPERMODEL GIRLFRIEND AT HER COLLEGE...
Belgium
GERMANY
Poland
France
★Tübingen
Czech Rep.
SHE'S BEEN GOING TO THE UNIVERSITY OF TÜBINGEN.. & I'VE BEEN SITTING IN ON HER AFRICAN-AMERICAN LIT. CLASS THIS PAST WEEK....
BRECHT - BAU
Universität Tübingen
WWWHHHHEEEEEEEE.WHHEEEEEEEEEEEEEEW
UNFORTUNATELY, THE BUILDING THE CLASS IS LOCATED IN SITS NEXT TO THE TOWN SLAUGHTERHOUSE...
..AND EACH MORNING THE STUDENTS ARE TREATED TO THE CONTINUOUS CRIES OF SWINE BEING DRAGGED TO THEIR IMMINENT DEATHS...
I SWEAR TO YOU.. I HAVE NEVER HEARD A MORE FRIGHTENING & DISTURBING NOISE IN ALL MY LIFE...
THEY SHRIEK AS IF THEY KNOW WHAT'S GOING TO HAPPEN.... THE INCESSANT SCREAMING GETS LOUDER & LOUDER UNTIL..
SILENCE...
AND THAT'S WHEN YOU REALLY START TO FEEL BAD.
Sigh
STOP

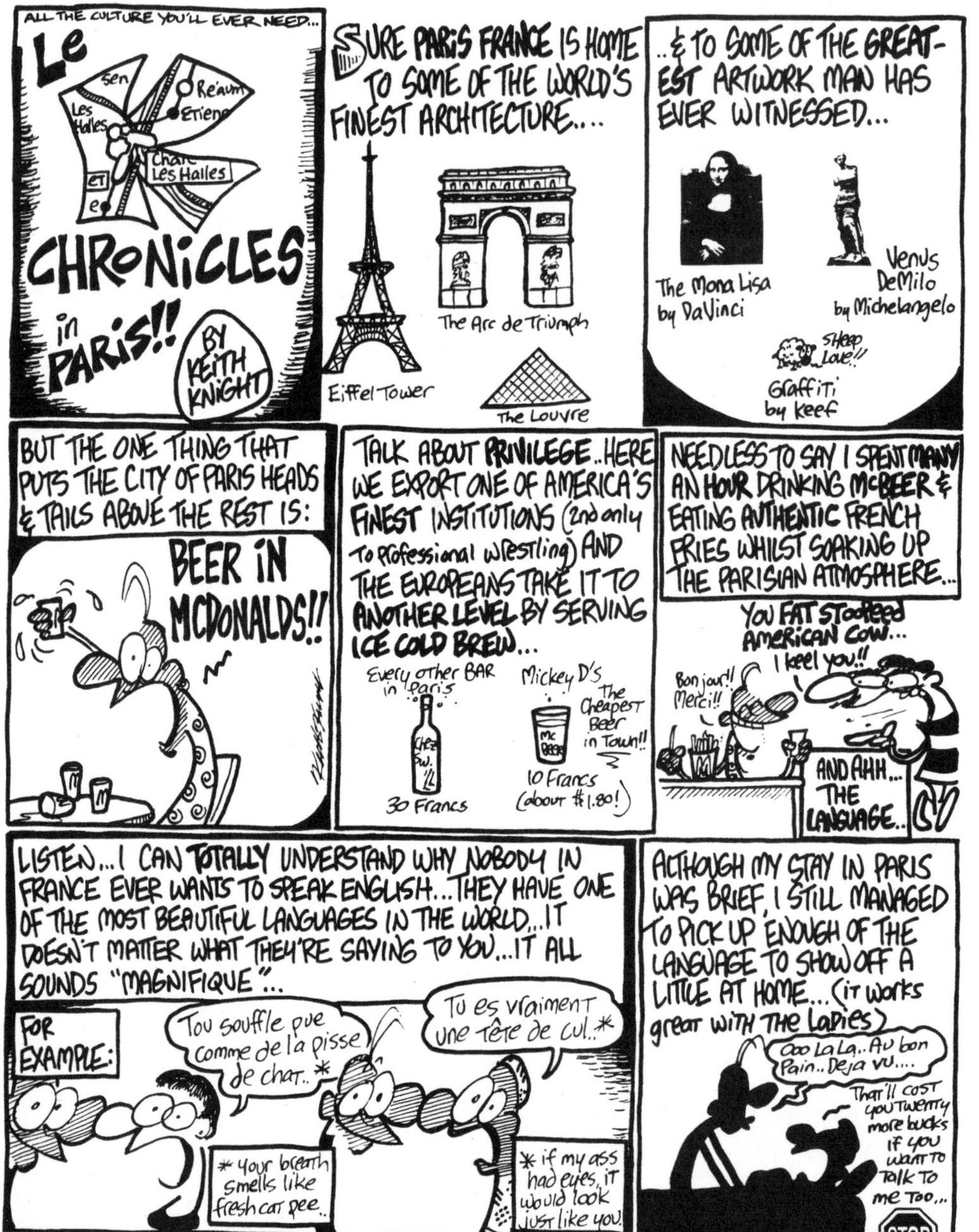

ALL THE CULTURE YOU'LL EVER NEED...

Le CHRONiCLES in PARiS!!

BY KEITH KNIGHT

Sen · Les Halles · Réaum · Etienne · Chart Les Halles · et · e

SURE PARIS FRANCE IS HOME TO SOME OF THE WORLD'S FINEST ARCHITECTURE....

Eiffel Tower

The Arc de Triumph

The Louvre

..& TO SOME OF THE GREATEST ARTWORK MAN HAS EVER WITNESSED...

The Mona Lisa by DaVinci

Venus DeMilo by Michelangelo

SHEEP LOVE!!

Graffiti by keef

BUT THE ONE THING THAT PUTS THE CITY OF PARIS HEADS & TAILS ABOVE THE REST IS:

BEER IN MCDONALDS!!

TALK ABOUT PRIVILEGE..HERE WE EXPORT ONE OF AMERICA'S FINEST INSTITUTIONS (2nd only to professional wrestling) AND THE EUROPEANS TAKE IT TO ANOTHER LEVEL BY SERVING ICE COLD BREW...

Every other BAR in paris

Chez Sw.

30 Francs

Mickey D's

The Cheapest Beer in Town!!

Mc Beer

10 Francs (about $1.80!)

NEEDLESS TO SAY I SPENT MANY AN HOUR DRINKING McBEER & EATING AUTHENTIC FRENCH FRIES WHILST SOAKING UP THE PARISIAN ATMOSPHERE...

YOU FAT STOOPED AMERICAN COW... I keel you!!

Bonjour!! Merci!!

AND AHH... THE LANGUAGE..

LISTEN...I CAN **TOTALLY** UNDERSTAND WHY NOBODY IN FRANCE EVER WANTS TO SPEAK ENGLISH...THEY HAVE ONE OF THE MOST BEAUTIFUL LANGUAGES IN THE WORLD...IT DOESN'T MATTER WHAT THEY'RE SAYING TO YOU...IT ALL SOUNDS "MAGNIFIQUE"...

FOR EXAMPLE:

Tou souffle pue comme de la pisse de chat..*

* your breath smells like fresh cat pee..

Tu es vraiment une tête de cul..*

* if my ass had eyes, it would look just like you!

ALTHOUGH MY STAY IN PARIS WAS BRIEF, I STILL MANAGED TO PICK UP ENOUGH OF THE LANGUAGE TO SHOW OFF A LITTLE AT HOME...(it works great WITH THE LADIES)

Ooo La La..Au bon Pain..Deja vu....

That'll cost you twenty more bucks if you want to talk to me too,..

STOP

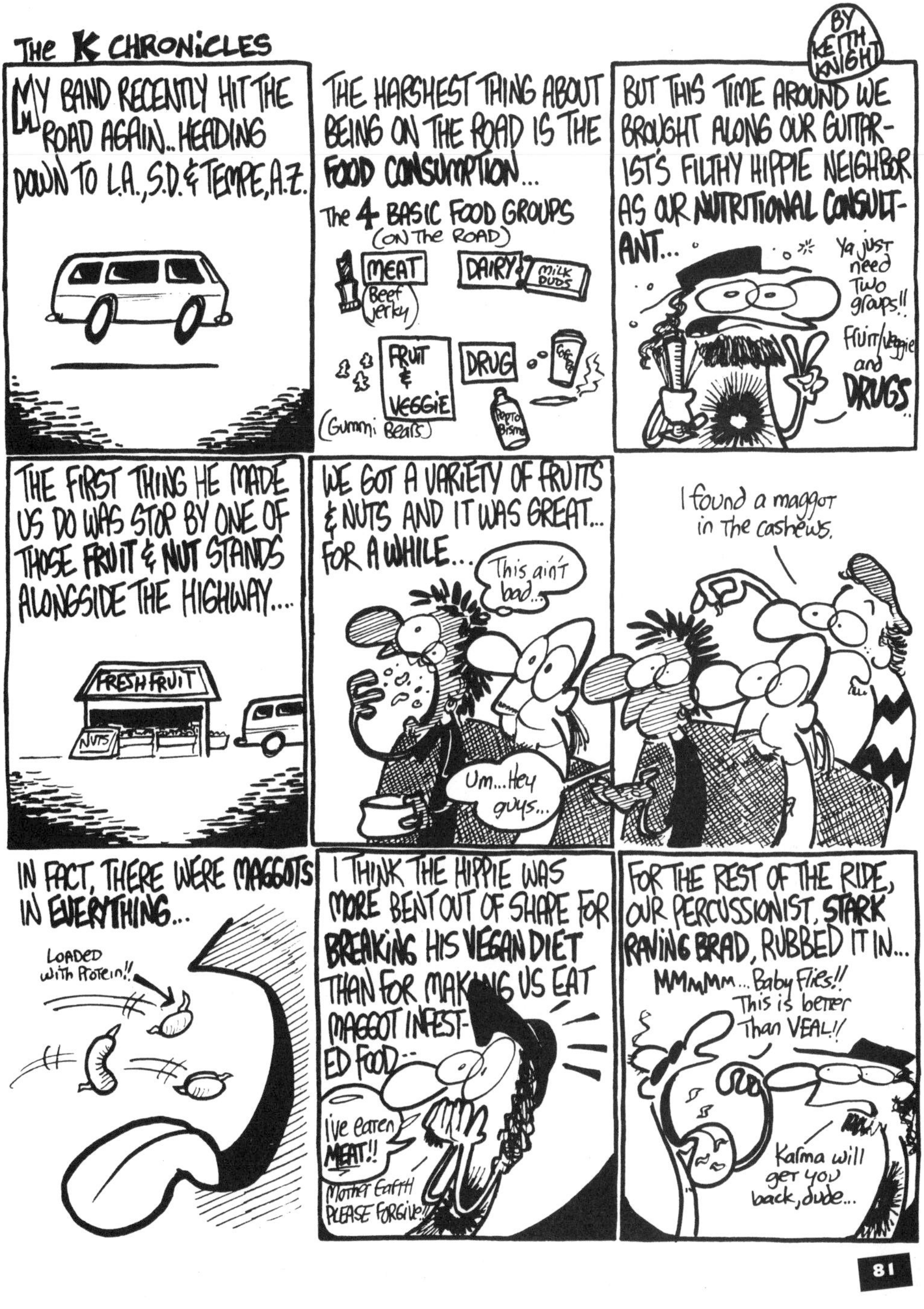

THE K CHRONICLES
BY KEITH KNIGHT
MY BAND RECENTLY HIT THE ROAD AGAIN.. HEADING DOWN TO L.A., S.D. & TEMPE, A.Z.
THE HARSHEST THING ABOUT BEING ON THE ROAD IS THE FOOD CONSUMPTION...
The 4 BASIC FOOD GROUPS (ON THE ROAD)
MEAT
Beef jerky
DAIRY
MILK DUDS
FRUIT & VEGGIE
(Gummi Bears)
DRUG
Pepto Bismol
BUT THIS TIME AROUND WE BROUGHT ALONG OUR GUITARIST'S FILTHY HIPPIE NEIGHBOR AS OUR NUTRITIONAL CONSULTANT...
Ya just need Two groups!! Fruit/Veggie and DRUGS..
THE FIRST THING HE MADE US DO WAS STOP BY ONE OF THOSE FRUIT & NUT STANDS ALONGSIDE THE HIGHWAY....
FRESH FRUIT
NUTS
WE GOT A VARIETY OF FRUITS & NUTS AND IT WAS GREAT... FOR A WHILE...
This ain't bad...
Um...Hey guys...
I found a maggot in the cashews.
IN FACT, THERE WERE MAGGOTS IN EVERYTHING...
LOADED with Protein!!
I THINK THE HIPPIE WAS MORE BENT OUT OF SHAPE FOR BREAKING HIS VEGAN DIET THAN FOR MAKING US EAT MAGGOT INFESTED FOOD...
I've eaten MEAT!!
Mother Earth PLEASE FORGIVE!!
FOR THE REST OF THE RIDE, OUR PERCUSSIONIST, STARK RAVING BRAD, RUBBED IT IN...
MMMMM... Baby Flies!! This is better than VEAL!!
Karma will get you back, dude...

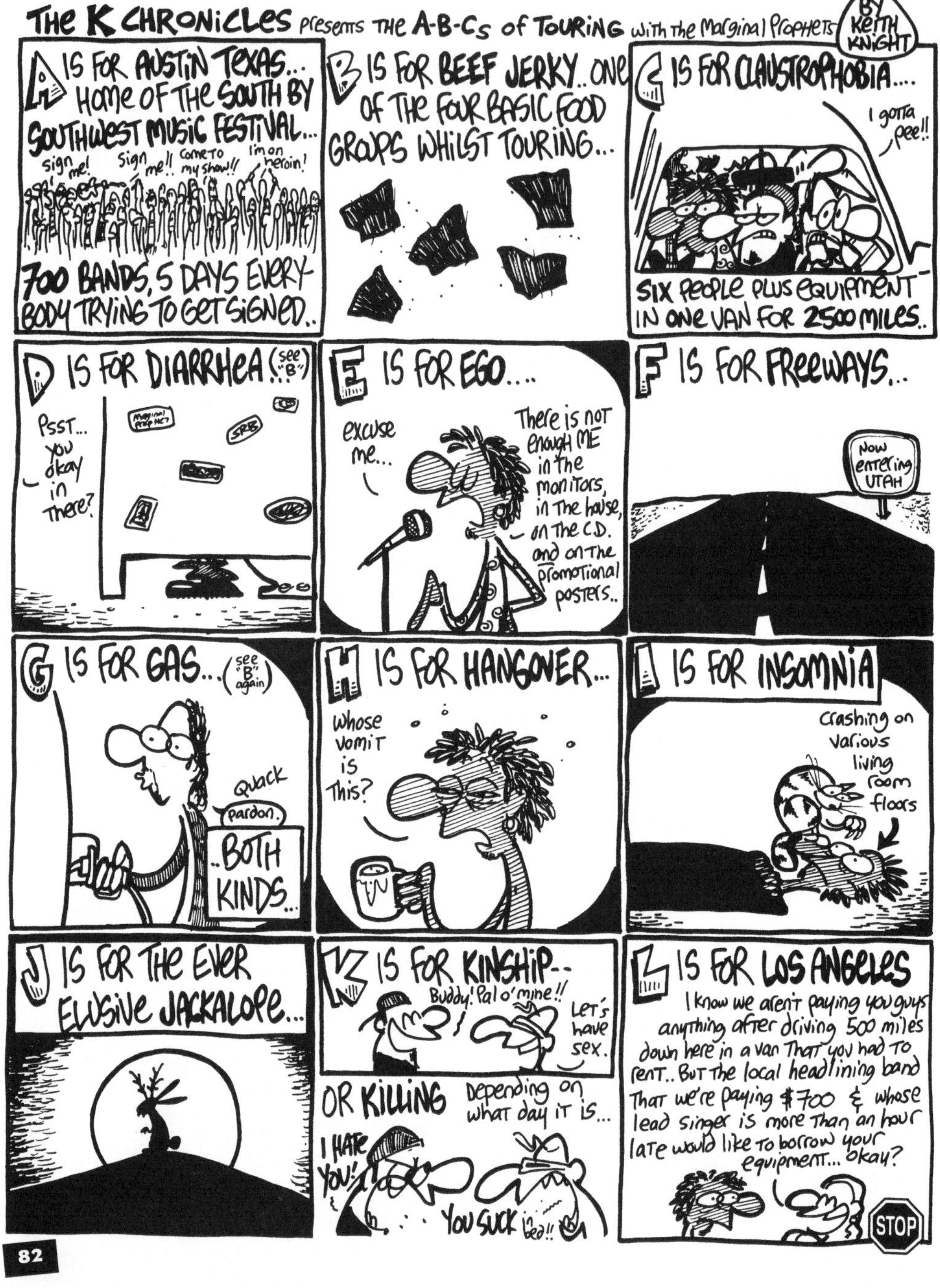
THE K CHRONICLES presents THE A-B-Cs of TOURING with the Marginal Prophets
BY KEITH KNIGHT
A IS FOR AUSTIN TEXAS... HOME OF THE SOUTH BY SOUTHWEST MUSIC FESTIVAL...
sign me!
sign me!!
come to my show!!
i'm on heroin!
700 BANDS, 5 DAYS EVERYBODY TRYING TO GET SIGNED..
B IS FOR BEEF JERKY.. ONE OF THE FOUR BASIC FOOD GROUPS WHILST TOURING...
C IS FOR CLAUSTROPHOBIA....
I gotta pee!!
SIX PEOPLE PLUS EQUIPMENT IN ONE VAN FOR 2500 MILES..
D IS FOR DIARRHEA!! (see "B")
PSST... you okay in there?
Marginal Prophet
SRB
E IS FOR EGO....
excuse me...
There is not enough ME in the monitors, in the house, on the C.D. and on the promotional posters..
F IS FOR FREEWAYS...
Now entering UTAH
G IS FOR GAS... (see "B" again)
Quack
pardon.
..BOTH KINDS..
H IS FOR HANGOVER...
Whose vomit is this?
I IS FOR INSOMNIA
Crashing on various living room floors
J IS FOR THE EVER ELUSIVE JACKALOPE...
K IS FOR KINSHIP--
Buddy! Pal o'mine!!
Let's have sex.
OR KILLING depending on what day it is...
I HATE YOU!
YOU SUCK in bed!!
L IS FOR LOS ANGELES
I know we aren't paying you guys anything after driving 500 miles down here in a van that you had to rent.. But the local headlining band that we're paying $700 & whose lead singer is more than an hour late would like to borrow your equipment... okay?
STOP

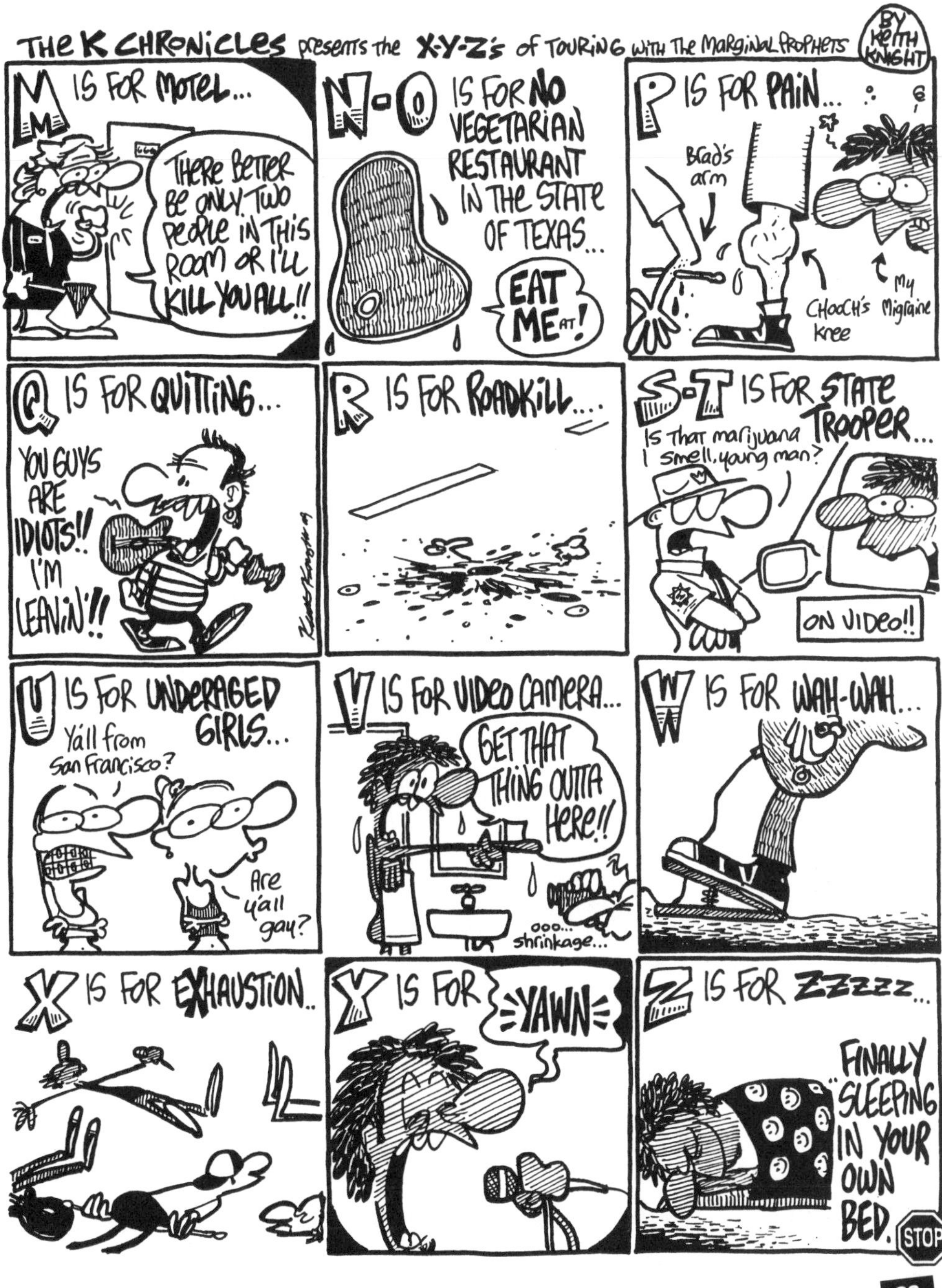
THE K CHRONICLES presents the X-Y-Z's of TOURING with The Marginal Prophets
BY KEITH KNIGHT
M IS FOR MOTEL...
THERE BETTER BE ONLY TWO PEOPLE IN THIS ROOM OR I'LL KILL YOU ALL!!
N-O IS FOR NO VEGETARIAN RESTAURANT IN THE STATE OF TEXAS...
EAT MEAT!
P IS FOR PAIN...
Brad's arm
CHOoCH's knee
My Migraine
Q IS FOR QUITTING...
YOU GUYS ARE IDIOTS!! I'M LEAVIN'!!
R IS FOR ROADKILL....
S-T IS FOR STATE TROOPER...
Is that marijuana I smell, young man?
ON VIDEO!!
U IS FOR UNDERAGED GIRLS...
Y'all from San Francisco?
Are y'all gay?
V IS FOR VIDEO CAMERA...
GET THAT THING OUTTA HERE!!
ooo... shrinkage...
W IS FOR WAH-WAH...
X IS FOR EXHAUSTION..
Y IS FOR YAWN
Z IS FOR ZZZZZ...
...FINALLY SLEEPING IN YOUR OWN BED.
STOP

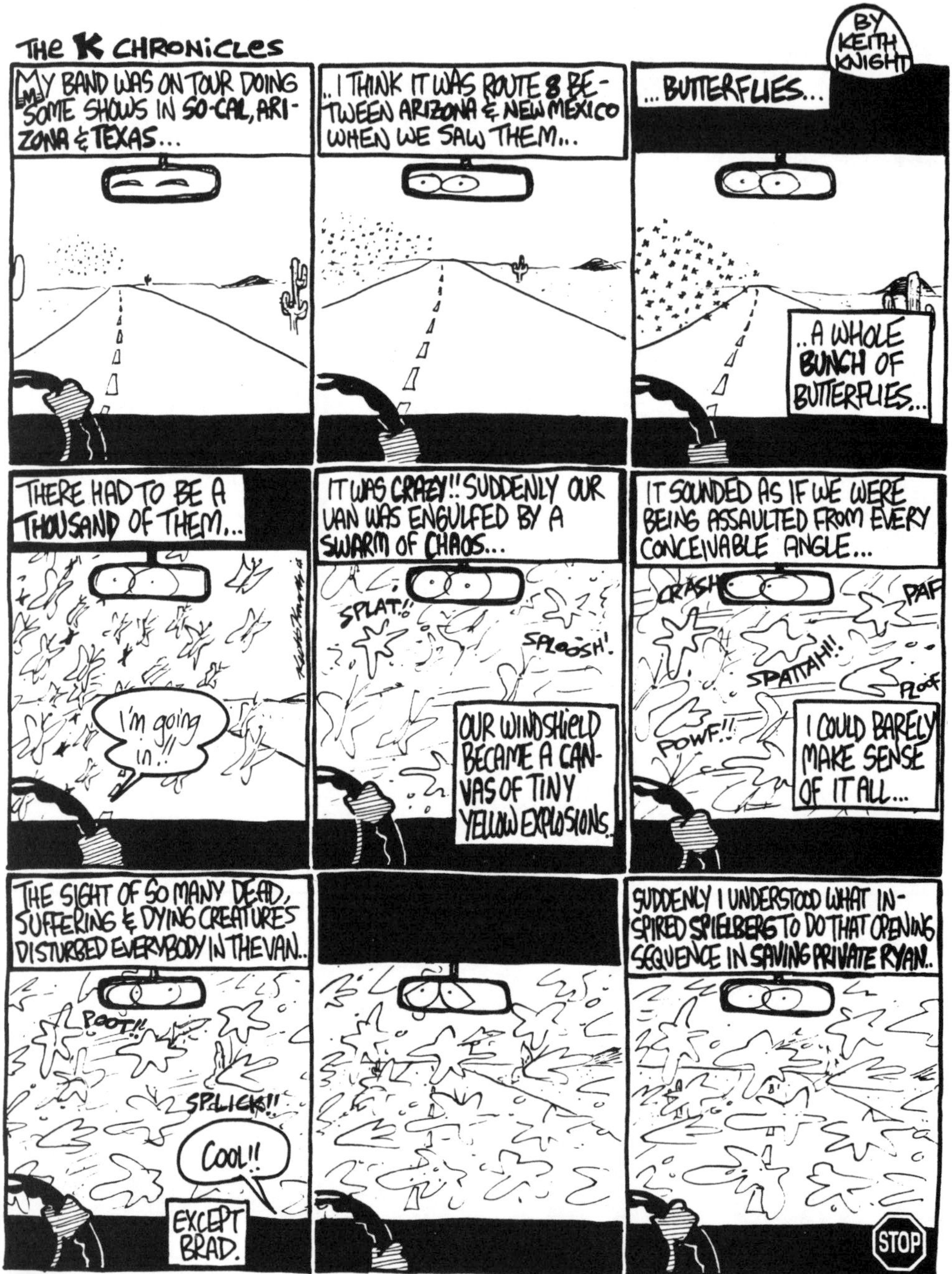
THE K CHRONICLES
BY KEITH KNIGHT
MY BAND WAS ON TOUR DOING SOME SHOWS IN SO-CAL, ARIZONA & TEXAS...
..I THINK IT WAS ROUTE 8 BETWEEN ARIZONA & NEW MEXICO WHEN WE SAW THEM...
...BUTTERFLIES...
..A WHOLE BUNCH OF BUTTERFLIES...
THERE HAD TO BE A THOUSAND OF THEM...
I'm going in!!
IT WAS CRAZY!! SUDDENLY OUR VAN WAS ENGULFED BY A SWARM OF CHAOS...
SPLAT!!
SPLOOSH!
OUR WINDSHIELD BECAME A CANVAS OF TINY YELLOW EXPLOSIONS.
IT SOUNDED AS IF WE WERE BEING ASSAULTED FROM EVERY CONCEIVABLE ANGLE...
CRASH
PAF
SPATTAH!!
PLOOF
POWF!!
I COULD BARELY MAKE SENSE OF IT ALL...
THE SIGHT OF SO MANY DEAD, SUFFERING & DYING CREATURES DISTURBED EVERYBODY IN THE VAN..
POOT!!
SPLICK!!
COOL!!
EXCEPT BRAD.
SUDDENLY I UNDERSTOOD WHAT INSPIRED SPIELBERG TO DO THAT OPENING SEQUENCE IN SAVING PRIVATE RYAN..
STOP

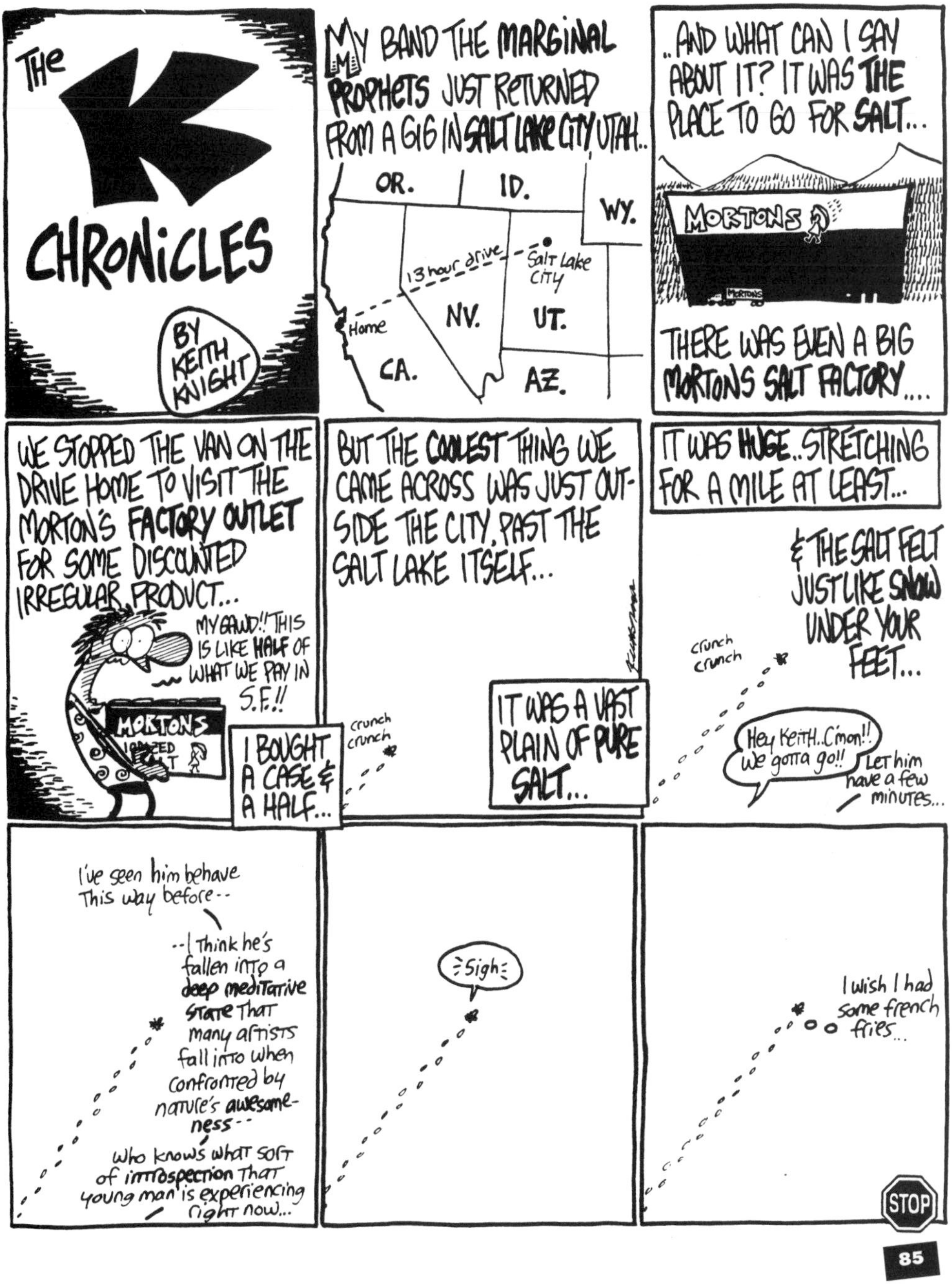
THE K CHRONICLES
BY KEITH KNIGHT
MY BAND THE MARGINAL PROPHETS JUST RETURNED FROM A GIG IN SALT LAKE CITY, UTAH..
OR.
ID.
WY.
13 hour drive
Salt Lake City
Home
NV.
UT.
CA.
AZ.
..AND WHAT CAN I SAY ABOUT IT? IT WAS THE PLACE TO GO FOR SALT...
MORTONS
THERE WAS EVEN A BIG MORTONS SALT FACTORY....
WE STOPPED THE VAN ON THE DRIVE HOME TO VISIT THE MORTON'S FACTORY OUTLET FOR SOME DISCOUNTED IRREGULAR PRODUCT...
MY GAWD!! THIS IS LIKE HALF OF WHAT WE PAY IN S.F.!!
MORTONS
I BOUGHT A CASE & A HALF...
BUT THE COOLEST THING WE CAME ACROSS WAS JUST OUTSIDE THE CITY, PAST THE SALT LAKE ITSELF...
crunch crunch
IT WAS A VAST PLAIN OF PURE SALT...
IT WAS HUGE..STRETCHING FOR A MILE AT LEAST...
& THE SALT FELT JUST LIKE SNOW UNDER YOUR FEET...
crunch crunch
Hey KeiTH..C'mon!! We gotta go!!
Let him have a few minutes...
I've seen him behave This way before--
--I Think he's fallen into a deep meditative state That many artists fall into when confronted by nature's awesomeness--
Who knows what sort of introspection That young man is experiencing right now...
Sigh
I wish I had some french fries...
STOP

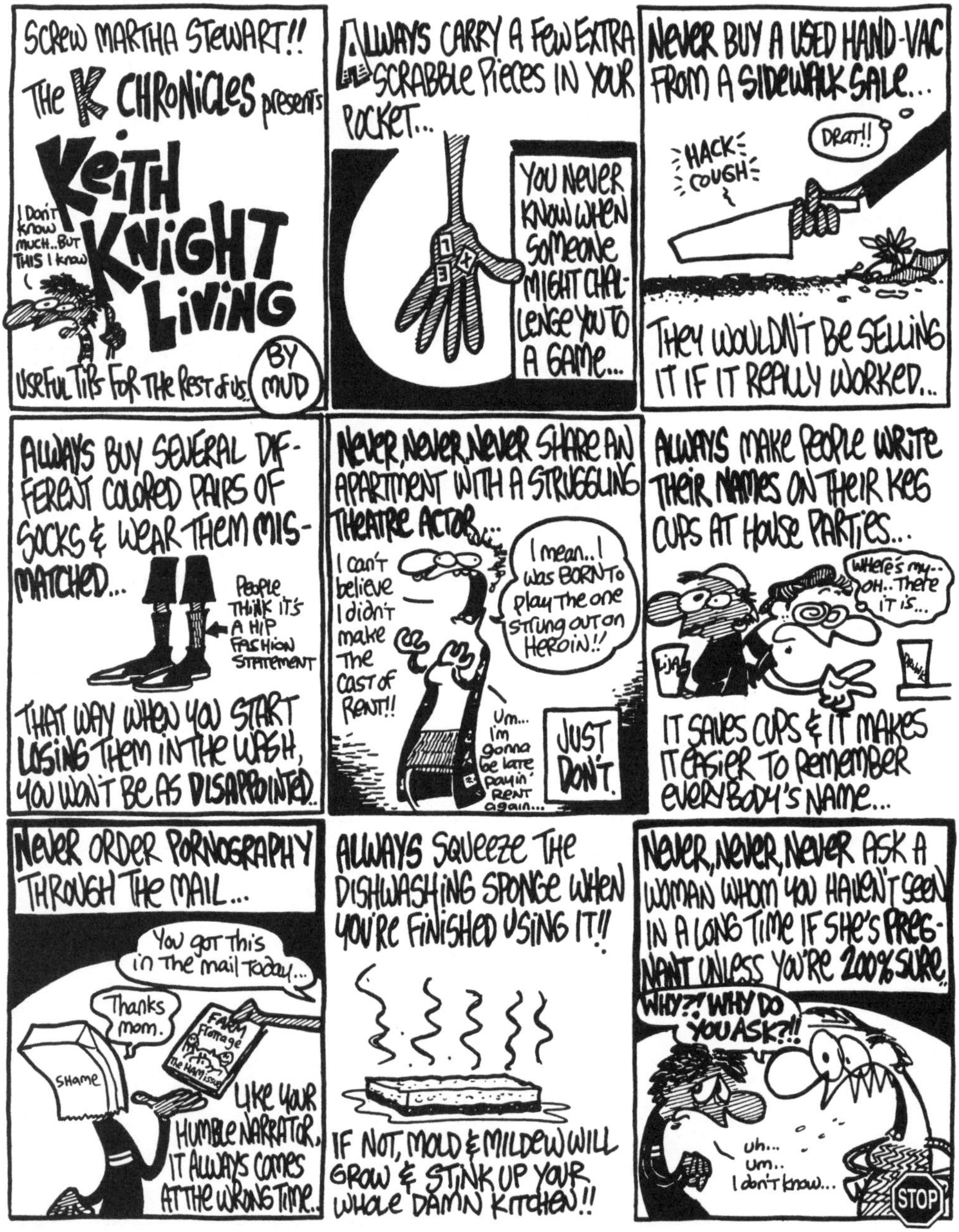
SCREW MARTHA STEWART!!
THE K CHRONICLES presents
KEITH KNIGHT LIVING
I DON'T KNOW MUCH.. BUT THIS I KNOW
USEFUL TIPS FOR THE REST OF US..
BY MUD
ALWAYS CARRY A FEW EXTRA SCRABBLE PIECES IN YOUR POCKET...
YOU NEVER KNOW WHEN SOMEONE MIGHT CHALLENGE YOU TO A GAME...
NEVER BUY A USED HAND-VAC FROM A SIDEWALK SALE...
HACK COUGH
DRAT!!
THEY WOULDN'T BE SELLING IT IF IT REALLY WORKED...
ALWAYS BUY SEVERAL DIFFERENT COLORED PAIRS OF SOCKS & WEAR THEM MISMATCHED...
PEOPLE THINK IT'S A HIP FASHION STATEMENT
THAT WAY WHEN YOU START LOSING THEM IN THE WASH, YOU WON'T BE AS DISAPPOINTED..
NEVER, NEVER, NEVER SHARE AN APARTMENT WITH A STRUGGLING THEATRE ACTOR...
I can't believe I didn't make the cast of RENT!!
I mean.. I was BORN TO play the one strung out on HEROIN!!
Um... I'm gonna be late payin' RENT again...
JUST DON'T.
ALWAYS MAKE PEOPLE WRITE THEIR NAMES ON THEIR KEG CUPS AT HOUSE PARTIES...
Where's my.. OH.. There it is...
IT SAVES CUPS & IT MAKES IT EASIER TO REMEMBER EVERYBODY'S NAME...
NEVER ORDER PORNOGRAPHY THROUGH THE MAIL...
You got this in the mail today...
Thanks mom.
SHAME
FARM Frottage The HAM issue
LIKE YOUR HUMBLE NARRATOR, IT ALWAYS COMES AT THE WRONG TIME..
ALWAYS SQUEEZE THE DISHWASHING SPONGE WHEN YOU'RE FINISHED USING IT!!
IF NOT, MOLD & MILDEW WILL GROW & STINK UP YOUR WHOLE DAMN KITCHEN!!
NEVER, NEVER, NEVER ASK A WOMAN WHOM YOU HAVEN'T SEEN IN A LONG TIME IF SHE'S PREGNANT UNLESS YOU'RE 200% SURE.
WHY?! WHY DO YOU ASK?!!
uh... um.. I don't know...
STOP

Move over Martha Stewart...

The K Chronicles presents

more!!

KEITH KNIGHT LIVING

Useful tips for the rest of us!!

BY MUD

Never underestimate the stupidity of the American populace...

Hey!! George Bush is running again?!! Well that makes it easy!!

He's already got the experience!!

VOTING BOOTH

Always wear a party hat on your birthday all day long

Free Drinks!!

Free Toll!!

Free Admission!!

Discounted rates on prostitution!!

IT'S LIKE HAVING A FREE PASS FOR THE DAY..

Never believe that you can win at three card monty...

Just pick the right card...

If you see anybody winning.. they're in on it with the dealer...

Always reach way in the back for milk & orange juice....

OCT. 7 ORANGE JUICE

OCT. 7 ORANGE JUICE

OCT. 31 ORANGE JUICE

OCT. 31 ORANGE JUICE

That's where they put all the freshest stuff...

Never!! Never!! Never walk into a video rental shop, undecided, with a group of ex-film school snobs...

What about this one? Oh my gawd!! That wretched hack?!! C'mon you guys!! It's been an hour already!!

You'll be there all night.

Always take a female date dancing to a gay men's club..

I'll be over at the bar if you need me...

The music is better.. the drinks are cheaper... and no one will hit on her...

Never take acid in Disneyland...

JUST DON'T.

And, last but not least: If you're desperate to lose a few pounds...

..Always remember that you only need one kidney! STOP

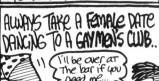

87

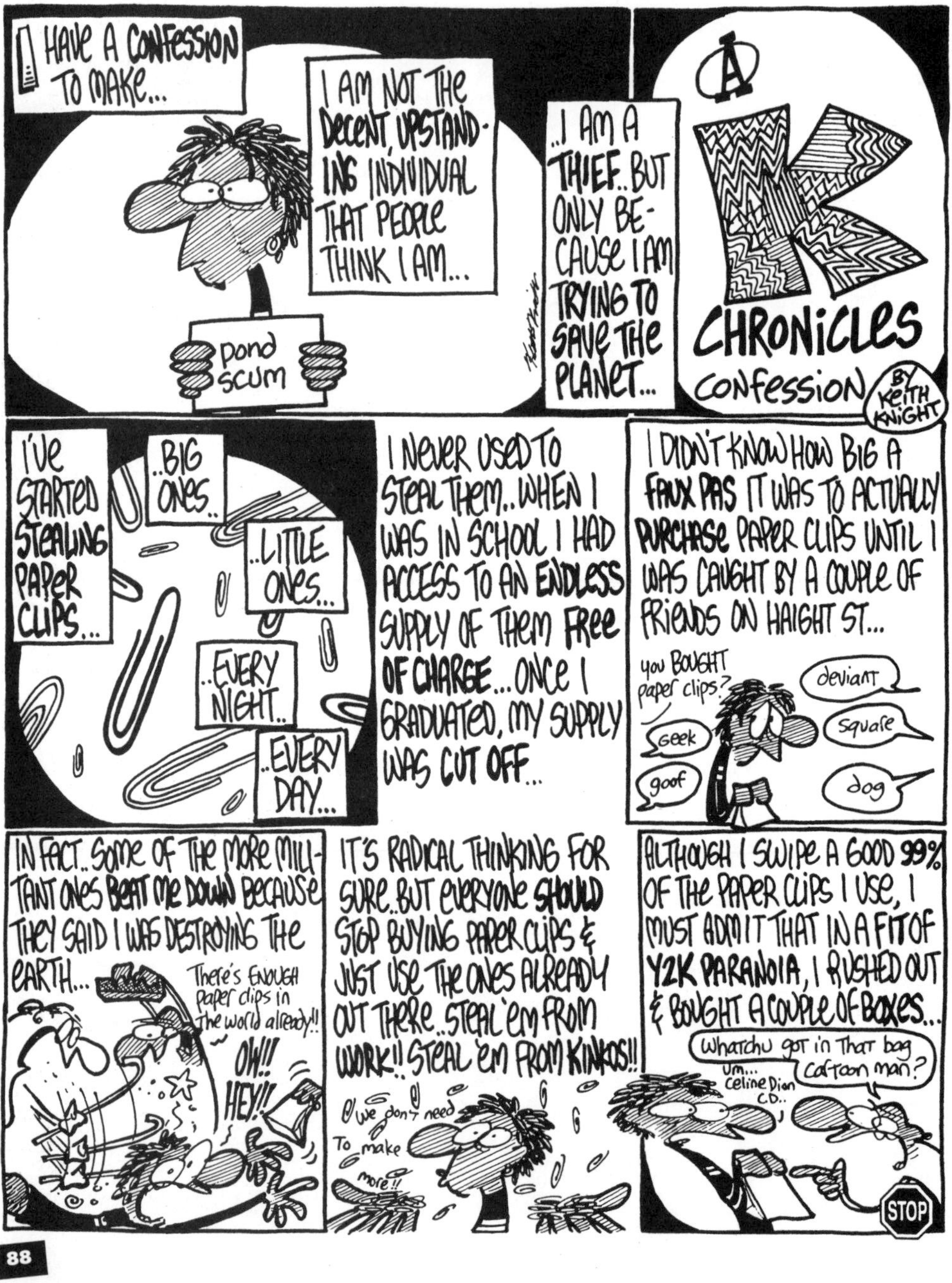
I HAVE A CONFESSION TO MAKE...
I AM NOT THE DECENT, UPSTANDING INDIVIDUAL THAT PEOPLE THINK I AM...
pond scum
...I AM A THIEF.. BUT ONLY BECAUSE I AM TRYING TO SAVE THE PLANET...
K CHRONICLES
CONFESSION
BY KEITH KNIGHT
I'VE STARTED STEALING PAPER CLIPS...
..BIG ONES..
..LITTLE ONES...
..EVERY NIGHT..
..EVERY DAY...
I NEVER USED TO STEAL THEM.. WHEN I WAS IN SCHOOL I HAD ACCESS TO AN ENDLESS SUPPLY OF THEM FREE OF CHARGE... ONCE I GRADUATED, MY SUPPLY WAS CUT OFF...
I DIDN'T KNOW HOW BIG A FAUX PAS IT WAS TO ACTUALLY PURCHASE PAPER CLIPS UNTIL I WAS CAUGHT BY A COUPLE OF FRIENDS ON HAIGHT ST...
you BOUGHT paper clips?
deviant
geek
square
goof
dog
IN FACT.. SOME OF THE MORE MILITANT ONES BEAT ME DOWN BECAUSE THEY SAID I WAS DESTROYING THE EARTH...
There's ENOUGH paper clips in the world already!!
OW!!
HEY!!
IT'S RADICAL THINKING FOR SURE.. BUT EVERYONE SHOULD STOP BUYING PAPER CLIPS & JUST USE THE ONES ALREADY OUT THERE.. STEAL 'EM FROM WORK!! STEAL 'EM FROM KINKOS!!
we don't need To make more!!
ALTHOUGH I SWIPE A GOOD 99% OF THE PAPER CLIPS I USE, I MUST ADMIT THAT IN A FIT OF Y2K PARANOIA, I RUSHED OUT & BOUGHT A COUPLE OF BOXES...
Whatchu got in That bag cartoon man?
Um... Celine Dion C.D..
STOP

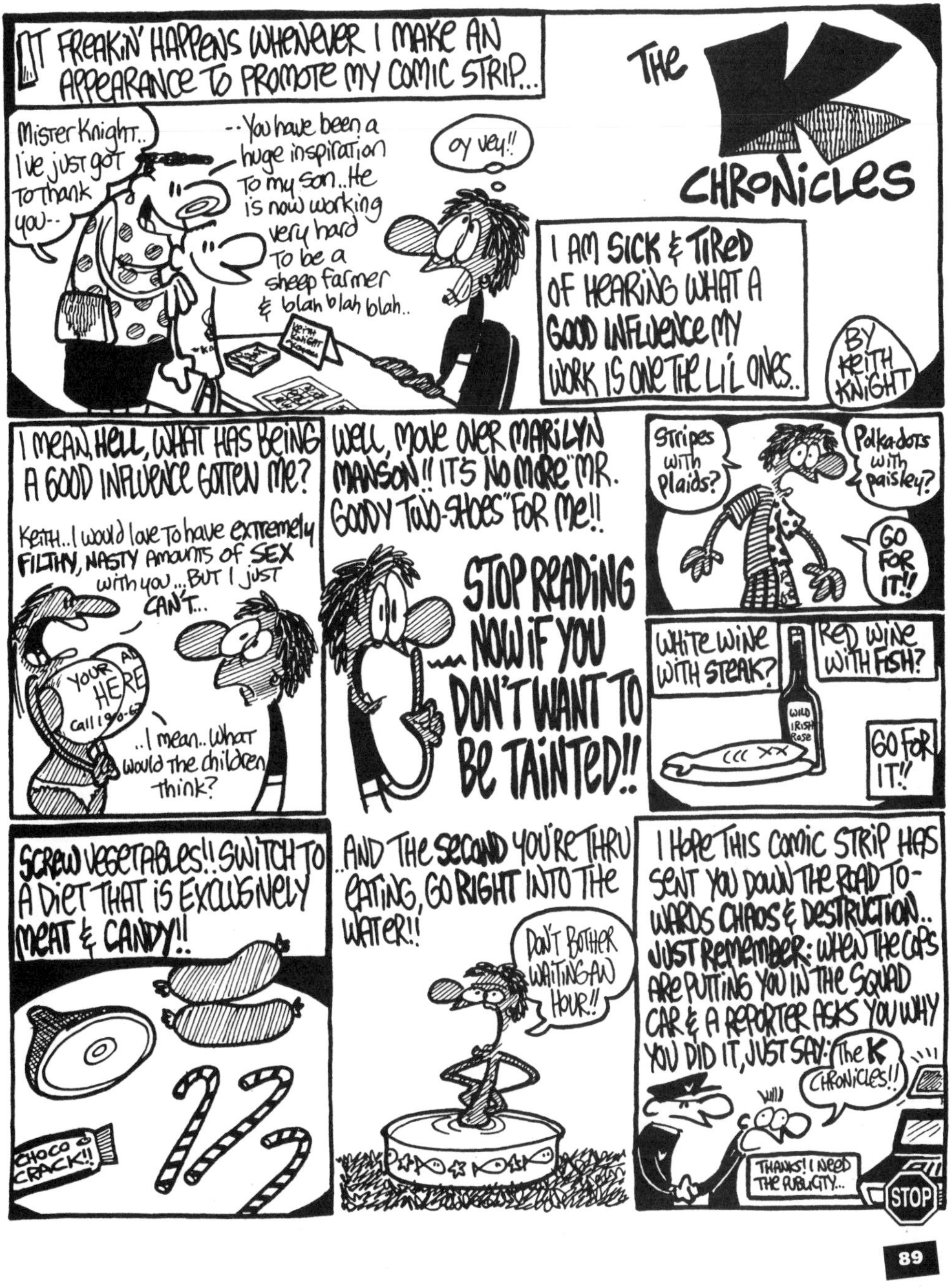
IT FREAKIN' HAPPENS WHENEVER I MAKE AN APPEARANCE TO PROMOTE MY COMIC STRIP...
Mister Knight.. I've just got to thank you--..
--You have been a huge inspiration to my son.. He is now working very hard to be a sheep farmer & blah blah blah..
oy vey!!
THE K CHRONICLES
I AM SICK & TIRED OF HEARING WHAT A GOOD INFLUENCE MY WORK IS ON THE LI'L ONES..
BY KEITH KNIGHT
I MEAN, HELL, WHAT HAS BEING A GOOD INFLUENCE GOTTEN ME?
Keith.. I would love to have extremely FILTHY, NASTY amounts of SEX with you... BUT I JUST CAN'T...
..I mean.. What would the children think?
WELL, MOVE OVER MARILYN MANSON!! IT'S NO MORE "MR. GOODY TWO-SHOES" FOR ME!!
...STOP READING NOW IF YOU DON'T WANT TO BE TAINTED!!
Stripes with plaids?
Polka-dots with paisley?
GO FOR IT!!
WHITE WINE WITH STEAK?
RED WINE WITH FISH?
WILD IRISH ROSE
GO FOR IT!!
SCREW VEGETABLES!! SWITCH TO A DIET THAT IS EXCLUSIVELY MEAT & CANDY!!..
CHOCO CRACK!!
..AND THE SECOND YOU'RE THRU EATING, GO RIGHT INTO THE WATER!!
DON'T BOTHER WAITING AN HOUR!!
I HOPE THIS COMIC STRIP HAS SENT YOU DOWN THE ROAD TOWARDS CHAOS & DESTRUCTION.. JUST REMEMBER: WHEN THE COPS ARE PUTTING YOU IN THE SQUAD CAR & A REPORTER ASKS YOU WHY YOU DID IT, JUST SAY:
The K CHRONICLES!!
THANKS! I NEED THE PUBLICITY...
STOP

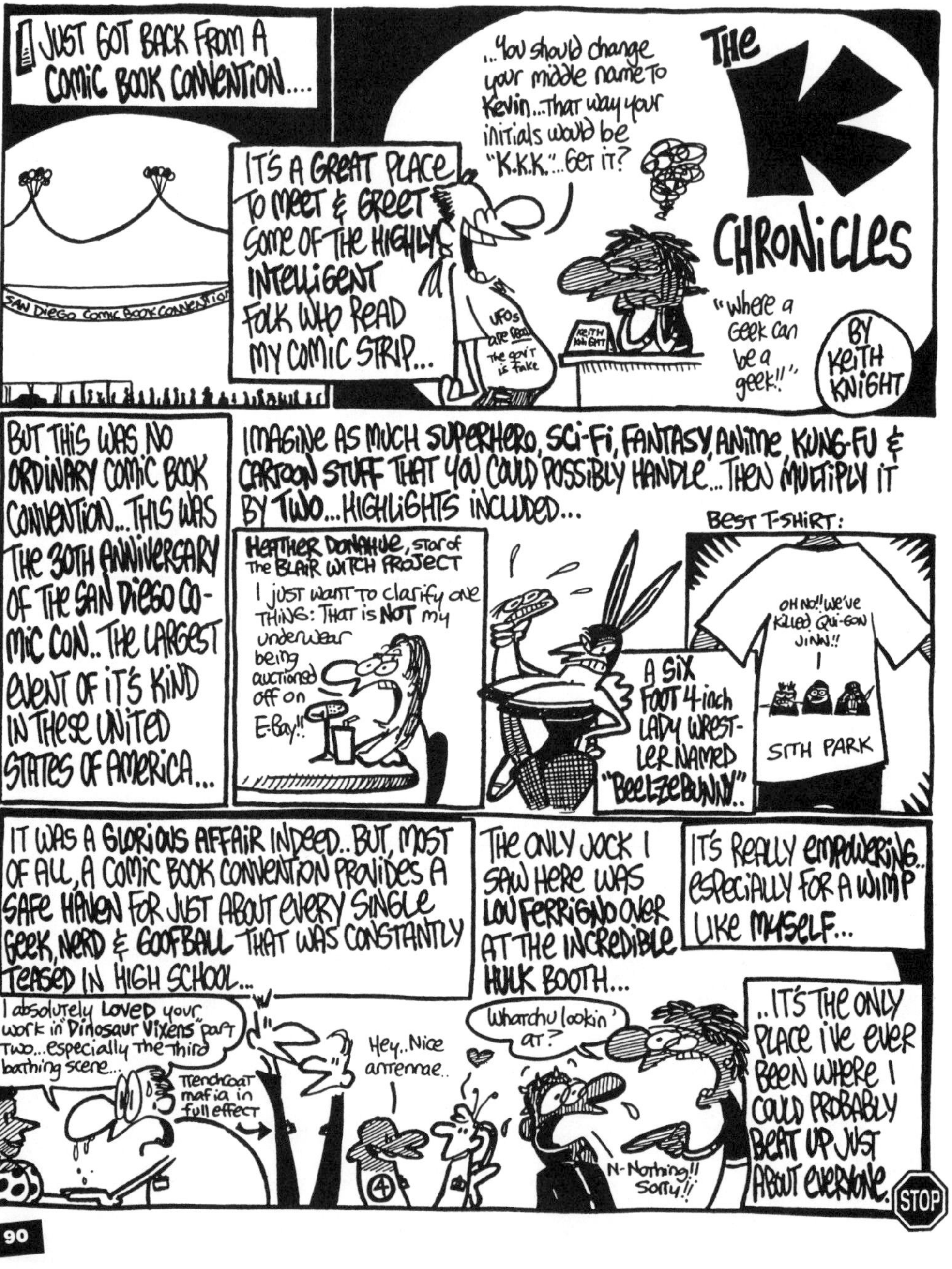
I JUST GOT BACK FROM A COMIC BOOK CONVENTION....
SAN DIEGO COMIC BOOK CONVENTION
IT'S A GREAT PLACE TO MEET & GREET SOME OF THE HIGHLY INTELLIGENT FOLK WHO READ MY COMIC STRIP...
...You should change your middle name to Kevin...That way your initials would be "K.K.K."...Get it?
UFOs are real
The gov't is fake
KEITH KNIGHT
THE K CHRONICLES
"where a geek can be a geek!!"
BY KEITH KNIGHT
BUT THIS WAS NO ORDINARY COMIC BOOK CONVENTION... THIS WAS THE 30TH ANNIVERSARY OF THE SAN DIEGO COMIC CON.. THE LARGEST EVENT OF IT'S KIND IN THESE UNITED STATES OF AMERICA...
IMAGINE AS MUCH SUPERHERO, SCI-FI, FANTASY, ANIME, KUNG-FU & CARTOON STUFF THAT YOU COULD POSSIBLY HANDLE... THEN MULTIPLY IT BY TWO... HIGHLIGHTS INCLUDED...
HEATHER DONAHUE, star of The BLAIR WITCH PROJECT
I just want to clarify one thing: That is NOT my underwear being auctioned off on E-Bay!!
A SIX FOOT 4 inch LADY WRESTLER NAMED "BEELZEBUNNY"..
BEST T-SHIRT:
OH NO!! We've killed Qui-Gon Jinn!!
SITH PARK
IT WAS A GLORIOUS AFFAIR INDEED.. BUT, MOST OF ALL, A COMIC BOOK CONVENTION PROVIDES A SAFE HAVEN FOR JUST ABOUT EVERY SINGLE GEEK, NERD & GOOFBALL THAT WAS CONSTANTLY TEASED IN HIGH SCHOOL...
THE ONLY JOCK I SAW HERE WAS LOU FERRIGNO OVER AT THE INCREDIBLE HULK BOOTH...
IT'S REALLY EMPOWERING.. ESPECIALLY FOR A WIMP LIKE MYSELF...
I absolutely LOVED your work in "Dinosaur Vixens" part Two... especially the third bathing scene...
Trenchcoat mafia in full effect
Hey.. Nice antennae..
Whatchu lookin' at?
N-Nothing!! Sorry!!
..IT'S THE ONLY PLACE I'VE EVER BEEN WHERE I COULD PROBABLY BEAT UP JUST ABOUT EVERYONE.
STOP

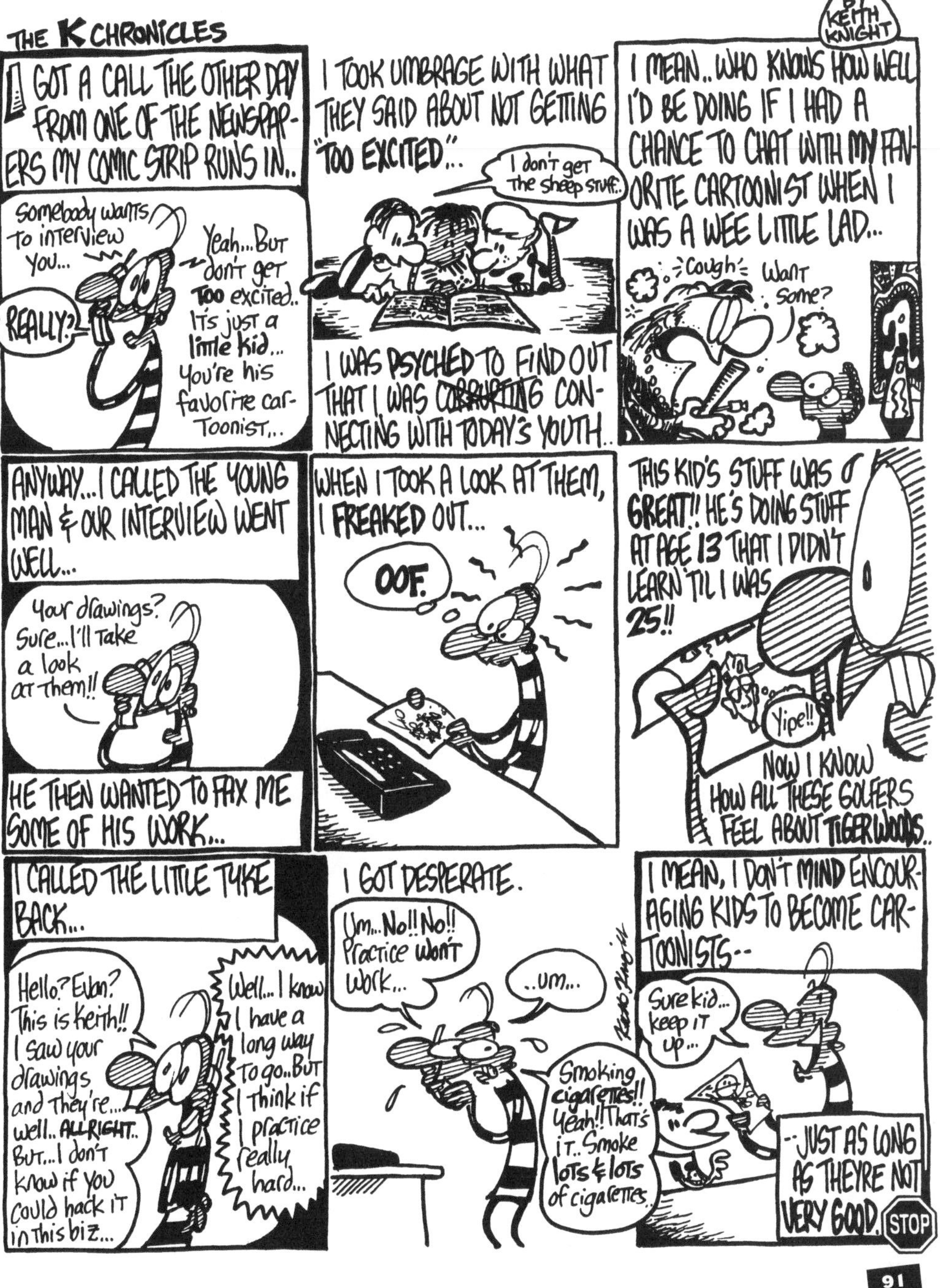
THE K CHRONICLES
BY KEITH KNIGHT
I GOT A CALL THE OTHER DAY FROM ONE OF THE NEWSPAPERS MY COMIC STRIP RUNS IN..
Somebody wants to interview you...
REALLY?
Yeah... But don't get TOO excited.. It's just a little kid... You're his favorite cartoonist...
I TOOK UMBRAGE WITH WHAT THEY SAID ABOUT NOT GETTING "TOO EXCITED"...
I don't get the sheep stuff..
I WAS PSYCHED TO FIND OUT THAT I WAS CORRUPTING CONNECTING WITH TODAY'S YOUTH..
I MEAN.. WHO KNOWS HOW WELL I'D BE DOING IF I HAD A CHANCE TO CHAT WITH MY FAVORITE CARTOONIST WHEN I WAS A WEE LITTLE LAD...
Cough
Want some?
ANYWAY... I CALLED THE YOUNG MAN & OUR INTERVIEW WENT WELL...
Your drawings? Sure... I'll take a look at them!!
HE THEN WANTED TO FAX ME SOME OF HIS WORK...
WHEN I TOOK A LOOK AT THEM, I FREAKED OUT...
OOF.
THIS KID'S STUFF WAS GREAT!! HE'S DOING STUFF AT AGE 13 THAT I DIDN'T LEARN 'TIL I WAS 25!!
Yipe!!
NOW I KNOW HOW ALL THESE GOLFERS FEEL ABOUT TIGER WOODS..
I CALLED THE LITTLE TYKE BACK...
Hello? Evan? This is Keith!! I saw your drawings and they're... well.. ALLRIGHT.. But... I don't know if you could hack it in this biz...
Well... I know I have a long way to go.. But I think if I practice really hard...
I GOT DESPERATE.
Um... No!! No!! Practice won't work...
..um...
Smoking cigarettes!! Yeah!! That's it.. Smoke lots & lots of cigarettes..
I MEAN, I DON'T MIND ENCOURAGING KIDS TO BECOME CARTOONISTS--
Sure kid... keep it up...
--JUST AS LONG AS THEY'RE NOT VERY GOOD.
STOP

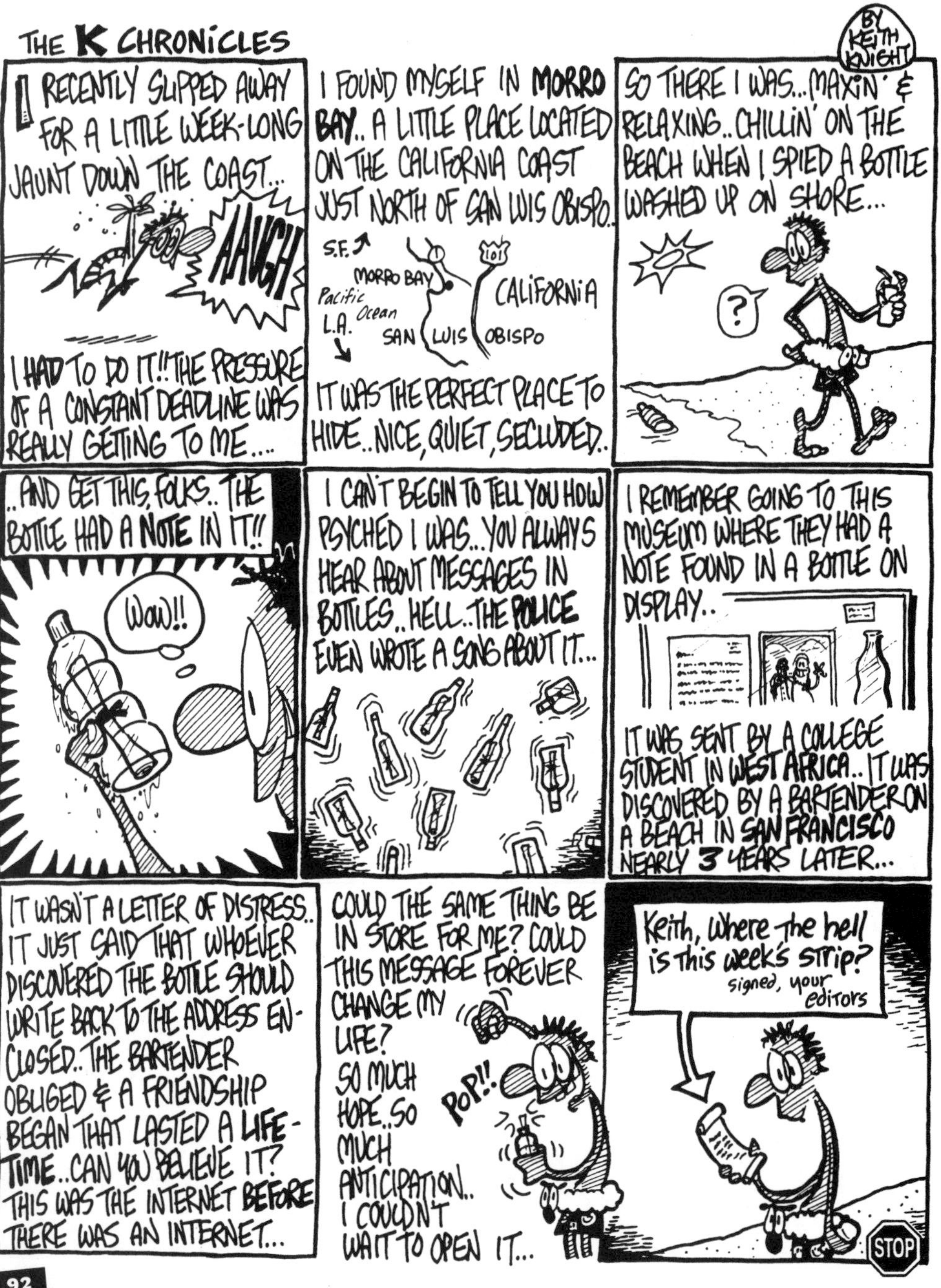
THE K CHRONICLES
BY KEITH KNIGHT
I RECENTLY SLIPPED AWAY FOR A LITTLE WEEK-LONG JAUNT DOWN THE COAST...
AAUGH
I HAD TO DO IT!! THE PRESSURE OF A CONSTANT DEADLINE WAS REALLY GETTING TO ME....
I FOUND MYSELF IN MORRO BAY.. A LITTLE PLACE LOCATED ON THE CALIFORNIA COAST JUST NORTH OF SAN LUIS OBISPO..
S.F.
MORRO BAY
101
CALIFORNIA
Pacific Ocean
L.A.
SAN LUIS OBISPO
IT WAS THE PERFECT PLACE TO HIDE.. NICE, QUIET, SECLUDED..
SO THERE I WAS... MAXIN' & RELAXING.. CHILLIN' ON THE BEACH WHEN I SPIED A BOTTLE WASHED UP ON SHORE...
?
..AND GET THIS, FOLKS.. THE BOTTLE HAD A NOTE IN IT!!
WOW!!
I CAN'T BEGIN TO TELL YOU HOW PSYCHED I WAS... YOU ALWAYS HEAR ABOUT MESSAGES IN BOTTLES.. HELL.. THE POLICE EVEN WROTE A SONG ABOUT IT...
I REMEMBER GOING TO THIS MUSEUM WHERE THEY HAD A NOTE FOUND IN A BOTTLE ON DISPLAY..
IT WAS SENT BY A COLLEGE STUDENT IN WEST AFRICA.. IT WAS DISCOVERED BY A BARTENDER ON A BEACH IN SAN FRANCISCO NEARLY 3 YEARS LATER...
IT WASN'T A LETTER OF DISTRESS.. IT JUST SAID THAT WHOEVER DISCOVERED THE BOTTLE SHOULD WRITE BACK TO THE ADDRESS EN-CLOSED.. THE BARTENDER OBLIGED & A FRIENDSHIP BEGAN THAT LASTED A LIFE-TIME.. CAN YOU BELIEVE IT? THIS WAS THE INTERNET BEFORE THERE WAS AN INTERNET...
COULD THE SAME THING BE IN STORE FOR ME? COULD THIS MESSAGE FOREVER CHANGE MY LIFE?
SO MUCH HOPE.. SO MUCH ANTICIPATION.. I COULDN'T WAIT TO OPEN IT...
POP!!
Keith, Where the hell is this week's strip?
signed, your editors
STOP

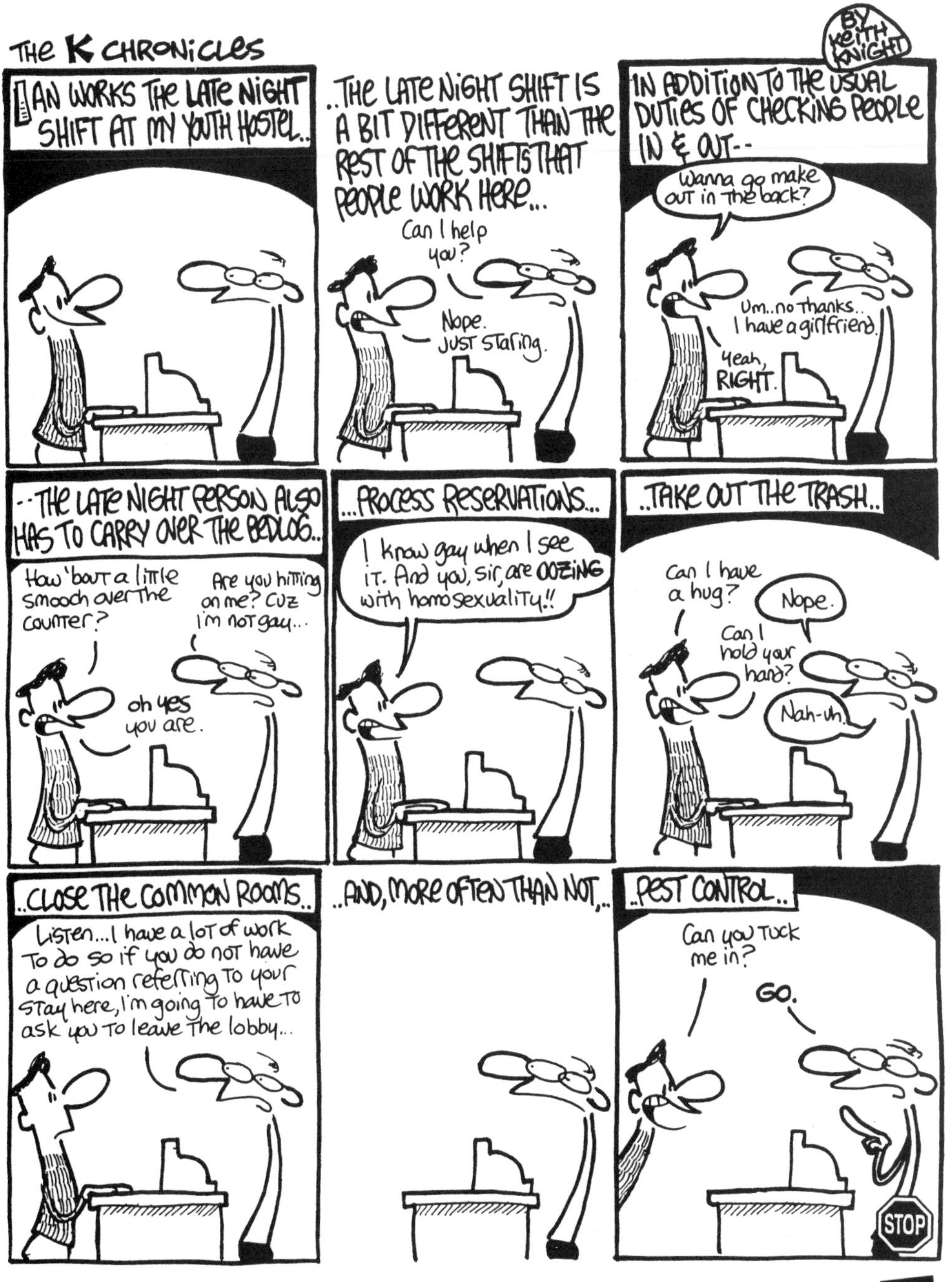
THE K CHRONICLES
BY KEITH KNIGHT
IAN WORKS THE LATE NIGHT SHIFT AT MY YOUTH HOSTEL..
..THE LATE NIGHT SHIFT IS A BIT DIFFERENT THAN THE REST OF THE SHIFTS THAT PEOPLE WORK HERE...
Can I help you?
Nope. JUST STARING.
IN ADDITION TO THE USUAL DUTIES OF CHECKING PEOPLE IN & OUT--
Wanna go make out in the back?
Um..no thanks.. I have a girlfriend.
Yeah, RIGHT.
--THE LATE NIGHT PERSON ALSO HAS TO CARRY OVER THE BEDLOG..
How 'bout a little smooch over the counter?
Are you hitting on me? Cuz I'm not gay...
oh yes you are.
...PROCESS RESERVATIONS...
I know gay when I see it. And you, sir, are OOZING with homosexuality!!
..TAKE OUT THE TRASH..
Can I have a hug?
Nope.
Can I hold your hand?
Nah-uh.
..CLOSE THE COMMON ROOMS..
Listen...I have a lot of work to do so if you do not have a question referring to your stay here, I'm going to have to ask you to leave the lobby...
..AND, MORE OFTEN THAN NOT,..
..PEST CONTROL..
Can you tuck me in?
GO.
STOP

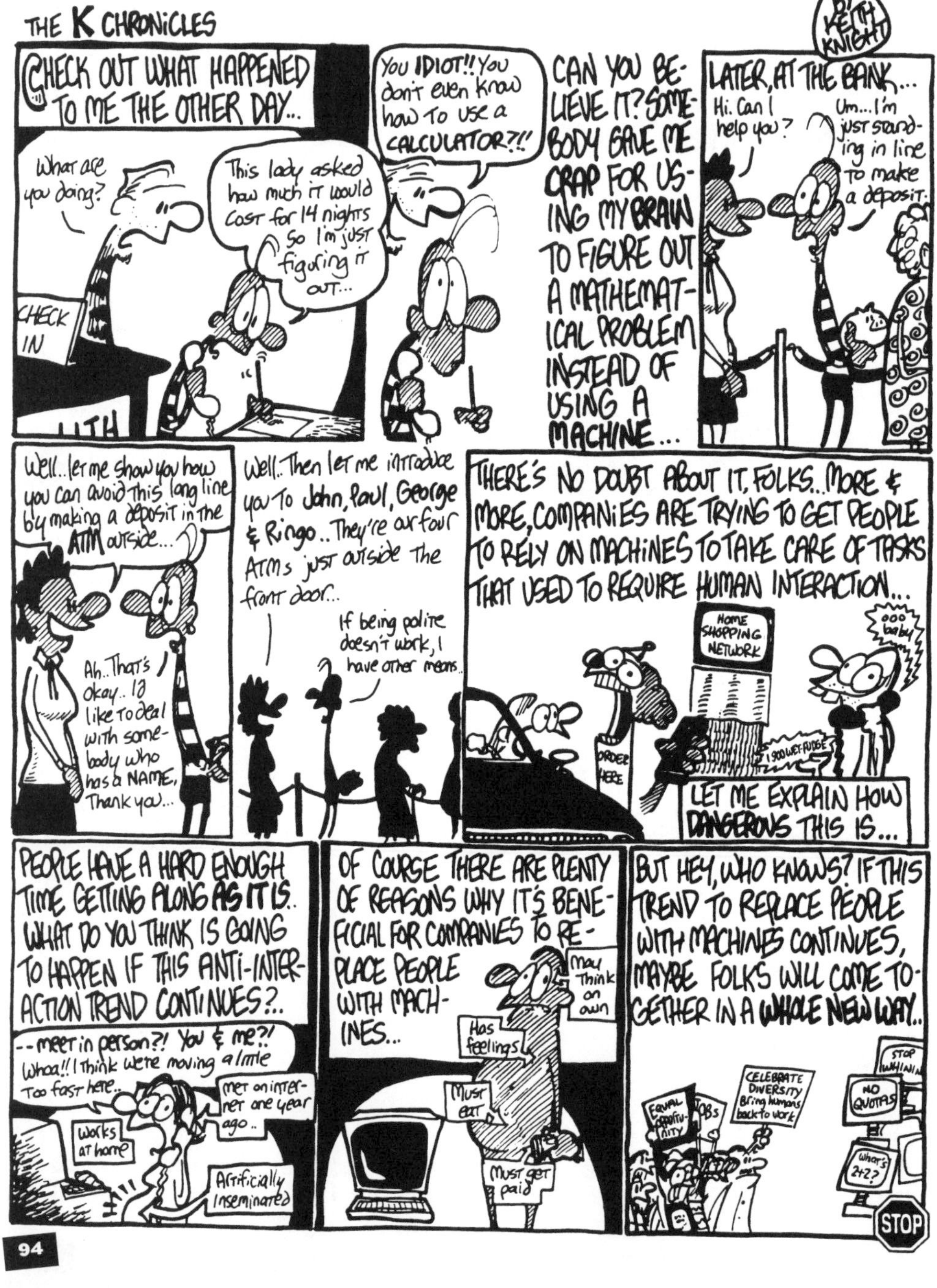
THE K CHRONICLES
BY KEITH KNIGHT
CHECK OUT WHAT HAPPENED TO ME THE OTHER DAY...
What are you doing?
This lady asked how much it would cost for 14 nights so I'm just figuring it out...
CHECK IN
You IDIOT!! You don't even know how to use a CALCULATOR?!!
CAN YOU BELIEVE IT? SOMEBODY GAVE ME CRAP FOR USING MY BRAIN TO FIGURE OUT A MATHEMATICAL PROBLEM INSTEAD OF USING A MACHINE...
LATER, AT THE BANK...
Hi. Can I help you?
Um...I'm just standing in line to make a deposit.
Well..let me show you how you can avoid this long line by making a deposit in the ATM outside...
Ah..That's okay.. I'd like to deal with somebody who has a NAME, Thank you...
Well.. Then let me introduce you to John, Paul, George & Ringo.. They're our four ATMs just outside the front door...
If being polite doesn't work, I have other means..
THERE'S NO DOUBT ABOUT IT, FOLKS...MORE & MORE, COMPANIES ARE TRYING TO GET PEOPLE TO RELY ON MACHINES TO TAKE CARE OF TASKS THAT USED TO REQUIRE HUMAN INTERACTION...
HOME SHOPPING NETWORK
ooo baby
ORDER HERE
1 900 WET-FUDGE
LET ME EXPLAIN HOW DANGEROUS THIS IS...
PEOPLE HAVE A HARD ENOUGH TIME GETTING ALONG AS IT IS.. WHAT DO YOU THINK IS GOING TO HAPPEN IF THIS ANTI-INTERACTION TREND CONTINUES?..
--meet in person?! You & me?! Whoa!! I think we're moving a little too fast here..
Met on internet one year ago..
Works at home
Artificially Inseminated
OF COURSE THERE ARE PLENTY OF REASONS WHY IT'S BENEFICIAL FOR COMPANIES TO REPLACE PEOPLE WITH MACHINES...
May Think on own
Has feelings
Must eat
Must get paid
BUT HEY, WHO KNOWS? IF THIS TREND TO REPLACE PEOPLE WITH MACHINES CONTINUES, MAYBE FOLKS WILL COME TOGETHER IN A WHOLE NEW WAY...
EQUAL OPPORTUNITY
JOBS
CELEBRATE DIVERSITY Bring humans back to work
STOP WHINING
NO QUOTAS
What's 2+2?
STOP

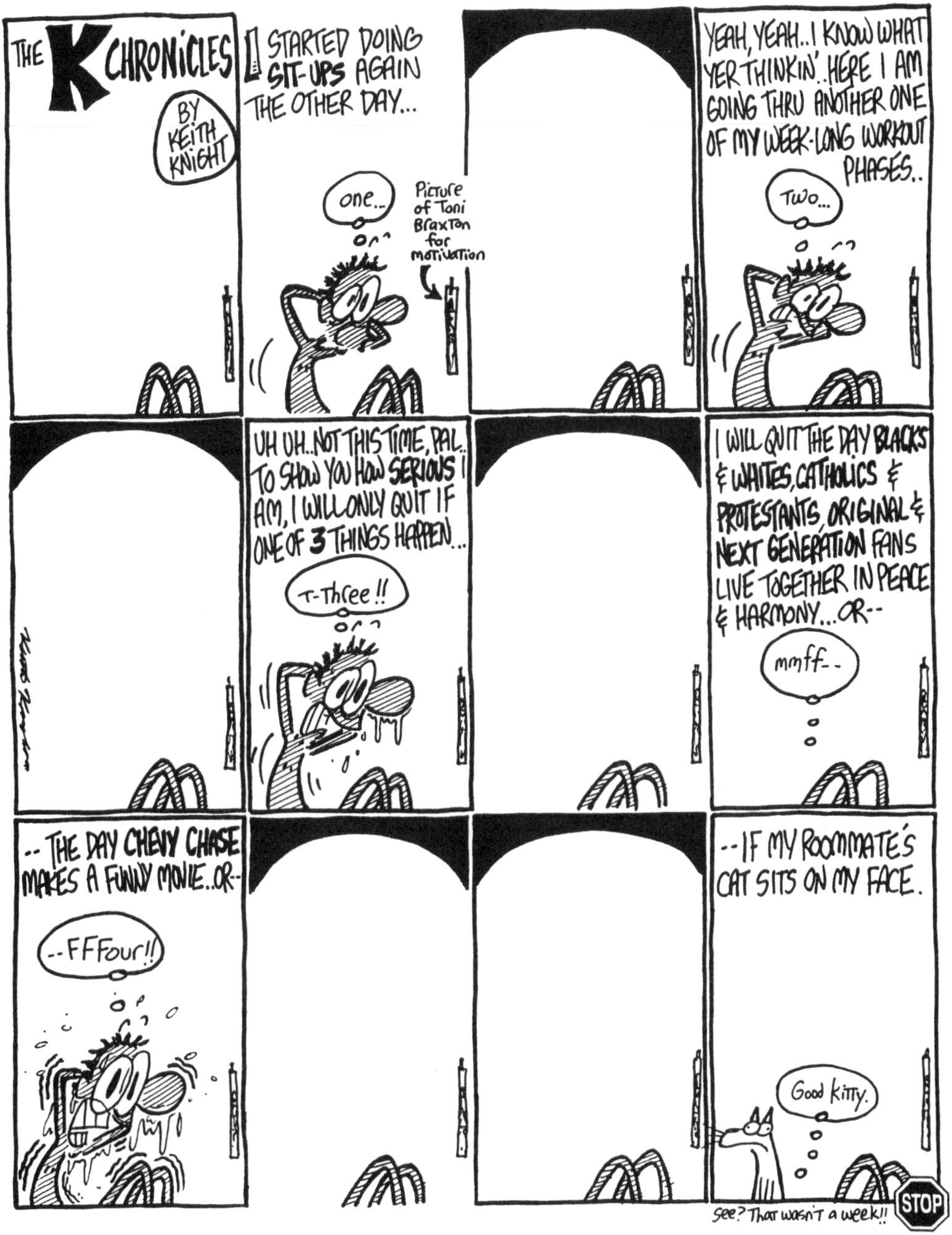
THE K CHRONICLES
BY KEITH KNIGHT
I STARTED DOING SIT-UPS AGAIN THE OTHER DAY...
one...
Picture of Toni Braxton for motivation
YEAH, YEAH..I KNOW WHAT YER THINKIN'..HERE I AM GOING THRU ANOTHER ONE OF MY WEEK-LONG WORKOUT PHASES..
Two...
UH UH..NOT THIS TIME, PAL.. TO SHOW YOU HOW SERIOUS I AM, I WILL ONLY QUIT IF ONE OF 3 THINGS HAPPEN...
T-Three!!
I WILL QUIT THE DAY BLACKS & WHITES, CATHOLICS & PROTESTANTS, ORIGINAL & NEXT GENERATION FANS LIVE TOGETHER IN PEACE & HARMONY...OR--
mmff--
--THE DAY CHEVY CHASE MAKES A FUNNY MOVIE..OR--
--FFFour!!
--IF MY ROOMMATE'S CAT SITS ON MY FACE..
Good kitty.
STOP
See? That wasn't a week!!

THE K CHRONICLES

BY Keith Knight

Me & my homie went to the casket shoppe the other day...

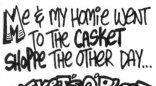

CASKETS 'O' PLENTY

FOLKS ARE DYING TO GET INTO OUR COFFINS!!

50%-70% OFF!

I'm not expecting any-one I know to die soon.. it's just that the whole industry of death fascinates me...

$ Caskets!! $ Flowers!!
$ Limo!!
Burial!! $ Headstons!!
$

There are a whole lot of folks making a killing in it...

The caskets that we were looking at were guaranteed to be the lowest prices in the area...

Jiminy Crickets!!

Mahogany wood with velvet interior

$7495

Some of the bronze ones went for $7000 too!!!

Hell.. if I was gonna spend 7 grand on something like that, I'm certainly not going to stick it in the ground right away...

..I'd show it off on my front lawn for at least 3 weeks..

..or maybe add some wheels & put an engine in it & drive it around town...

I'd never want to do the whole burial thing anyway... it costs too much money & takes up too much space...

RIP RIP RIP RIP RIP

When I die, either cremate me & toss the ashes into the sea, or dump my body in the woods & let the animals have their way...

As far as cremation goes, why not do it yourself?

Cremation for Dummies

I'm sure there's a "Dummies" guide for it...

..and screw paying any-where from $75 to $1500 for an urn to put the ashes in...

K.F.C, Pizza Hut & Taco Bell have been selling urns all summer for $1.99 a piece.

STOP

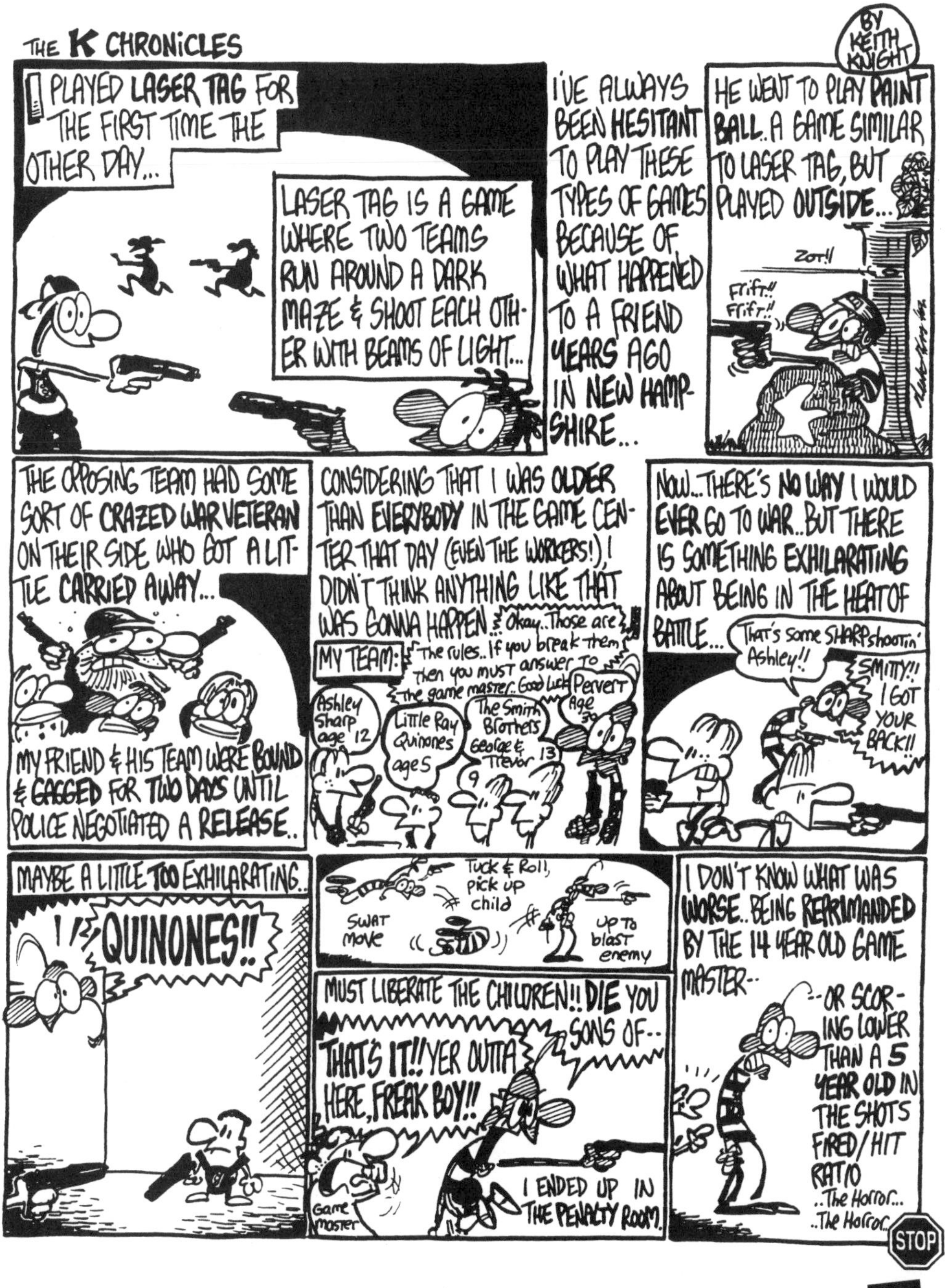
THE K CHRONICLES
BY KEITH KNIGHT
I PLAYED LASER TAG FOR THE FIRST TIME THE OTHER DAY...
LASER TAG IS A GAME WHERE TWO TEAMS RUN AROUND A DARK MAZE & SHOOT EACH OTHER WITH BEAMS OF LIGHT...
I'VE ALWAYS BEEN HESITANT TO PLAY THESE TYPES OF GAMES BECAUSE OF WHAT HAPPENED TO A FRIEND YEARS AGO IN NEW HAMPSHIRE...
HE WENT TO PLAY PAINT BALL.. A GAME SIMILAR TO LASER TAG, BUT PLAYED OUTSIDE...
ZOT!!
Frift!! Frift!!
THE OPPOSING TEAM HAD SOME SORT OF CRAZED WAR VETERAN ON THEIR SIDE WHO GOT A LITTLE CARRIED AWAY...
MY FRIEND & HIS TEAM WERE BOUND & GAGGED FOR TWO DAYS UNTIL POLICE NEGOTIATED A RELEASE..
CONSIDERING THAT I WAS OLDER THAN EVERYBODY IN THE GAME CENTER THAT DAY (EVEN THE WORKERS!), I DIDN'T THINK ANYTHING LIKE THAT WAS GONNA HAPPEN...
Okay.. Those are the rules.. If you break them then you must answer to the game master.. Good Luck
MY TEAM:
Ashley Sharp age 12
Little Ray Quinones age 5
The Smith Brothers George & Trevor 9 13
Pervert Age 30
NOW... THERE'S NO WAY I WOULD EVER GO TO WAR.. BUT THERE IS SOMETHING EXHILARATING ABOUT BEING IN THE HEAT OF BATTLE...
That's some SHARPshootin' Ashley!!
SMITTY!! I GOT YOUR BACK!!
MAYBE A LITTLE TOO EXHILARATING..
!! QUINONES!!
Tuck & Roll, pick up child
SWAT move
Up to blast enemy
MUST LIBERATE THE CHILDREN!! DIE YOU SONS OF--
THAT'S IT!! YER OUTTA HERE, FREAK BOY!!
Game master
I ENDED UP IN THE PENALTY ROOM.
I DON'T KNOW WHAT WAS WORSE.. BEING REPRIMANDED BY THE 14 YEAR OLD GAME MASTER--
--OR SCORING LOWER THAN A 5 YEAR OLD IN THE SHOTS FIRED/HIT RATIO
..The Horror... ..The Horror..
STOP

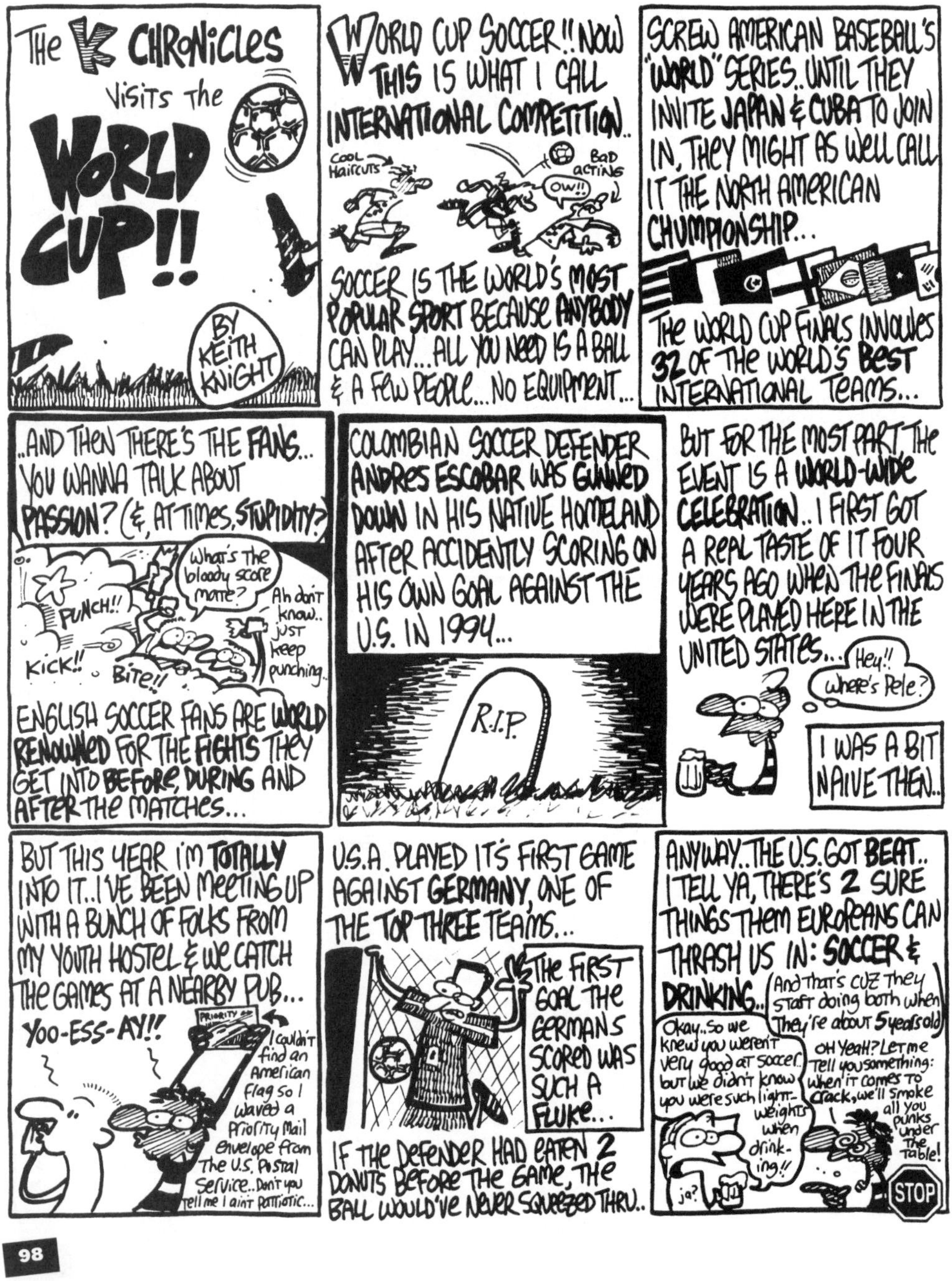

The K Chronicles visits the WORLD CUP!!
BY KEITH KNIGHT
WORLD CUP SOCCER!! NOW THIS IS WHAT I CALL INTERNATIONAL COMPETITION..
COOL HAIRCUTS
BAD ACTING
OW!!
SOCCER IS THE WORLD'S MOST POPULAR SPORT BECAUSE ANYBODY CAN PLAY... ALL YOU NEED IS A BALL & A FEW PEOPLE... NO EQUIPMENT...
SCREW AMERICAN BASEBALL'S "WORLD" SERIES.. UNTIL THEY INVITE JAPAN & CUBA TO JOIN IN, THEY MIGHT AS WELL CALL IT THE NORTH AMERICAN CHUMPIONSHIP...
THE WORLD CUP FINALS INVOLVES 32 OF THE WORLD'S BEST INTERNATIONAL TEAMS...
..AND THEN THERE'S THE FANS... YOU WANNA TALK ABOUT PASSION? (&, AT TIMES, STUPIDITY?)
What's the bloody score mate?
Ah don't know.. just keep punching..
PUNCH!!
KICK!!
BITE!!
ENGLISH SOCCER FANS ARE WORLD RENOWNED FOR THE FIGHTS THEY GET INTO BEFORE, DURING AND AFTER THE MATCHES...
COLOMBIAN SOCCER DEFENDER ANDRES ESCOBAR WAS GUNNED DOWN IN HIS NATIVE HOMELAND AFTER ACCIDENTLY SCORING ON HIS OWN GOAL AGAINST THE U.S. IN 1994...
R.I.P.
BUT FOR THE MOST PART, THE EVENT IS A WORLD-WIDE CELEBRATION.. I FIRST GOT A REAL TASTE OF IT FOUR YEARS AGO WHEN THE FINALS WERE PLAYED HERE IN THE UNITED STATES...
Hey!! where's Pele?
I WAS A BIT NAIVE THEN..
BUT THIS YEAR I'M TOTALLY INTO IT.. I'VE BEEN MEETING UP WITH A BUNCH OF FOLKS FROM MY YOUTH HOSTEL & WE CATCH THE GAMES AT A NEARBY PUB...
YOO-ESS-AY!!
PRIORITY
I couldn't find an American flag so I waved a Priority Mail envelope from the U.S. Postal Service.. Don't you tell me I ain't patriotic...
U.S.A. PLAYED IT'S FIRST GAME AGAINST GERMANY, ONE OF THE TOP THREE TEAMS...
THE FIRST GOAL THE GERMANS SCORED WAS SUCH A FLUKE...
IF THE DEFENDER HAD EATEN 2 DONUTS BEFORE THE GAME, THE BALL WOULD'VE NEVER SQUEEZED THRU..
ANYWAY.. THE U.S. GOT BEAT.. I TELL YA, THERE'S 2 SURE THINGS THEM EUROPEANS CAN THRASH US IN: SOCCER & DRINKING..
(And that's cuz they start doing both when they're about 5 years old)
Okay.. So we knew you weren't very good at soccer.. but we didn't know you were such light-weights when drink-ing!!
OH YEAH? Let me tell you something: when it comes to crack, we'll smoke all you punks under the table!
ja?
STOP

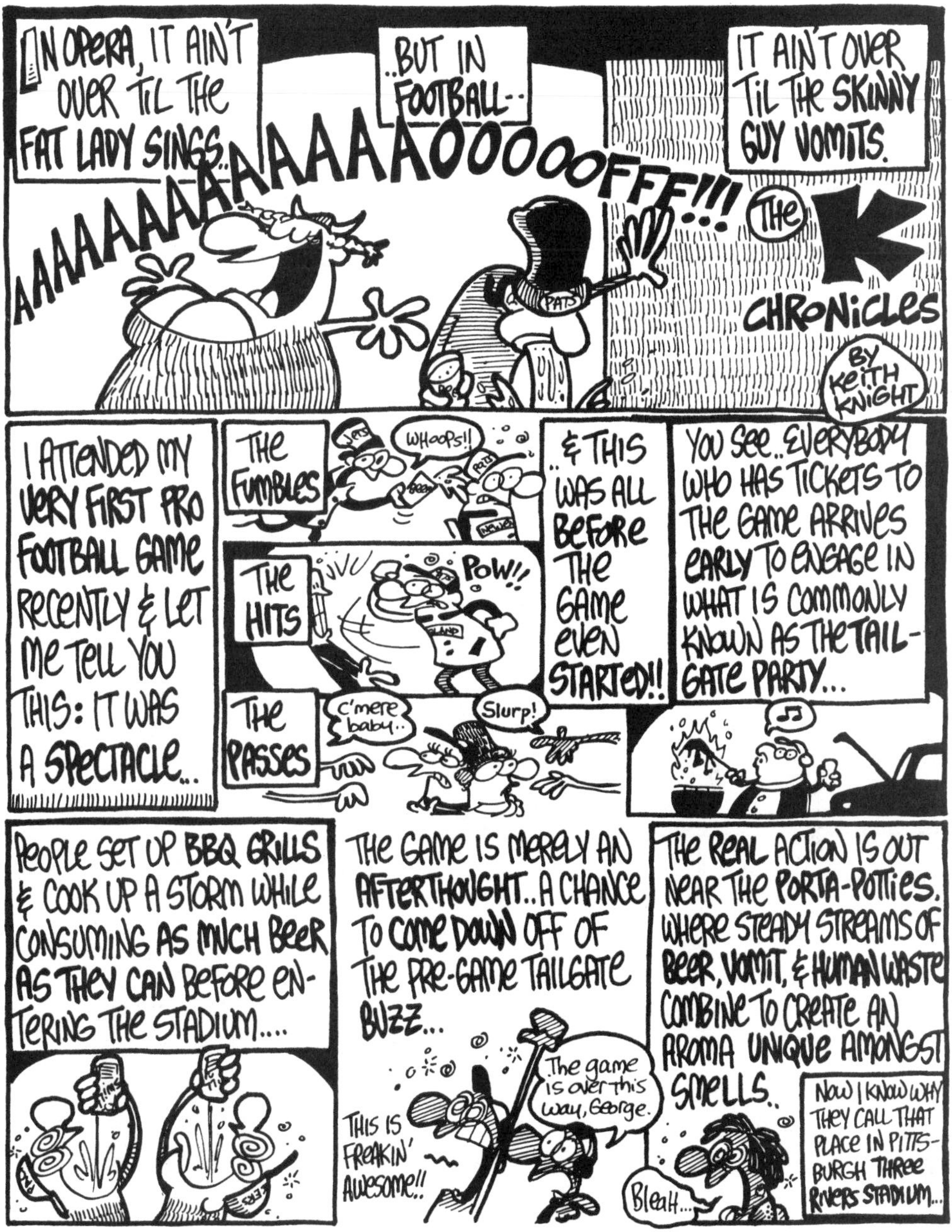
IN OPERA, IT AIN'T OVER TIL THE FAT LADY SINGS...
..BUT IN FOOTBALL..
IT AIN'T OVER TIL THE SKINNY GUY VOMITS.
AAAAAAAAAAAAAAAAAOOOOOOFFF!!!
PATS
THE K CHRONICLES
BY KEITH KNIGHT
I ATTENDED MY VERY FIRST PRO FOOTBALL GAME RECENTLY & LET ME TELL YOU THIS: IT WAS A SPECTACLE...
THE FUMBLES
WHOOPS!!
THE HITS
POW!!
THE PASSES
C'mere baby..
Slurp!
..& THIS WAS ALL BEFORE THE GAME EVEN STARTED!!
YOU SEE..EVERYBODY WHO HAS TICKETS TO THE GAME ARRIVES EARLY TO ENGAGE IN WHAT IS COMMONLY KNOWN AS THE TAIL-GATE PARTY...
PEOPLE SET UP BBQ GRILLS & COOK UP A STORM WHILE CONSUMING AS MUCH BEER AS THEY CAN BEFORE EN-TERING THE STADIUM....
THE GAME IS MERELY AN AFTERTHOUGHT..A CHANCE TO COME DOWN OFF OF THE PRE-GAME TAILGATE BUZZ...
THIS IS FREAKIN' AWESOME!!
The game is over this way, George.
THE REAL ACTION IS OUT NEAR THE PORTA-POTTIES. WHERE STEADY STREAMS OF BEER, VOMIT, & HUMAN WASTE COMBINE TO CREATE AN AROMA UNIQUE AMONGST SMELLS..
Bleah...
NOW I KNOW WHY THEY CALL THAT PLACE IN PITTS-BURGH THREE RIVERS STADIUM...

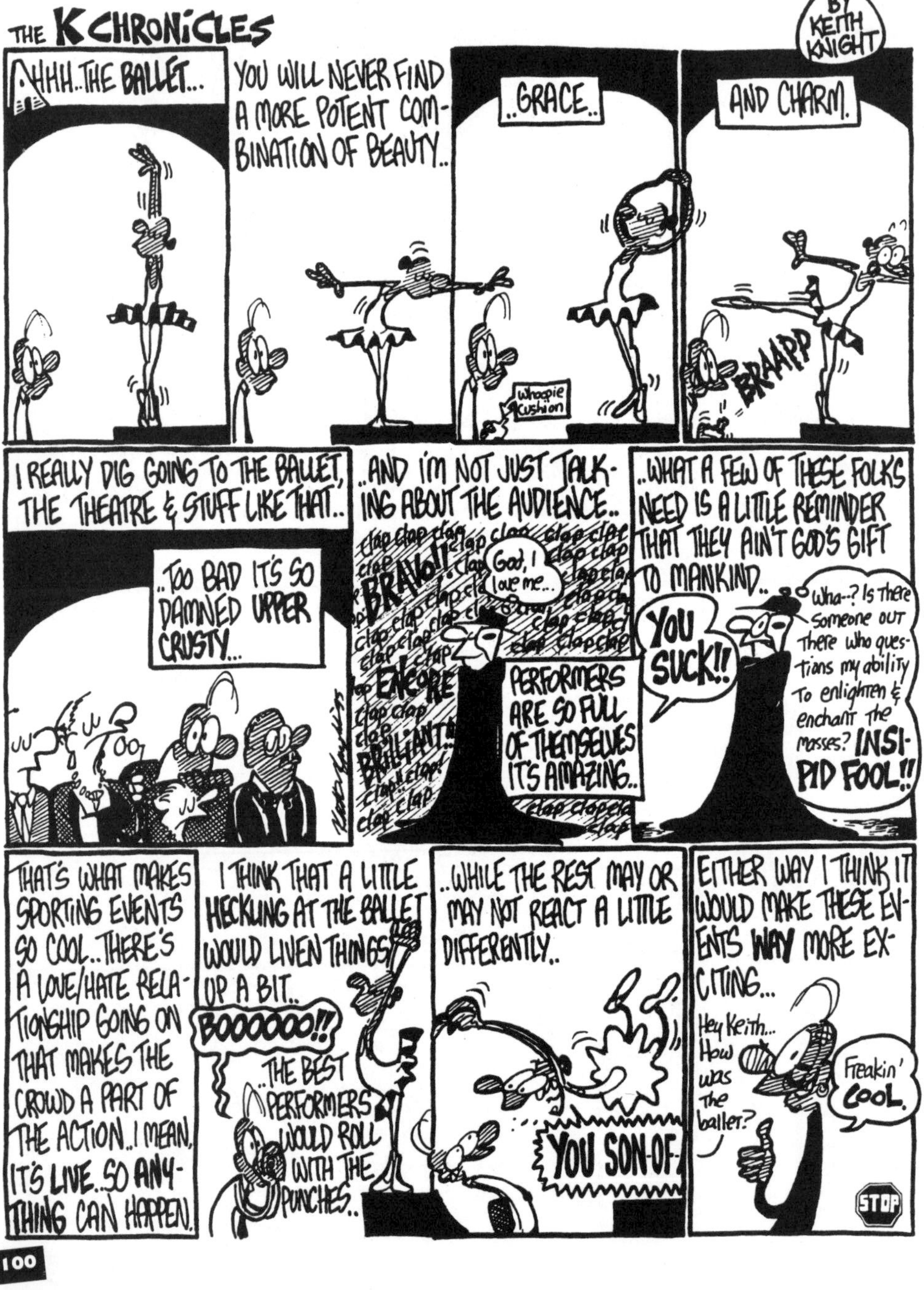
THE K CHRONICLES
BY KEITH KNIGHT
AHHH..THE BALLET...
YOU WILL NEVER FIND A MORE POTENT COMBINATION OF BEAUTY..
..GRACE..
Whoopie Cushion
AND CHARM.
BRAAPP
I REALLY DIG GOING TO THE BALLET, THE THEATRE & STUFF LIKE THAT..
..TOO BAD IT'S SO DAMNED UPPER CRUSTY...
..AND I'M NOT JUST TALKING ABOUT THE AUDIENCE..
clap clap clap clap
BRAVO!!
God, I love me...
ENCORE
BRILLIANT!!
PERFORMERS ARE SO FULL OF THEMSELVES IT'S AMAZING..
..WHAT A FEW OF THESE FOLKS NEED IS A LITTLE REMINDER THAT THEY AIN'T GOD'S GIFT TO MANKIND..
YOU SUCK!!
Wha--? Is there someone out there who questions my ability to enlighten & enchant the masses? INSIPID FOOL!!
THAT'S WHAT MAKES SPORTING EVENTS SO COOL..THERE'S A LOVE/HATE RELATIONSHIP GOING ON THAT MAKES THE CROWD A PART OF THE ACTION..I MEAN, IT'S LIVE..SO ANYTHING CAN HAPPEN.
I THINK THAT A LITTLE HECKLING AT THE BALLET WOULD LIVEN THINGS UP A BIT..
BOOOOOOO!!
..THE BEST PERFORMERS WOULD ROLL WITH THE PUNCHES..
..WHILE THE REST MAY OR MAY NOT REACT A LITTLE DIFFERENTLY..
YOU SON-OF-
EITHER WAY I THINK IT WOULD MAKE THESE EVENTS WAY MORE EXCITING...
Hey Keith... How was the ballet?
Freakin' COOL.
STOP

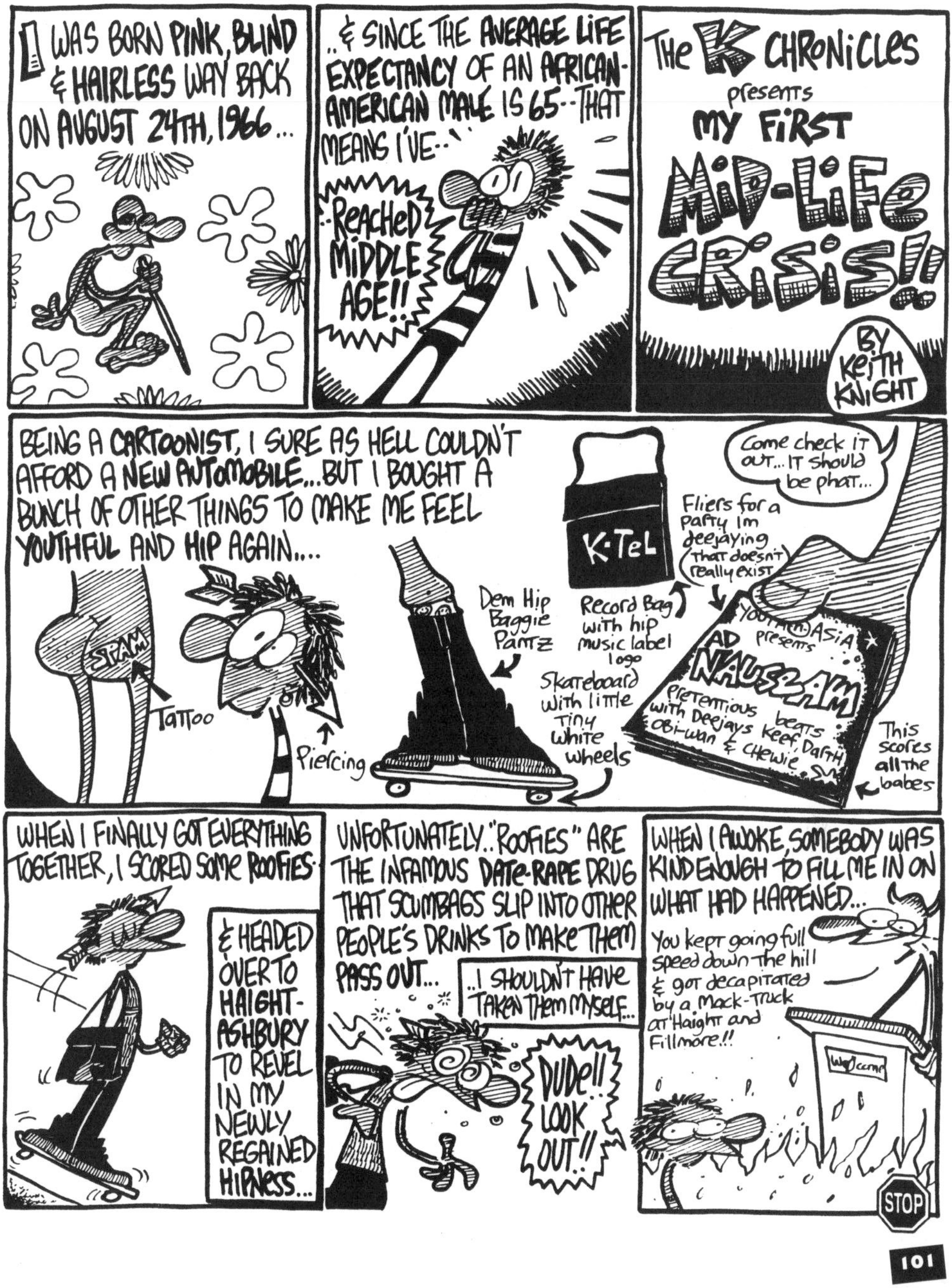
I WAS BORN PINK, BLIND & HAIRLESS WAY BACK ON AUGUST 24TH, 1966...
..& SINCE THE AVERAGE LIFE EXPECTANCY OF AN AFRICAN-AMERICAN MALE IS 65--THAT MEANS I'VE--
REACHED MIDDLE AGE!!
THE K CHRONICLES
presents
MY FIRST
MID-LIFE CRISIS!!
BY KEITH KNIGHT
BEING A CARTOONIST, I SURE AS HELL COULDN'T AFFORD A NEW AUTOMOBILE... BUT I BOUGHT A BUNCH OF OTHER THINGS TO MAKE ME FEEL YOUTHFUL AND HIP AGAIN....
Tattoo
Piercing
Dem Hip Baggie Pantz
K-TeL
Record Bag with hip music label logo
Fliers for a party I'm deejaying (that doesn't really exist)
Come check it out... it should be phat...
YOUTH(IN)ASIA presents
AD NAUSEAM
Pretentious beats with Deejays Keef, Darth, Obi-wan & Chewie
Skateboard with little tiny white wheels
This scores all the babes
WHEN I FINALLY GOT EVERYTHING TOGETHER, I SCORED SOME ROOFIES-
& HEADED OVER TO HAIGHT-ASHBURY TO REVEL IN MY NEWLY REGAINED HIPNESS...
UNFORTUNATELY.."ROOFIES" ARE THE INFAMOUS DATE-RAPE DRUG THAT SCUMBAGS SLIP INTO OTHER PEOPLE'S DRINKS TO MAKE THEM PASS OUT...
..I SHOULDN'T HAVE TAKEN THEM MYSELF...
DUDE!! LOOK OUT!!
WHEN I AWOKE, SOMEBODY WAS KIND ENOUGH TO FILL ME IN ON WHAT HAD HAPPENED...
You kept going full speed down the hill & got decapitated by a Mack-Truck at Haight and Fillmore!!
STOP

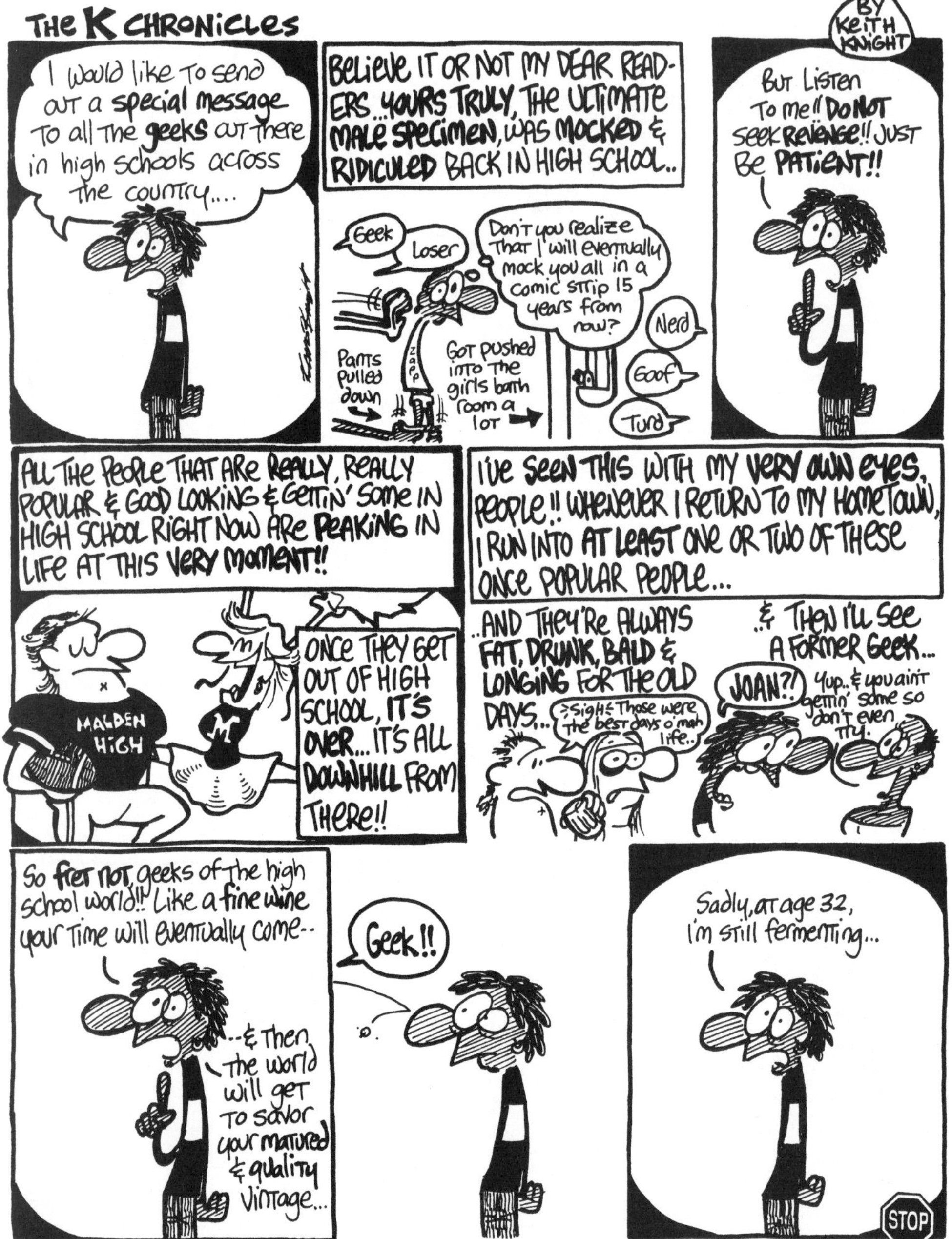
THE K CHRONICLES
BY KEITH KNIGHT
I would like to send out a special message to all the geeks out there in high schools across the country....
BELIEVE IT OR NOT MY DEAR READERS... YOURS TRULY, THE ULTIMATE MALE SPECIMEN, WAS MOCKED & RIDICULED BACK IN HIGH SCHOOL..
Geek
Loser
Don't you realize That I will eventually mock you all in a comic strip 15 years from now?
Nerd
Goof
Turd
Pants pulled down
Got pushed into The girls bath room a lot
But Listen To me!! DO NOT seek REVENGE!! JUST Be PATIENT!!
ALL THE PEOPLE THAT ARE REALLY, REALLY POPULAR & GOOD LOOKING & GETTIN' SOME IN HIGH SCHOOL RIGHT NOW ARE PEAKING IN LIFE AT THIS VERY MOMENT!!
MALDEN HIGH
ONCE THEY GET OUT OF HIGH SCHOOL, IT'S OVER... IT'S ALL DOWNHILL FROM THERE!!
I'VE SEEN THIS WITH MY VERY OWN EYES, PEOPLE!! WHENEVER I RETURN TO MY HOMETOWN, I RUN INTO AT LEAST ONE OR TWO OF THESE ONCE POPULAR PEOPLE...
..AND THEY'RE ALWAYS FAT, DRUNK, BALD & LONGING FOR THE OLD DAYS...
Sigh Those were the best days o' mah life..
..& THEN I'LL SEE A FORMER GEEK...
JOAN?!
Yup.. & you ain't gettin' some so don't even try.
So fret not, geeks of the high school world!! Like a fine wine your time will eventually come..
..& Then the world will get to savor your matured & quality vintage...
Geek!!
Sadly, at age 32, I'm still fermenting...
STOP

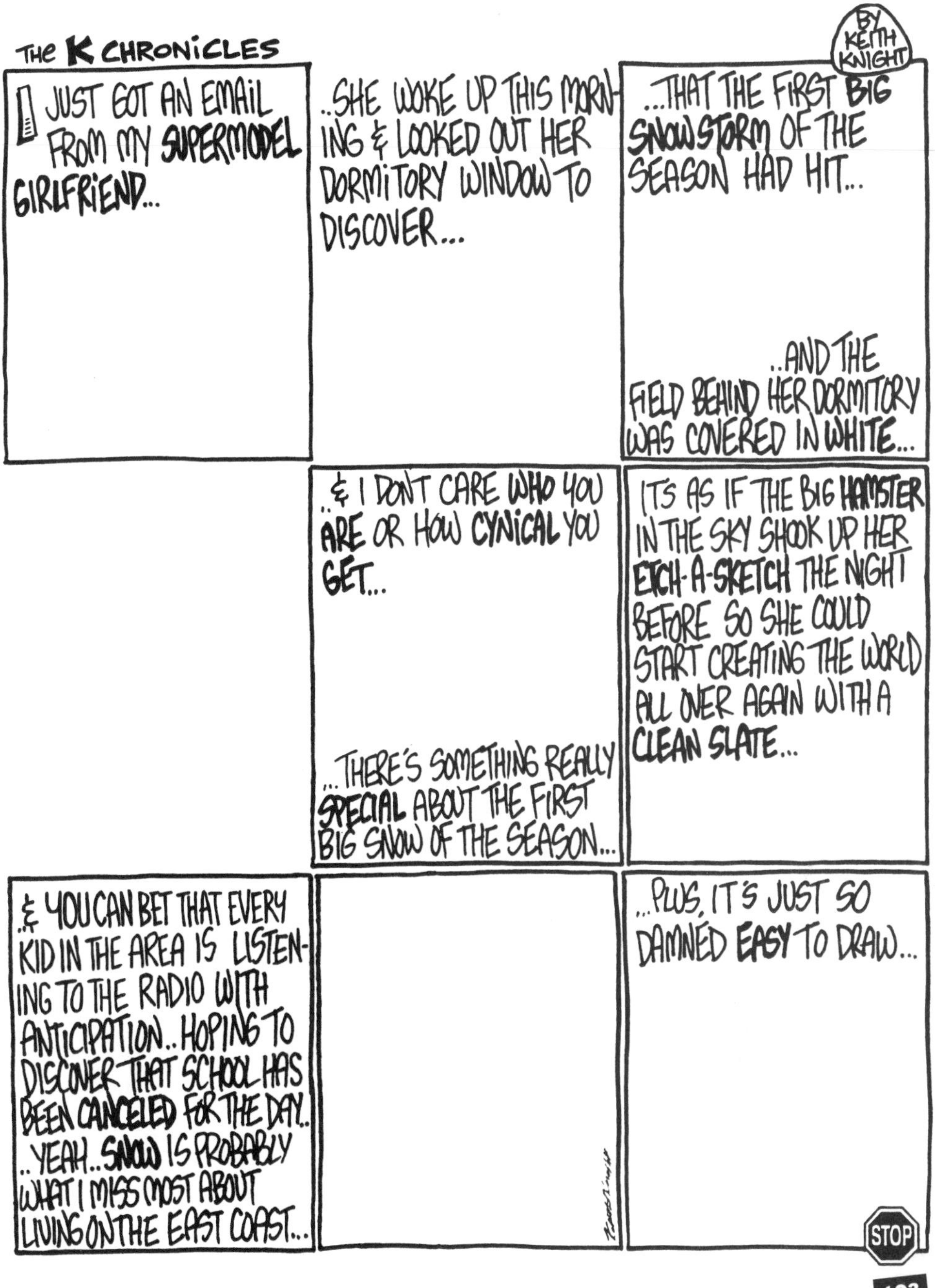
THE K CHRONICLES
BY KEITH KNIGHT
I JUST GOT AN EMAIL FROM MY SUPERMODEL GIRLFRIEND...
..SHE WOKE UP THIS MORNING & LOOKED OUT HER DORMITORY WINDOW TO DISCOVER...
...THAT THE FIRST BIG SNOWSTORM OF THE SEASON HAD HIT...
..AND THE FIELD BEHIND HER DORMITORY WAS COVERED IN WHITE...
..& I DON'T CARE WHO YOU ARE OR HOW CYNICAL YOU GET...
...THERE'S SOMETHING REALLY SPECIAL ABOUT THE FIRST BIG SNOW OF THE SEASON...
IT'S AS IF THE BIG HAMSTER IN THE SKY SHOOK UP HER ETCH-A-SKETCH THE NIGHT BEFORE SO SHE COULD START CREATING THE WORLD ALL OVER AGAIN WITH A CLEAN SLATE...
..& YOU CAN BET THAT EVERY KID IN THE AREA IS LISTENING TO THE RADIO WITH ANTICIPATION.. HOPING TO DISCOVER THAT SCHOOL HAS BEEN CANCELED FOR THE DAY..
..YEAH..SNOW IS PROBABLY WHAT I MISS MOST ABOUT LIVING ON THE EAST COAST...
...PLUS, IT'S JUST SO DAMNED EASY TO DRAW...
STOP

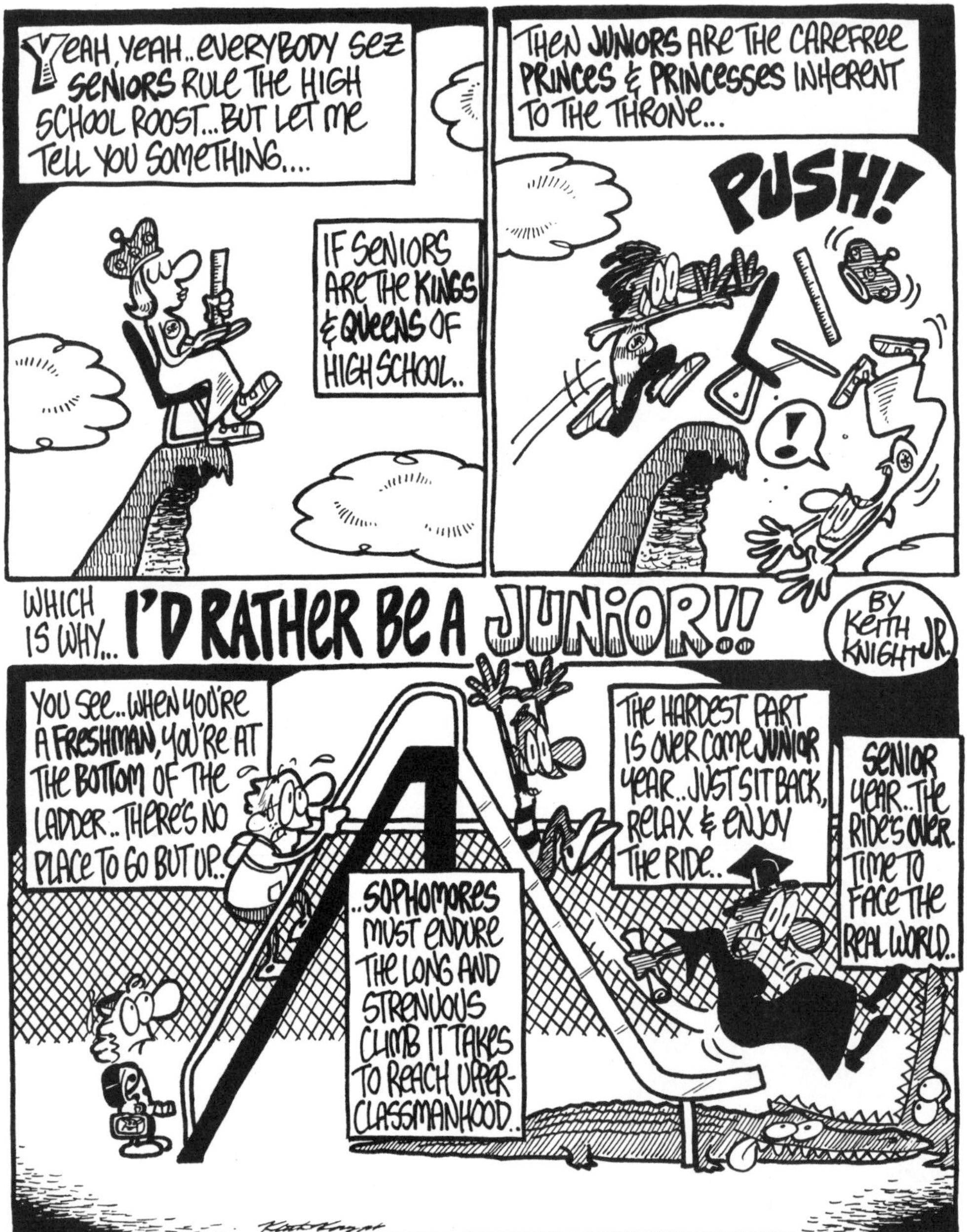
YEAH, YEAH.. EVERYBODY SEZ SENIORS RULE THE HIGH SCHOOL ROOST... BUT LET ME TELL YOU SOMETHING....
IF SENIORS ARE THE KINGS & QUEENS OF HIGH SCHOOL..
THEN JUNIORS ARE THE CAREFREE PRINCES & PRINCESSES INHERENT TO THE THRONE...
PUSH!
!
WHICH IS WHY... I'D RATHER BE A JUNIOR!!
BY KEITH KNIGHT JR.
YOU SEE.. WHEN YOU'RE A FRESHMAN, YOU'RE AT THE BOTTOM OF THE LADDER.. THERE'S NO PLACE TO GO BUT UP..
..SOPHOMORES MUST ENDURE THE LONG AND STRENUOUS CLIMB IT TAKES TO REACH UPPER-CLASSMANHOOD..
THE HARDEST PART IS OVER COME JUNIOR YEAR.. JUST SIT BACK, RELAX & ENJOY THE RIDE..
SENIOR YEAR.. THE RIDE'S OVER. TIME TO FACE THE REAL WORLD..

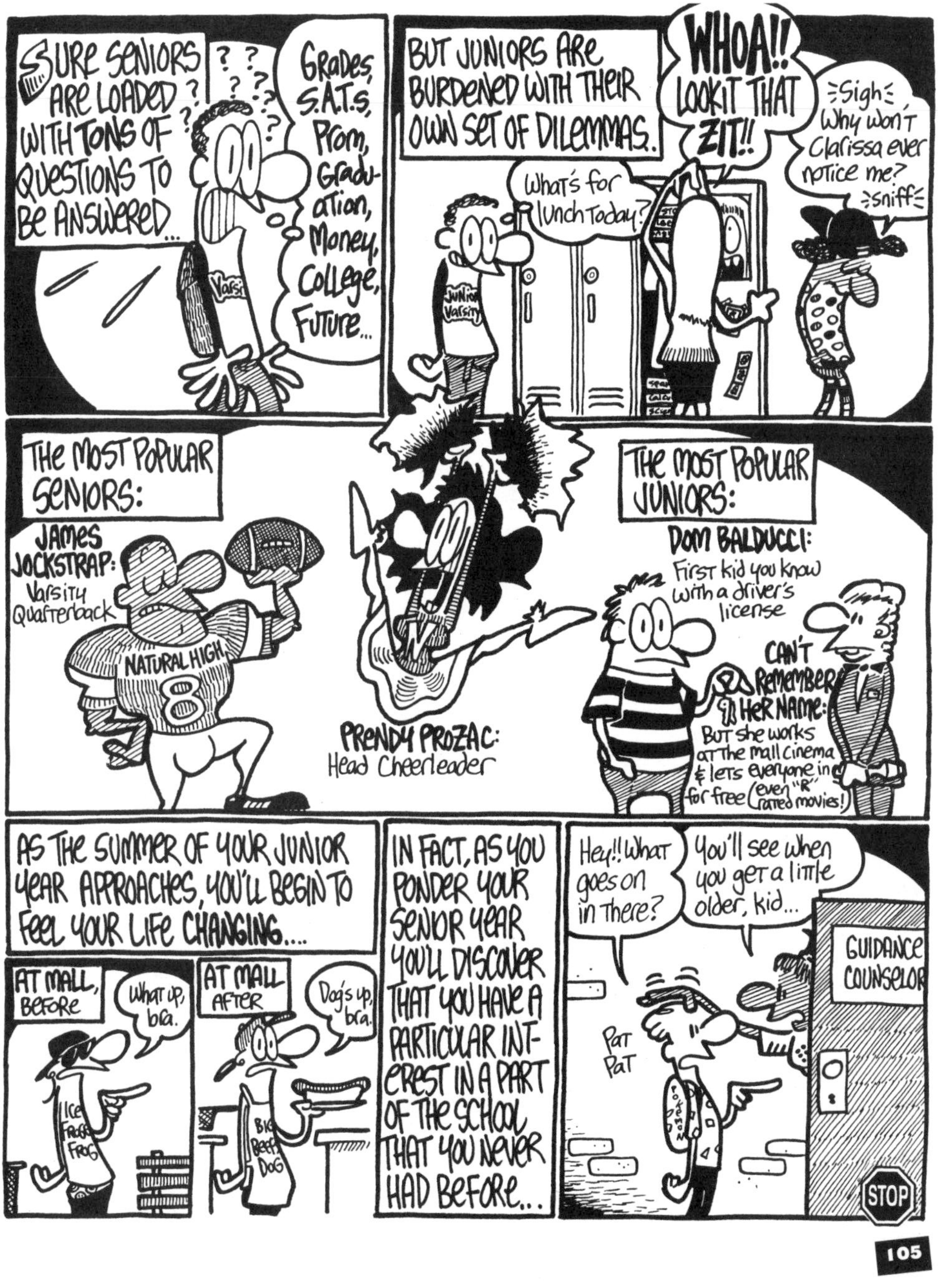

SURE SENIORS ARE LOADED WITH TONS OF QUESTIONS TO BE ANSWERED...
Grades, S.A.T.s, Prom, Graduation, Money, College, Future...
Varsi
BUT JUNIORS ARE BURDENED WITH THEIR OWN SET OF DILEMMAS.
What's for lunch Today?
Junior Varsity
WHOA!! LOOKIT THAT ZIT!!
Sigh, Why won't Clarissa ever notice me? sniff
THE MOST POPULAR SENIORS:
JAMES JOCKSTRAP: Varsity Quarterback
NATURAL HIGH 8
PRENDY PROZAC: Head Cheerleader
THE MOST POPULAR JUNIORS:
DOM BALDUCCI: First kid you know with a driver's license
CAN'T REMEMBER HER NAME: But she works at The mall cinema & lets everyone in for free (even "R" rated movies!)
AS THE SUMMER OF YOUR JUNIOR YEAR APPROACHES, YOU'LL BEGIN TO FEEL YOUR LIFE CHANGING....
AT MALL, BEFORE
What up, bra.
Ice Frog Frog
AT MALL AFTER
Dog's up, bra.
Big Beef Dog
IN FACT, AS YOU PONDER YOUR SENIOR YEAR YOU'LL DISCOVER THAT YOU HAVE A PARTICULAR INTEREST IN A PART OF THE SCHOOL THAT YOU NEVER HAD BEFORE...
Hey!! What goes on in There?
You'll see when you get a little older, kid...
Pat Pat
GUIDANCE COUNSELOR
POKEMON
STOP

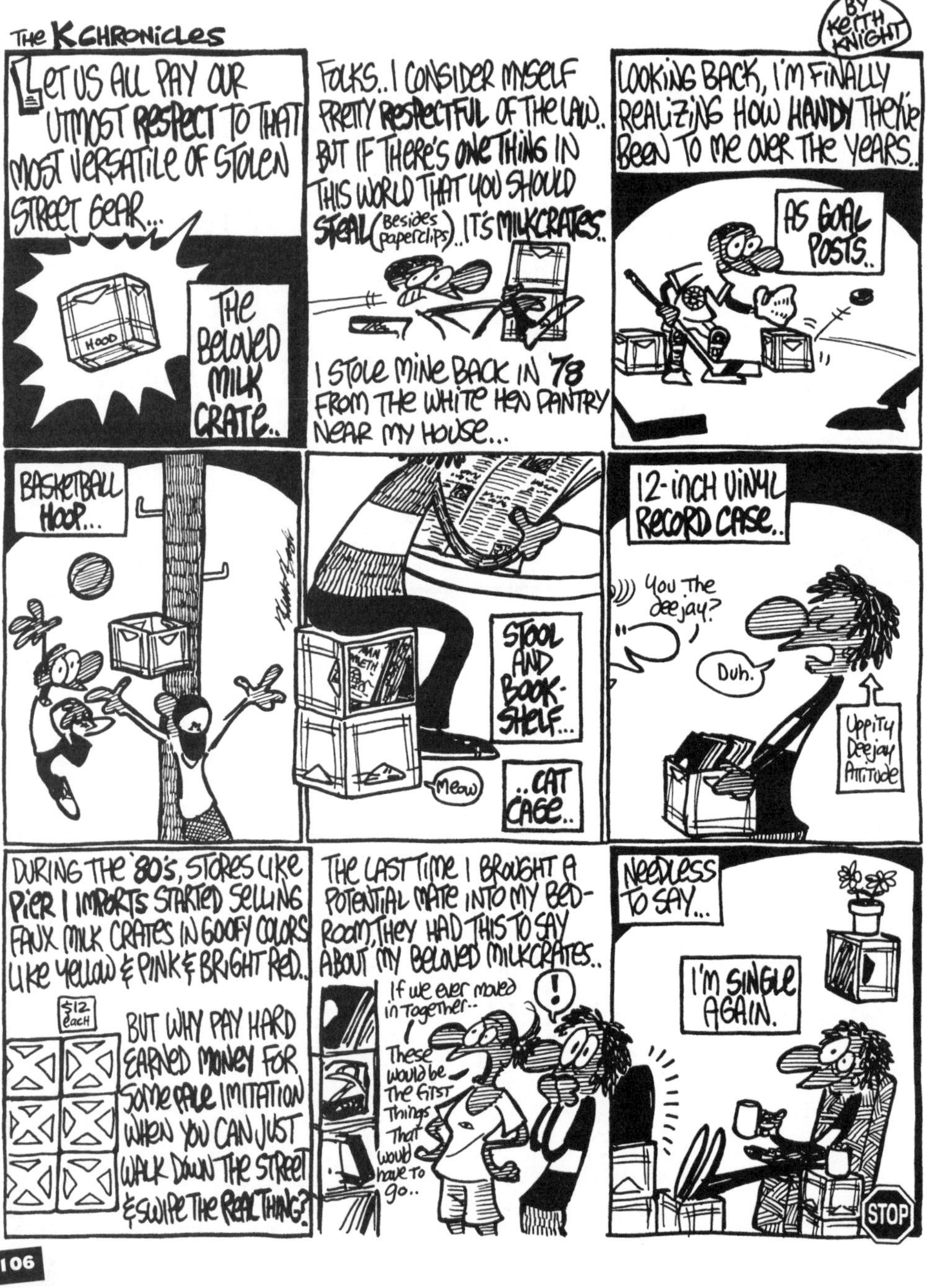
THE K CHRONICLES
BY KEITH KNIGHT
LET US ALL PAY OUR UTMOST RESPECT TO THAT MOST VERSATILE OF STOLEN STREET GEAR...
HOOD
THE BELOVED MILK CRATE..
FOLKS.. I CONSIDER MYSELF PRETTY RESPECTFUL OF THE LAW.. BUT IF THERE'S ONE THING IN THIS WORLD THAT YOU SHOULD STEAL (Besides paperclips).. IT'S MILKCRATES..
I STOLE MINE BACK IN '78 FROM THE WHITE HEN PANTRY NEAR MY HOUSE...
LOOKING BACK, I'M FINALLY REALIZING HOW HANDY THEY'VE BEEN TO ME OVER THE YEARS..
AS GOAL POSTS..
BASKETBALL HOOP...
STOOL AND BOOK-SHELF...
Meow
..CAT CAGE..
12-INCH VINYL RECORD CASE..
You The deejay?
Duh.
Uppity Deejay Attitude
DURING THE '80'S, STORES LIKE PIER I IMPORTS STARTED SELLING FAUX MILK CRATES IN GOOFY COLORS LIKE YELLOW & PINK & BRIGHT RED..
$12 each
BUT WHY PAY HARD EARNED MONEY FOR SOME PALE IMITATION WHEN YOU CAN JUST WALK DOWN THE STREET & SWIPE THE REAL THING?
THE LAST TIME I BROUGHT A POTENTIAL MATE INTO MY BED-ROOM, THEY HAD THIS TO SAY ABOUT MY BELOVED MILKCRATES..
If we ever moved in Together..
These would be The first Things That would have to go..
!
NEEDLESS TO SAY...
I'M SINGLE AGAIN.
STOP

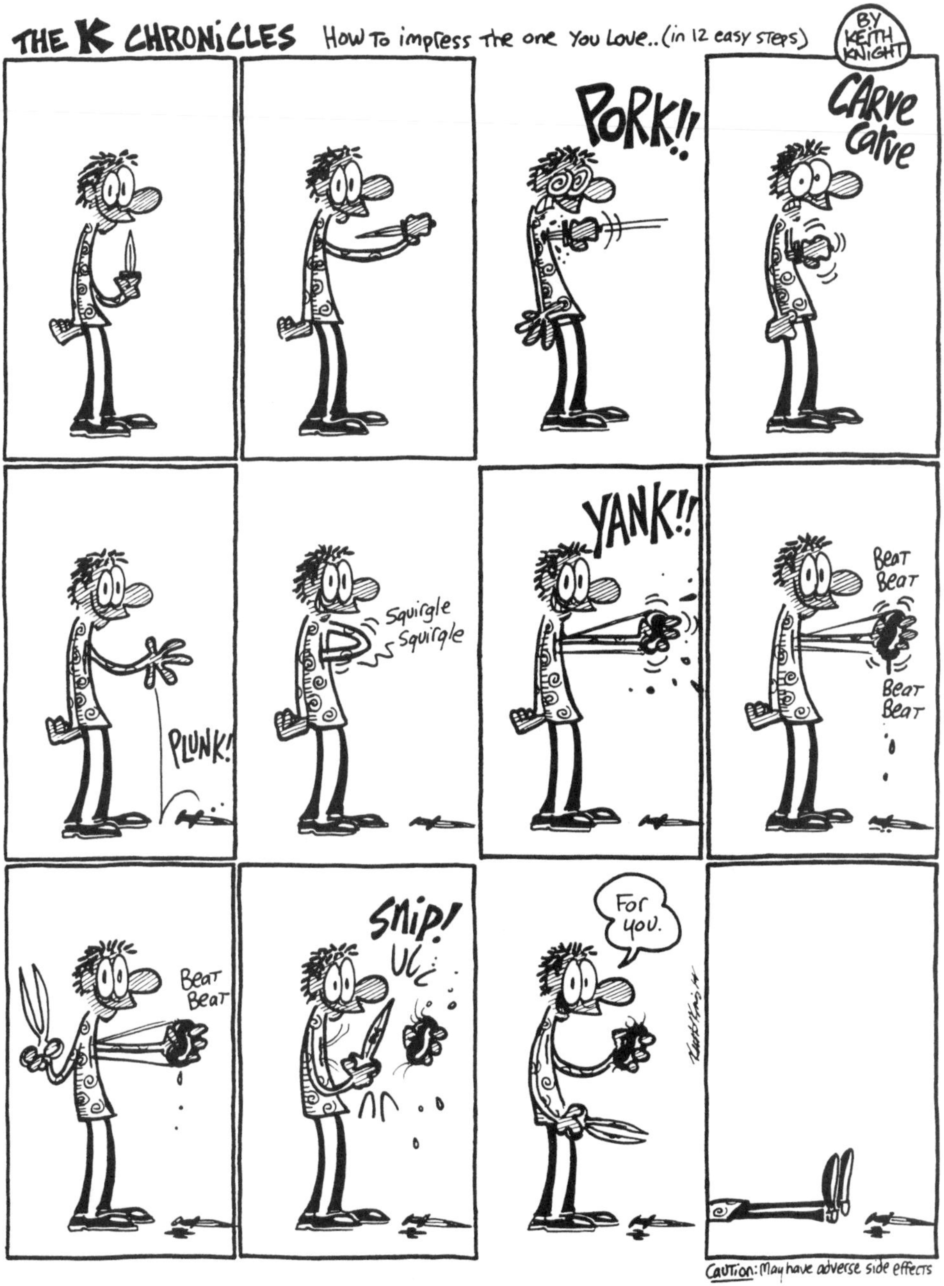
THE K CHRONICLES
How To impress The one You Love.. (in 12 easy steps)
BY KEITH KNIGHT
PORK!!
CARVE CARVE
PLUNK!
squirgle squirgle
YANK!!
Beat Beat
Beat Beat
Beat Beat
SNIP!
For you.
CAUTION: May have adverse side effects

The K CHRONICLES

BY KEITH KNIGHT

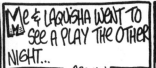

Me & LaQuisha went to see a play the other night...

Are you leaving?

Nope.

She insisted on taking her car...

& I don't know if you're familiar with driving in San Francisco--

Is that one?

Naw... Bus stop.

BUS

--but trying to park here is worse than smoking cigarettes...

How 'bout there?

Driveway.

--it's expensive...

How much is it?

#8⁰⁰ an hour...

PARKIN

Screw that!!

--you experience a lack of confidence & low self esteem..

Here's one.

I'll never be able to fit in there

Yes you can.

No I can't!!

I bet you can!! I'll get out & help..

It's stressful...

See?! I told you I couldn't fit!! And now all these cars are backed up behind us for nothing!!

What are you talking about? You've got it!! And stop worrying about everybody else...

Beep Beep

It diminishes sex drive...

See?! I told you so!! Now to collect on the bet--

Don't you kiss me you smug bastard!!

..you waste 20 minutes of your life every time you do it..

The play starts in five minutes & we're 20 blocks away...

Taxi!!

STOP

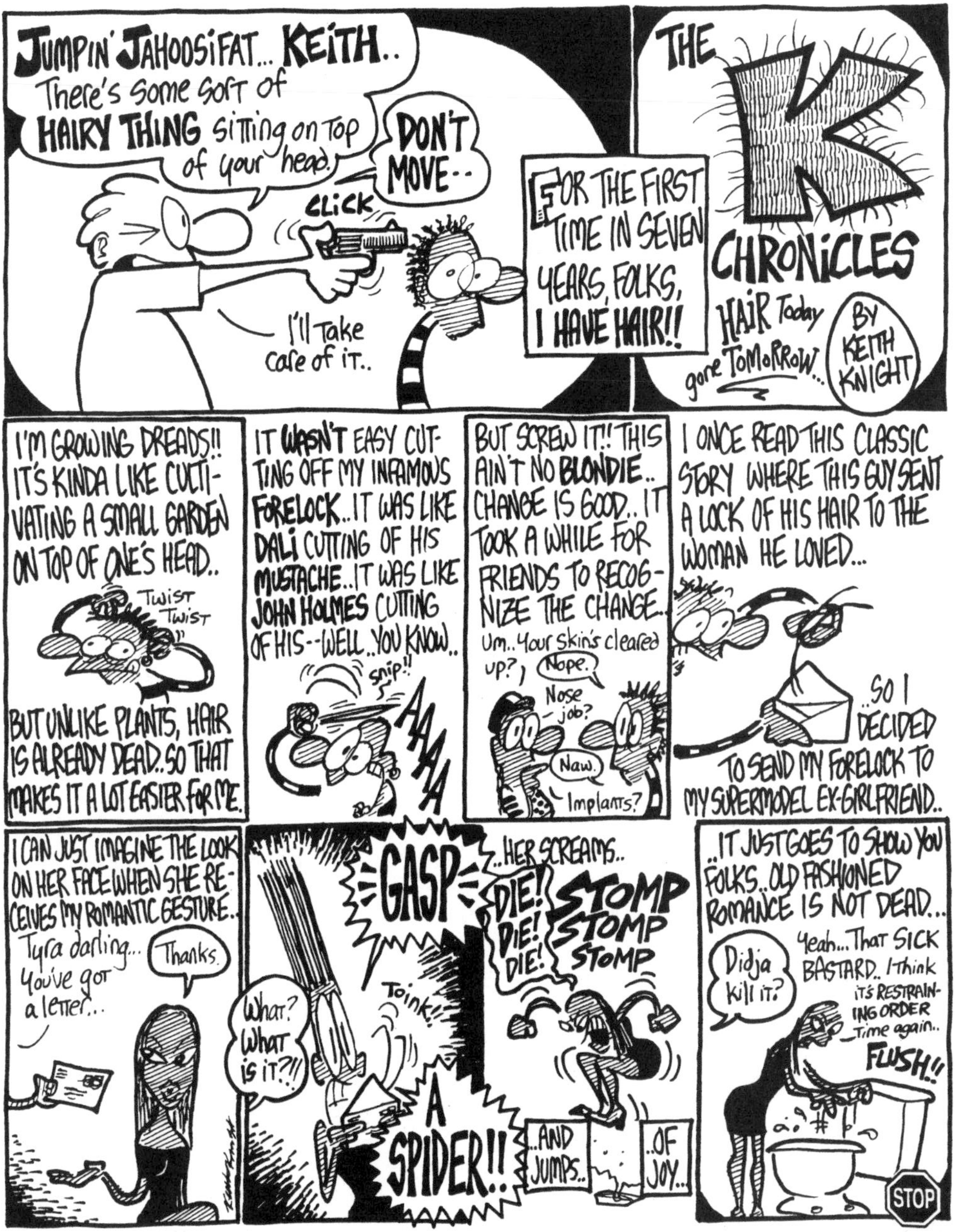

JUMPIN' JAHOOSIFAT... KEITH.. There's some sort of HAIRY THING sitting on top of your head.
DON'T MOVE--
CLICK
I'll take care of it..
FOR THE FIRST TIME IN SEVEN YEARS, FOLKS, I HAVE HAIR!!
THE K CHRONICLES
HAIR Today gone TOMORROW...
BY KEITH KNIGHT
I'M GROWING DREADS!! IT'S KINDA LIKE CULTIVATING A SMALL GARDEN ON TOP OF ONE'S HEAD..
TWIST TWIST
BUT UNLIKE PLANTS, HAIR IS ALREADY DEAD.. SO THAT MAKES IT A LOT EASIER FOR ME.
IT WASN'T EASY CUTTING OFF MY INFAMOUS FORELOCK.. IT WAS LIKE DALI CUTTING OF HIS MUSTACHE.. IT WAS LIKE JOHN HOLMES CUTTING OF HIS--WELL..YOU KNOW..
snip!!
AAAAAA
BUT SCREW IT!! THIS AIN'T NO BLONDIE.. CHANGE IS GOOD.. IT TOOK A WHILE FOR FRIENDS TO RECOGNIZE THE CHANGE..
Um.. Your skin's cleared up?
Nope.
Nose job?
Naw.
Implants?
I ONCE READ THIS CLASSIC STORY WHERE THIS GUY SENT A LOCK OF HIS HAIR TO THE WOMAN HE LOVED...
..SO I DECIDED TO SEND MY FORELOCK TO MY SUPERMODEL EX-GIRLFRIEND..
I CAN JUST IMAGINE THE LOOK ON HER FACE WHEN SHE RECEIVES MY ROMANTIC GESTURE..
Tyra darling... You've got a letter...
Thanks.
GASP
What? What is it?!!
Toink!!
A SPIDER!!
..HER SCREAMS..
DIE! DIE! DIE!
STOMP STOMP STOMP
..AND JUMPS..
..OF JOY...
..IT JUST GOES TO SHOW YOU FOLKS..OLD FASHIONED ROMANCE IS NOT DEAD...
Didja kill it?
Yeah... That SICK BASTARD.. I think it's RESTRAINING ORDER time again..
FLUSH!!
STOP

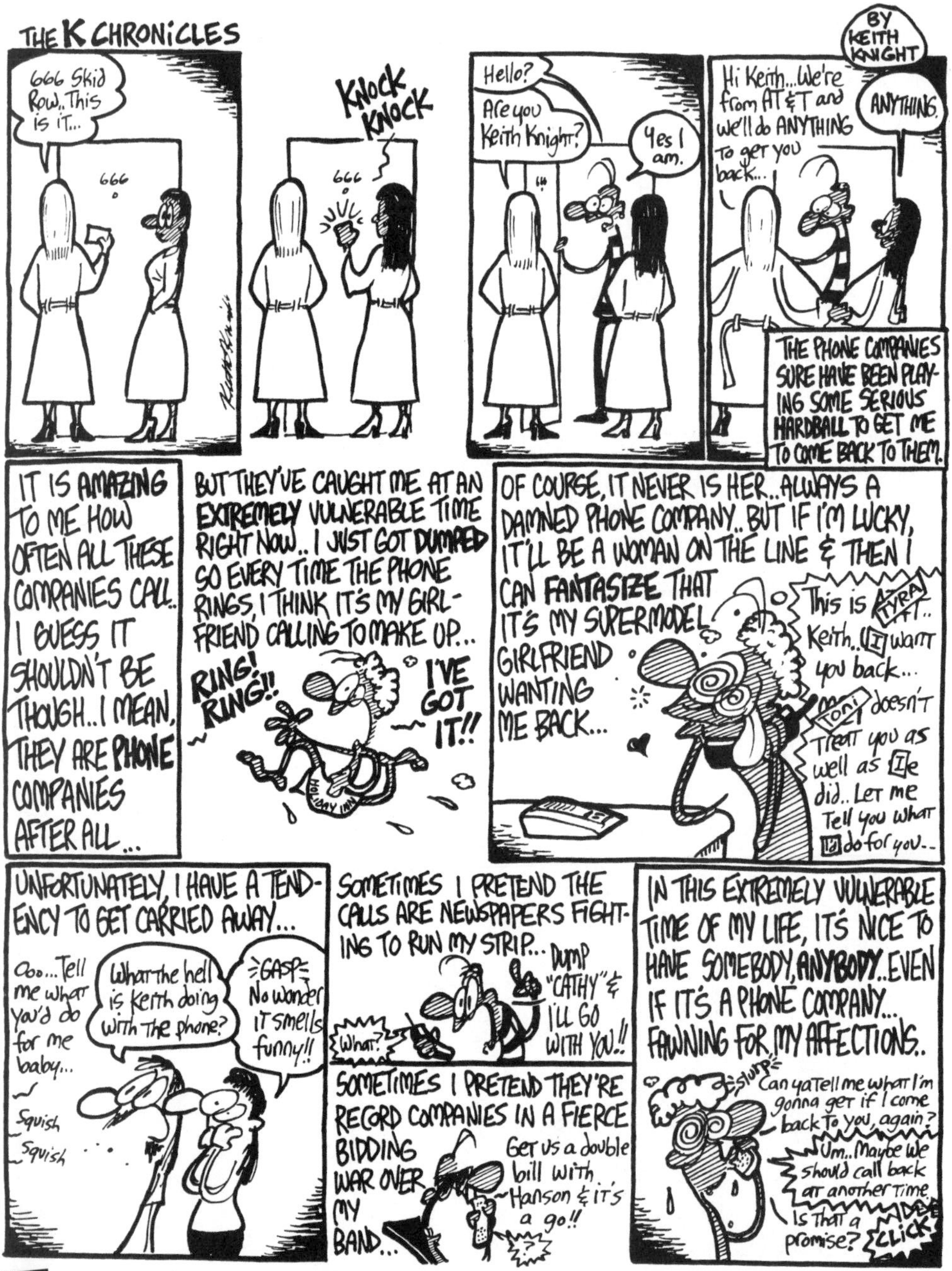

THE K CHRONICLES
BY KEITH KNIGHT
666 Skid Row.. This is iT...
666
KNOCK KNOCK
Hello?
Are you Keith Knight?
Yes I am.
Hi Keith...We're from AT&T and we'll do ANYTHING to get you back...
ANYTHING.
THE PHONE COMPANIES SURE HAVE BEEN PLAYING SOME SERIOUS HARDBALL TO GET ME TO COME BACK TO THEM.
IT IS AMAZING TO ME HOW OFTEN ALL THESE COMPANIES CALL.. I GUESS IT SHOULDN'T BE THOUGH...I MEAN, THEY ARE PHONE COMPANIES AFTER ALL...
BUT THEY'VE CAUGHT ME AT AN EXTREMELY VULNERABLE TIME RIGHT NOW.. I JUST GOT DUMPED SO EVERY TIME THE PHONE RINGS, I THINK IT'S MY GIRLFRIEND CALLING TO MAKE UP...
RING! RING!!
I'VE GOT IT!!
HOLIDAY INN
OF COURSE, IT NEVER IS HER...ALWAYS A DAMNED PHONE COMPANY.. BUT IF I'M LUCKY, IT'LL BE A WOMAN ON THE LINE & THEN I CAN FANTASIZE THAT IT'S MY SUPERMODEL GIRLFRIEND WANTING ME BACK...
This is TYRA.. Keith.. I want you back...
Toni doesn't treat you as well as I did.. Let me tell you what I'd do for you..
UNFORTUNATELY, I HAVE A TENDENCY TO GET CARRIED AWAY...
Ooo...Tell me what you'd do for me baby...
Squish Squish
What the hell is Keith doing with the phone?
GASP No wonder it smells funny!!
SOMETIMES I PRETEND THE CALLS ARE NEWSPAPERS FIGHTING TO RUN MY STRIP...
Dump "CATHY" & I'LL GO WITH YOU!!
What?
SOMETIMES I PRETEND THEY'RE RECORD COMPANIES IN A FIERCE BIDDING WAR OVER MY BAND...
Get us a double bill with Hanson & it's a go!!
?
IN THIS EXTREMELY VULNERABLE TIME OF MY LIFE, IT'S NICE TO HAVE SOMEBODY, ANYBODY...EVEN IF IT'S A PHONE COMPANY... FAWNING FOR MY AFFECTIONS..
slurp
Can ya tell me what I'm gonna get if I come back to you, again?
Um.. Maybe we should call back at another time.
Is that a promise?
CLICK

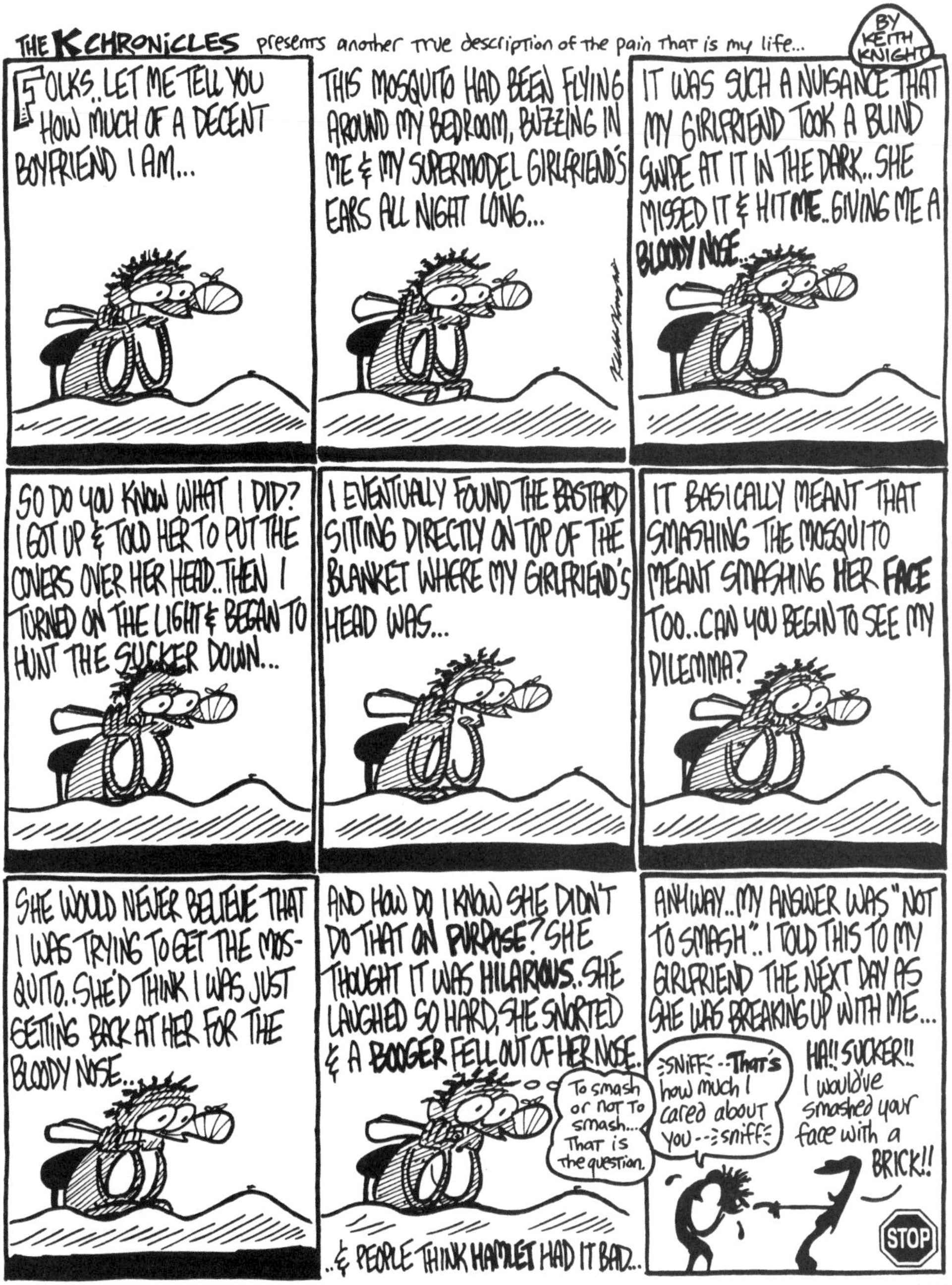
THE K CHRONICLES presents another true description of the pain that is my life...
BY KEITH KNIGHT
FOLKS..LET ME TELL YOU HOW MUCH OF A DECENT BOYFRIEND I AM...
THIS MOSQUITO HAD BEEN FLYING AROUND MY BEDROOM, BUZZING IN ME & MY SUPERMODEL GIRLFRIEND'S EARS ALL NIGHT LONG...
IT WAS SUCH A NUISANCE THAT MY GIRLFRIEND TOOK A BLIND SWIPE AT IT IN THE DARK..SHE MISSED IT & HIT ME..GIVING ME A BLOODY NOSE...
SO DO YOU KNOW WHAT I DID? I GOT UP & TOLD HER TO PUT THE COVERS OVER HER HEAD..THEN I TURNED ON THE LIGHT & BEGAN TO HUNT THE SUCKER DOWN...
I EVENTUALLY FOUND THE BASTARD SITTING DIRECTLY ON TOP OF THE BLANKET WHERE MY GIRLFRIEND'S HEAD WAS...
IT BASICALLY MEANT THAT SMASHING THE MOSQUITO MEANT SMASHING HER FACE TOO..CAN YOU BEGIN TO SEE MY DILEMMA?
SHE WOULD NEVER BELIEVE THAT I WAS TRYING TO GET THE MOSQUITO..SHE'D THINK I WAS JUST GETTING BACK AT HER FOR THE BLOODY NOSE...
AND HOW DO I KNOW SHE DIDN'T DO THAT ON PURPOSE? SHE THOUGHT IT WAS HILARIOUS..SHE LAUGHED SO HARD, SHE SNORTED & A BOOGER FELL OUT OF HER NOSE.
To smash or not to smash... That is the question.
..& PEOPLE THINK HAMLET HAD IT BAD...
ANYWAY..MY ANSWER WAS "NOT TO SMASH"..I TOLD THIS TO MY GIRLFRIEND THE NEXT DAY AS SHE WAS BREAKING UP WITH ME...
=SNIFF= --That's how much I cared about you--=sniff=
HA!! SUCKER!! I would've smashed your face with a BRICK!!
STOP

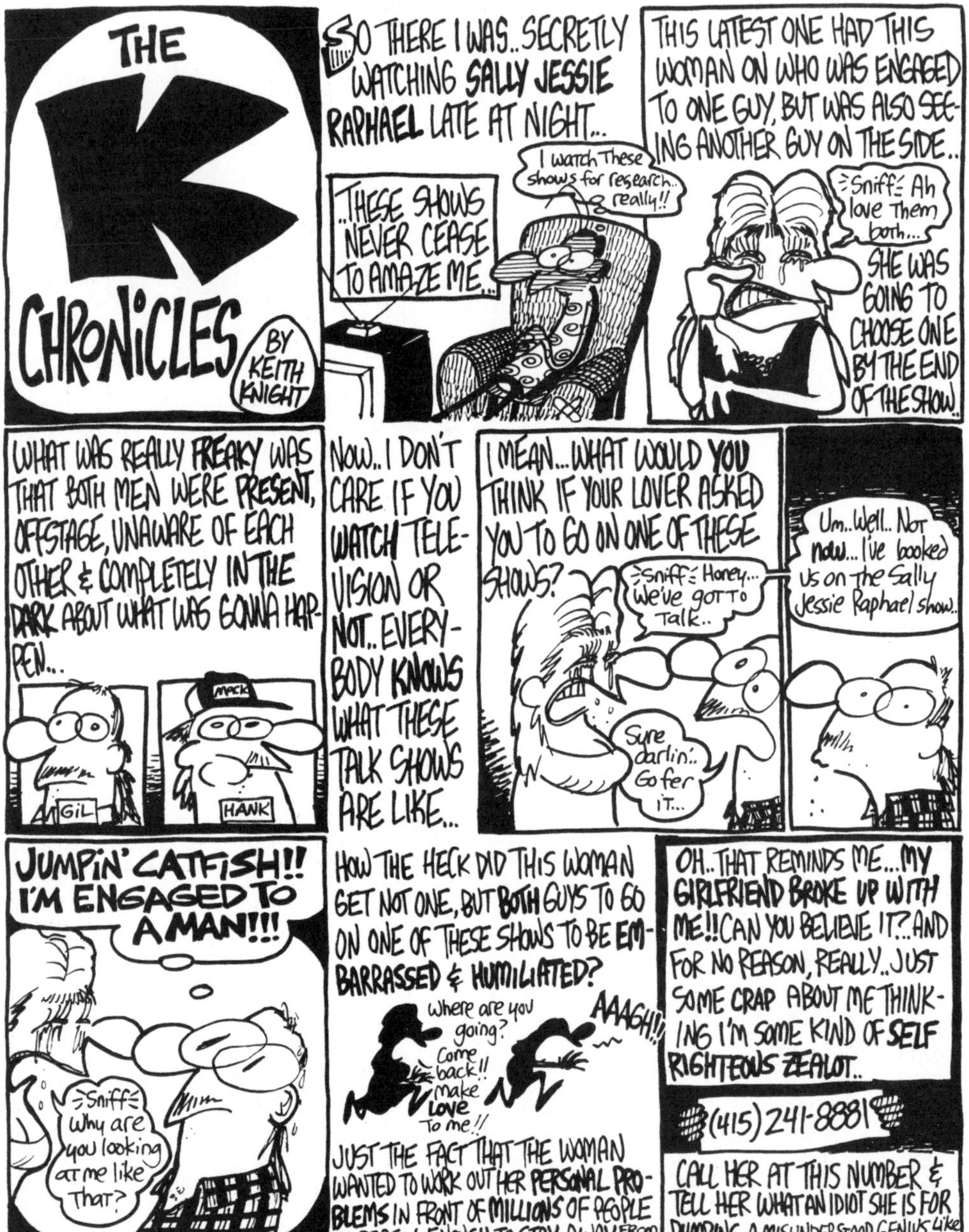

THE K CHRONICLES
BY KEITH KNIGHT
SO THERE I WAS.. SECRETLY WATCHING SALLY JESSIE RAPHAEL LATE AT NIGHT...
..THESE SHOWS NEVER CEASE TO AMAZE ME..
I watch These shows for research.. really!!
THIS LATEST ONE HAD THIS WOMAN ON WHO WAS ENGAGED TO ONE GUY, BUT WAS ALSO SEEING ANOTHER GUY ON THE SIDE..
Sniff Ah love Them both...
SHE WAS GOING TO CHOOSE ONE BY THE END OF THE SHOW..
WHAT WAS REALLY FREAKY WAS THAT BOTH MEN WERE PRESENT, OFFSTAGE, UNAWARE OF EACH OTHER & COMPLETELY IN THE DARK ABOUT WHAT WAS GONNA HAPPEN...
MACK
GIL
HANK
NOW.. I DON'T CARE IF YOU WATCH TELEVISION OR NOT.. EVERYBODY KNOWS WHAT THESE TALK SHOWS ARE LIKE...
I MEAN... WHAT WOULD YOU THINK IF YOUR LOVER ASKED YOU TO GO ON ONE OF THESE SHOWS?
Sniff Honey... We've gotta Talk..
Sure darlin'.. Go fer IT...
Um.. Well.. Not now... I've booked us on the Sally Jessie Raphael show..
JUMPIN' CATFISH!! I'M ENGAGED TO A MAN!!!
Sniff Why are you looking at me like That?
HOW THE HECK DID THIS WOMAN GET NOT ONE, BUT BOTH GUYS TO GO ON ONE OF THESE SHOWS TO BE EMBARRASSED & HUMILIATED?
Where are you going? Come back!! Make LOVE To me!!
AAAGH!!
JUST THE FACT THAT THE WOMAN WANTED TO WORK OUT HER PERSONAL PROBLEMS IN FRONT OF MILLIONS OF PEOPLE IS REASON ENOUGH TO STAY AWAY FROM HER..
OH.. THAT REMINDS ME... MY GIRLFRIEND BROKE UP WITH ME!! CAN YOU BELIEVE IT?.. AND FOR NO REASON, REALLY.. JUST SOME CRAP ABOUT ME THINKING I'M SOME KIND OF SELF RIGHTEOUS ZEALOT..
(415) 241-8881
CALL HER AT THIS NUMBER & TELL HER WHAT AN IDIOT SHE IS FOR DUMPING A MISUNDERSTOOD GENIUS like myself

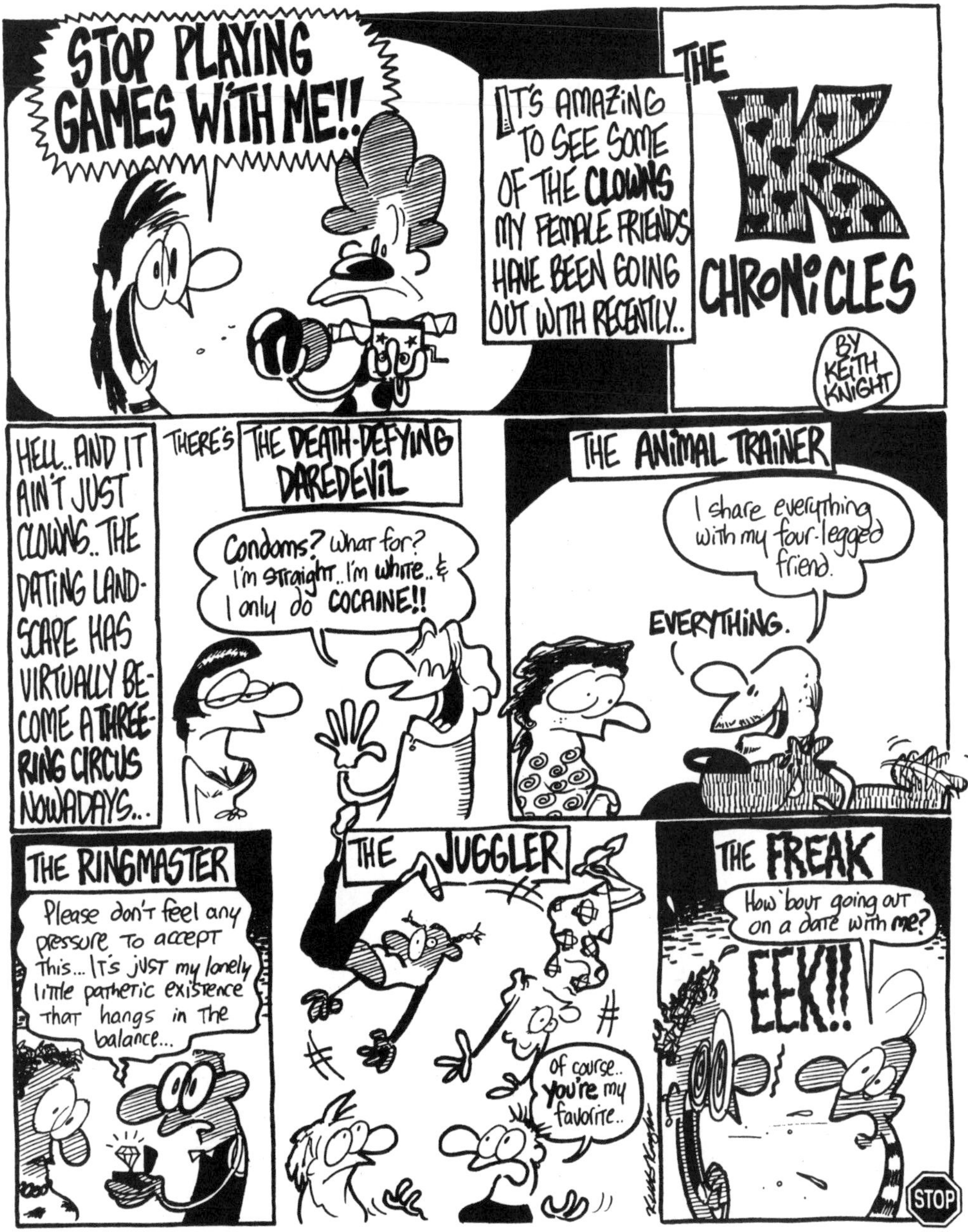
STOP PLAYING GAMES WITH ME!!
IT'S AMAZING TO SEE SOME OF THE CLOWNS MY FEMALE FRIENDS HAVE BEEN GOING OUT WITH RECENTLY..
THE K CHRONICLES
BY KEITH KNIGHT
HELL.. AND IT AIN'T JUST CLOWNS.. THE DATING LAND-SCAPE HAS VIRTUALLY BE-COME A THREE-RING CIRCUS NOWADAYS...
THERE'S
THE DEATH-DEFYING DAREDEVIL
Condoms? what for? I'm straight.. I'm white.. & I only do COCAINE!!
THE ANIMAL TRAINER
I share everything with my four-legged friend.
EVERYTHING.
THE RINGMASTER
Please don't feel any pressure to accept this... It's just my lonely little pathetic existence that hangs in the balance...
THE JUGGLER
Of course.. you're my favorite..
THE FREAK
How 'bout going out on a date with me?
EEK!!
STOP

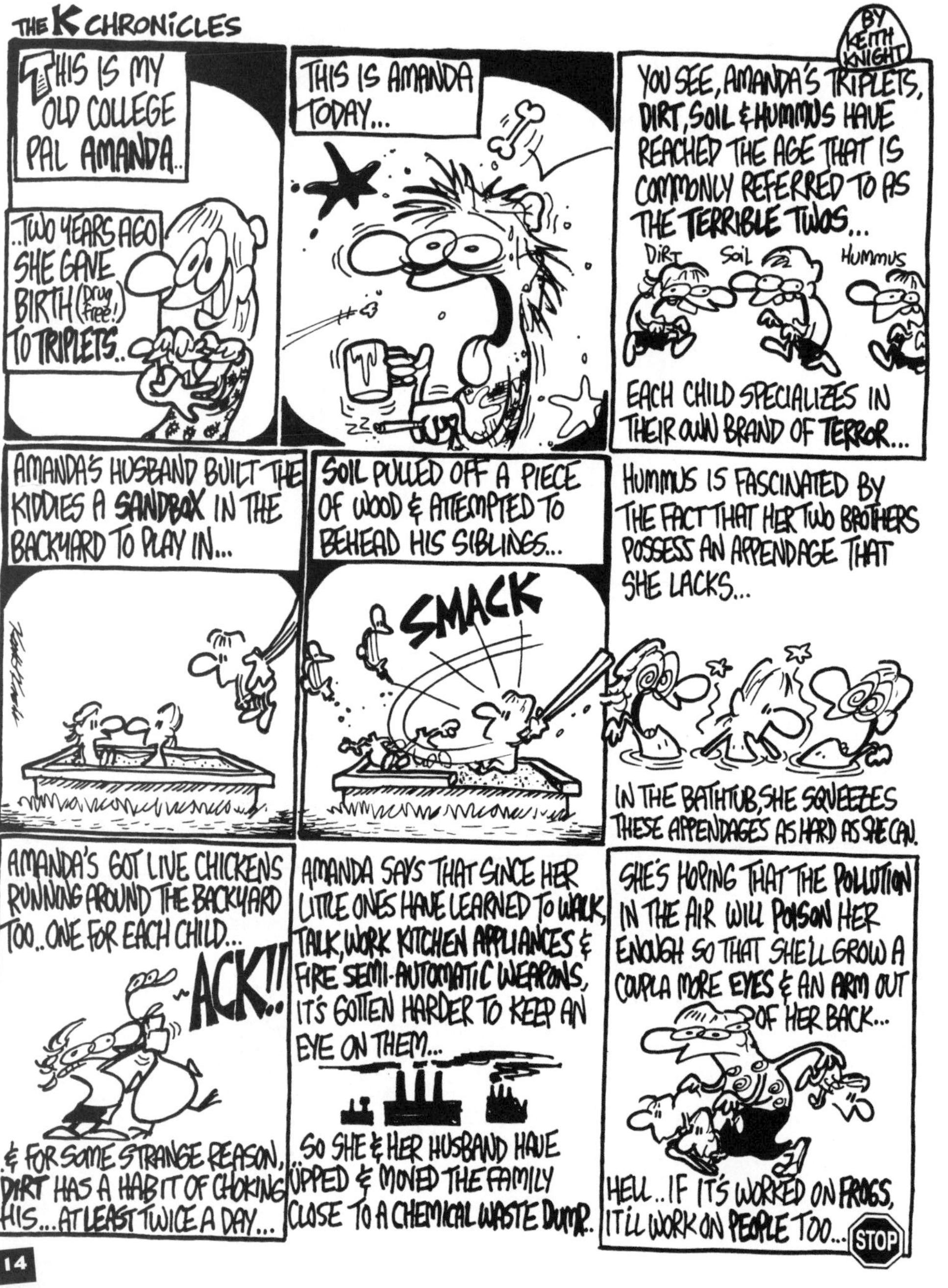
THE K CHRONICLES
BY KEITH KNIGHT
THIS IS MY OLD COLLEGE PAL AMANDA..
..TWO YEARS AGO SHE GAVE BIRTH (drug free!) TO TRIPLETS..
THIS IS AMANDA TODAY...
YOU SEE, AMANDA'S TRIPLETS, DIRT, SOIL & HUMMUS HAVE REACHED THE AGE THAT IS COMMONLY REFERRED TO AS THE TERRIBLE TWOS...
DIRT
SOIL
HUMMUS
EACH CHILD SPECIALIZES IN THEIR OWN BRAND OF TERROR...
AMANDA'S HUSBAND BUILT THE KIDDIES A SANDBOX IN THE BACKYARD TO PLAY IN...
SOIL PULLED OFF A PIECE OF WOOD & ATTEMPTED TO BEHEAD HIS SIBLINGS...
SMACK
HUMMUS IS FASCINATED BY THE FACT THAT HER TWO BROTHERS POSSESS AN APPENDAGE THAT SHE LACKS...
IN THE BATHTUB, SHE SQUEEZES THESE APPENDAGES AS HARD AS SHE CAN.
AMANDA'S GOT LIVE CHICKENS RUNNING AROUND THE BACKYARD TOO..ONE FOR EACH CHILD...
ACK!!..
..& FOR SOME STRANGE REASON, DIRT HAS A HABIT OF CHOKING HIS...AT LEAST TWICE A DAY...
AMANDA SAYS THAT SINCE HER LITTLE ONES HAVE LEARNED TO WALK, TALK, WORK KITCHEN APPLIANCES & FIRE SEMI-AUTOMATIC WEAPONS, IT'S GOTTEN HARDER TO KEEP AN EYE ON THEM...
SO SHE & HER HUSBAND HAVE UPPED & MOVED THE FAMILY CLOSE TO A CHEMICAL WASTE DUMP..
SHE'S HOPING THAT THE POLLUTION IN THE AIR WILL POISON HER ENOUGH SO THAT SHE'LL GROW A COUPLA MORE EYES & AN ARM OUT OF HER BACK...
HELL..IF IT'S WORKED ON FROGS, IT'LL WORK ON PEOPLE TOO...
STOP

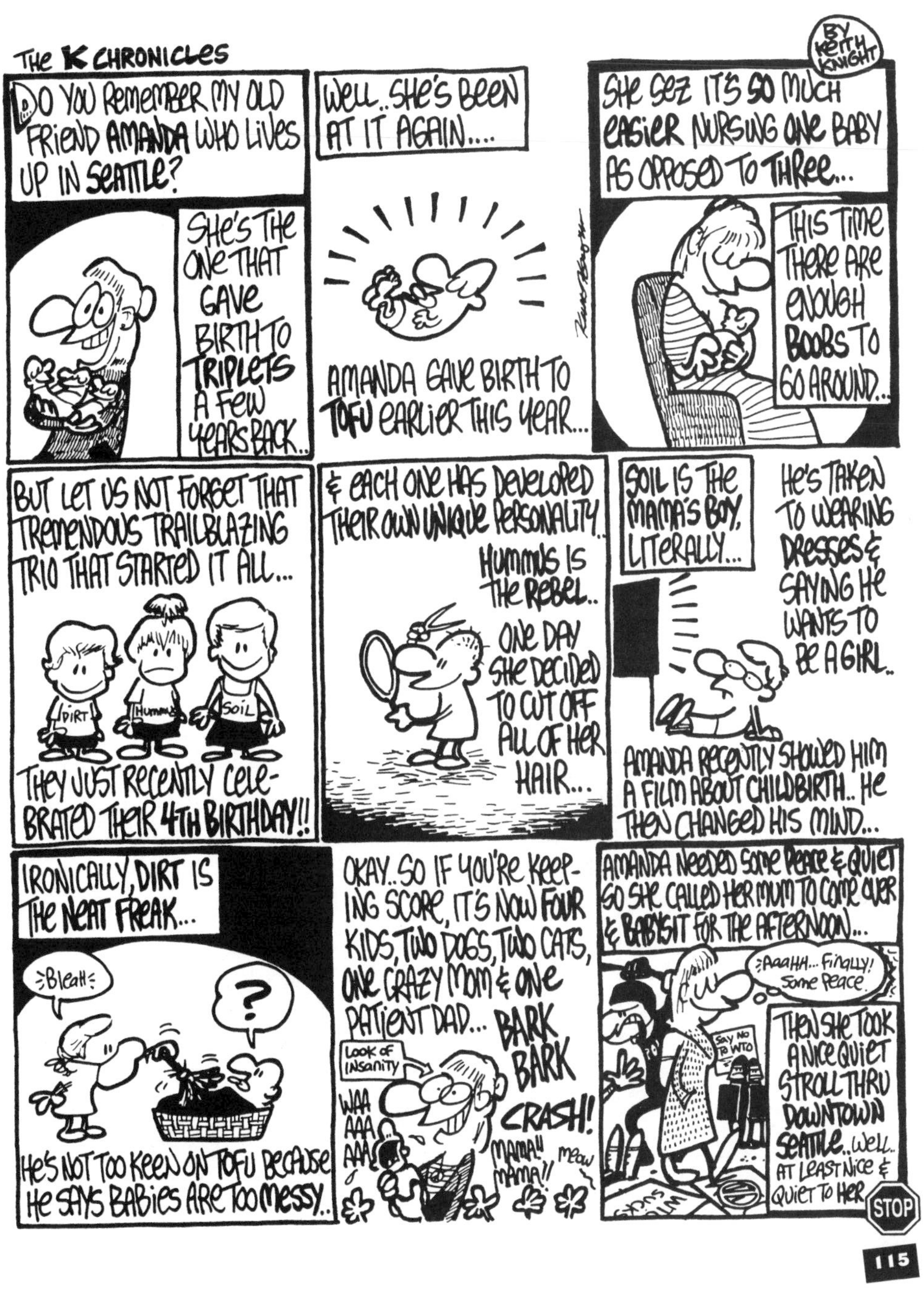
THE K CHRONICLES
BY KEITH KNIGHT
DO YOU REMEMBER MY OLD FRIEND AMANDA WHO LIVES UP IN SEATTLE?
SHE'S THE ONE THAT GAVE BIRTH TO TRIPLETS A FEW YEARS BACK..
WELL.. SHE'S BEEN AT IT AGAIN....
AMANDA GAVE BIRTH TO TOFU EARLIER THIS YEAR...
SHE SEZ IT'S SO MUCH EASIER NURSING ONE BABY AS OPPOSED TO THREE...
THIS TIME THERE ARE ENOUGH BOOBS TO GO AROUND...
BUT LET US NOT FORGET THAT TREMENDOUS TRAILBLAZING TRIO THAT STARTED IT ALL...
DIRT
SOIL
THEY JUST RECENTLY CELEBRATED THEIR 4TH BIRTHDAY!!
& EACH ONE HAS DEVELOPED THEIR OWN UNIQUE PERSONALITY..
HUMMUS IS THE REBEL..
ONE DAY SHE DECIDED TO CUT OFF ALL OF HER HAIR...
SOIL IS THE MAMA'S BOY, LITERALLY...
HE'S TAKEN TO WEARING DRESSES & SAYING HE WANTS TO BE A GIRL..
AMANDA RECENTLY SHOWED HIM A FILM ABOUT CHILDBIRTH.. HE THEN CHANGED HIS MIND...
IRONICALLY, DIRT IS THE NEAT FREAK...
BLEAH
?
HE'S NOT TOO KEEN ON TOFU BECAUSE HE SAYS BABIES ARE TOO MESSY..
OKAY.. SO IF YOU'RE KEEPING SCORE, IT'S NOW FOUR KIDS, TWO DOGS, TWO CATS, ONE CRAZY MOM & ONE PATIENT DAD...
BARK BARK
LOOK OF INSANITY
WAA AAA AAA
CRASH!
MAMA!! MAMA!!
MEOW
AMANDA NEEDED SOME PEACE & QUIET SO SHE CALLED HER MUM TO COME OVER & BABYSIT FOR THE AFTERNOON...
AAAHH... FINALLY! SOME PEACE.
SAY NO TO WTO
WTO SUCKS
THEN SHE TOOK A NICE QUIET STROLL THRU DOWNTOWN SEATTLE.. WELL.. AT LEAST NICE & QUIET TO HER
STOP

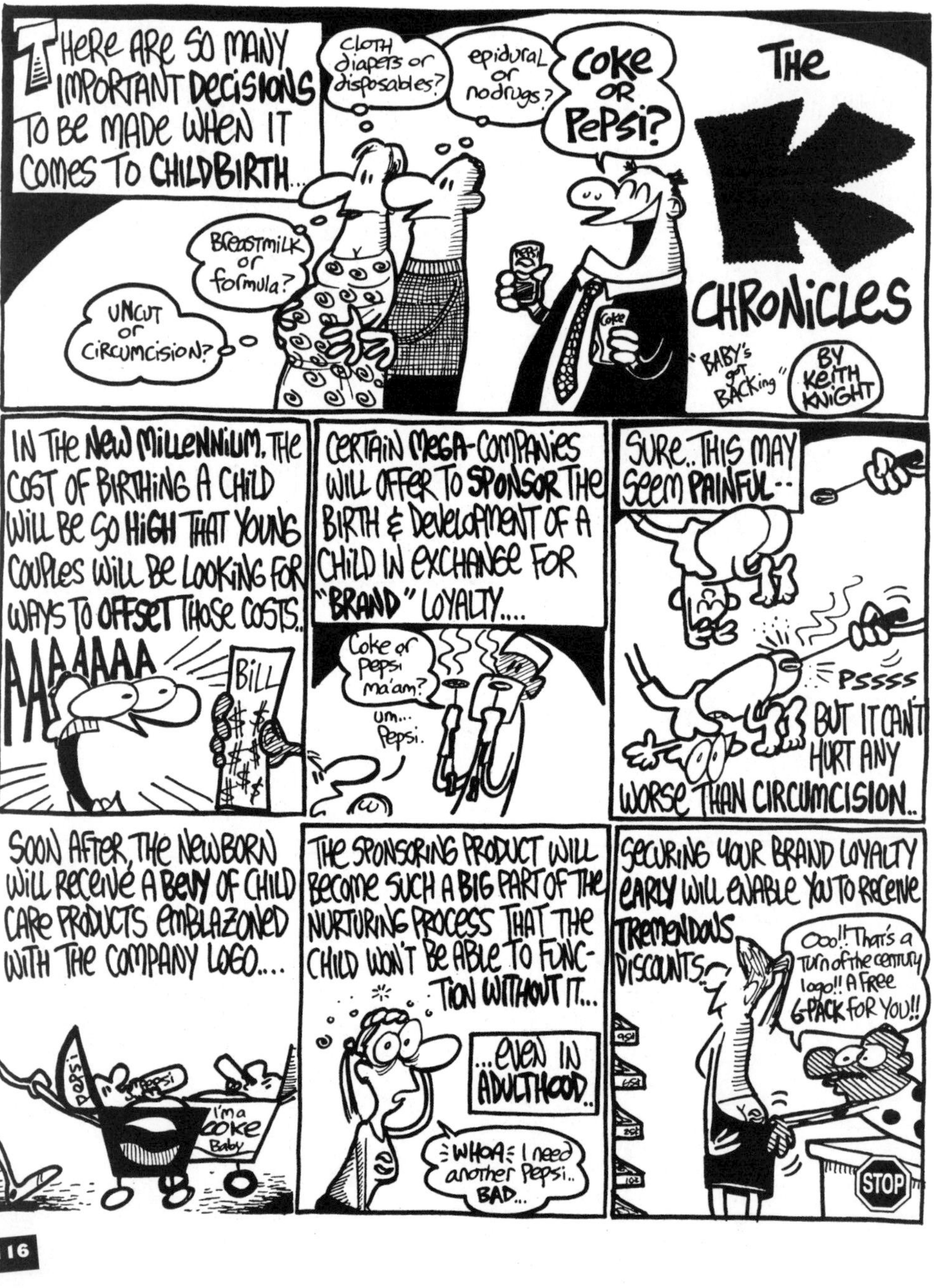

THERE ARE SO MANY IMPORTANT DECISIONS TO BE MADE WHEN IT COMES TO CHILDBIRTH...
Cloth diapers or disposables?
epidural or nodrugs?
COKE OR PEPSI?
THE K CHRONICLES
Breastmilk or formula?
UNCUT or CIRCUMCISION?
Pepsi
Coke
"BABY'S got BACKing"
BY KEITH KNIGHT
IN THE NEW MILLENNIUM, THE COST OF BIRTHING A CHILD WILL BE SO HIGH THAT YOUNG COUPLES WILL BE LOOKING FOR WAYS TO OFFSET THOSE COSTS...
AAAAAAA
BILL
CERTAIN MEGA-COMPANIES WILL OFFER TO SPONSOR THE BIRTH & DEVELOPMENT OF A CHILD IN EXCHANGE FOR "BRAND" LOYALTY....
Coke or Pepsi ma'am?
um... Pepsi.
SURE.. THIS MAY SEEM PAINFUL...
PSSSS
BUT IT CAN'T HURT ANY WORSE THAN CIRCUMCISION..
SOON AFTER, THE NEWBORN WILL RECEIVE A BEVY OF CHILD CARE PRODUCTS EMBLAZONED WITH THE COMPANY LOGO....
Pepsi
Pepsi
I'm a Coke Baby
THE SPONSORING PRODUCT WILL BECOME SUCH A BIG PART OF THE NURTURING PROCESS THAT THE CHILD WON'T BE ABLE TO FUNCTION WITHOUT IT...
...EVEN IN ADULTHOOD..
WHOA! I need another Pepsi.. BAD...
SECURING YOUR BRAND LOYALTY EARLY WILL ENABLE YOU TO RECEIVE TREMENDOUS DISCOUNTS..
Ooo!! That's a Turn of the century logo!! A Free 6-PACK FOR YOU!!
STOP

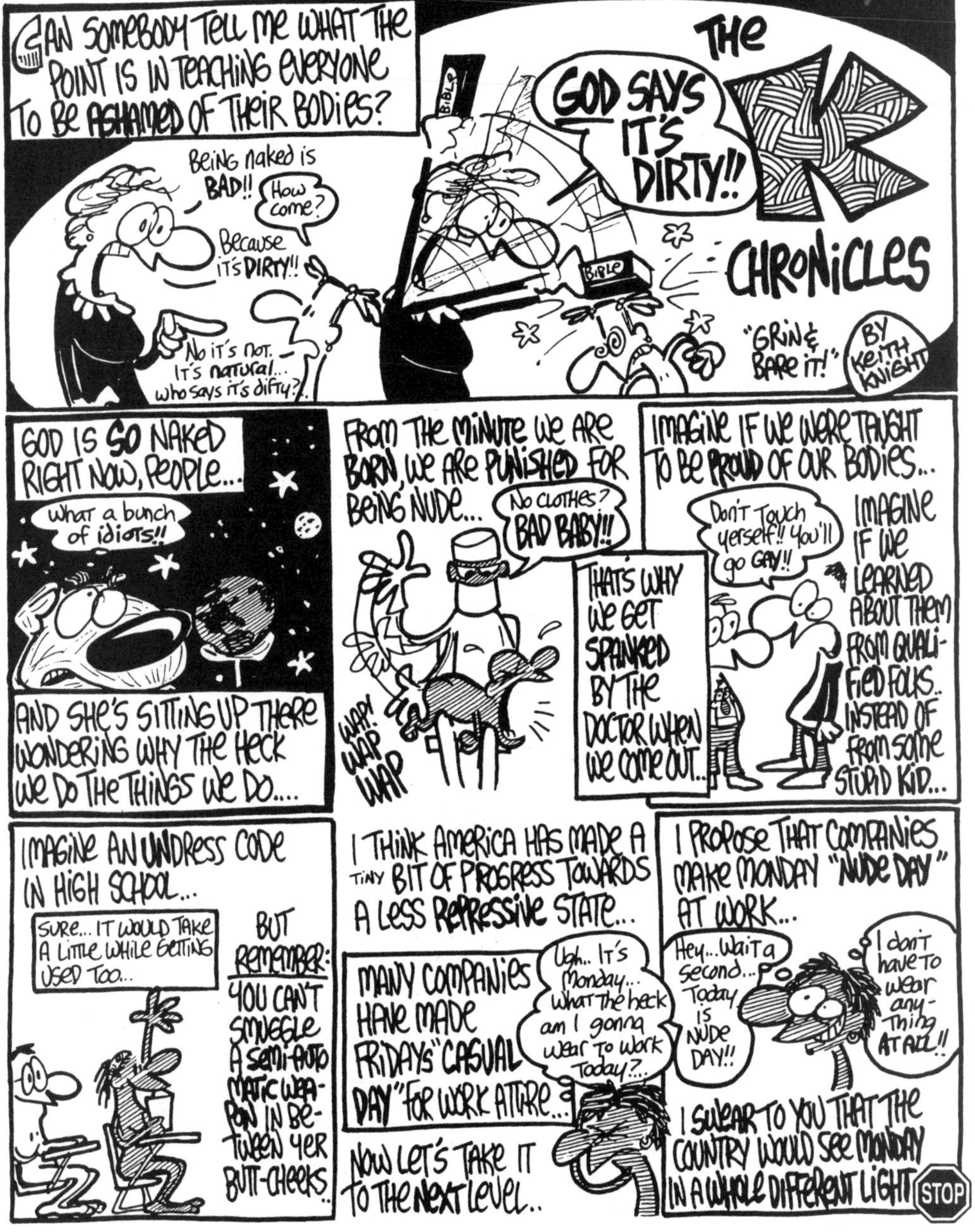

CAN SOMEBODY TELL ME WHAT THE POINT IS IN TEACHING EVERYONE TO BE ASHAMED OF THEIR BODIES?
THE K CHRONICLES
"GRIN & BARE IT!"
BY KEITH KNIGHT
Being naked is BAD!!
How come?
Because it's DIRTY!!
No it's not. It's natural... who says it's dirty?
GOD SAYS IT'S DIRTY!!
BIBLE
BIBLE
GOD IS SO NAKED RIGHT NOW, PEOPLE...
What a bunch of idiots!!
AND SHE'S SITTING UP THERE WONDERING WHY THE HECK WE DO THE THINGS WE DO....
FROM THE MINUTE WE ARE BORN, WE ARE PUNISHED FOR BEING NUDE...
No CLOTHES? BAD BABY!!
WAP! WAP WAP
THAT'S WHY WE GET SPANKED BY THE DOCTOR WHEN WE COME OUT...
IMAGINE IF WE WERE TAUGHT TO BE PROUD OF OUR BODIES...
Don't Touch yerself!! You'll go GAY!!
IMAGINE IF WE LEARNED ABOUT THEM FROM QUALIFIED FOLKS.. INSTEAD OF FROM SOME STUPID KID...
IMAGINE AN UNDRESS CODE IN HIGH SCHOOL...
SURE... IT WOULD TAKE A LITTLE WHILE GETTING USED TOO...
BUT REMEMBER: YOU CAN'T SMUGGLE A SEMI-AUTOMATIC WEAPON IN BETWEEN YER BUTT-CHEEKS...
I THINK AMERICA HAS MADE A TINY BIT OF PROGRESS TOWARDS A LESS REPRESSIVE STATE...
MANY COMPANIES HAVE MADE FRIDAYS "CASUAL DAY" FOR WORK ATTIRE...
Ugh.. It's Monday... What the heck am I gonna wear to work Today?...
NOW LET'S TAKE IT TO THE NEXT LEVEL..
I PROPOSE THAT COMPANIES MAKE MONDAY "NUDE DAY" AT WORK...
Hey... Wait a second... Today is NUDE DAY!!
I don't have to wear anything AT ALL!!
I SWEAR TO YOU THAT THE COUNTRY WOULD SEE MONDAY IN A WHOLE DIFFERENT LIGHT
STOP

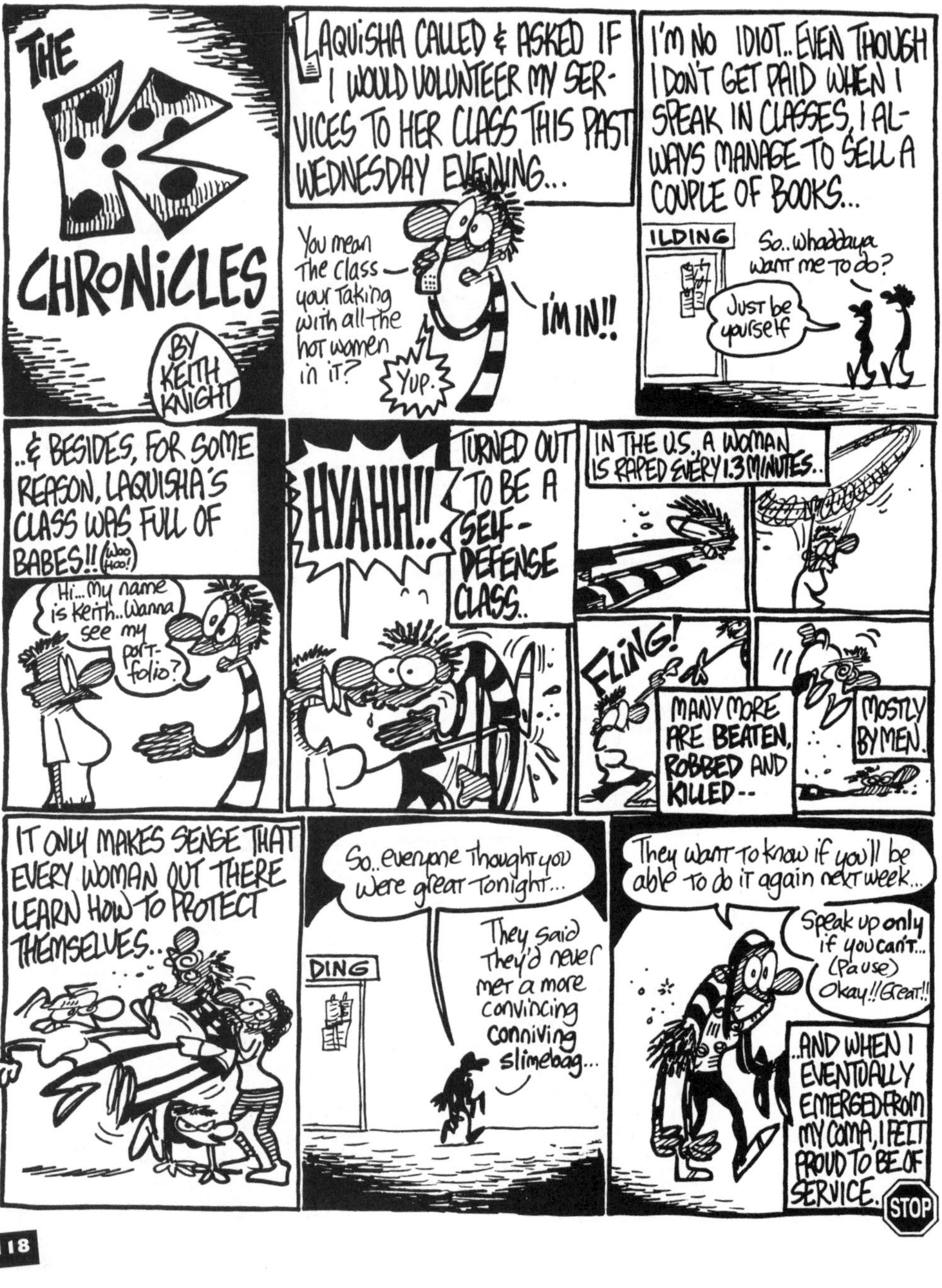
THE K CHRONICLES
BY KEITH KNIGHT
LAQUISHA CALLED & ASKED IF I WOULD VOLUNTEER MY SERVICES TO HER CLASS THIS PAST WEDNESDAY EVENING...
You mean the class your taking with all the hot women in it?
YUP.
I'M IN!!
I'M NO IDIOT.. EVEN THOUGH I DON'T GET PAID WHEN I SPEAK IN CLASSES, I ALWAYS MANAGE TO SELL A COUPLE OF BOOKS...
ILDING
So.. whaddaya want me to do?
Just be yourself
..& BESIDES, FOR SOME REASON, LAQUISHA'S CLASS WAS FULL OF BABES!! (Woo Hoo!)
Hi... my name is Keith.. Wanna see my portfolio?
HYAHH!!..
TURNED OUT TO BE A SELF-DEFENSE CLASS..
IN THE U.S., A WOMAN IS RAPED EVERY 1.3 MINUTES..
FLING!
MANY MORE ARE BEATEN, ROBBED AND KILLED--
MOSTLY BY MEN.
IT ONLY MAKES SENSE THAT EVERY WOMAN OUT THERE LEARN HOW TO PROTECT THEMSELVES...
So.. everyone thought you were great tonight...
They said they'd never met a more convincing conniving slimebag...
DING
They want to know if you'll be able to do it again next week...
Speak up only if you can't... (Pause) Okay!! Great!!
..AND WHEN I EVENTUALLY EMERGED FROM MY COMA, I FELT PROUD TO BE OF SERVICE.
STOP

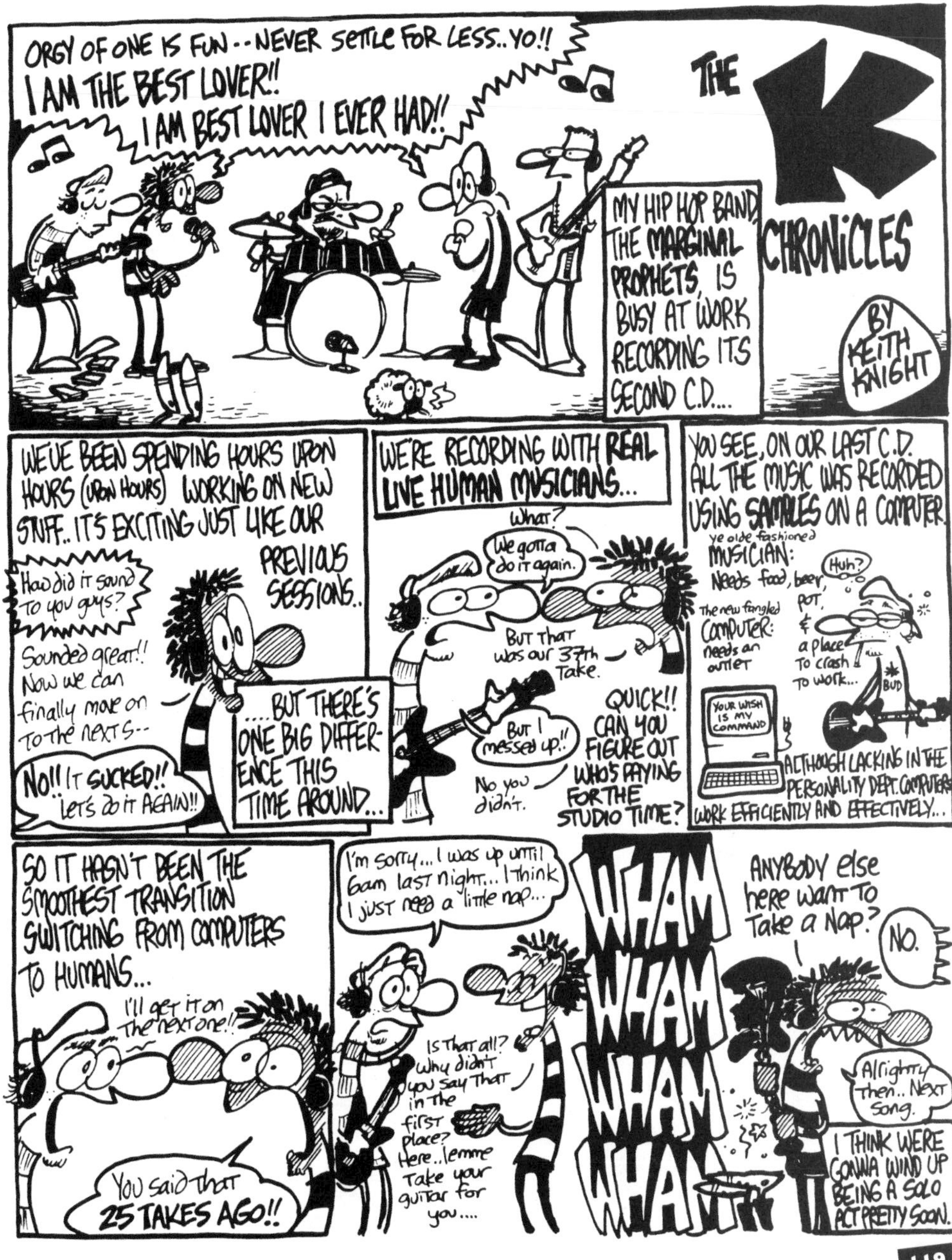

ORGY OF ONE IS FUN--NEVER SETTLE FOR LESS..YO!!
I AM THE BEST LOVER!!
I AM BEST LOVER I EVER HAD!!
THE K CHRONICLES
BY KEITH KNIGHT
MY HIP HOP BAND THE MARGINAL PROPHETS, IS BUSY AT WORK RECORDING ITS SECOND C.D....
WE'VE BEEN SPENDING HOURS UPON HOURS (UPON HOURS) WORKING ON NEW STUFF.. IT'S EXCITING JUST LIKE OUR PREVIOUS SESSIONS..
How did it sound to you guys?
Sounded great!! Now we can finally move on to the next s--
NO!! IT SUCKED!! Let's do it AGAIN!!
....BUT THERE'S ONE BIG DIFFERENCE THIS TIME AROUND...
WE'RE RECORDING WITH REAL LIVE HUMAN MUSICIANS...
What?
We gotta do it again.
But that was our 37th Take.
But I messed up!!
No you didn't.
QUICK!! CAN YOU FIGURE OUT WHO'S PAYING FOR THE STUDIO TIME?
YOU SEE, ON OUR LAST C.D. ALL THE MUSIC WAS RECORDED USING SAMPLES ON A COMPUTER.
ye olde fashioned MUSICIAN: Needs food, beer, pot, & a place to crash to work...
Huh?
The new fangled COMPUTER: needs an outlet
YOUR WISH IS MY COMMAND
BUD
ALTHOUGH LACKING IN THE PERSONALITY DEPT. COMPUTERS WORK EFFICIENTLY AND EFFECTIVELY...
SO IT HASN'T BEEN THE SMOOTHEST TRANSITION SWITCHING FROM COMPUTERS TO HUMANS...
I'll get it on the next one!!
You said that 25 TAKES AGO!!
I'm sorry... I was up until 6am last night... I think I just need a little nap...
Is that all? Why didn't you say that in the first place? Here.. lemme take your guitar for you....
WHAM WHAM WHAM WHAM WHAM
ANYBODY else here want to take a nap?
NO.
Alrighty then.. Next Song.
I THINK WE'RE GONNA WIND UP BEING A SOLO ACT PRETTY SOON..

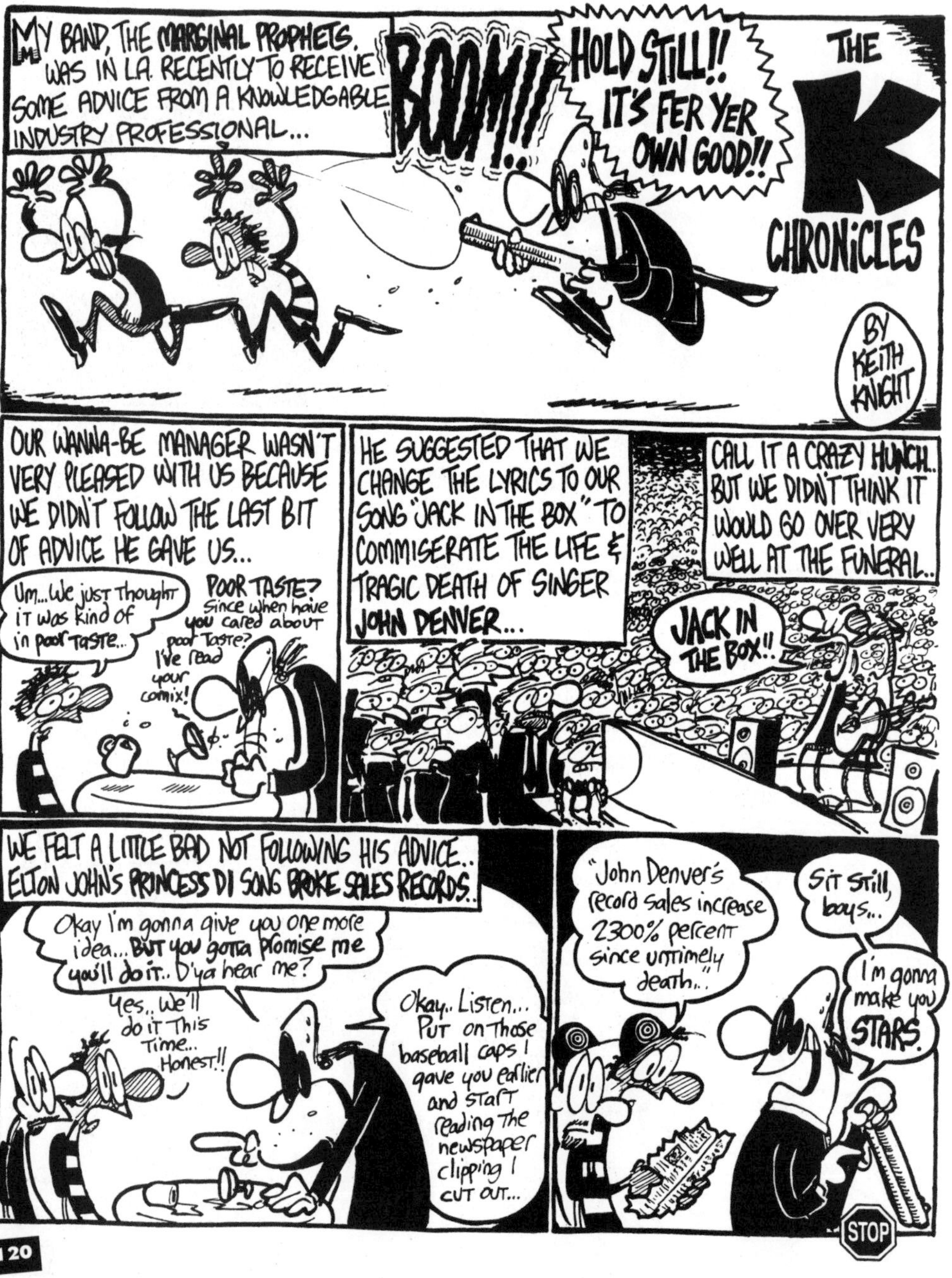

THE K CHRONICLES
BY KEITH KNIGHT
MY BAND, THE MARGINAL PROPHETS, WAS IN L.A. RECENTLY TO RECEIVE SOME ADVICE FROM A KNOWLEDGABLE INDUSTRY PROFESSIONAL...
BOOM!!
HOLD STILL!! IT'S FER YER OWN GOOD!!
OUR WANNA-BE MANAGER WASN'T VERY PLEASED WITH US BECAUSE WE DIDN'T FOLLOW THE LAST BIT OF ADVICE HE GAVE US...
Um... We just thought it was kind of in poor taste...
POOR TASTE? Since when have you cared about poor taste? I've read your comix!
HE SUGGESTED THAT WE CHANGE THE LYRICS TO OUR SONG "JACK IN THE BOX" TO COMMISERATE THE LIFE & TRAGIC DEATH OF SINGER JOHN DENVER...
CALL IT A CRAZY HUNCH.. BUT WE DIDN'T THINK IT WOULD GO OVER VERY WELL AT THE FUNERAL..
JACK IN THE BOX!!
WE FELT A LITTLE BAD NOT FOLLOWING HIS ADVICE.. ELTON JOHN'S PRINCESS DI SONG BROKE SALES RECORDS..
Okay I'm gonna give you one more idea... BUT you gotta promise me you'll do it.. D'ya hear me?
Yes.. We'll do it This Time... Honest!!
Okay.. Listen... Put on those baseball caps I gave you earlier and start reading the newspaper clipping I cut out...
"John Denver's record sales increase 2300% percent since untimely death.."
Sit still, boys...
I'm gonna make you STARS.
STOP

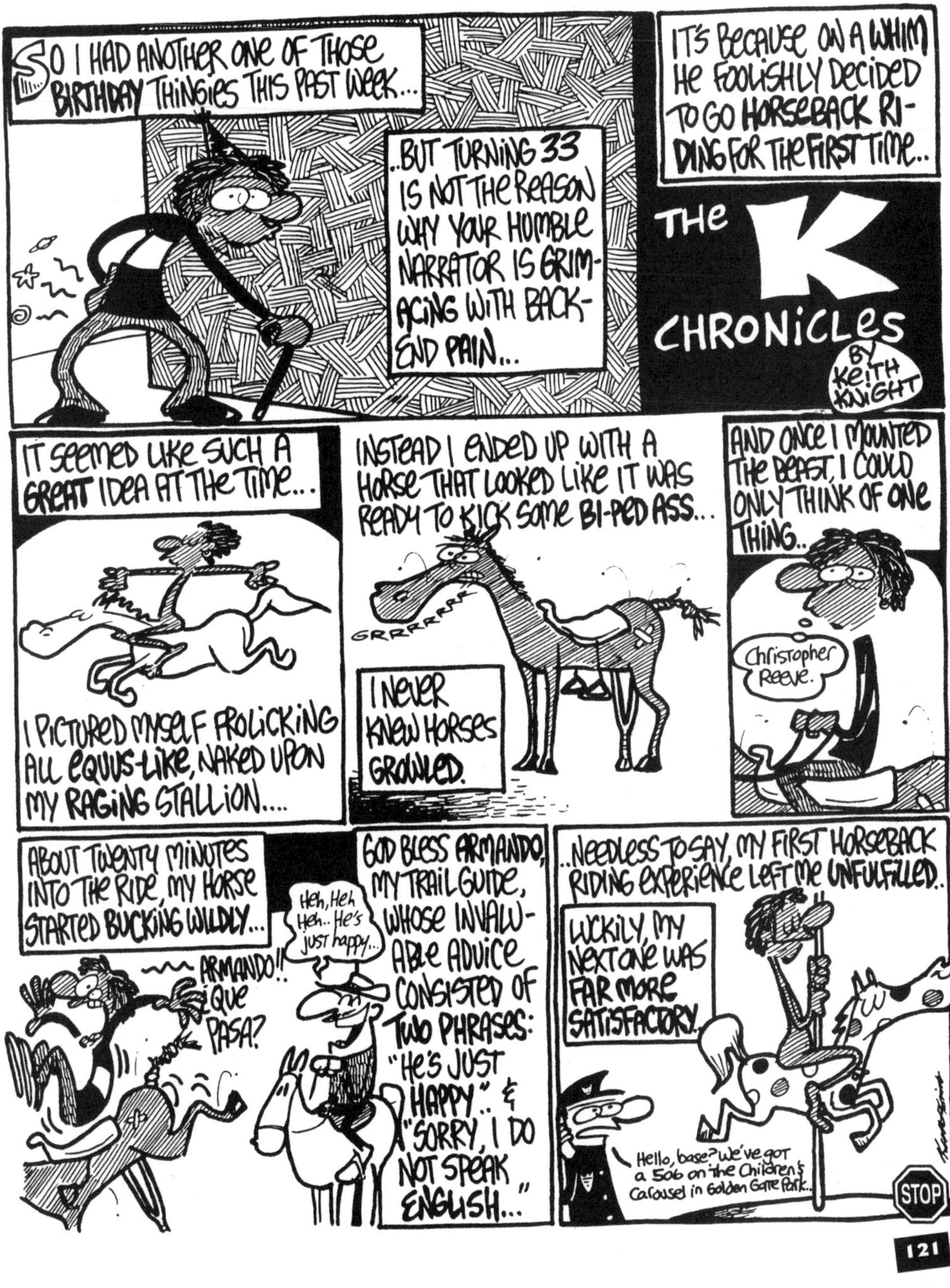
SO I HAD ANOTHER ONE OF THOSE BIRTHDAY THINGIES THIS PAST WEEK...
..BUT TURNING 33 IS NOT THE REASON WHY YOUR HUMBLE NARRATOR IS GRIMACING WITH BACK-END PAIN...
IT'S BECAUSE ON A WHIM HE FOOLISHLY DECIDED TO GO HORSEBACK RIDING FOR THE FIRST TIME..
THE K CHRONICLES
BY KEITH KNIGHT
IT SEEMED LIKE SUCH A GREAT IDEA AT THE TIME...
I PICTURED MYSELF FROLICKING ALL EQUUS-LIKE, NAKED UPON MY RAGING STALLION....
INSTEAD I ENDED UP WITH A HORSE THAT LOOKED LIKE IT WAS READY TO KICK SOME BI-PED ASS...
GRRRRRRRR
I NEVER KNEW HORSES GROWLED.
AND ONCE I MOUNTED THE BEAST, I COULD ONLY THINK OF ONE THING..
Christopher Reeve.
ABOUT TWENTY MINUTES INTO THE RIDE, MY HORSE STARTED BUCKING WILDLY...
~~ ARMANDO!! ¿QUE PASA?
Heh, Heh Heh.. He's just happy...
GOD BLESS ARMANDO, MY TRAIL GUIDE, WHOSE INVALUABLE ADVICE CONSISTED OF TWO PHRASES: "HE'S JUST HAPPY".. & "SORRY, I DO NOT SPEAK ENGLISH..."
..NEEDLESS TO SAY, MY FIRST HORSEBACK RIDING EXPERIENCE LEFT ME UNFULFILLED..
LUCKILY, MY NEXT ONE WAS FAR MORE SATISFACTORY.
Hello, base? We've got a 506 on the Children's Carousel in Golden Gate Park..
STOP

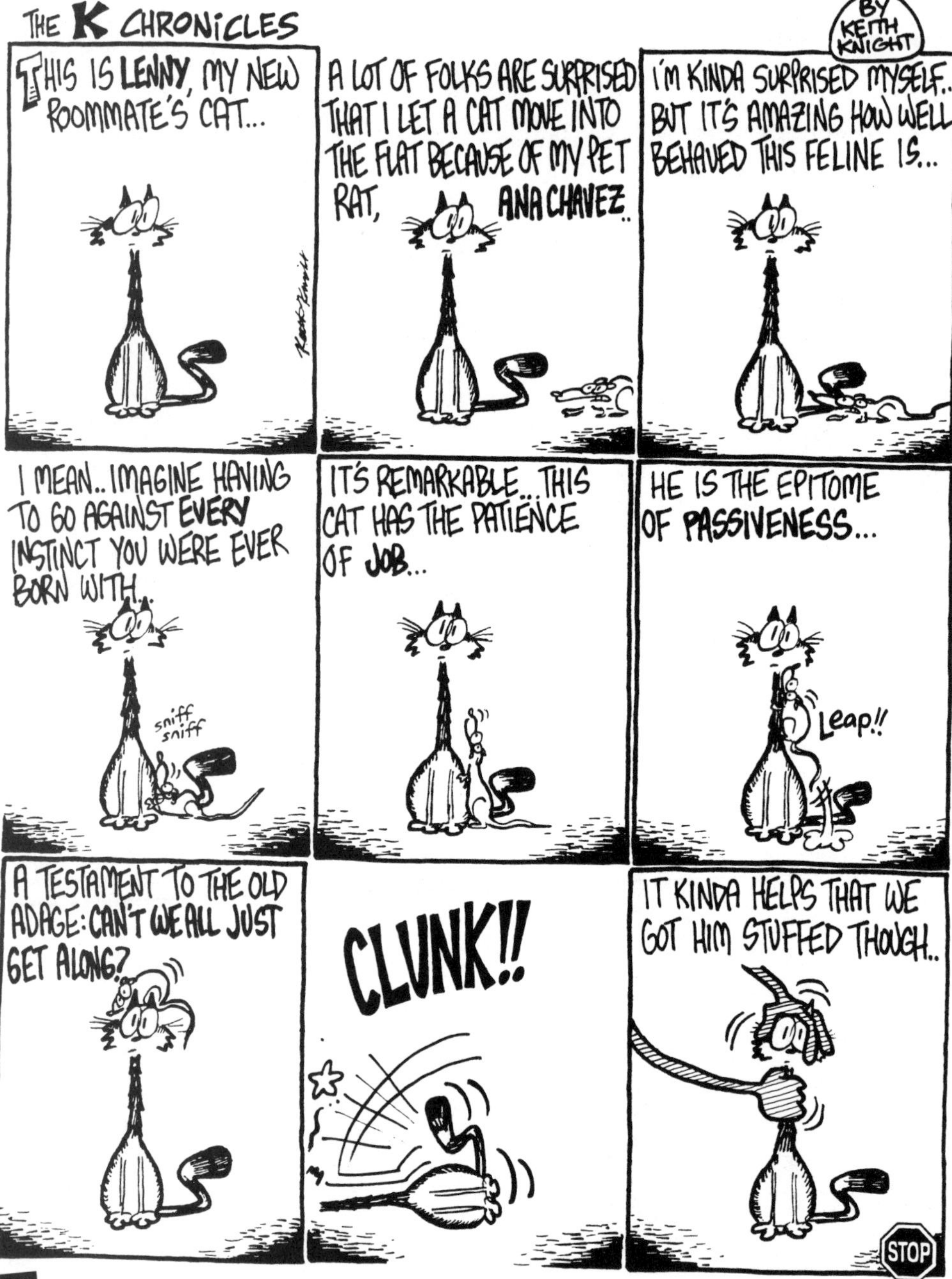

THE K CHRONICLES
BY KEITH KNIGHT
THIS IS LENNY, MY NEW ROOMMATE'S CAT...
A LOT OF FOLKS ARE SURPRISED THAT I LET A CAT MOVE INTO THE FLAT BECAUSE OF MY PET RAT, ANA CHAVEZ..
I'M KINDA SURPRISED MYSELF.. BUT IT'S AMAZING HOW WELL BEHAVED THIS FELINE IS...
I MEAN.. IMAGINE HAVING TO GO AGAINST EVERY INSTINCT YOU WERE EVER BORN WITH...
sniff sniff
IT'S REMARKABLE... THIS CAT HAS THE PATIENCE OF JOB...
HE IS THE EPITOME OF PASSIVENESS...
Leap!!
A TESTAMENT TO THE OLD ADAGE: CAN'T WE ALL JUST GET ALONG?
CLUNK!!
IT KINDA HELPS THAT WE GOT HIM STUFFED THOUGH..
STOP

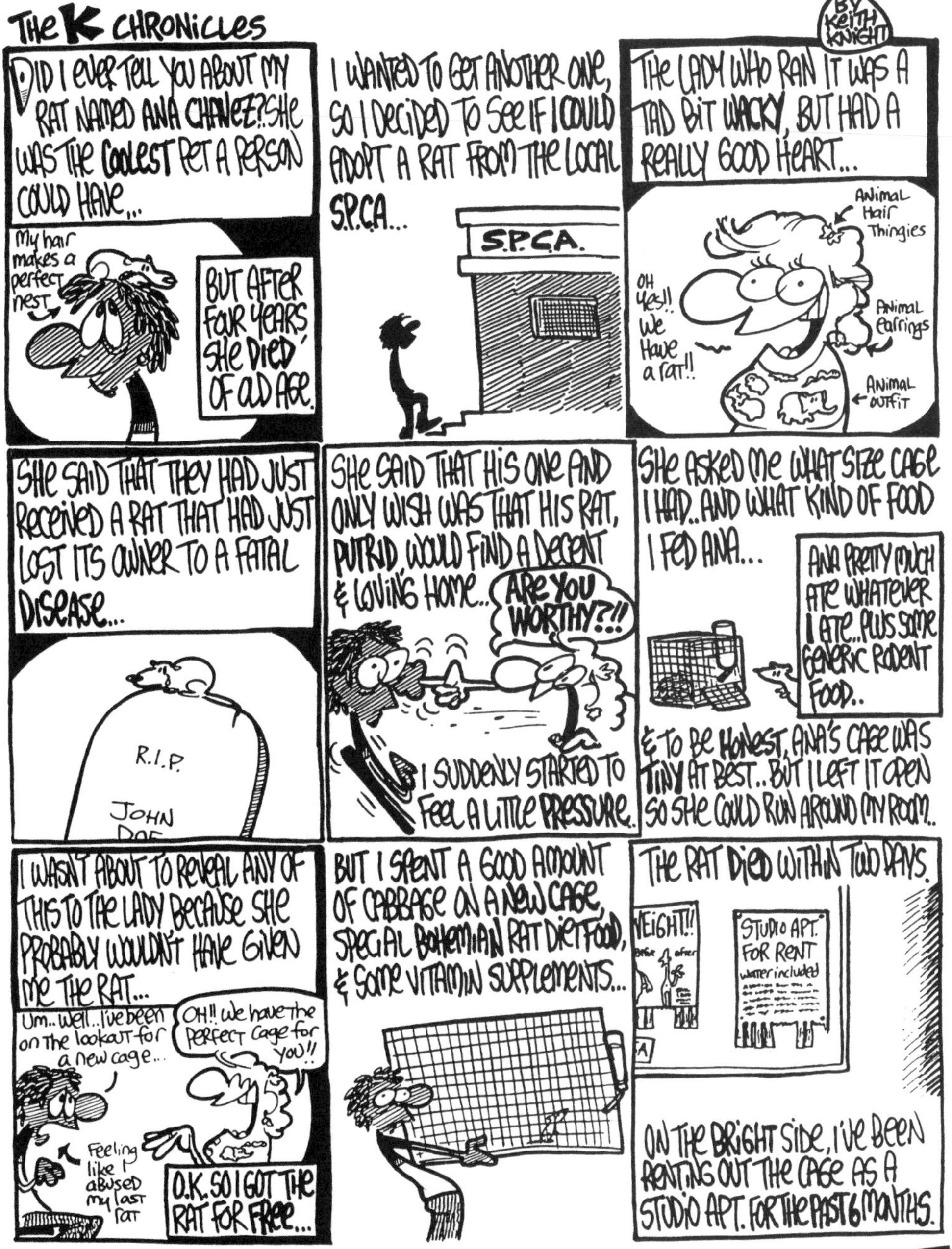
THE K CHRONICLES
BY KEITH KNIGHT
DID I EVER TELL YOU ABOUT MY RAT NAMED ANA CHAVEZ?..SHE WAS THE COOLEST PET A PERSON COULD HAVE...
My hair makes a perfect nest
BUT AFTER FOUR YEARS, SHE DIED OF OLD AGE.
I WANTED TO GET ANOTHER ONE, SO I DECIDED TO SEE IF I COULD ADOPT A RAT FROM THE LOCAL S.P.C.A...
S.P.C.A.
THE LADY WHO RAN IT WAS A TAD BIT WACKY, BUT HAD A REALLY GOOD HEART...
Animal Hair Thingies
OH YES!! WE HAVE A RAT!!
Animal Earrings
Animal outfit
SHE SAID THAT THEY HAD JUST RECEIVED A RAT THAT HAD JUST LOST ITS OWNER TO A FATAL DISEASE...
R.I.P.
JOHN DOE
SHE SAID THAT HIS ONE AND ONLY WISH WAS THAT HIS RAT, PUTRID, WOULD FIND A DECENT & LOVING HOME...
ARE YOU WORTHY?!!
I SUDDENLY STARTED TO FEEL A LITTLE PRESSURE.
SHE ASKED ME WHAT SIZE CAGE I HAD.. AND WHAT KIND OF FOOD I FED ANA...
ANA PRETTY MUCH ATE WHATEVER I ATE.. PLUS SOME GENERIC RODENT FOOD..
& TO BE HONEST, ANA'S CAGE WAS TINY AT BEST.. BUT I LEFT IT OPEN SO SHE COULD RUN AROUND MY ROOM..
I WASN'T ABOUT TO REVEAL ANY OF THIS TO THE LADY BECAUSE SHE PROBABLY WOULDN'T HAVE GIVEN ME THE RAT...
Um.. Well.. I've been on the lookout for a new cage...
OH!! We have the perfect cage for you!!
Feeling like I abused my last rat
O.K. SO I GOT THE RAT FOR FREE...
BUT I SPENT A GOOD AMOUNT OF CABBAGE ON A NEW CAGE, SPECIAL BOHEMIAN RAT DIET FOOD, & SOME VITAMIN SUPPLEMENTS...
THE RAT DIED WITHIN TWO DAYS.
WEIGHT!!
Before after
STUDIO APT. FOR RENT
water included
ON THE BRIGHT SIDE, I'VE BEEN RENTING OUT THE CAGE AS A STUDIO APT. FOR THE PAST 6 MONTHS.

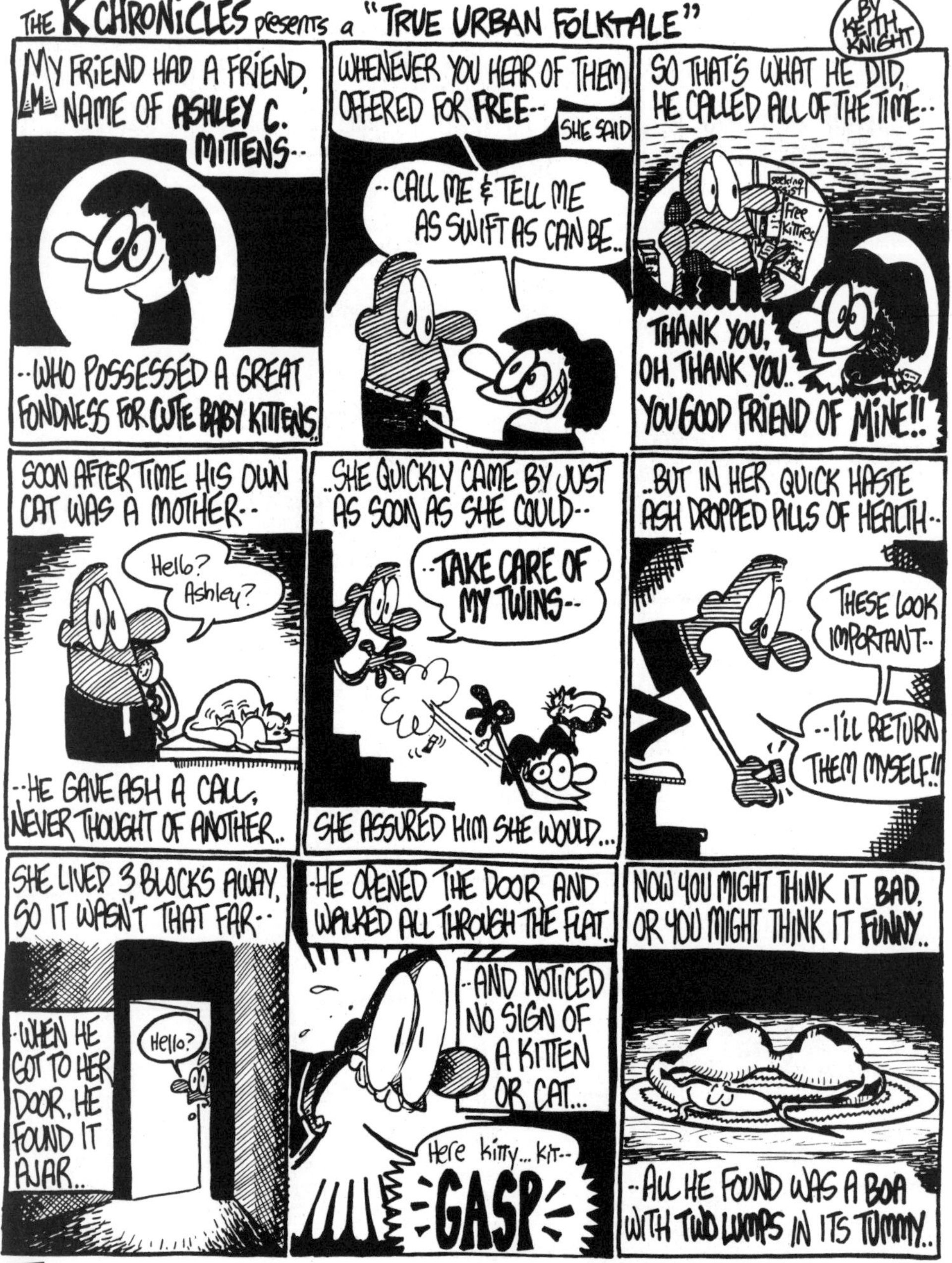
THE K CHRONICLES presents a "TRUE URBAN FOLKTALE"
BY KEITH KNIGHT
MY FRIEND HAD A FRIEND, NAME OF ASHLEY C. MITTENS..
..WHO POSSESSED A GREAT FONDNESS FOR CUTE BABY KITTENS..
WHENEVER YOU HEAR OF THEM OFFERED FOR FREE--
SHE SAID
..CALL ME & TELL ME AS SWIFT AS CAN BE..
SO THAT'S WHAT HE DID, HE CALLED ALL OF THE TIME..
seeking assist
Free Kitties
THANK YOU, OH, THANK YOU.. YOU GOOD FRIEND OF MINE!!
SOON AFTER TIME HIS OWN CAT WAS A MOTHER--
Hello? Ashley?
--HE GAVE ASH A CALL, NEVER THOUGHT OF ANOTHER..
..SHE QUICKLY CAME BY JUST AS SOON AS SHE COULD--
..TAKE CARE OF MY TWINS--
SHE ASSURED HIM SHE WOULD...
..BUT IN HER QUICK HASTE ASH DROPPED PILLS OF HEALTH..
THESE LOOK IMPORTANT..
--I'LL RETURN THEM MYSELF!!
SHE LIVED 3 BLOCKS AWAY, SO IT WASN'T THAT FAR--
-WHEN HE GOT TO HER DOOR, HE FOUND IT AJAR..
Hello?
-HE OPENED THE DOOR AND WALKED ALL THROUGH THE FLAT..
--AND NOTICED NO SIGN OF A KITTEN OR CAT...
Here kitty... kit--
GASP
NOW YOU MIGHT THINK IT BAD, OR YOU MIGHT THINK IT FUNNY..
--ALL HE FOUND WAS A BOA WITH TWO LUMPS IN ITS TUMMY..

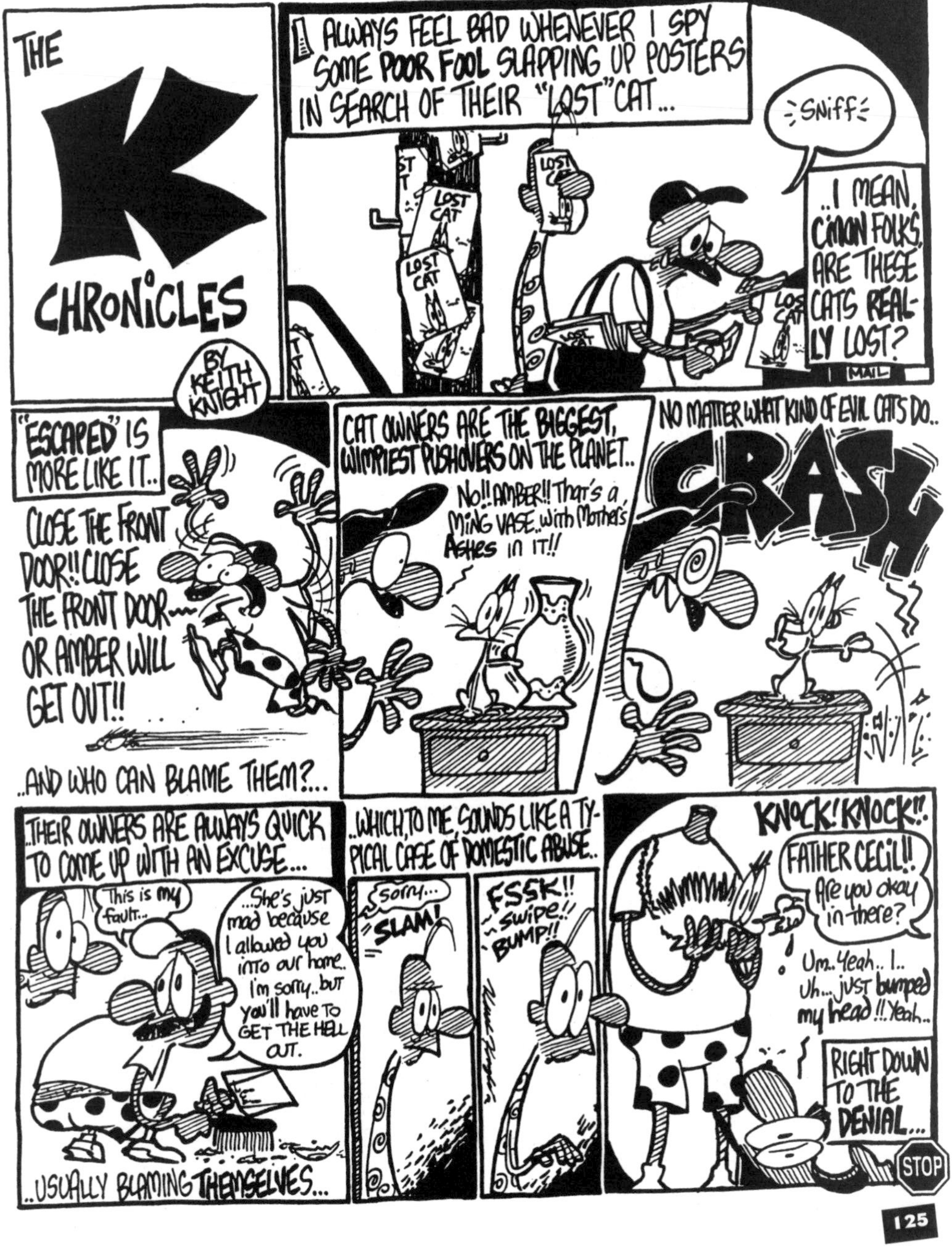

THE K CHRONICLES
BY KEITH KNIGHT
I ALWAYS FEEL BAD WHENEVER I SPY SOME POOR FOOL SLAPPING UP POSTERS IN SEARCH OF THEIR "LOST" CAT...
LOST CAT
Sniff
..I MEAN, C'MON FOLKS, ARE THESE CATS REAL-LY LOST?
MAIL
"ESCAPED" IS MORE LIKE IT..
CLOSE THE FRONT DOOR!! CLOSE THE FRONT DOOR--- OR AMBER WILL GET OUT!!
..AND WHO CAN BLAME THEM?...
CAT OWNERS ARE THE BIGGEST, WIMPIEST PUSHOVERS ON THE PLANET..
No!! AMBER!! That's a MING VASE.. with Mother's Ashes in it!!
NO MATTER WHAT KIND OF EVIL CATS DO..
CRASH
..THEIR OWNERS ARE ALWAYS QUICK TO COME UP WITH AN EXCUSE...
This is my fault...
...She's just mad because I allowed you into our home.. I'm sorry.. but you'll have to GET THE HELL OUT.
..USUALLY BLAMING THEMSELVES...
..WHICH, TO ME, SOUNDS LIKE A TY-PICAL CASE OF DOMESTIC ABUSE..
sorry...
SLAM!
FSSK!!
swipe!!
BUMP!!
KNOCK! KNOCK!!
FATHER CECIL!! Are you okay in there?
Um.. Yeah.. I.. Uh... just bumped my head!! Yeah...
RIGHT DOWN TO THE DENIAL...
STOP

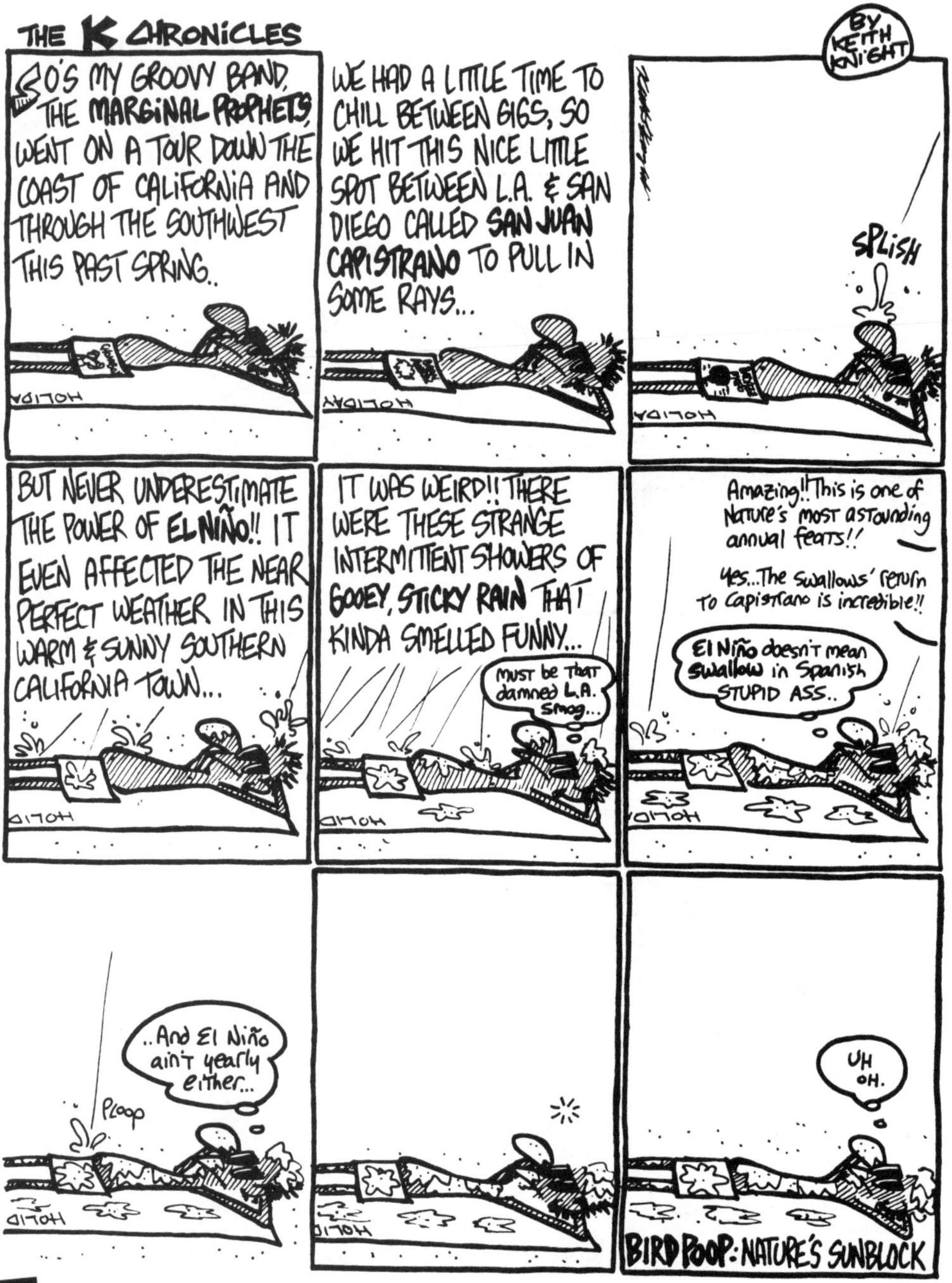
THE K CHRONICLES
BY KEITH KNIGHT
SO'S MY GROOVY BAND, THE MARGINAL PROPHETS, WENT ON A TOUR DOWN THE COAST OF CALIFORNIA AND THROUGH THE SOUTHWEST THIS PAST SPRING..
WE HAD A LITTLE TIME TO CHILL BETWEEN GIGS, SO WE HIT THIS NICE LITTLE SPOT BETWEEN L.A. & SAN DIEGO CALLED SAN JUAN CAPISTRANO TO PULL IN SOME RAYS...
SPLISH
BUT NEVER UNDERESTIMATE THE POWER OF EL NIÑO!! IT EVEN AFFECTED THE NEAR PERFECT WEATHER IN THIS WARM & SUNNY SOUTHERN CALIFORNIA TOWN...
IT WAS WEIRD!! THERE WERE THESE STRANGE INTERMITTENT SHOWERS OF GOOEY, STICKY RAIN THAT KINDA SMELLED FUNNY...
Must be that damned L.A. Smog...
Amazing!! This is one of Nature's most astounding annual feats!!
Yes...The swallows' return to Capistrano is incredible!!
El Niño doesn't mean swallow in Spanish STUPID ASS..
..And El Niño ain't yearly either...
PLOOP
UH OH.
BIRD POOP: NATURE'S SUNBLOCK

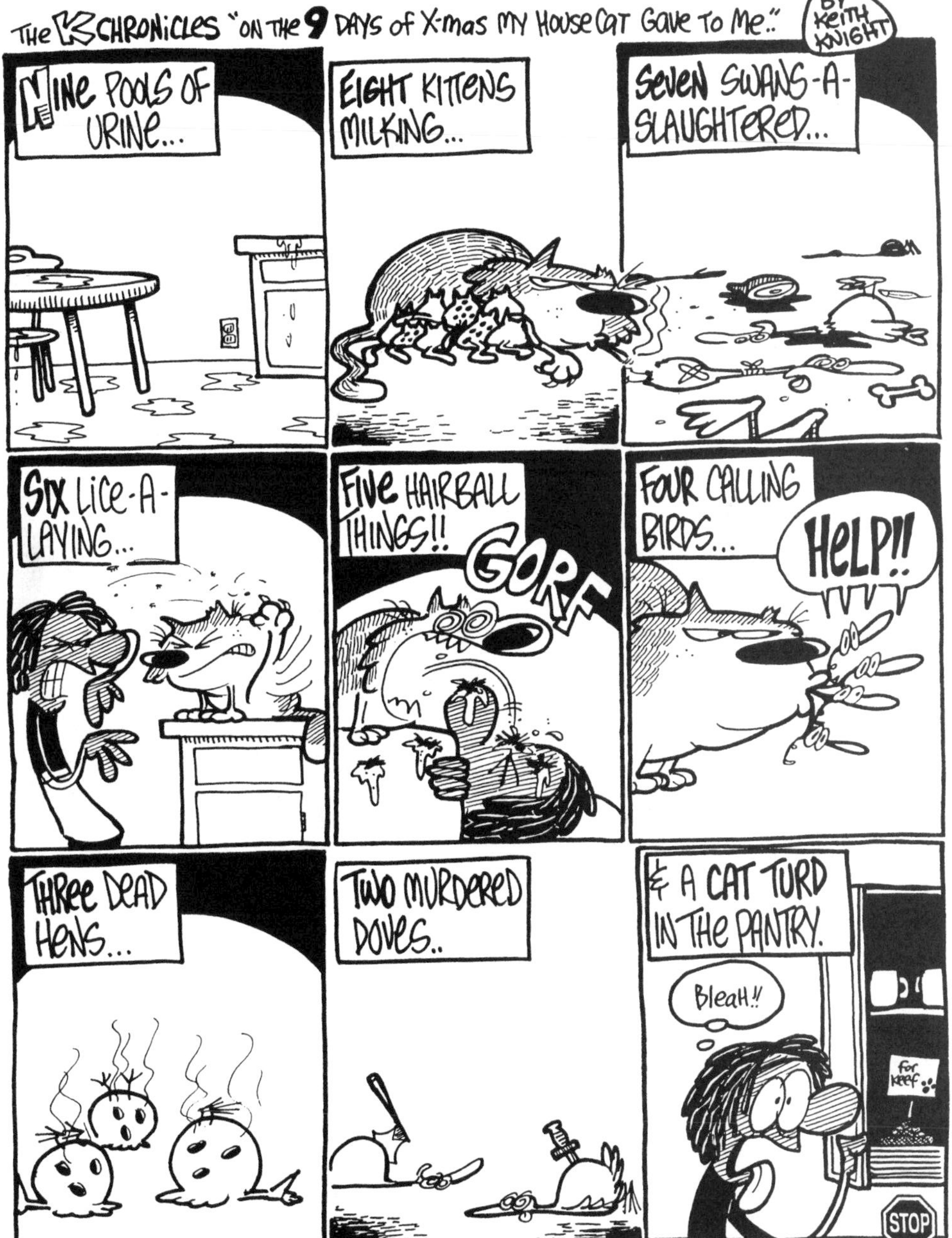
THE K CHRONICLES "ON THE 9 DAYS OF X-MAS MY HOUSECAT GAVE TO ME.."
BY KEITH KNIGHT
NINE POOLS OF URINE...
EIGHT KITTENS MILKING...
SEVEN SWANS-A-SLAUGHTERED...
SIX LICE-A-LAYING...
FIVE HAIRBALL THINGS!!
GORF
FOUR CALLING BIRDS...
HELP!!
THREE DEAD HENS...
TWO MURDERED DOVES..
& A CAT TURD IN THE PANTRY.
BleaH!!
for keef
STOP

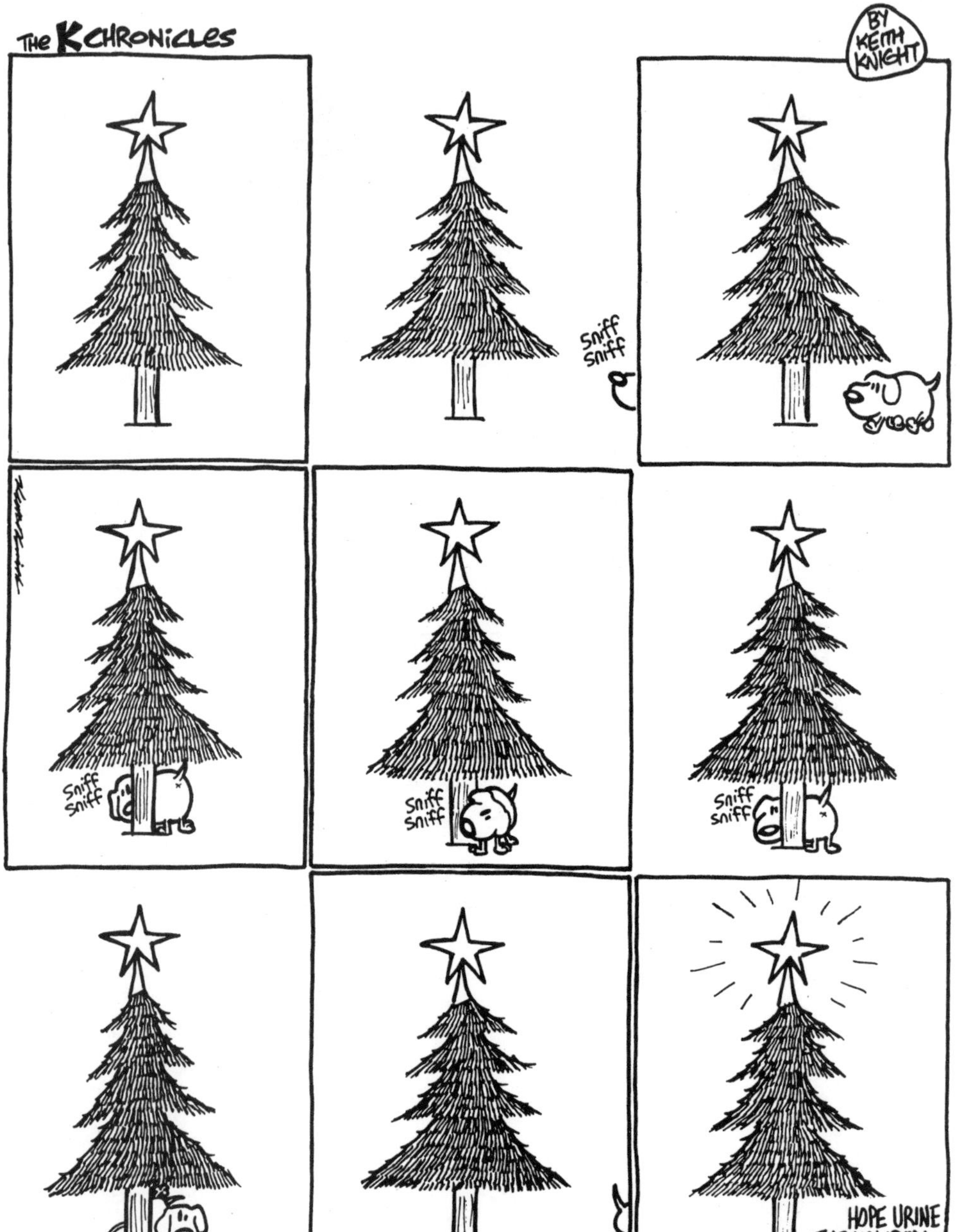
THE K CHRONICLES
BY KEITH KNIGHT
Sniff sniff
Sniff sniff
Sniff sniff
Sniff sniff
HOPE URINE THE HOLIDAY SPIRIT!!
STOP